SINGLE PARENT FAMILIES

SINGLE PARENT FAMILIES

Perspectives on Research and Policy

Edited by Joe Hudson and Burt Galaway

THOMPSON EDUCATIONAL PUBLISHING, INC.

Requests for permission to make copies of any part of the work should be directed to the publisher. Additional copies of this book may be obtained from the publisher.

Orders may be sent to:

Canada
11 Briarcroft Road
Toronto, Ontario
M6S 1H3

United States
240 Portage Road
Lewiston, New York
14092

For faster delivery, please send your order by telephone or fax to:
Tel (416) 766–2763 / Fax (416) 766–0398

Canadian Cataloguing in Publication Data

Main entry under title:

Single parent families : Perspectives on research and policy

Includes bibliographical references and index.
ISBN 1-55077-046-2
1. Single parent family - Canada. I. Hudson,
Joe. II Galaway, Burt, 1937-

HQ759.915.S55 1993   306.85'6'0971   C93-093548-9

Cover photo: Family and Rainstorm by Alex Colville, 1955,
National Gallery of Canada. Reproduced by permission of Alex Colville.

Printed and bound in Canada by John Deyell Company Limited.
1 2 3 4   96 95 94 93

Table of Contents

PART V

SOCIALIZATION EXPERIENCES OF CHILDREN

PART VI

CONCLUSIONS

Acknowledgments

Earlier versions of the papers presented in this volume were developed for a Research and Policy Workshop funded by National Welfare Grants, Health and Welfare Canada. The Workshop was co-sponsored by The University of Calgary Faculty of Social Work, University of Manitoba Faculty of Social Work, The Vanier Institute of the Family, and the Ontario Child, Youth and Family Policy Research Centre. We extend our deepest appreciation to Michel Smith and David Thornton of National Welfare Grants, Laura Johnson of the Child, Youth and Family Policy Research Centre, and Robert Glossop of The Vanier Institute of the Family for their support, encouragement, and assistance in planning both the Workshop and this publication. The book is only possible because of the hard work of the authors whose papers are presented here. We thank them for their efforts and appreciate the spirit of cooperation as we worked under tight timelines for both the Workshop and the publication. A special word of thanks is due to many people whose hard work was essential to the production of this volume: Karen Braid, Barb Messenger, and Kathy Penner, University of Calgary, Faculty of Social Work (Edmonton Division), prepared volumes of correspondence and other materials in preparation for the Workshop; Claudette Cormier of the University of Manitoba Faculty of Social Work, was responsible for manuscript production; and Raymond Arcand and Carmen Landry did both English/French and French/English translations for the work. Finally, we appreciate the assistance of Keith Thompson, Thompson Educational Publishing, who helped move this project from manuscript to book. This volume is a collaborative responsibility and would not have been possible without the assistance of many people. Ideas and points of view expressed in the chapters, however, are solely the responsibility of the various authors. Materials presented in this volume do not necessarily represent the policies or views of National Welfare Grants or any of the sponsoring organizations.

Foreword

The idea for this book grew from a national conference held in Alberta, Canada, March 18–21, 1992. Twelve months in the planning, the National Research and Policy Workshop on the Single Parent Family brought together forty-six researchers and senior policy makers. The researchers came from Canada, the United States, France and Britain. The senior policy makers came from the Canadian federal, provincial and territorial governments as well as from the voluntary sector. The Workshop was an opportunity for outstanding scholars and decision makers to meet and interact around a substantively important topic and to establish new partnerships in the hope of contributing to the development of more effective policies for single parent families and families in general.

Single Parent Families: Perspectives on Research and Policy not only provides an authoritative overview of current research on single parent families, it also outlines what many books have failed to address: the identification of policy and research implications and the identification of a research agenda for the immediate future.

As Director of the National Welfare Grants Division, Social Service Programs Branch, Health and Welfare Canada, who funded and co-sponsored the Workshop, I am delighted with the book's outcome and pleased to have been associated with this project. I would be remiss if I did not express my sincere appreciation to the Workshop's organizing committee members who made a significant contribution to its success. They are: Drs. Joe Hudson and Burt Galaway, co-directors of the Workshop, Dr. Robert Glossop, Vanier Institute of the Family, Dr. Laura Johnson, Child, Youth and Family Policy Research Centre and Mr. Michel Smith, National Welfare Grants, who successfully identified and coordinated the participation of eighteen key federal/provincial/territorial policy makers.

While the significance of the problems associated with the single parent family are becoming increasingly evident and while there has been increasing research devoted to this topic, *Single Parent Families: Perspectives on Research and Policy* is the first book entirely devoted to pulling together and synthesizing the current research and policy issues surrounding this growing family type. I have no doubts this book will become required reading for anyone concerned with the well-being of single parent families. I commend everyone associated with this book and the preceding Workshop for their commitment and vision.

David Thornton, Ph.D.
Director
National Welfare Grants
Health and Welfare Canada

Contributors

LOIS BROCKMAN. Professor, Department of Family Studies, University of Manitoba, Winnipeg, Manitoba.

KIM CLARE. Assistant Professor, Faculty of Social Work, Winnipeg Education Centre, University of Manitoba, Winnipeg, Manitoba.

SUSAN CLARK. Vice President (Academic), Brock University, St. Catharines, Ontario.

MARTIN DOOLEY. Associate Professor, Department of Economics, McMaster University, Hamilton, Ontario.

MARGRIT EICHLER. Professor, Department of Sociology in Education, Ontario Institute for Studies in Education, Toronto, Ontario.

ELSA FERRI. Senior Research Fellow, Social Statistics Research Unit, City University, London, England.

BURT GALAWAY. Professor, Faculty of Social Work, University of Manitoba, Winnipeg, Manitoba.

IRWIN GARFINKEL. Professor, School of Social Work, Columbia University, New York, New York.

ELLEN M. GEE. Professor, Department of Sociology and Anthropology, Simon Fraser University, Burnaby, British Columbia.

ROBERT GLOSSOP. Director of Programs, Vanier Institute of the Family, Ottawa, Ontario.

CAROLYNE GORLICK. Assistant Professor, Department of Social Work, King's College, The University of Western Ontario, London, Ontario.

JOE HUDSON. Professor, Faculty of Social Work, The University of Calgary (Edmonton Division), Edmonton, Alberta.

LAURA JOHNSON. Visiting Expert in Residence, Centre for Future Studies, Canada Mortgage and Housing Corporation.

FRAN KLODAWSKY. Assistant Professor, Departments of Women's Studies and Geography, and Director, Institute of Women's Studies, Carleton University, Ottawa, Ontario.

LISE LAVOIE. Policy Director, Children's Bureau, Health and Welfare Canada, Ottawa, Ontario.

NADINE LEFAUCHEUR. Sociologue, Centre National de la Recherche Scientifique, Paris, France.

DONNA LERO. Associate Professor, Department of Family Studies, University of Guelph, Guelph, Ontario.

NICOLE MARCIL-GRATTON. Researcher, Groupe de recherche sur la démographie québécoise, Département de démographie, Université de Montréal, Montréal, Québec.

CLAUDE MARTIN. Professor of Sociology. École Nationale de la Santé Publique, Rennes, France.

SUSAN A. MCDANIEL. Professor, Department of Sociology, University of Alberta, Edmonton, Alberta.

FRAN MCININCH. Consultant, National Welfare Grants, Health and Welfare Canada, Ottawa.

CRAIG MCKIE. Professor, Department of Sociology and Anthropology, Carleton University, and Editor, Canadian Social Trends, Statistics Canada, Ottawa.

SARA MCLANAHAN. Professor, Department of Sociology, Princeton University, Princeton, New Jersey.

ELIZABETH MCNAUGHTON. Director, Policy Planning and Research, Nova Scotia Department of Community Services, Halifax, Nova Scotia.

E. DIANE PASK. Professor, Faculty of Law, The University of Calgary, Calgary, Alberta.

MARYANNE PENTICK. Consultant, National Welfare Grants, Health and Welfare Canada, Ottawa.

ALAN D. POMFRET. Professor, Department of Sociology, King's College, The University of Western Ontario, London, Ontario.

ARON N. SPECTOR. Ark Research Associates, Ottawa, Ontario.

ELLEN ZWIEBEL. Professor, Faculty of Law, University of Ottawa, Ottawa, Ontario.

Introduction

Burt Galaway and Joe Hudson

This volume was developed to present contemporary Canadian research findings, identify the public policy implications of the research, and to identify future research needs in regard to the single parent family. The scholars whose work is represented in this volume are in disagreement as to whether the term single parent family or lone parent family is the preferred descriptor for these families. Single parent family is the older, and more established term. Some of the authors object to this term, and prefer the term lone parent family, because they believe the term single confuses marital status and family structure. They correctly point out that many persons come to this family form through routes other than single parenthood. Proponents of the term single note that the word derives from the Latin singulus, and has a usage that is well beyond referring to marital status. Further, the word lone can also imply that the family is alone in the sense of being cutoff from forms of social support. This is clearly not the case with most of these families. Although this debate may be of interest, to deal with it in a protracted manner would detract from the purpose of this volume. Thus, we are adopting the term single parent family in the title because this is the more established and commonly used term although it may not be the preferred term among Canadian scholars. In the chapters, both the terms lone and single are used reflecting the preferences of the original writers.

Introductory papers by Elsa Ferri, Sara McLanahan and Irving Garfinkel, and Nadine Lafaucheur and Claude Martin present information regarding the single parent family in Britain, the United States, and France and provide an international perspective for the Canadian papers. The sections that follow present research regarding the demographics of the single parent family, Canadian public policy impacts on the single parent family, support needs of the single parent family, and the socialization experiences of children in single parent families. Each of the major parts of the volume is concluded with a summary chapter that identifies major themes, notes policy implications, and suggests an agenda for future research.

The demographic papers suggest that the number of single parent families in Canada now exceeds one million, and is growing three times as fast as husband and wife families. Craig McKie notes that single parent families now constitute about 14% of the total. Nicole Marcil-Gratton estimates that, over their life time, 34% of mothers will have spent time as a single parent and that an increasing number of children will experience a period of time in a single parent family. Donna Lero, as well as other authors, reports that single parent families tend to be part of the population with a high rate of child and family poverty. Martin Dooley notes that lone mothers under thirty-five are characterized by falling market earnings and rising transfers income. Married mothers under thirty-five are more likely to be employed than are single mothers; 54% of mother headed and 22% of father headed single parent families are below the poverty line. These families are predominantly headed by mothers, although McKie notes that 18% of the single parent families are father headed.

Margarit Eichler argues that the single parent familyhood is largely a transitory phenomena, with people moving in and out of this status because of remarriage and cohabitation. Single parenthood may not be an appropriate unit for analysis; what is needed is a family policy, rather than a policy specifically oriented towards single parents. Examination of tax policy by Ellen Zweibel suggests that tax treatment of child support increases economic disparity between custodial mothers and dependent children and non-custodial fathers. E. Diane Pask argues that there is no coherent body of policy which guides the development of statutes and jurisprudence relating to family law and Susan McDaniel suggests that public policy in single parents is familized, based on dependency, misses the diversity of the realities faced by single mothers, and builds in contradictory notions of intentionality and victimization.

Support needs of single parent families relate to the condition of resource deficit that comes about because responsibilities usually carried out by two adults become the responsibility of a single adult. Susan Clark provides information from a longitudinal study of women who were single at the time of their first birth compared to those who were married. Many of the single mothers subsequently married but their income levels and employment remains lower than for women who began motherhood married. Donna Lero examines the child care arrangements for employed single parent families as well as employed dual parent families. Only a minority of both groups receive daycare from regulated facilities; the single parent families are more likely to use regulated facilities, relatives, or other children than the dual parent families who more typically rely upon the other parent. Aaron Spector and Fran Klodawsky analyze the housing arrangements of the lone parent families in a relation to fourteen established criteria; housing and related income and support issues are particularly critical for single parent families headed by women in their thirties and forties who have become single parent through separation or divorce. Carolyne Gorlick and D. Alan Pomfret examine the role of social support in single parents' likelihood in engaging in documentable strategies designed to secure exit from social assistance; documentable strategies include activities such as securing employment, training, education, and so forth. Informational support is particularly important; single parents tend to receive support primarily from female companions and relatives.

Elsa Ferri analyzes data from a birth cohort in England to study the effects on children who were raised in a single parent family. Young people who have experienced such situations do less well than peers from unbroken homes on a range of measures including educational attainment and social emotional behaviour in school years but the differences are largely explained by social and economic disadvantage. Ellen Gee examines the adult adjustment of people who, at age fifteen, were living with both parents, lost a parent as a result of death, or lost a parent as a result of divorce or separation. She finds only small differences across the groups on a series of behavioral and attitudinal measures. Elizabeth McNaughton reports on the relationship between mother's marital status at the time of the child's birth and the socialization and developmental experiences of children at age ten. Several differences emerged although much of the difference can be attributed to low income.

A final, summary chapter pulls together the major themes of this volume, identifies the policy implications, and suggests directions for future research. The most consistently identified research need is for a large scale longitudinal study to permit more detailed study of the transitions through which Canadian families move. More use needs to be made of existing data sources and multiple research methods are necessary to generate comprehensive information about Canadian families. Family policies and programs should be more carefully evaluated with attention to both expected and unexpected results. Further research is required to identify the factors that contribute to successful outcomes, especially for children of single parent families. Finally, researchers and policy makers need to identify the ways in which research findings can be more effectively communicated and used for policy making.

PART I

INTERNATIONAL RESEARCH AND POLICY PERSPECTIVES

1

An Overview of Research and Policy on the Lone Parent Family in Britain

Elsa Ferri

Just over twenty years ago the British government set up the Finer committee of enquiry to consider the problems facing lone parent families. The ensuing report (Department of Health and Social Security, 1974) made numerous recommendations in relation to family law, social security and other income sources, employment, day care, and housing. In a climate of increasing restraint on public expenditure, however, comparatively few changes were subsequently introduced. Nevertheless, a sociological review of the lone parent family in the mid–1970s anticipated an amelioration in its position (Chester, 1977). This was expected to stem from improved financial circumstances resulting from greater occupational opportunities for women, and from more tolerant social attitudes towards divorce and births outside marriage. Almost two decades later, however, the picture is less encouraging. Despite a reduction in stigmatization, lone parent families have recently re-emerged as a major social problem. Rapid growth in numbers, and an even greater increase in the proportions dependent upon financial support from the state, have led the government to consider once again its policy towards lone parent households.

Recent Demographic Trends

The number of lone parent families in Britain has more than doubled in the past twenty years. Figures from the 1990 General Household Survey showed that 19% of families with dependent children is now headed by a lone parent, involving a total of almost two million children (Office of Population Census and Surveys, 1990). Nine out of ten of these families are headed by a lone mother; the sharpest rise in numbers has occurred among female headed households. However, this overall increase masks different trends in the causes of lone mother status. The number of families headed by widowed mothers has actually declined; the growth is due to increased rates of divorce and to births to single mothers.

Apart from a temporary slowdown in the early 1980s, divorce rates have risen inexorably since the Divorce Reform Act of 1969. Britain currently has the second highest divorce rate in Europe (after Denmark). Estimates are that 37 per cent of marriages will be dissolved and one child in five will experience parental divorce by the age of sixteen if present rates continue (Kiernan and Wicks, 1990). Much remains to be learned about the causes and correlates of marital breakdown; among the demographic factors associated with divorce are younger age at marriage (Haskey,1988) and the birth of the first child earlier in marriage (Ermisch,1990).

Currently, 25% of all births in Britain are to single mothers, representing a fourfold increase since 1971. Not all of these contribute to the lone parent family population as approximately half are registered by both parents living at the same address. This represents an equally dramatic rise in cohabitation as part of the increasingly diverse pattern of family life in contemporary British society. Nonetheless, the proportion of children living with a single mother alone has also shown a marked upward trend. This group tends to be younger on average than other lone mothers; Ermisch (1990) found that early exit from the education system was also associated with single motherhood.

Other Correlates of Lone Parenthood

Families headed by lone parents have, in the context of a general decline in family size over the last two decades, remained smaller on average (1.6 children) than two-parent families (1.8). Lone mothers tend to have more children than lone fathers (1.6 and 1.4 on average respectively). Only in the sub-group of single mothers, however, has the trend in family size not been in a downward direction.

Assessing the social class background of one-parent families is somewhat problematic, insofar as lone mother families by definition lack a male head of household, whose occupational status is the conventional measure of social class. In the National Child Development Study (a continuing follow-up of one week's births in 1958), father's occupation at the time of the child's birth showed that both motherless and fatherless children at eleven were more likely to come from semiskilled or unskilled backgrounds. The only exception was the widowed mother group, which did not differ significantly from two-parent families. Haskey (1984) used a sample drawn from divorce records and also found that divorce rates rose as the social class scale descended. Britain is a multicultural society; the prevalence of lone motherhood differs among the various minority ethnic groups. There is a higher than average proportion of lone motherhood among the Afro-Caribbean population, which is younger than the population as a whole, while Asian and Chinese groups contain fewer than average (Leonard and Speakman, 1986).

Dynamics of Lone Parenthood

Views taken at particular points in time underestimate the numbers who will ever experience lone parenthood. Family formation, dissolution, and reconstitution is a dynamic process; Ermisch (1986) notes that half of those who become lone parents marry or remarry within five years. However, higher failure rates attach to second (and subsequent) marriages (Ferri, 1984). Bradshaw and Millar (1991) found that 14% of their sample of divorced and single parents had experienced more than one episode of lone parenthood, and half had at least one child by a second partner.

Much more needs to be known about movement in and out of different family situations and the factors which influence this. The lack of data in the census and other demographic sources presents a problem. Longitudinal data sets, such as the National Child Development Study, furnish valuable information on those who enter and leave different family status groups. The demographic picture currently available indicates that family life, for a large and growing number of children and parents in Britain, will involve one or more dramatic changes in household composition, lifestyle, and relationships.

Policy and Its Impact

Britain has not so much a family policy as a series of not always consistent policies that affect families. The official approach to lone parent families, nearly two decades after the Finer Committee, remains 'one of the most uncertain and surely unsatisfactory areas of social policy' (Kiernan & Wicks, 1990, p.33). This uncertainty can be traced to considerable public ambivalence towards the role of lone parents, especially mothers, as parents or workers; this ambivalence also applies to mothers in general, but becomes particularly problematic in relation to those who are unsupported.

Income and Employment

Whether or not lone parents enter or stay in the labour market will be influenced both by specific policy measures and prevailing social attitudes, especially those that reinforce gender differences in the roles of men and women as parents. Thus, the great majority of lone fathers pursue the traditional male breadwinner role through full-time employment, although more are registered as unemployed than is the case among fathers in general, and there is also evidence that their level of earnings and career advancement are curtailed by their domestic responsibilities (Ferri and Robinson, 1976).

There is much less clarity and consensus for lone mothers, both in terms of social expectation and relevant policy measures regarding which of two full-time roles — earning a living and caring for children — they are to undertake. Thus, official policy, as expressed by the Department of Social Security, purports to a position of neutrality:

> Social security benefits are structured so that while not requiring lone parents with children up to the age of 16 to be available for work, they nevertheless do not unduly discourage lone parents from working if they wish to (National Audit Office, 1990: 6).

The implication of this policy stance is that it is up to individual parents to decide which source or combination of income provision is most appropriate to their family's needs. The actual operation of the benefit system and other policies influencing labour market participation, however, shows that the choice facing a high proportion of lone mothers is between two routes to poverty.

During a period when employment rates of mothers generally have shown a consistent rise, those of lone mothers have actually fallen, so that they are now less likely to be in work than their married counterparts. The proportion of lone mothers in part-time work has remained considerably lower, while the number in full-time jobs has dropped to a level equal to that of all mothers. The operation of the current benefit system has clearly contributed to this situation. For married women, part-time work, although usually poorly paid, represents a supplement to the earnings of a male partner. For divorced, separated or single mothers, however, Income Support (the benefit available to the unemployed or to part-time workers) is reduced £ for £ after the first £15 (approximately $30) of earnings. This contrasts with the Widowed Mother's Allowance which carries no such loss of benefit and thus places this group of lone mothers in a comparatively advantaged position. Part-time employment is not financially worthwhile, taking into account the costs of work, such as child care and travel. Lone mothers in full-time work may be eligible for Family Credit, which boosts the income of those in low-paid occupations. However, this is likely to mean the loss of other benefits linked to receipt of Income Support, as well as the increased child care costs of longer working hours, so that a switch to full-time employment could entail a net loss in disposable income. A recent study of the operation of the benefit system concluded that:

> ... the balance of gaining or losing by working will vary according to the number and age of children, the level of earnings, housing costs, maintenance payments made by liable relatives and work-related expenses. Quite small changes in personal circumstances can tip the financial balance either way (National Audit Office, 1990: 18).

It is hardly surprising that other researchers have found many parents to be unaware of the levels and conditions attaching to different benefits and unable to arrive at rational decisions regarding the advantages or otherwise of employment (Joshi,1990).

Several studies have examined the interaction of factors affecting the employment behaviour of lone mothers. Bradshaw and Millar (1991), in a recent investigation of over 1800 divorced, separated, or single parents, found that those most likely to be economically active were older, with school age children, previously married (rather than single), with some educational or vocational qualifications, living in owner-occupied accommodation and receiving some maintenance from their former partner. The same study showed that the factors predictive of full-time employment were higher anticipated wage rates, access to child care and having older, school age children. Factors affecting employment behaviour of lone parents can be grouped under three broad headings relating to: (1) the individual attributes and skills of the parent, (2) parental responsibilities (especially for child care), and (3) the material circumstances of the family, in particular accommodation and income. Various areas of public policy impinge directly or indirectly on all of these factors.

How does policy relating to maintenance payments by former partners affect the employment situation of lone parents? Studies have consistently shown that maintenance represents a small and unreliable proportion of the income of lone mother families (Maclean and Ekelaar, 1986; Millar, 1989), reflecting the unwillingness and/or inability of ex-partners to provide support. This has recently become a salient policy issue in the context of political concern over the increasing dependence of lone parent families on the social security system, and is leading to the introduction of procedures to recover more maintenance from errant fathers. Even if successful such measures will have little impact on the financial position of families receiving Income Support, since recovered maintenance will be deducted from benefit payments. Opposition has also been voiced by mothers who, under the new regulations, will be required to name the father of their child, under penalty of reduction in benefit, in order that pursuit of maintenance can take place.

The major sources of income available to lone parents are state benefits, earnings, and maintenance. The combination of earnings and maintenance represents, under current conditions, the greatest potential for raising family finances above the poverty level since the two other combinations contain in-built ceilings on obtainable income.

Housing

Housing policy has considerable impact on lone parent families, through its linkage with other socio-economic factors. The Finer Report (Department of Health and Social Security, 1974) concluded that, after financial difficulties, housing was the most serious problem facing lone parent families. It could be argued that the success of housing policy is measured by the extent to which households enjoy choice in terms of accommodation. The experience of lone parent families is more likely to be characterized by constraint than by the availability of options; the disadvantage suffered is greater in families headed by lone mothers (Family Policy Studies Centre, no date; Ferri, 1976).

The housing disadvantage of lone parents is linked to what happens at the time of family dissolution and to subsequent, longer term trends in their housing careers. The break in the family may mean the loss of the family home — Bradshaw and Millar (1991) found that 58% of the families in their study had to move as a result — although some lone parent families may retain the home at this point. The latter situation is more likely to occur in the publicly rented sector, where transfers of tenancy are available to enable the caring parent and children to remain in the home, whereas the division of assets among home owners may mean the loss of such accommodation; the National Child Development Study found that only 67% of divorced or separated lone mother families had remained in owned housing compared with 95% of intact families (Ferri, 1976). Lone parent households are less likely to be owner occupiers and more likely to be tenants. The long term trend in their housing careers is downwardly mobile, i.e., towards the public sector and away from owner occupation.

Housing studies have also revealed discriminatory policies in the public sector, with lone parent families being housed in the poorest accommodation and the least desirable localities (Austerberry and Watson, 1985). This may reflect a perception of lone parent households as problem families or the undeserving poor (Karn and Henderson, 1983). The situation has been exacerbated in the last ten years or so by the central government policy of offering public housing for sale to tenants. This policy, ostensibly aimed at reversing social polarization between home owners and municipal tenants, has had the opposite effect. The sales drive has focused on the most marketable sections of public housing but other policy measures have resulted in very little new additions to the public housing stock. Lone parent families are heavily over-represented among the poorer public housing tenants who could not afford to buy and may have little wish to purchase the inferior accommodation in which they have been placed. The resulting intensified segregation of the poorest (Karn and Henderson, 1983) concentrates lone parent families geographically, either in inner city or perimeter overspill estates, where limited employment opportunities further reinforce the vicious circle of disadvantage in which so many become trapped.

Support Needs of Lone Parent Families

A wealth of evidence has accumulated demonstrating the economic and social disadvantage suffered by lone parent families, in particular the difficulties such parents face in achieving adequate living standards (Finer, 1974; Hunt et al., 1973; Millar, 1989). Research findings also reveal marked differences between lone parent families according to the sex of the parent and the reason for their situation. Lone father families, although disadvantaged by comparison with two-parent families, are considerably better off in material terms than those headed by lone mothers (Townsend, 1979); within the latter group, widows' families fare better than those of divorced, separated, or single mothers (Ferri, 1976).

The economic and social support needs of all families centre on the resources required to fulfil the multiple tasks of parenting — providing satisfactory living standards as well as the time, care, and attention needed to foster children's growth and development. The diminution of adult resources intensifies the problems faced by lone parent families in undertaking these often competing roles; the need for extra-familial support is correspondingly greater.

Perhaps the most significant, incontrovertible social fact relating to lone parenthood, and especially lone motherhood, is its association with poverty, both absolute and relative. The number of one-parent families (in particular those headed by divorced and single mothers) dependent upon state benefits has increased faster than both the prevalence of lone parenthood and the total numbers in receipt of benefits (Millar, 1989). By 1985, 73% of lone parent families were living on the margins of poverty, defined as not more than 40% above the level of Income Support (Department of Health and Social Security, 1988). The 1989 Family Expenditure Survey showed that the net disposable income of lone parent families was just 39% that of couples with two children (Office of Population Census and Surveys, 1990). Social security was the main source of income of two-thirds of lone parent families, compared with just one in eight intact families (Family Policy Studies Centre, no date).

A recent study of the material circumstance of lone parent families concluded that the most likely routes out of poverty are repartnering (although the outcome here depends upon the employment status of the new partner) or obtaining sufficiently remunerative employment. A key area of support to lone parent families thus involves assistance in participating in the labour market. Lone parents' opportunities in this area are affected by both formal policy measures and informal support systems.

Child Care

The issue of child care is of crucial significance to the employment behaviour of lone parents and one in which social policy in Britain has long been conspicuous for its passivity. There is a striking contradiction in current employment policy, which seeks to encourage mothers into the work force, and social welfare policy, which maintains that it is not the role of the state to encourage the abrogation of maternal responsibility by providing day care for the children of those who respond to the call. As a result, Britain is one of the poorest providers of publicly funded child care in Europe; Moss (1991) estimates that there is only one public day care place for every hundred children under three.

Working mothers are expected both to find and finance private solutions. Surveys have shown that, under these circumstances, married mothers are heavily reliant on their partners and other relatives to provide child care; in one example, fathers cared for 47% of preschool-aged children and 57% of school-aged children while mothers were at work (Martin and Roberts, 1984). In the absence of a partner, the child care dilemma is particularly acute. Bradshaw and Millar (1991) found that the number of lone mothers who said they would work if they had child care would have raised their employment rate to that of women generally. One-third of those unemployed and on Income Support said that the lack of child care was their main reason for not working. Moreover, three-quarters of those in employment claimed that they would have to give up work immediately if their child care arrangements broke down.

Where there is little subsidized provision, the cost of child care is an even greater constraint on employment than its availability. Bradshaw and Millar (1991) found that only 42% of lone mothers using child care actually paid for it. This reflected their very high level of dependence upon the informal care provided by relatives (especially grandmothers), friends, and neighbours. Seventy-five percent of preschool children of lone mothers were cared for in this way, and the figure rose to 81% for children of school age. An important question is whether the continuing trend for women to re-enter the labour market will seriously reduce this vital supply of substitute child care.

Skills and Training

The route out of poverty via employment is contingent upon the possession of skills and experience which will lead to adequate earnings. In a labour market situation in which women generally still experience discrimination and disadvantage (Millar and Glendinning, 1987), lone mothers earn less than their married counterparts (Bradshaw and Millar, 1991), yet work longer hours (Roll, 1988). There is thus a clear need for support measures that will equip them to improve their position through the acquisition of marketable skills.

The response to this need has been limited. An Employment Training Scheme that began in 1988 included 5000 places for lone parents who had claimed Income Support for at least six months and had school-aged children; there were an estimated that there were 389,000 lone parents in this situation. Child care costs up to £50 per week were met by the scheme. Bradshaw and Millar (1991) found that only two percent of the lone parents had been on the scheme; although 68% expressed an interest in it, only 30% knew how to apply and just 13% knew that child care costs would be met.

Here, as in other areas, lack of knowledge could act as a barrier to obtaining relevant support. Considerable stress has been laid on the contribution of voluntary, community and self-help groups. For example, a central government grant of £1 million has recently been allocated to the National Council for One-Parent Families to provide six-day return to work courses for lone parents wishing to re-enter the labour market.

Employment Practice

Employment practice is a further important aspect of support for labour market participation. This is also an area in which lone parents are likely to experience disadvantage. Maclean and Ekelaar (1986) found that attitudes among employers confirmed the claims of discrimination voiced by a sample of divorced mothers. Two approaches were identified: family aware employers would not appoint applicants whose domestic situation they considered rendered them unreliable; family averse employers disregarded domestic circumstances when appointing but were likely to dismiss those who experienced difficulty in fulfilling their contractual terms of employment. Employment practice, through inflexibility of hours, lack of provision for parental leave, and so on, currently fails to offer adequate and much needed support for the family responsibilities of workers, particularly those attempting to combine the dual roles of worker and parent.

Housing

Housing represents a problem for many lone parent families and formal policies in this area can have adverse consequences for them. Here, too, informal support, provided by the extended family in particular, is of importance, especially in relation to preventing or hiding homelessness. Research has shown that lone parent families are heavily over-represented among those officially identified as homeless. Greve and Currie (1990) noted that 40% of those accepted as homeless by local authorities were lone parents. Other studies have pointed to lone parents' reliance on relatives for accommodation, suggesting that the official figures conceal a high level of hidden homelessness. The Family Policy Studies Centre (no date) reported that 12% of lone mothers, and a third of single mothers, were living with their own parents. Other studies have confirmed the importance of kinship networks in providing accommodation, but have also noted that the reality of such situations can be fraught with tension and strained relationships (Cashmore, 1985).

The Need for Social and Emotional Support

The research literature has paid comparatively little attention to the need which lone parents have for social and emotional support in the difficult and often isolated task of bringing up children single-handedly. This includes the need for adult companionship and relationships as well as some sharing of the responsibilities of childrearing. Qualitative research into the experiences of lone parents suggests that they are particularly likely to detect problems in their children's development and to attribute these to their family situation and their own perceived inadequacies as parents (Ferri and Robinson, 1976). The last two decades have seen a mushrooming of self-help support groups aimed at meeting these needs and of pressing for policies that will promote the welfare of lone parent families. A number of parents interviewed in the study said that only others with similar experiences could offer them the support they sought. This is likely to reflect the difficulties faced by lone parents in reintegrating into social activities and relationships which are so firmly predicated on the participation of couples.

Socialization of Children from Lone Parent Families

What are the effects of lone parenting on the welfare and development of children? It would be gratifying if the considerable body of relevant research could be encapsulated in a few unequivocal statements. That this is not the case partly reflects the inherent complexity of the subject. The diverse situations and experiences subsumed under the umbrella heading of lone parent family need to be considered in assessing its impact. Factors such as the reason for the family situation, the sex of the lone parent and children concerned, and the age of the children both at the time of assessment and when the lone parent family was created, all need to be taken into account in examining relationships, both short and long term, between family experience and a wide range of developmental outcomes. Effects attributable to the family situation must also be disentangled from those due to other social and environmental factors that influence development.

Although the picture is not altogether clear, some consistent and important findings have emerged from studies equipped to address the complexity of the issue. The most rigorous investigations have been based on the longitudinal National Child Development Study, which has collected a wealth of information at five follow-up surveys about the background and development of the 17,000 or so individuals born in one week of 1958. Multivariate analyses using this data have compared the educational achievement and social/emotional behaviour of children from different family situations, while allowing for variations in their social and economic background. Briefly, the results have revealed the significant contribution of the disadvantaged circumstances suffered by lone parent families (including low income and housing difficulties) in explaining the poorer overall performance of their children (Ferri, 1976; Essen, 1979). A tendency remained for children with divorced/separated mothers or lone fathers to have done less well than their counterparts in intact homes, but the differences were comparatively small in magnitude. The contribution of socio-economic factors to developmental differences are inextricably linked to issues of policy and support. Thus, the disadvantages suffered by lone parent families in terms of income, housing, and weakness in the labour market are amenable to change through social policy measures aimed at strengthening the lone parent family as a child-rearing environment.

Conclusion

Dramatic growth in the number of lone parent families in Britain over the past two decades has been a major contributory factor in the fundamental change that has taken place in family structure. The traditional stereotype of the family unit comprising an employed father, home-based mother, and two dependent children now applies to only a minority of British households. The lone parent family is also one of the fastest growing groups in Britain living in, or on the margins of, poverty. This is especially so in the case of the largest groups of lone parent families, those headed by a divorced, separated or single mother. The reasons can be traced to the continuing gender inequality in our society and also to policy measures that fail to address the interrelated needs of lone parent families in a way which would assist families to break out of a vicious circle of deprivation.

Policies explicitly concerned with the material support of lone parent families are grounded in a narrow economic perspective in which the dominant concerns are the interests of the labour market and the public purse. As a result, inadequate recognition is given to the problem of reconciling work and family life — a problem which becomes especially acute in lone parent households, and one which would receive far greater prominence in a policy approach that took as its starting point the needs of children and families. Such a strategy would produce a package of integrated measures, in which the links between the three key institutions of work, family, and state were recognized and facilitated. It could also shift the current policy preoccupation with reducing dependency through a reappraisal of the conventional, but arbitrary, distinction between what is and is not considered work. A move away from the traditional view of childrearing as merely another unskilled and unrewarded component in the repertoire of maternal domestic activity could produce a different perception of the appropriate public response to the support needed by lone parents to fulfil their multiple roles.

Research to date has amply demonstrated the wide-ranging disadvantages experienced by lone parent families in terms of their living standards and the important part played by this disadvantage in explaining the relatively poor developmental outcomes for children growing up in such families. The societal response to the needs of lone parent families has been inadequate and increases the risk that children in such families will fail to fulfil their potential. Research evidence as to the nature and extent of the problems facing lone parent families, and their unmet needs for support, provides an informed basis for the development of more effective policy measures aimed at alleviating their disadvantage and promoting the welfare of their children.

2

Single Motherhood in the United States: Growth, Problems, and Policies

Sara McLanahan and Irwin Garfinkel

This chapter examines single mother families in the United States, including their growth and composition, the problems they confront, and the ways in which public policy affects their economic situation. Families headed by unmarried mothers increased dramatically in the U.S. during the past three decades. Whereas in 1960 about 8% of all families with children were headed by single mothers, by 1990 the number was nearly 25%. Moreover, the 25% figure understates by half, the proportion of all children who will spend a part of their childhood in a family headed by a single mother. The composition of mother-only families also changed during this period, with the proportion of widowed mothers declining and the proportion of divorced and never married mothers increasing.

The major problems faced by single mother families in the U.S. are poverty and economic insecurity. Nearly half of single mothers live below the poverty line and a large proportion of those who are not poor experience considerable economic instability. There is growing evidence that single motherhood has long term negative consequences for children and that many of these consequences are due to low (and perhaps insecure) income. Economic insecurity in mother-only families has three proximate causes: the low earning capacity of the mothers, the inadequate and irregular child support from nonresident fathers, and the low level of public support for children in general.

Poverty arising from mothers' low earnings capacity can be reduced by investing in mothers' human capital and by enhancing their earnings through child care subsidies and earnings subsidies. The states and the federal government have been slow to put money into work and training programs for single mothers despite evidence that employment and training investments have a positive, albeit modest, return to both taxpayers and beneficiaries. The Family Support Act of 1988 offers matching funds to the states for work/training programs, and Senator Moynihan has recently proposed increasing federal funding from $1 billion to $5 billion for such programs. The U.S. has done better at creating instruments that compensate mothers with low earnings: the earned income tax credit (EITC) and child care benefits were all developed and expanded during the 1970s and 1980s.

During the 1970s and 1980s the U.S. moved aggressively towards strengthening and rationalizing the private child support system. A series of amendments to the Social Security Act, beginning in the mid 1970s and culminating in the Family Support Act of 1988, were designed by the federal government to put pressure on states to expand child support awards to all eligible children, including children born out-of-wedlock, to standardize and update award levels, and to increase collections by withholding child support obligations from fathers' earnings.

Substantial reductions in the poverty and economic insecurity of families headed by single mothers will require additional increases in public support. The benefits can be targeted only on the poorest children who live with single mothers or upon all children. In general, the less targeted on the poor, the more helpful the benefit will be in reducing dependence upon cash welfare assistance. Benefits for all children — like a refundable tax credit for children in the income tax or some form of national health insurance — or benefits for all children potentially eligible for child support — like an assured child support benefit — would, like the EITC, help make work pay and would make life outside welfare much more economically secure.

The Growth of Single Parent Family in the United States

In 1990, approximately 6 million families in the United States were headed by single mothers, nearly 25% of all families with children. Among Whites, mother-only families accounted for 17% of all families with children, and among African-Americans they accounted for 53% of all families (U.S. Bureau of the Census, 1991b). These figures are based on cross-sectional data and therefore they understate the proportion of children that will ever live in a mother-only family. Demographers estimate that about half of all children born in the 1980s will live in a mother-only family before reaching age eighteen — 45% of Whites and 85% of African-Americans (Bumpass, 1984). The median length of time spent in a mother-only family is about six years, it is over ten years for children born to unmarried mothers. The trend in the proportion of families headed by single mothers is shown in Figure 2-1 for the period 1940 to 1990. The line was flat between 1940 and 1950, rose gradually during the 1950s, and increased markedly after 1960. The acceleration of growth after 1960 coincided with the increase in divorce rates and the decline in marriage rates that occurred in the sixties.

Historically, widowhood was the most common form of single parenthood in the United States. In 1900, about 80% of children living with a single parent were living with a widowed mother or father (Gordon and McLana-

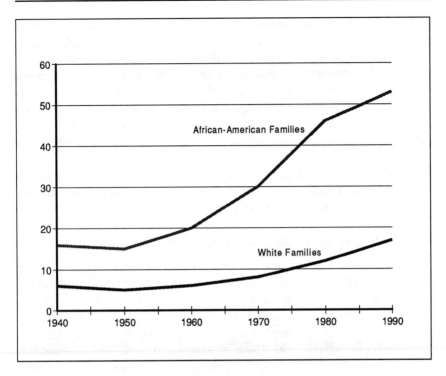

Figure 2-1:
Proportion of Mother-Only Families in the United States,
1940-1990

han, 1991). Since World War II, divorce and premarital birth have become increasingly important factors in accounting for the growth in single parenthood and this pattern continues through the present. In 1970, 6.8% of all children living with a single mother were living with a never married mother, whereas in 1984 the figure was 24%. The composition varies considerably by race, African-American children are more likely to live with unmarried mothers, whereas Anglo children are more likely to live with divorced mothers (Ellwood, 1988). The distinction among the different types of single motherhood is important because of the variation across groups in access to economic and social resources. Widows have higher incomes than other single mothers, and they experience less social disapproval. In contrast, unmarried mothers have the fewest resources and are most likely to be stigmatized of all single mothers.

Numerous explanations have been put forward to account for the growing number of mother-only families in the United States. The four most common are the increase in women's employment (women's economic independence), the decrease in men's employment, the increase in government assistance, and changing social values. To date, the empirical evidence is most consistent with the first hypothesis, that the increase in single parenthood is due to women's growing economic independence. There is some evidence that the expansion of public assistance and increase in benefits that occurred between 1960 and 1975 may have contributed to single parenthood by reducing remarriage (Garfinkel and McLanahan, 1986). But government transfers appear to have had only a minor effect on divorce and out-of-wedlock births, accounting for no more that 15% of the overall growth and no more than 30% of the growth among low income couples. Similarly, the change in public attitudes toward divorce and single mothers appears to have followed rather than preceded the growth in mother-only families in the 1960s (Garfinkel and McLanahan, 1986).

The Problems of Single Mother Families

Single mother families face a much higher risk of poverty than other demographic groups. Roughly 45% of these families are poor, according to the official government definition of poverty (U.S. Census Bureau, 1991a). Figure 2-2 shows the trend in the poverty rate for single mother families as compared to two-parent families and aged persons in the United States for the years 1959 through 1990. These measures of poverty take into account the assistance provided by the major government income support programs, except the value of in-kind transfers such as food stamps and medical insurance. (If the in-kind value is counted, the absolute figures are lower, but the trends are similar.) Women and children in single mother families are the poorest of all these groups, and the gap between single mothers and the elderly has actually increased. This is because social security benefits paid to elderly people are indexed to increases in the cost of living whereas Aid to Families with Dependent Children (AFDC) benefits paid to single mothers are not. Both the relative and the absolute condition of single mothers has deteriorated since 1970 due to a 30% decline in the real value of welfare benefits. Poverty is but the most extreme form of economic insecurity. Most single mothers who escape poverty still suffer from severe economic instability. The average income of the more fortunate half of single mothers is equal to only 60% of their pre-divorce income. At least part of the income loss following divorce is due to the loss of economies of scale; it costs more to support two households than one household. The costs of divorce, however, are not equally distributed among parents and children. Whereas the standard of living of the entire group of single mothers declines after the family breaks up, fathers' living standard goes up slightly (Duncan and Hoffman, 1985).

Following a divorce, women and children undergo numerous other changes in roles and social position that involve insecurity stemming from the loss of social status as well as loss of family and friends. Changes in

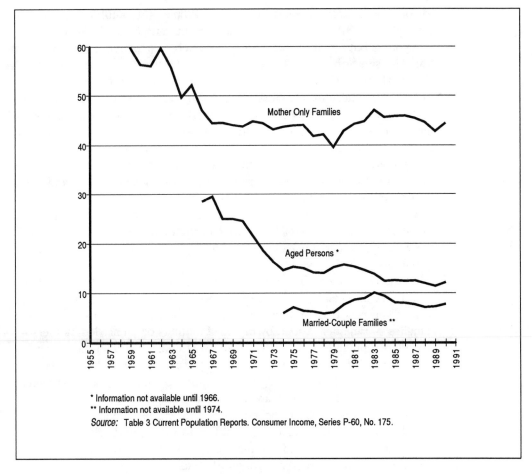

Figure 2-2:

Poverty Rates for Mother-Only Families, Aged Person and Married-Couple Families, 1959-1990

residence are perhaps the most common form of social instability in newly formed mother-only families. One study shows that about 38% of divorced mothers and their children move their residence during the first year after a divorce (McLanahan, 1983). Changes in residence require adjustment to new neighbourhoods and living conditions, and may also mean the loss of important social networks and support.

Changes in employment are also common among single mothers. Many mothers enter the labour force for the first time or increase their working hours in an effort to recoup some of their income loss after divorce. Duncan and Hoffman (1985) found that the proportion of mothers who worked 1000 or more hours per year increased from 51% before divorce to 73% after divorce. A substantial change in working hours is stressful for the mother as well as her children. Child care arrangements must be made if her children are young; both mother and children are likely to experience anxiety about the new situation.

Social and economic instability have direct implications for the mental health of mothers and children. Changes in social roles or status may lead to increases in psychological distress and anxiety. Undesirable and involuntary changes are thought to be the most stressful, particularly when they involve the disruption of social networks and support systems. Not surprisingly, epidemiological surveys show that single mothers report substantially higher rates of anxiety and depression than do married women and men; facility utilization statistics show that mother-only families with children consume a disproportionate share of community mental health services (Guttentag, Salassin, and Belle, 1980). Much of the variation in psychological distress appears to be caused by differences in income and economic instability.

Perhaps the most far reaching consequence of family disruption is its effect on child well-being. Numerous studies conducted in the United States during the past decade show that children who grow up in mother only families — whether headed by divorced mothers or unmarried mothers — are disadvantaged in a number of ways as compared with children who grow up with both parents (McLanahan and Booth, 1989). The former are less likely to graduate from high school (and from college), are more likely to have children as teenagers and to give birth out-of-wedlock, and are more likely to be involved in delinquency and crime. While some of this disadvantage is likely due to family differences that pre-date the divorce, at least part of it is caused by the disruption itself. Estimates based on longitudinal studies that have followed children through adolescence and young adulthood indicate that as much as half of the lower achievement of children in single parent families is due to low income (McLanahan, 1985). No one has attempted to estimate what proportion of the gap is due to unstable income.

The Proximate Causes of Low Income

Why do single mothers in the United States have such high poverty rates given the strong relationship between income and children's well-being? A comparison of income sources in single mother and two-parent families sheds some light on the question. Table 2-1 reports the sources of income for two-parent and mother-only families in the United States in 1982 (Garfinkel and McLanahan, 1986). The average income of two-parent families in 1982 was about two-and-one-half times as large as the average income of mother-only families. For white families, total income was $30,814 for two-parent families, compared with $12,628 for families headed by single

Table 2-1:

Average Income Receipts of Two-Parent and Mother-Only Families in 1982, by Race

	White		African-American	
	Married Couple Families	*Mother-Only Families*	*Married Couple Families*	*Mother-Only Families*
Total Cash Income	30,814	12,628	23,913	9,128
Head's Earned Income	21,932	7,666	13,508	5,363
Other's Earnings	6,377	928	8,096	827
Alimony and Child Support	227	1,246	253	322
Social Security, Pensions, Other Unearned	2,171	1,782	1,720	907
Public Assistance and Food Stamps	174	1,399	1,838	2,573

Source: Garfinkel and McLanahan, 1986.♦

mothers. For African-American families the pattern was much the same although income levels were lower in both types of families. The median income for black two-parent families was $23,913, compared with $9,128 for mother-only families. The ratios based on the 1990 Current Population Survey are even higher. The median income of white two-parent families was $41,685 as compared with $14,868 for single parent families. The median income of black two-parent families was $35,721 as compared with $10,306 for single parent families.

Low Earnings Capacity

The major source of income for both two-parent families and mother-only families is the earnings of the primary breadwinner. Since approximately 60% to 70% of total income comes from this source, the ability of single women to earn income is a critical determinant of their economic status. Even if men and women worked and earned identical amounts, single parent families would have only half the earnings capacity of two-parent families. This inequality is exacerbated because of gender differences in labour force participation and wages; female breadwinners earn only 35% as much as fathers in two-parent families.

Single mothers participate in the labour force substantially less than married fathers. Labour force participation ranges from 34% of black widows to 81% of divorced white mothers. The significance of not working is profound. Ellwood (1988) has shown that only about 6% of single mothers who worked full-time year-round were poor in any given year, as compared with more than 70% of nonworking women. These findings should not be interpreted to mean that if all single mothers worked full time, only 6% of them would be poor. To some extent, the apparent advantage of working mothers reflects the selection process that channels women with higher earnings capacity into the labour force and women with lower earnings capacity into homemaker status.

Why are earnings of single mothers so low? In part it is because they are mothers and as such have invested a substantial amount of their time and energy in child rearing. Compared with fathers, mothers are less likely to have worked continuously since leaving school and they are less likely to have received on-the-job training, both of which have a strong positive effect on wage rates. Differences in education and work experience, however, cannot account for all of the difference in the wages of fathers and mothers; thus some of the lower earnings of single mothers must be due to other factors. Among full-time year-round workers, women earn about 60% as much as men; this ratio, although it has narrowed somewhat in the 1980s especially for younger cohorts of workers, has remained relatively constant for the past thirty years. Estimates of the proportion of the wage gap due to differences in human capital (education, work experience, and work commitment) generally range from 10% to 44%, which suggests that over half of the gender wage gap is due to something else.

Inadequate Child Support

That non-resident fathers do not pay much child support is a second factor contributing to the economic insecurity of single mothers. Not only does the major breadwinner in a single mother family have a lower earnings capacity than the major breadwinner in a two-parent family (usually the father), but the ratio of dependents to earners is higher in the former than in the latter. Table 2-1 shows that a substantial portion of income in two-parent families comes from earnings by other family members which are usually the mothers.

Alimony and Child Support are the Contribution from Father

Only about 40% of white fathers and 19% of absent African-American fathers pay child support. The average amount contributed, of those who pay, is much lower than the amount contributed by the secondary earner in two-parent families. Exactly what share of the cost of raising a child should be borne by the absent parent depends, of course, on value judgements. Regardless of how one calculates the amount owed, however, fathers do not appear to be contributing their fair share.

Meagre Public Support

A final cause of poverty in mother-only families is the relatively meagre transfer benefits provided by the government to such families. The United States is the only industrialized nation that does not provide cash allowances for all children. Instead, the U.S. has a deduction of $2000 per child for the purposes of calculating federal income tax liability. The deduction is worth about $300 per year for taxpayers with the lowest income tax liabilities, about $700 per year for taxpayers in the top tax bracket, and is worth nothing to the poorest families whose incomes are so low that they owe no taxes. The major U.S. health care program for families with children, Medicaid, limits nearly all of its benefits to poor single mother families receiving AFDC, a means tested public assistance program. Finally, the U.S. spends less on day care than many other industrialized nations.

Single mothers who are widowed receive Survivors Insurance (SI), regardless of whether or not they are poor. All other single mothers receive nothing, unless they are poor, in which case they are eligible for welfare (AFDC). Welfare benefits are much smaller than SI benefits. Moreover, by drastically reducing benefits as earnings increase, income tested programs like AFDC replace rather than supplement earnings. The AFDC program is a poverty trap for single mothers since it discourages work by imposing a high tax rate on earnings and does not provide sufficient income for a nonworking mother and child to live above the poverty line. Thus single mothers with low earnings capacity in the U.S. are forced to choose between working full time, living at the poverty line, and having no time for their children or not working, living below the poverty line, and having time with their children. Widows are better off than other single mothers, not because they work more, but because they receive more generous benefits. The U.S. has not been willing to extend such generosity to non-widowed single mothers, partly out of fear of negative incentives with respect to work and marriage.

Policies for Single Mother Families

The United States has the highest proportion of mother-only families of all the highly industrialized countries. Sweden has a higher proportion of unmarried mothers, but about half of these women are living with the fathers of their children. Moreover, single mothers in the U.S. have the next to highest poverty rates of single mothers in all the major industrialized countries. Only Australia has higher rates (McLanahan and Garfinkel, 1991). The two phenomenon are related; the growth and poverty of single mother families gives rise to great concern that too much and too little is being done to help these families. The high poverty rate of single mother families reflects a dilemma among policy makers and among all Americans about how to aid single mother families without encouraging their prevalence and economic dependence. Values of compassion and community argue for making single parenthood more secure, but many fear that making single-parenthood more comfortable will encourage the formation of such families and promote dependence on government. Values of self reliance and self interest suggest making single parenthood more austere and thereby discouraging prevalence and dependence, but many fear that doing so will harm mothers and have long term negative consequences for children. For the last forty years, Americans have struggled with how to resolve this dilemma within the welfare system. Between 1950 and 1970 cash and in kind welfare benefits were substantially raised. Poverty rates declined and welfare caseloads soared. Between 1970 and 1990, welfare benefits were reduced; the proportion of single mothers dependent on welfare decreased and poverty rates increased. American society is not willing to support single mothers to stay at home and raise their children — especially in a time when married mothers are increasing their labour force participation. The Nation began enacting legislation to reduce long term dependence upon welfare even as cash and in kind welfare benefits increased to unprecedented levels during the 1960s. Yet Americans have been unwilling to provide the services necessary to allow poor single mothers to earn enough to support their families through paid employment.

Recently there has been movement toward changing policies so that single mothers are less dependent and better off and so that values of compassion and self reliance are both satisfied. This new movement is taking place on three fronts: investments in raising the earnings capacity of poor single mothers, compensating for low earnings capacity, and strengthening child support. A major thrust of all these policies is to increase the economic security of all single mothers outside the welfare system. These are desirable policy directions and should be forwarded via a refundable tax credit for children, a child support assurance system, and some form of national health insurance — all of which have been endorsed by the National Commission on Children — a bi-partisan Commission appointed by President Reagan and the Congress and chaired by Senator Jay Rockefeller.

Policies for Increasing Low Earnings Capacity

Some policies for increasing low earnings capacity, such as reforms of the public education system, fall outside the realm of income transfer policy, narrowly construed. Others, such as more general employment and training programs, were never really very important relative to cash assistance and were cut to the bone during the Reagan Administration. Most of the action with respect to employment and training within the last decade has taken place within welfare. The primary thrust of the work and training provisions of the Family Support Act of 1988 is to encourage single mothers to increase their human capital so that they will be able to enter the labour force and support their families. AFDC, when established in 1935, was intended to provide support for widows in a society where most married mothers did not work outside the home. The situation had changed dramatically by the 1960s. Most single mothers were not widows and most married mothers worked at least part time outside the home. Thus conservatives and liberals alike came to view AFDC as a poor mechanism for supporting single mothers. In 1967 the federal government tried to induce AFDC mothers to work by creating work incentives within AFDC. When this failed to have much impact on either work or caseloads, Congress began legislating work requirements for mothers with children over age six. The Reagan Administration rejected the approach of creating work incentives within the AFDC program, and instead, sought to cut benefits to working mothers and to force nonworking mothers to work in exchange for their benefits. The Family Support Act of 1988 tightened work requirements for mothers with children over three and provided increased federal funding for services such as job training and day care. Mothers who become employed are offered free child-care and free health care for up to one year after leaving welfare. But the states must put up approximately 50% of the cost of these services and states have not provided much new funding. Senator Moynihan has proposed increasing the federal appropriations for job services within AFDC from $1 billion to $5 billion. In the absence of such a large increase, the Family Support Act of 1988 will not have much impact on the earnings capacity or welfare dependence of single mothers now dependent on AFDC.

Policies for Compensating for Low Earnings Capacity

There are several ways that policy can compensate for low earnings capacity. Child support and child care are two obvious remedies to the extent that low capacity is due to the absence of a parent. The former secures a share of the earnings of the nonresident parent while the latter allows the resident parent to secure her own earnings. Finally, an earnings supplement such as the earned income tax credit (EITC), compensates for low earnings capacity, whatever the source. EITC is the most well developed American policy for compensating for low earnings capacity. EITC is a refundable tax credit available to all families with earnings below a certain level. It began in the mid 1970s as a means of increasing the earnings of low wage workers by offsetting payroll taxes of poor families. The credit was expanded in 1986 and again in 1990 so that it represents a substantial income supplement to poor or near poor families. EITC has three components: an earnings credit, a child-care credit, and a health insurance credit. In 1991, the basic credit paid 17 cents for each dollar earned up to about $7,000. The maximum benefit was $1,192 for a family with one child and $1,235 for a family with two or more children. In 1994, the maximum benefit increases to $1,854 and

$2,015 respectively. The child-care credit provides an additional credit of 5% of earned income to families with a child under the age of one, so long as the family does not claim a child care deduction for the child. The maximum credit in 1991 was $357 and increases to $403 in 1994. Finally, the EITC provides families with an additional 6% on earned income to cover the cost of purchasing health insurance.

The earned income tax credit is attractive as compared to welfare because of its simplicity and its anonymity. It is administered through the income tax system, there is only one form to fill out, and families that receive benefits are not stigmatized. But this form and the administration of the EITC have been criticized for being over-complicated. Moreover, the EITC is popular with the general population because it rewards work. A mother with no earnings receives no subsidy. The more a mother earns, up to a certain amount, the more she receives. Unlike AFDC, which many citizens view as isolating and encouraging dependency, the EITC is seen as promoting work and integrating single mothers into mainstream society. The popularity of the EITC reflects the fact that most Americans now believe that single mothers should earn money to help support their families once their children are in school. In 1985 about 41% of single mothers worked full time and another 25% worked part time during the year (Ellwood, 1986).

Child care is a second policy that is critical to increasing single mothers' earnings. Child care in the United States is expensive. Only about 20% of all mothers who work outside the home are able to obtain free child care. In 1985, families who purchased child care for a child under age five spent an average of $36.69 per week. The cheapest source of care, a relative, was nearly as much as the most expensive source, a child care provider — $34.57 versus $38.80. Families who used the more expensive form purchased fewer hours of care than families who relied on relatives and therefore both groups ended up spending about the same amount. Child care expenses represent about 17% of the budgets of single mothers who pay for care and represent about 25% of the budgets of poor single mothers.

The bulk of the subsidies provided by federal government for child care expenditures goes to middle and upper middle income families in the form of the dependent care tax credit, in the federal income tax. Families can subtract from their tax liability between 20% and 30% of child care expenditures up to a maximum of $480 for one child and $960 for two or more children. The credit is worth nothing for families whose earnings are so low that they owe no taxes. In 1986, this program accounted for about $3.5 billion of the $5.5 billion in federal expenditures on child care. That leaves only about $2.0 billion in expenditures for subsidizing the child care of low income families, including single mothers. Legislation in 1990 provides for federal grants amounting to about three-quarters of a billion dollars to states for child care.

The Family Support Act of 1988 provides child care support for single mothers who are participating in work or training programs. According to the law, mothers who get a job will receive child care benefits for up to one year after they leave welfare. After that, however, there are no special child care provisions for single mothers, other than the tax credit, which is regressive and does nothing for single mothers with low earnings.

Policies for Increasing and Regularizing Child Support

A second major cause of poverty and insecurity among single mothers is the low level and irregularity of private child support. The United States has also begun to increase and regularize fathers' economic contributions to their children to remedy this problem. The country has taken steps in terms of securing universal paternity and child support awards, standardizing award levels, routinizing withholding and other collection procedures, and even establishing an assured child support benefit. In 1975 the Federal Office of Child Support Enforcement was established along with regional offices at the state and county levels. The 1984 child support legislation was passed by a unanimous Congress. The two most important provisions require the states to adopt numerical child support guidelines for the purposes of determining child support awards and to withhold child support obligations from the wages of parents who had become more than one month delinquent in their payments of child support. The Family Support Act of 1988 went even further in strengthening child support enforcement. The state guidelines are now a presumption from which judges can depart only if they make a written justification for doing so. The 1988 legislation requires income withholding from the outset in all cases by 1994 instead of waiting for a delinquency. Finally the Family Support Act establishes performance standards for the states with respect to establishing paternity. The 1984 act gave the state of Wisconsin a waiver that permitted use of federal funds, otherwise devoted to AFDC, to help fund an assured child support benefit. A similar waiver for the state of New York was enacted in 1988. New York has begun piloting a very limited version of an assured child support benefit; Wisconsin has yet to make use of its waiver which will expire in 1993.

Increasing Public Support for Children in Single Mother Families

Improving single mothers' earning capacity and strengthening fathers' child support obligations go a long way toward reducing poverty and economic insecurity in single mother families. Still missing, however, is the public obligation. Caring for children is the public's responsibility as well as the responsibility of individual parents. Public benefits can be targeted on the poorest children or on all children. In general, the less targeted on the poor, the more helpful the benefits will be in reducing dependence on cash welfare assistance. Three proposals increase public contributions toward the support of children: a refundable tax credit, national health insurance, and child support assurance, including a minimum child support benefit. A major thrust of all these policies is to increase the economic security of all single mothers. Like the EITC, all these benefits help make work pay and make life outside welfare much more economically secure. All have been endorsed by the National Commission on Children (1991) — a bi-partisan Commission appointed by President Reagan and the Congress and chaired by Senator Jay Rockefeller.

All industrialized countries except for the U.S. have a child allowance and there is some evidence that the U.S. is moving in this direction. The refundable child tax credit of $1000 per child proposed by the National Commission on Children would replace the current child deduction in the income tax is worth about $300 to families in the lowest tax bracket, about $700 to families in the highest bracket, and nothing to families who are too poor to pay taxes. In economic terms, a refundable tax credit is equivalent to a child allowance although administration of the programs differ. Child allowances are mailed to all families on a weekly or monthly basis, whereas families with a worker would receive the credit during the year in the form of an offset to taxes withheld, and families with no wage earners would be required to apply for the refundable credit.

Some form of national health insurance is a second step toward increasing public responsibility for children. Currently, health insurance coverage for most working parents is provided by the employer. Many single mothers who work outside the home, however, are not covered, either because they work part time or because their jobs do not provide medical benefits. Single mothers on welfare are covered through Medicaid which is income-tested. The income test provides a strong disincentive for leaving welfare by going to work and, therefore, operates to lower single mothers earning capacity. Single mothers with low earning capacity cannot afford to leave welfare and give up their medicaid benefits; yet staying on welfare means staying below the poverty line. Current proposals for increasing medical insurance range from provision of tax credits for the purchase of private health insurance to proposals for a full fledged national health insurance system along the lines of the Canadian system.

The Child Support Assurance System (CSAS) as developed by Garfinkel (1992) and his colleagues at the University of Wisconsin, is the final proposal for increasing public support for children. The CSAS proposal, since it is the most targeted on single mothers, from a budget point of view, costs the least. Child Support Assurance would be a new social security program. All nonresident parents would be required to share their income with their children. The sharing rate is a proportion of the nonresident parent's gross income and is determined by legislation. The resulting child support obligation is withheld routinely from income just as income and payroll taxes are withheld. The child receives either the full amount owed or a minimum benefit set by legislation and provided by the government, whichever is higher. Like Survivors' Insurance, which is part of the current social security system, Child Support Assurance aids children of all income classes who suffer an income loss due to the absence of a parent. The cause of the absence differs of course. Survivors' Insurance compensates for the loss of income arising from widowhood. Child Support Assurance compensates for the loss arising from divorce, separation, and nonmarriage. The percentage-of-income standard, in conjunction with routine income withholding, makes the bulk of the financing of Child Support Assurance similar to a proportional payroll tax, which is used to finance all American social insurance programs. In the Child Support Assurance, however, the tax applies only to those who are legally liable for child support. The assured-benefit component of Child Support Assurance makes the benefit structure of the system like all other social insurance programs in that it provides greater benefits to low-income families than are justified on the basis of the family's contributions or taxes. The assured benefit encourages work and reduces welfare dependence. Unlike welfare, it is not reduced by one dollar for each dollar of earnings. Thus it simultaneously reduces economic insecurity and welfare dependence. Private child support is irregular. An assured benefit will provide a secure base of child support that will be of value to single mothers from all income classes but especially to single mothers with low earnings capacity.

The U.S. has already taken giant strides towards a CSAS on the collection side. But the task has not been completed. Despite the adoption of guidelines, the courts are still heavily involved in determining child support obligations. Few states have yet implemented universal routine withholding of child support obligations. All states are a long way from universal establishment of paternity. Crossing state lines still remains a very effective way to avoid a child support obligation. Finally, neither the federal government nor any state has adopted an assured child support benefit. Although Wisconsin applied for and received a federal waiver to use federal AFDC funds to help finance an assured benefit, the current Governor is opposed to the concept and the initiative has been stalled since he took office. New York state is currently piloting a restricted version of an assured benefit which is limited to low income families who qualify for AFDC. The National Commission on Children and the National Commission on Interstate Child Support Enforcement have recommended that the federal government enact legislation to encourage the states to experiment with an assured child support benefit.

3

Lone Parent Families in France: Situation and Research

Nadine Lefaucheur and Claude Martin

The expression *familles monoparentales* (lone parent families) was introduced in France during the late 1970s and became generally accepted throughout the ensuing decade (Lefaucheur, 1985; LeGall and Martin, 1987). The so-called *familles monoparentales* had been included under the category of dissociated families (Lefaucheur, 1989) by criminology and psychopathology specialists who, for almost a century, considered the breakup of parental couples as a major factor leading to juvenile delinquency and behaviourial problems in children; they generally included in this category all conjugal households comprising a parental couple that did not seem normal, particularly those including an in-law (Lefaucheur, 1987b). Up until the 1970s, legislators and public opinion did not give widowhood, divorce, and illegitimacy cases the same treatment. Widows and single mothers were often placed at opposite extremes on the scale of social consideration and feminine dignity. The introduction and diffusion of the lone parent families category occurred in a specific context characterized by a general awareness of an existing family crisis, development of a new form of poverty resulting from a rise in unemployment, the French government's strong family policy and the infrastructure responsible for its implementation, namely the *Caisses d'allocations familiales* (CAF) (Family Allowance Funds).

Family Crisis and Lone Parent Type Families

The expression, one-parent families, was introduced in France during the late 1970s, by feminist sociologists who sought to promote recognition of the fact that women were " ... extremely capable of raising their children alone" (Michel, 1978: 204), whatever their marital status and had equally legitimate rights, as any man, to be a head of household. Further, their households should be considered as real families, of a specific sociological type, but just as noble and perhaps more modern than the traditional family which appeared to be threatened by the evolution in moral standards, a process which, in France as in most of the developed countries, is clearly reflected through variations in demographic indicators as well as legislative changes (INSEE, 1991; Lefaucheur, 1992b).

The fertility indicator, for example, declined sharply from 3, in 1964, to less than 1.8 in 1983, while the number of children born out of wedlock rose from less than 6% to over 12% in 1983 and 28% in 1989; however, recognition by both parents of these children was on the increase. There was a marked tendency among couples to cohabitate prior to, or instead of, getting married. More and more opted for divorce (the annual divorce rate doubled since 1975) and, after a shorter period together, as well. Furthermore, an increasing number of women were choosing to work outside the home; the employment rate of those living in couples (married or unmarried) rose from 32% in the early 1960s, to 43% in 1975, 54% in 1982, and 67% in 1989. More women were claiming their equal rights to men on all issues dealing with family, professional, and social life, including free access to contraception and abortion. In most instances, the law was inclined to adopt or favour this new legislation; in 1970, paternal authority gave way to a parental authority jointly exercised by both spouses (or by the mother alone, when the parents are not married and didn't ask for exercising it jointly); in 1972, natural children were granted the same status as legitimate children; in 1975, voluntary pregnancy termination became legal, as well as divorce by mutual consent.

The lone parent family category began to show up in French literature on sociology at a time when traditional forms of conjugal life were being seriously questioned. The designation "lone parents" was concurrently introduced by policy-makers when dealing with social and family issues.

Family Policy and Lone Parents

Fear of depopulation in France, at the close of the nineteenth century, led to the adoption of a progressive family policy aimed at protecting motherhood, encouraging childbirth and ensuring a certain horizontal redistribution of income among households, based on the number of dependants. The main instrument used to implement this policy was the establishment of the *caisses d'allocations familiales* (CAF) or Family Allowance Funds which became part of the general Social Security system in 1946 and are funded through automatic payroll deductions. These funds are administered by a council of representatives of family associations, salaried employees, employers and independent workers. The main purpose of these *caisses* is to distribute family allowance benefits and to create or finance social services and equipment (e.g., housing benefits, holiday benefits, homecare workers, participation in the social equipment: kindergarten, neighbourhood centres, daycare centres, nurseries, etc.). The amount and eligibility to such benefits — as is the case for employer/employee contributions — are determined by law. The National Family Allowance Funds represent also one of the major funding sources for all research on family issues.

In 1946, the family allowance system was based on the provision of four benefits: a family allowance starting at the birth of a second child, a single-income allowance for families where the mother does not work outside the home, a prenatal allowance, and a maternity allowance. Other benefits were later added, including a rental allowance in 1948. Table 3-1 summarizes current benefits. Since the late 1970s and subsequent to a rise in unemployment, distribution of family allowance benefits has gradually become less universal, although the head of household is no longer required to work in order to be eligible, and these benefits are more frequently income-tested and/or destined to parents of young children or specific categories such as the handicapped and lone parents (Table 3-1). Two special benefits were created for the latter category.

The first, an Orphan's Allowance (recently renamed *allocation de soutien familial* or Family Maintenance Allowance) was created in 1970 for children having lost one or both parents, or those born of single mothers and unrecognized by their fathers. In 1975, this allowance was extended to include paternally recognized children living with the mother but morally abandoned by the father who provides no maintenance. Since 1986, the CAF has made payments of this allowance to lone parents who have not received child support from the non-custodial parent for at least two months. The CAF is responsible for recovery of unpaid child support (INED, 1986).

The second special benefit called *allocation de parent isolé* or API (the Lone Parent Allowance) was created in 1976. It is a differential and transitory benefit which, for a limited period (1 to $3\frac{1}{2}$ years, depending on the child's age) helps round out the lone parent's income to the minimum level required to face the material consequences resulting from death, divorce, or abandonment. The rapid increase in the number of API beneficiaries (from 50,000 in 1979 to 130,000 in 1989) has revealed the high level of poverty risk to which lone parent families are exposed, particularly when the lone parent is a woman with no professional skills or who is disqualified due to a prolonged absence from the job market. This group of families, to which the family crisis in France gave rise, has also come to symbolize the new form of poverty created by the economic crisis. One of the reasons for the common acceptance of the expression lone parent family in the eighties was its ability to crystallize most social representations linked to this double crisis in France. Another factor that led to the coining of the expression was its introduction in the households/families nomenclature used by the Institut

Table 3-1:
Family Allowance

Benefit	Year of Creation	Amount (% of SMIC)	Number of Beneficiaries		Requirements			Total Amount paid by C.A.F. in 1989 (million FF)
			All Families	Lone Parents	Family	Parents	Children	
Maintenance								
Actual Family Benefit	(1932) 1946	2 C: 11% S 3 C: 26% S 4 C: 40% S 5 C: 55% S C > 10: +3% S C > 15: +6% S	3,600,000 families	300,000			2 children or more under age 17	49,500 M FF
New School Year	1974	7% S per child	2,000,000 children		Eligible for at least one means-test benefit		Schooled	
Family Supplement	1978	15% S	730,000 families	100,000	Income lower than about twice a SMIC		3 children or more under age 3	
Young Children								
Young Child Benefit	1985	16% S	440,000 families			Pregnant mother	or 1 child under 3 months of age	21,300 M FF
			1,2000,000 families	500,000	Income lower than about twice a SMIC		1 child over 3 months and under 3 years of age	
Parenting Leave	1983	From 25% S to 50% S	160,000 families			1 parent having stopped working or reduced his or her working time	3 children or more—last one under age 3	
Child Cared at Home Benefit	1986	Employer's social security contribution on the payroll				both parents employed	child cared for at home	

Housing

Family Housing Benefit	1948	Depending on income and housing	1,000,000 families	Conditions of income and of size, rent level and comfort of housing		One child or more	38,900 M FF
Personalized Housing Benefit	1977	Depending on income and housing	2,100,000 households	Conditions of income and of size, rent level and kind of housing			

Handicapped People

Specialized Education Benefit	(1963) (1970) 1975	11% S to 37% S	75,000 children	Income lower than 55% SMIC		Handicapped	14,100 M FF
Handicapped Adult Benefit	(1971) 1975		464,000 persons		Handi-capped parent	Handicapped child over age 20	

Lone Parents

Family Maintenance Allowance	(1970) (1973)	10% S (benefit or advance on unpaid alimonies)	400,000		Alone	(Semi-) orphan, or recognized by only one parent; unpaid alimony	6,600 M FF
Lone-Parent Benefit	1976	Pregnant: 53% S lone parent: 53% S + 18% S per child	130,000	Income lower than guaranteed one	Alone	At least one child expected or living	
Guaranteed Minimum for Insertion	1988	1 person: 40% S 3 persons: 60% S others: 11% S (each person)	About 75,000 persons	Income lower than guaranteed one			

Table 3-2:

Lone Parent Families 1968-1989
(rate, number and marital status)

	1968	1989	
% Lone parents within families with children <25 with children <18	9.3%	12.6%	11%
Number of lone parent families with children <25 with children <18	719,700	1,097,500	770,000
Lone mothers with children Widows Never married Divorced or separated	< 25 56% 9% 35%	< 25 21% 21% 58%	< 18 14% 26% 60%

Source: INSEE, Census of population, 1968; Employment and Income Survey, 1989.♦

National de la Statistique et des Études Économiques (INSEE) to present results of demographic census and various other survey findings.

A Statistical Rubric

The lone parent families rubric found in the INSEE's households/families nomenclature includes data on households comprising a person living without a spouse and at least one dependent child, under twenty-five years of age, who is single, spouseless, and childless. The introduction of such a rubric has generated considerable data production concerning the socio-demographic structure and circumstances in one-parent families.

Comparison of the data used to determine the percentage of lone parent families among all households/families and their distribution in terms of marital status with the previous available statistics of the single parent population indicates that the 1970s constituted a demographic revolution for the lone parent population. The frequency rate did not show a marked increase; the percentage of lone parent families among all households with children was even slightly lower in 1975 (9.4%) than in 1962 (9.6%). But the ways lone parents were formed changed markedly and shifted a decrease in deaths of one of the spouses to a growing rate of separation which has become the main generating factor of the so-called lone parent situations. The widows to divorcees ratio has been inverted among the lone parent population. In 1968, among all women heads-of-households, 56% were

Table 3-3:

Lone Mothers by Age Groups and Number of Children

Lone mothers with children <18	All lone mothers	Never-married mothers
Median age	37	31
Under age 20	0.2%	0.7%
Age 20-24	4.8%	14.8%
Age 25-34	32.6%	50.0%
Over age 35	62.4%	34.5%

Source: INSEE, Employment and Income Survey 1989.

Average number of children under age 25		
one	56%	77%
two	27%	15%
three or more	17%	8%

Source: INSEE, Census of Population, 1982. ♦

widows, 35% were divorced or separated, and 9% were single women. In 1982, only 32% of these were widows, whereas the rate for single women rose to 17% and to 53% for divorced or separated women. Table 3-2 shows that lone parent families now represent 12.5% of all households which include single children under twenty-five years of age. Approximately 1,500,000 children, or dependants, are under the care of 1,150,000 lone parents of whom 87% are women. Almost 60% of these are divorced or separated and, among the remaining portion, there are just as many single mothers (with a higher rate of children born in a common-law conjugal setting and recognized by the father) as there are widows.

Information about the age of lone parents and the age and number of children is presented in Tables 3-3 and 3-4. The reduction, within the lone parent population, in the number of widows and widowers was accompanied by a moderate decrease in its age range. The median age for single mothers went from forty-seven in 1962, to forty in 1989; and for their dependants, it varied from fourteen in 1968, to thirteen in 1982. In France, a lone mother and her children are rarely very young. Among lone mothers with at least one dependant under eighteen years of age, only 5% are

Table 3-4:

Number of Lone Parent Families
By Age of Only or Last Child

	0-2	3-6	7-16	17-24
All lone parent families	65,820	121,840	412,900	286,480
Women-headed	60,360	109,940	354,140	233,300
never married	33,120	32,320	47,860	15,760
divorced	13,220	48,000	170,660	67,420
married-separated	10,700	19,580	46,460	22,540
widows	3,320	10,040	89,160	127,580
Men-headed	5,460	11,900	58,760	53,180
never married	1,180	1,400	2,740	1,860
divorced	620	4,060	22,500	14,280
married-separated	2,880	4,600	14,440	11,340
widowers	780	1,840	19,080	25,700

Source: INSEE, Census of Population, 1982.♦

younger than twenty-five, while 62% are over thirty-five, and barely 5% of their children are under three years old. Although the rate of increase in the percentage of lone parent families among all households/families, measured at any given time since the late 1960s, was relatively low (from 9.5% to 12.5%), the probability of becoming a lone parent, for a certain period, has undoubtedly increased sharply, concurrent with growing rate of separations, legal or not. An estimated one out of four children and one out of six women is likely to experience such a situation, at least temporarily.

Context for Research

The importance given in France to family policy, the major role played by the CNAF in the field of research on family issues, particularly that of lone parent families, and the following factors have contributed to the development of research in the field of lone parent families:

- the adoption of a lone parent families rubric by the INSEE and abundance of available data on these families;
- the liberalization of legislature governing families, sexuality, demographic growth in divorce, and illegitimate birth rates;

- the creation of specific benefits for lone parents; and
- the cumulative impediments to job access.

The research has been directed towards specific themes such as the circumstances, living conditions, and socio-economic vulnerability of these households, the effectiveness of family policies, social action and transfer payments on their behalf, as well as the effects of a lone parent household structure on the socialization of children (Lefaucheur, 1991).

Lone Parenthood and Poverty

Poverty, socio-economic dependence, and inadequate socialization of children are some of the major issues most frequently associated with lone parent families. However, research results produced in France during the past twenty years indicate that lone parenthood is far from producing these effects on all households included in the lone parent families category.

Lone Parenthood, Poverty and Impoverishment

Comparative studies on the variations between one-parent and two-parent families, in terms of income and standard of living (CERC, 1987; Lefaucheur, 1988a), or between members of these families prior to their lone parenthood situation (ACT, 1987; Bastard and Cardia-Vonèche, 1988a, 1988b; CERC, 1986, 1989; Festy, 1988b, 1991; Festy and Valetas, 1987, 1990; Languin et al., 1990; Lefaucheur, 1987a) have all resulted in outlining the globally unfavourable conditions of lone parent families. But they also reveal a broad diversity in these families' circumstances and show that the variation in their relative level of poverty or impoverishment was largely dependent on the factors of duration of the lone parenthood situation, sex, age, marital status and activity of the head-of-household, number and age of dependants, family's socio-professional trajectories, type of relationship established with the non-custodial parent, and strategies adopted to cope as a lone parent.

For some, entering lone parenthood can entail a dramatic reduction in their standard of living, but for others it may be momentary or non-existent. For example, seven months after the death of a spouse under sixty years of age, widows and their families may see their per capita income reduced by 5%; in one-third of the cases, this reduction can even exceed 20%. However, in a few cases the per capita income increases and, for 50% of widows, after nineteen months of widowhood, is at least equal to what it was prior to the spouse's death. For one-fourth of these widows, the average income level is reduced by 30%, while for another fourth, widowhood gives rise to an income increase of 30%. This stability or progression in young widow's standard of living are guaranteed by transfer payments which constitute almost half of the average income for these families (CERC, 1986, 1989).

Studies concerning lone parent families resulting from a divorce (ACT, 1987; Bastard and Cardia-Vonèche, 1984, 1987, 1988a, 1988b, 1991) show that the incidence of poverty is more prevalent among divorced mothers who were not professionally active at the time of the divorce. Other women also experience a sharp decline in their income level that is more severe for them than for the non-custodial divorced fathers because of disparity in their resources due both to unequal sharing of child maintenance expenses and to sexual discrimination on the job market. Approximately one-third of all child support payments are unpaid by the non-custodial father, or paid on an irregular basis, and the amount represents a mere 10% of a lone parent family's income (where the mother works) (CERC, 1987; Festy, 1988a; INED, 1986; Lefaucheur, 1988a).

If evaluations of the economic impact of divorce show that the reduction in a family's resources, as a result of a husband's loss of income, is not compensated by an equivalent increase in the wife's personal resources (Bastard and Cardia-Vonèche, 1987: 112) nor by the husband's alimony payments, a family's income, however, is not the only criteria to consider when attempting to determine the economic impact of a divorce. The loss of income can often be compensated by improved control over these resources; for some women, the impoverishment resulting from a divorce provides an opportunity to gain more control over the family's finances, allowing them to manage their own more limited resources without having to negotiate with or fear the ex-spouse's financial activities (Bastard and Cardia-Vonèche, 1988a: 116). Bastard and Cardia-Vonèche (1988a; 1988b) have also pointed out the various adaptation strategies developed by lone parents, subsequent to a divorce. Some women primarily seek to defend their rights (legal, social, or moral) by making claims to the ex-spouse and/or society. Others start by mobilizing their personal and environmental resources in order to restore or maximize their job-accessibility potential. Certain women, particularly among well-to-do families where divorce did not lead to a total breakup of the parental couple, tend to adopt a strategy of combined resource mobilization with their ex-spouse for the children's custodial maintenance. By adopting one, or even several of these strategies, subsequent to a divorce, the majority of lone parent families manage to limit or compensate for the resulting impoverishment and, in some instances, may improve their situation.

Economic Vulnerability and Dependence: Importance of a Professional Activity

One out of four lone parent families do remain poor or dependent for a certain period. Information regarding labour force participation by both lone and married parents is presented in Tables 3-5 and 3-6; 22% of lone fathers are inactive (15%) or unemployed (7%). One-third of lone mothers are

Table 3-5:

*Labour Force Participation and Unemployment Rates of Mothers, by Family
Situation and Marital Status, 1989*

	Coupled Mothers	Lone Mothers			
		All	*Never-married*	*Divorced & separated*	*Widows*
Labour force participation rate of mothers with children					
under age of 18	65%	85%	81%	83%	70%
under age of 25	64%	81%			
Unemployment rate of mothers with children under age 25	11%	17%			
Distribution of mothers with children under age 25 and:					
unemployed	7%	14%			
working	57%	67%			
non-working	36%	19%			
all	100%	100%			

Source: INSEE, Employment Survey, 1989. ♦

professionally inactive (19%) or unemployed (14%); 13% receive the API
and 12% the RMI (revenu minimum d'insertion). RMI is a differential benefit
guaranteeing an income that is equivalent to approximately one-half of the
guaranteed minimum wage, a much lower income than that provided by
the API (see Table 3-1). The rate of professionally active lone mothers in
France (85%) is much higher than in other developed countries and exceeds
that of mothers living with a conjugal partner (65%). Among the former
group, there are twice as many unemployed (14%) than among the latter,
but in total, over two-thirds of all lone mothers are employed compared to
57% of the married mothers.

Information about wages of mothers, according to their family situation,
is presented in Table 3-7; lone mothers have the highest average wage rate.

Table 3-6:

*Labour Force Participation and Unemployment Rates of
Mothers, by Family Situation and Age Groups, 1989*

	Coupled Mothers		Lone Mothers	
	< 25	*> 25*	*< 25*	*> 25*
Labour force participation rate	58%	64%	68%	82%
unemployment rate	34%	10%	54%	15%
Distribution				
working	38%	58%	31%	70%
unemployed	20%	6%	37%	12%
non-working	42%	36%	32%	18%
all	100%	100%	100%	100%
Number of families	255,200	7,583,430	34,550	915,980

Source: INSEE, Employment Survey, 1989 (mothers with children under age 25). ♦

Nevertheless, lone mothers — unlike other women living with a spouse, who have the possibility of choosing to stay home — are often obliged to seek and accept unpleasant, low-paying jobs, often involving constraints in terms of schedules and transportation. Results of a study undertaken by the CERC on the economic vulnerability of families indicated that among the population's most socio-economically vulnerable families where the mother is exercising a professional activity under constraining conditions, lone parent families were 2.5 more numerous than in the rest of the population (CERC, 1987). Further, lone parents rarely work part-time (this form of work being less prevalent in France) and tend to remain in the work force for longer periods than other mothers.

Lone mothers who were engaged in a conjugal relationship for the briefest period (single mothers) receive the highest average wages, whereas those who were engaged for a longer period (widows, married but separated mothers) tend to fall in the lowest average wage bracket. This is because the widows and married women had, prior to their lone parenthood, most frequently and for longer periods, interrupted their professional activities to take care of their families. The possibilities for lone mothers to adopt effective strategies aimed at maximizing or restoring their job market potential and the effectiveness of these strategies, are largely dependent on the actual state of the market. A comparative study of average wages for

Table 3-7:

*Mean Monthly Salary, by Age, Sex, Marital Status
and Family Situation, 1984*

	Female				**Male**			
	Total	*< 30 years*	*30-39 years*	*40-59 years*	*Total*	*< 30 years*	*30-39 years*	*40-59 years*
Total households	78	75	84	79	121	89	140	143
never married	81	73	103	113	86	78	117	102
divorced	90	86	91	91	127	99	131	134
married	76	78	79	74	138	108	145	149
widowed	73	59	89	75	136	-	166	141
Lone person households	100	92	118	108	115	106	135	114
never married	106	92	121	137	111	106	139	104
divorced	101	96	114	101	130	99	127	137
married	102	99	93	120	126	-	129	125
widowed	74	-	-	59	101	-	-	109
Lone parent households	85	79	88	84	133	91	143	141
never married	93	77	100	108	89	87	-	-
divorced	86	83	88	87	128	-	133	128
married	70	-	66	79	140	-	-	-
widowed	77	-	87	74	166	-	-	164
Family households	77	79	80	74	138	107	146	150
never married	84	80	107	81	112	100	136	141
divorced	89	92	85	94	137	96	142	155
married	76	78	79	73	139	108	146	150
widowed	58	-	-	55	132	-	-	-

Source: INSEE, Employment Survey, 1984 (100 = mean salary of all French salaried workers).

mothers, according to age group, marital status and family situation, shows a marked difference between wages earned during the mid 1980s by single mothers over thirty years of age who entered the job market prior to 1973 during a period of full employment and high demand for female workers, compared to those who entered after 1973 in a context of economic crisis, rising unemployment and major changes in job qualification requirements. The average wage for the first group was among the highest, the second among the lowest (Lefaucheur, 1988c).

Studies aimed at determining the disposable income per capita indicate that, for lone mothers, it was 25% lower on average than for mothers living with a spouse; among the former, the amount for the inactive group is barely half of the active lone mother's income. But these studies also show that the latter is almost 20% higher than that of a two-parent household, where the mother is inactive, and on average, three-quarters of an active lone mother's income stems from her professional activity. Transfer payments to these mothers represent 15% of their disposable income, whereas for married families where only one parent works, they account for 20% of income (CERC, 1987; Table 3-8). Furthermore, over one-third of lone parents having at least one dependant under twenty-five years of age, and one-tenth of those having one dependant under eighteen years of age, receive no family allowance benefits, either because they have only one child over three years old and the other living parent has not morally abandoned the child, or because the children are too old to qualify for such benefits. Among the latter there are many whose income is too low to be taxable; thus, they cannot take advantage of the supplementary half portion (or 1–1/2 for widows and widowers) of the family quotient granted to lone parents as a tax credit. So, although one-fourth of all lone parents in France are highly dependent and socially assisted, almost as many receive no family benefits whatsoever nor can they take advantage of any tax credits.

Public policy programs can alter the circumstances of lone parent families through means in addition to direct financial assistance. The French legislature appears to be relatively successful in preventing or minimizing the pauperization generally associated with lone parenthood (Baker, 1991; Lefaucheur, 1992a, 1992b) and for many reasons generates a higher rate of employment activity among lone mothers, thereby encouraging them to become financially independent. Child care is highly socialized. Almost every child between the ages of three and six, and one-third of all two-year olds, are placed in some form of nursery school which generally includes a canteen service at lunch time. One-third of working mothers' children under three years of age are placed in the care of nursery schools, daycare centres, or home day-care which are subject to medical surveillance and, in most cases, are government-funded, either directly or indirectly (Norvez, 1990; Villeneuve-Gokalp, 1989). The high rate of professionally active mothers

Table 3-8:

Sources of Income by Family Type, 1981

	Couples		Lone Mothers	
	Dual earner	*Single earner*	*Working*	*Unemployed or non-working*
Earnings (direct earnings or social security payments from previous work activity) of the father of the mother	57% 35%	78% 2%	76%	23%
Child support (by the father or by insurances when father is dead)	-	-	9%	21%
Family allowances and schooling grants	8%	20%	15%	56%
Total	100%	100%	100%	100%

Source: CERC, 1987 (families with children under age 25).♦

with young children is both a causal and consequential factor of the relative ease of access to daycare services: among all working women with at least one child under six years of age, three out of four mothers with one child, two out of three with two children and one out of three with three children are working.

Criticism of Lone Parent Benefit

Despite the high unemployment rate, full-time work is now the standard for all women in France, including mothers with young children. This probably accounts for much of the controversy surrounding the Lone Parent Benefit. The criticisms do not concern APIs granted to mothers with children over three years of age who become lone parents; it seems legitimate to provide temporary assistance to help them (one year maximum) cope with their new situation. What is strongly debated are the APIs provided to young mothers (single or separated) to the fraudulent (undisclosed cohabitant) and recidivist cases which the right to a guaranteed income, from early pregnancy up to the last dependent child's third birthday, can generate. In more scholarly terms, the controversy is on the deterrent effects of APIs on marriage and, particularly, on the willingness to become employed. The API was created in 1976 with a view to achieving three objectives: (1) provide financial assistance to widows or to women abandoned by their spouse or partner in coping with their new situation; (2) prevent a declining birth rate and increase in abortions (authorized the previous year); (3) allow young lone mothers to take care of their own children before they enter nursery school, in order to prevent emotional deficiency, delinquency or other problems generally associated with their status. But today, although APIs to young lone mothers meet some of these objectives, they are often considered immoral because they tend to dissuade them from remarrying or even choosing to live as a couple. Further, they seem to promote API dependants, who attempt to get pregnant every three years, to live off welfare for three years instead of striving for financial independence by looking for work or, at least, improving their skills to qualify for the job market once their benefits are terminated.

Representations concerning the perverse effects and immorality of the API are quite prevalent among social professionals (Decoin and Keil, 1983; LeGall and Martin, 1983, 1986; Tachon, 1989), although research tends to allay these fears (Bastard and Cardia-Vonèche, 1988a, 1988b; Gautier, 1989). Deterrent effects of the API appear limited and also difficult to prove (Ray, 1985; Ray et al., 1983, 1987, 1989) and the rate of fraud or recidivism cases is lower than generally estimated (ACT, 1984). Many social professionals strongly advocate compulsory training and social integration programs for API beneficiaries. Since the early 1980s, several such programs were established through public funding, particularly by the *Ministère des droits de la femme* (Department of Women's Rights); unemployed lone mothers are given priority access to paid on-the-job training programs (Lefaucheur, 1988b).

Socialization and Lone Parenthood

Criticisms of Scholarly Representations

Child socialization issues are clearly the most negative among social representations, including representations from scientific fields, dealing with lone parenthood. Criticisms of these scientific claims have constituted a major axis for French research efforts in three areas: (1) studies on the constitution and evolution of scientific representation correlating parental-couple dissolution with juvenile delinquency, academic failures, or personality and behaviourial problems (Lefaucheur, 1989); (2) inquiries contradicting such representation (Burguière and Seydoux, 1973; Léomant, 1974; Commaille, 1982); and (3) review of psychoanalytically inspired approaches to lone parenthood problems (Tort, 1987, 1988). Certain psychologists or sociologists (Poussin and Sayn, 1990; Degaulejac and Aubert, 1990) persist in viewing lone parenthood as the major source and, when it results from a divorce or illegitimacy, as a consequential factor related to socialization problems. However, most sociological studies on the correlation between lone parent households and socialization of children have focused mainly on the social and family networks within which these households evolve.

Socialization Networks and Lone Parenthood

Common usage of the expression lone parent families has helped to destigmatize those household categories most discredited by society. But it has also served to mask the heterogenous nature, complexity, and mobility of lone parenthood situations and, thus, has become less pertinent. The household, for lone parent families resulting from a divorce or separation (75% of all households classified in this category), is clearly a lone parent household, but it is a bifocal and biresidential one for the children who are part of such a family. Although 39% of children born of married and separated couples and 19% of those born of married and divorced couples never see their fathers again, and despite the fact that 20% of the former and 23% of the latter meet him less than once a month (Leridon and Villeneuve-Gokalp, 1988c: Table 3-9), the majority of children in lone parent families generally commute between their paternal and maternal domiciles.

While some researchers were developing criticism of representations that favoured the constitution of a specific lone parent families category featuring inherent and consequential problems (Lefaucheur, 1987a; 1988c), other extensive studies were attempting to research the social mobility and complexity of lone parent situations by using a longitudinal approach and analyzing family recomposition processes — especially the nature and evolution of parental networks and socialization (LeGall and Martin, 1988a, 1988b, 1990, 1991a, 1991b; Léridon and Villeneuve-Gokalp, 1988a, 1988b, 1988c, 1988d; Théry, 1987, 1991; Théry and Dravernas, 1991; Villeneuve-Gokalp, 1991). Some of these research findings indicate the various ways a child's family surroundings can impact on the socialization process, depending on sex and social environment of the lone parent (Neyrand and Guillot, 1988). Others have analyzed the evolution, subsequent to a family breakup, of parental networks, relationships, and communications established (or interrupted) between the family members and kins of both the custodian and non-custodian parents as well as other persons with whom they established new conjugal relationships which, in a large number of cases, were non-cohabiting partners.

The survey undertaken in 1987, by Didier LeGall and Claude Martin, with the collaboration of 1,100 separated or divorced and not remarried custodial parents, has indicated that two-thirds of them maintained relationships with the non-custodial parent. In 50% of these cases, contacts were limited to functional communications regarding children's visiting schedules or important decision-making on their behalf; but in almost 25% of the cases,

Table 3-9:

Frequency of Relations between Children and Their Father
When Parents Do Not Live Together (Not Only Lone Parents)

	Children who live with him full or half time	Children who meet him at least once a month or for all holidays	Children who meet him less than once a month	Children who never meet him	Total
All children who do not live with both their parents	15%	26%	21%	38%	100%
Children whose parents:					
were already separated at birth	7%	7%	12%	74%	100%
lived together but never married	23%	13%	20%	44%	100%
divorced	16%	34%	23%	27%	100%
divorced and were given joint custody	28%	30%	26%	16%	100%
Children aged:					
0-4	8%	22%	22%	48%	100%
5-8	15%	30%	23%	32%	100%
9-12	12%	26%	22%	40%	100%
13-16	21%	24%	18%	37%	100%

Source: Léridon and Villeneuve-Gokalp, 1988 c.♦

relationships between the two parents exceeded the functional level and were generally termed as friendly by the custodial parents. This was generally the case among parents with a higher socio-economic background. In almost five out of six cases, the non-custodial ex-spouse was living with a new companion, often a previously-married woman who, in one out of two cases, had borne one child or more during that previous marriage; in one out of four cases, these ex-spouses had fathered one child or more with their new companions. Resumption of conjugal living was much less frequent among custodial mothers. Only one out of six mothers had chosen to cohabitate with a partner and generally these mothers were in the higher socio-economic strata, almost 50% of their conjugal partners had previously

Table 3-10:

Family Situation of Custodian Mothers in 1987
Compared with 1990

	Family Situation in 1987			
	Without any partner	*Uncohabiting partner*	*Cohabiting partner*	*Total*
Family Situation in 1990 (Comparison)				
without any partner	(205) 89%	(33) 43%	(1) 5%	(239) 73%
uncohabiting partner	(16) 7%	(21) 28%	(3) 16%	(40) 12%
cohabiting partner	(5) 2%	(15) 20%	(8) 42%	(28) 9%
married or remarried	(5) 2%	(7) 9%	(7) 37%	(19) 6%
Total	(231) 100%	(76) 100%	(19) 100%	(326) 100%

Source: Martin, 1992 (custodian mothers divorced or separated in 1987).♦

been married and had often fathered children of which few had obtained custody. In approximately one out of five cases, these women had mothered one child or more with their new partner. Among custodial mothers living alone, more than one out of four admitted to having a regular companion who did not cohabitate with her on a daily basis (LeGall and Martin, 1988a, 1988b). One-third of these custodial parents were reinvestigated three years later. Nine-tenths of those living alone and not acknowledging a partner in 1987 were still without a partner in 1990. The situation remained unchanged for the majority of lone mothers living with a partner in 1987; four-fifths were living with a partner in 1990 but almost 50% of these women were now remarried. The situation for the lone mothers who, in 1987, were living alone but had admitted to having a regular companion, had changed in 1990: 43% were still living alone but no longer had a regular companion, 29% had formed a parental couple, and married in one-third of the cases (Martin, 1992: Table 3-10).

Conclusion

Cutting a lone parent family category out of the social field has permitted production of statistical data regarding these households and has brought to the fore their circumstances and the disadvantages they face in comparison with coupled parents. But more detailed examination of these data shows that there is a large variation in the impoverishment and circumstances of lone parent families, depending on different factors such as duration of the previous engagement in a conjugal relationship, duration of the lone parenthood situation, sex, age, marital status and activity of the head-of-household, number and age of dependants, family's socio-professional trajectories, type of relationship established with the non-custodial parent, benefits that the lone parents are allowed to receive according to these factors and strategies they adopt to cope. About two out of three French lone mothers are employed and cope — often better than two-parent households where the mother is not working — mainly with their own salary. About one out of four French lone mothers are highly dependent on transfer payments, mainly family allowances and two differential benefits, API, a lone parent transitory benefit, and RMI, a universal differential benefit guaranteeing an income that is equivalent to approximately one-half of the guaranteed minimum wage.

The importance attached to the lone parent family category by policy makers, social workers and family specialists follows partly from its ability to provide data, but also from its ability to crystallize social representations linked to the crisis of the welfare state and to the current changes in women's status and family life. But these changes lessen the relevance of the lone parent family category. Children who live in a lone parent household resulting from the high increase in divorce and separation have more and more often two parents alive and commute between their two domiciles. The evidence from recent studies demonstrates the complexity of relationships and multiplicity of persons likely to be involved in playing a parental role or representing parental figures of various types and degrees on behalf of children in lone parent households. Thus, research specialists, as well as social workers and policy makers, can no longer indiscriminately confuse households and families nor can they analyze lone parent families without taking into account the extent, nature, performance, and history of relational networks in which children evolve, and in which funds and services are provided.

PART II

DEMOGRAPHICS OF THE SINGLE PARENT FAMILY

4

An Overview of Lone Parenthood in Canada

Craig McKie

The number of lone parent families in Canada surpassed one million in total sometime in 1989, 1990, or 1991 depending on whether the Labour Force Survey, the General Social Survey, or the Inter-Censal Population estimates are used. Accelerating past rates of lone parenthood were last seen before the 1940s, an era when premature deaths created many widows and widowers. The Post-Censal Estimates suggest that in summer 1991 lone parent families comprised in excess of 14% of all family types continuing the sharp rise from 12.7% in 1986. Figure 4-1 and Table 4-1 show that the curve is both ascending and accelerating and has been doing so since a turning point reached in about 1976. Lone parents remain a heavily female group. The percentage of the total represented by males was 26% in 1941, dropped to a low of 17% in 1976, but has been rising ever since reaching an estimated 18% in 1991. This is still well below the mortality-based ratio of one in four in the 1930s. The proportion of Canadians eighteen to sixty-four years who have ever lived in a common law relationship is rising rapidly as well. In 1990, 28% of men had lived in such a relationship, up from 16% in 1984 at the time of the Family History survey. In like manner, the proportion for women rose to 29% from 17% over the same period (Stout, 1991: 19).

Changing Demographics of Lone Parenthood

Barring any countervailing force, the proportion of all families headed by a solitary adult seems destined to rise further in the future. A progressively larger proportion of Canadian children are reliant on the solitary parent's energies although there may be other adults in the household in a position to give some assistance. Canada has moved into a *terra incognita* of mass lone parenthood; what was once the exceptional has become pedestrian reality for many. Canadians have collectively surpassed the death-based proportions of the 1930s (12% of all families in 1931) and the rates of increasing incidence are themselves increasing in slope. For some, most

Table 4-1:

Number of Census Families in Canada by Type, 1941-1991 (000s) *

Year	Census Families	Husband-Wife	Lone Parent Families		
			Total	Male	Female
1941	2509.7	2202.7	307.0	80.7	226.3
1951	3287.4	2961.7	325.7	74.8	250.9
1956	3711.5	3393.1	318.7	75.0	243.5
1961	4147.4	3800.0	347.4	75.2	272.2
1966	4526.3	4154.4	371.4	71.5	300.4
1971	5070.7	4591.9	478.7	100.7	378.1
1976	5727.9	5168.6	559.3	95.0	464.3
1981	6325.0	5611.0	714.0	124.2	589.8
1986	6735.0	5881.3	853.6	151.7	701.9
1991*	7146.8	6124.8	1000.2	181.3	820.7

Source: Statistics Canada, 91-535E, Appendix Table 5.2, 1990, p.87.
* 1991 figures from Statistics Canada, Population Estimates, 91-204, Tables 1 & 7 for June 1, 1991.♦

notably John Conway (1990), this fact should be taken as nothing less than *prima facie* evidence of a crisis for Canadian society.

Though lone parenthood is not new, it now usually arrives in the guise of child rearing by never-married mothers (who are in some cases still children themselves) or through the dissolution of a family, whether it was based on a marriage or not, rather than through the death of a partner. Conway (1990: 99) reports that adolescent girls who keep their children add over 17,000 new single parent families in Canada annually. Further, female lone parents tend to have their first marital or common law union at a younger age than wives; 28% of the lone parents had been in a union before they were nineteen compared to 24% of the wives (Moore, 1987: 33). In earlier eras, as now, lone parenthood is associated with low income, a poor quality of life, restricted opportunities, high risks, and a low level of support (both ex-spousal and state-generated). Kevin McQuillan (1988) notes that the rapid increase in numbers of lone parents is associated with continuing high rates of divorce, decreasing numbers of children per family, fossilization of the sole-breadwinner family, and the episodic nature of contemporary family life. Conway estimates that between one and two million Canadian children have been touched by some form of marriage breakdown in the twenty years since the change in the divorce law (1990: 65).

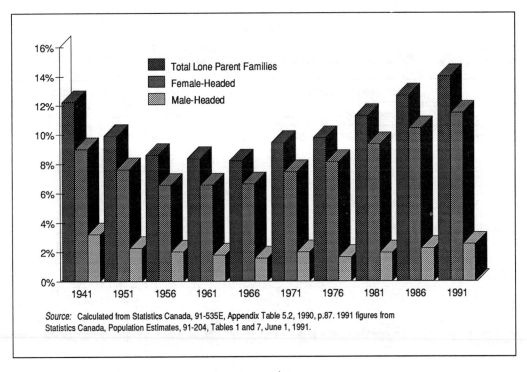

Figure 4-1:

Lone Parent Families in Canada by Type, 1941-1991

McQuillan (1988) identifies the growing heterogeneity of family types as occurring concurrent with a number of economic and social changes including much higher labour force participation rates for women, especially women with very young children. This increase has greatly stimulated unsatisfied demand for supervised daycare. "Between 1976 and 1986, the number of children under the age of six with either both parents working or an employed lone parent increased from just over 600,000 to 954,000 ... Over the same period, the total number of day-care spaces grew from 83,500 to 220,500" (Parliament, 1989: 4). Other changes occurring concurrently with increasing heterogeneity of family types are the emergence into relative dominance of the two-earner family as a social type, stable or declining real family incomes in consequence of higher rates of taxation occasioned by rapid aging of the population, more pressure and stress, longer hours of work if calculated on an inclusive family basis, more childless couples, sequential family formations, muddied genealogy, and conflicting emotional entanglements — "particularly in the case of families formed as a result of divorce, there are likely to be continuing emotional and financial connections with the parent who has left the home" (McQuillan, 1988: 3).

Table 4-2:

Lone Parent Families, Showing Sizes and
Jurisdictions, 1991 (000's)

Area	Lone Parent Families			Persons in Families			Average Family Size		
	Total	Male	Female	Total	Male	Female	Total	Male	Female
Canada	**1,002.0**	**181.3**	**820.7**	**2530.7**	**453.3**	**2077.4**	**2.5**	**2.5**	**2.5**
Newfoundland	18.8	3.8	15.0	51.3	10.5	40.8	2.7	2.7	2.7
Prince Edward Is.	4.7	0.9	3.7	12.1	2.5	9.6	2.6	2.7	2.6
Nova Scotia	34.5	5.9	28.6	87.7	15.0	72.6	2.5	2.5	2.5
New Brunswick	28.7	5.1	23.7	73.9	13.0	60.9	2.6	2.6	2.6
Quebec	301.4	54.1	247.3	744.2	133.2	611.0	2.5	2.5	2.5
Ontario	336.7	61.9	274.8	850.3	154.7	695.6	2.5	2.5	2.5
Manitoba	37.4	6.4	31.0	96.6	16.6	80.1	2.6	2.6	2.6
Saskatchewan	32.8	5.7	26.2	85.4	15.1	70.3	2.7	2.6	2.7
Alberta	88.9	15.6	73.3	229.3	39.4	189.9	2.6	2.5	2.6
British Columbia	118.9	21.7	97.2	299.9	53.3	246.6	2.5	2.5	2.5

Source: Statistics Canada, Population Estimates, 91-204, Table 8, June 1, 1991.♦

The notion of family identity (and within it the notion of personal identity) grows ever more problematic and questions, such as that of ethnic origin, more thorny as the accumulating layers of failed families and family fragments in Canadian society grow higher, the number of recombinant unions increases, and the incorporation of isolates proceeds. Genealogical terminology for multiple recombinant lineal relations is obdurate in the English language and graphically incomprehensible in many cases (ex-step-uncles for example). Consider the following wellspring. Whereas the never-married lone parent mother composed just 1% of lone parents in 1951, the proportion had risen to 15% by 1986 (McQuillan, 1988: Table 4-2) and will doubtless grow still further. By 1987, out-of-wedlock births had reached 12% of all births to women twenty-five and over, 31% of births to women aged twenty to twenty-four years, and 77% of births to women under twenty years of age; overall, 20% of births in 1987 were to unmarried women (McKie and Thompson, 1990: 128–129). Lone parent mothers are now younger; 16%

Table 4-3:

The Structure of Lone Parent Families as of June 1, 1991 (000s)

Lone Parent Families in Canada* as of June 1, 1991 (Estimated):	1,002,000

Of the above total:

387,100 families had all children over 18 years
 72,800 families had children over 18 years and at least one under 18 years
543,000 families had all children under 18 years
    143,200 families had all children under 6 years
    218,000 families had all children between 6 and 14 years
     68,000 families had all children between 15 and 17 years
     62,400 families had children under 6 years and between 6 and 14 years
      2,600 families had children under 6 years and between 15 and 17 years
     45,000 families had children between 6 and 14 years and between 15 and 17 years
      2,800 families had children under 6 years, between 6 and 14 years and
           between 15 and 17 years

Totals may not add up due to random rounding.
* Excludes Yukon and NWT
Source: Statistics Canada, Postcensal Population Estimates of Families, 91-204, Table 3.♦

were aged fifteen to thirty-four years in 1951 compared to 32% in 1986 (McQuillan, 1988: Table 4-3). These changes highlight the dissimilarity between lone parenthood early in this century which was based on mortality and the present era. The two eras are qualitatively dissimilar and are growing more so with the passage of time. For, as McQuillan put it, " ... the growing proportion of unmarried women in this age group [15 to 24 years] is largely responsible for the increase in overall female headship rates" (1988: 7). On the income side, McQuillan reported that "the majority of female lone parents in the youngest age category are not employed, and even among families where the mother is between twenty-five and thirty-four, the average number of earners is only .6   ... while their real income grew during the seventies by almost 20%, they continued to fall further behind husband-wife families. The early eighties have seen no real growth for either family type and consequently the gap has remained constant" (1988: 13–15).

Lone Parenting: Labels and Practice

Lone parents remain overwhelmingly female. Their relative poverty forms a continuing motif in the Canadian social welfare literature. Lone parent mothers have been shown to face problems such as shelter access and affordability and lack of access to a car with all that entails (Klodawsky, Spector and Rose, 1985). They are more likely to be renters than married women, to live in older apartments, and to have inferior household facilities relative to their married counterparts. Lone parents are less likely than dual parents to possess air conditioners, smoke detectors, fire extinguishers, microwave ovens, freezers, dishwashers, washing machines, dryers, and home entertainment systems (Moore, 1987: 34).

But it is important to distinguish between the transient label lone parent and the actual activity of lone parenting. Parents who have raised children on their own, and who have seen these children leave to form independent households, are still lone parents though their parental responsibilities have been reduced and transformed in nature. Likewise, lone parents who, after a period of parenting on their own, form new marital units, perhaps with new parenting responsibilities, nevertheless leave continuing threads of lone parenthood in the biographies of the children. These traces are seldom seen in the social record, an exception being the Family History Survey of 1984 (Statistics Canada, 1985 and 1986) which asked respondents to retrospectively record their biological and social parental careers. Quite a bit is known about the duration of lone parenting episodes. For instance, the average duration of lone parenthood for unwed mothers whose episode has ended by 1984 was 3.5 years (Moore, 1988: 41).

Financial sacrifices made in youth as a lone parent are lifelong in effect, being made manifest in continuing career damage, lack of accumulated assets, and lack of pension plan entitlements. Episodes of lone parenthood, though subsequently liquidated, leave a kind of mortgage on quality of life into the future. In this sense, lone parenthood is not just a current marital status; entry into it is a decisive and fateful turning point of life for many Canadians. Choosing or being forced into lone parenthood sets out a lifetime course.

Incidence

The numbers of lone parent families are increasing rapidly. For the year ending May 31, 1989, the 3.2% rate of annual growth in the number of lone parent families was a little over four times higher than the 0.8% rate for husband-wife families at the national level. Mothers provided the parental presence in 82% (797,900) of lone parent families. Females were over-represented in all age groups of parents, their proportions going from 75% (45–54 years) to 94% (15–24 years) (Statistics Canada 91–204, 1989: 6).

In the following two years the picture became more sharply defined with a continuation of the previous trends. In the year ending June 1, 1991, the number of lone parent families increased three-fold over that of husband-wife families (3.3% versus 1.0%, respectively). In June 1991, the number of lone parent families surpassed the million mark reaching 1,002,000 and representing 14% of all Census families compared to 12.7% in 1981 (Statistics Canada, 91–204, 1989). The most significant increase in this type of family occurred in British Columbia (+4.8% in 1990–91), followed closely by Alberta (+4.7%) and Newfoundland (+3.5%). Only these three provinces had annual growth rates in the number of lone parent families exceeding that of the national level (Statistics Canada 91–204, 1991: 7). Estimates of the number and characteristics of lone parent families based on contemporary surveys tend to indicate that the post censal estimates grounded on the findings of the 1986 Census are conservative with respect to the rate of increase in the number of lone parent families. Results from the 1990 General Social Survey suggest that by 1990 the number of lone parent families had exceeded 1 million. Figures from the Labour Force Survey indicate that the 1 million figure was exceeded as early as 1989.

Table 4-3 shows a comparable age breakdown of the ages of children in lone parent families as of the June 1, 1991 estimates. There are many families with children all over eighteen years (387,100) but more with all children under eighteen years (543,000). No typical pattern can be discerned except that, owing to the general decline in fertility, there are fewer children per family on average (1.5 overall) than there once were.

Little analysis has been conducted on ethnicity and lone parenthood although, in 1986, 23% of aboriginal families living off reserves were headed by a lone parent, almost twice the rate for all Canadians (McDonald, 1991: 4). Special tabulations from the 1986 Census done for the federal Employment Equity program indicated that lone parents in Canada, both male and female, are not conspicuously drawn from the visible minorities if the program's visible minority designation is accepted at face value. Of the 701,815 female lone parent families in Canada in 1986, only 50,770 were designated as being members of a visible minority. The comparable total for males was 9,115. These tabulations also show relatively few lone parent families in which there were children under the age of fifteen years who had immigrated to Canada (only 22,695 in total). Lone parenthood is a state that can be both entered and left. These survey results are estimates of the temporal balance between the processes of creation and liquidation of lone parent families. Even if creation continues at a constant rate, the current total will increase if the rate of liquidation declines. There is no real measure of the liquidation rate since it can take many forms. The creation of a new common-law union, for example, can take two lone parents away from the grand total of lone parent families.

Summary Overview on the Number of Lone Parent Families

The incidence of lone parent families in Canada has tended to increase as a proportion of all Census families over the past two decades. While tending to decline until 1976, the proportion has risen ever since, and the rate of rise is now accelerating. Remarriage and the creation of new common-law unions both remove families from the category over time; these rates have sharply increased in the last two decades (Burke, 1986: 8), and should place downward pressure on the total number of lone parent families.

Downward pressure, however, has been more than offset by the prolific creation of new lone parent families largely through the process of union dissolution and increasing custodial retention by never-married mothers.

Recent sample surveys confirm the increase is still underway. At any given time, the number of men and women in the current state of lone parenthood is but a fraction of all those who have spent a significant period of their lives in this condition. Nevertheless, the Census snapshot available every five years (the best single source of authoritative and accurate data available) shows a steady increase in the numbers of both men and women lone parents. These numbers are now higher, both in absolute terms and relative to the total number of census families than they were in 1941. In 1931, 13.6% of Census families were headed by a lone parent, a proportion higher than in 1986 (Graves, 1991: 6). No breakdown of men and women is available for 1931. Since very few divorces were granted in this period, and since many fewer unmarried women kept children born out of wedlock, we may presume that higher rates of adult mortality produced this higher proportion. For the purposes of contemporary analysis, the current era of lone parent-hood in Canada begins with the 1941 Census.

Historically, lone parent families headed by women have outnumbered those headed by men by a large factor. The ratio of the former to the latter has increased with time. It was 2.8: 1 in 1941 and by 1976 had increased steadily to 4.9: 1. In 1977, the ratio began to drop and is estimated to have stood at 4.5: 1 in 1991, still much above the 1941 ratio. This ratio is affected by many factors including the disposition of Canadian courts to award child custody to mothers (McKie, Prentice and Reed, 1983: 207), the differential rates of remarriage between men and women (Burke, 1986: 8), and the growing incidence of lone parenthood among never-married women. Lone parent families by 1991 were both more numerous (about 14% of all Census families) and more likely to be female than was the case in the 1940s and 1950s, the era immediately before divorce reform.

Lone Parent Mothers Compared To Lone Parent Fathers

Male Lone Parents

The heavy preponderance of female lone parents has tended to deflect attention and research efforts away from male lone parents. These are a small but growing proportion of the total of lone parents; the proportion reached 18% of the total in 1991 although this does not approach the 1941 proportion (26%). The proportion is lower still in the United States where the comparable rate is only 12% (Graves, 1991: 7). Graves also reports that in 1985, 26% of American families were headed by only one parent, a figure far higher than the 12.7% of Canadian single parent families. Much of the increase in numbers of male lone parents is also attributable to rising rates

Table 4-4:

Lone Parent Families Showing Family Size in Canada
as of June 1, 1991 (000s)

Sex and Age Group	Total Lone Parent Families	Families by Size			Persons in Families	Average Family Size
		Two	*Three*	*Four +*		
Male	**181.3**	**112.9**	**51.1**	**17.3**	**453.3**	**2.5**
15-24 years	3.5	2.7	0.7	0.2	8.2	2.3
25-34 years	21.8	13.0	6.6	2.1	55.0	2.5
35-44 years	58.1	31.4	20.1	6.6	151.3	2.6
45-54 years	45.0	27.0	13.2	4.8	114.0	2.5
55-64 years	31.4	21.7	7.3	2.5	76.0	2.4
65 years and over	21.5	17.2	3.2	1.1	48.8	2.3
Female	**820.7**	**483.0**	**257.8**	**79.9**	**2,077.4**	**2.5**
15-24 years	53.4	39.6	11.3	2.5	123.4	2.3
25-34 years	203.9	106.2	73.2	24.4	535.4	2.6
34-44 years	250.5	116.7	101.7	32.2	673.7	2.7
45-54 years	128.7	77.1	39.8	11.8	323.3	2.5
55-64 years	98.3	70.3	21.4	6.7	233.8	2.4
65 years and over	86.0	73.2	10.4	2.3	187.8	2.2
Total	**1,002.0**	**596.0**	**308.8**	**97.2**	**2,530.7**	**2.5**

Source: Statistics Canada, Population Estimates, 91-204, Table 7, June 1, 1991.♦

of marital dissolution of both legal and social types. Lone parenthood among fathers is likely to occur in the middle or late years of the life cycle; there is little representation of lone parent fathers in the two youngest age groups (18–24 and 25–29 years). The pattern shown in Table 4-4 shows a large proportion of male lone parents residing with children who are either teenagers or even young adults. Canadian courts tend to allow teenage children a voice in their residence patterns.

Graves has noted the lack of primary data regarding single fathers in Canada (1991). Most available information about single fathers has relied on questionnaires and interviews administered to small, non-random samples of single fathers (Hanson, 1985; Schnayer and Orr, 1988/89). Individual men move through the lone parent category as transients subject to quick remarriage and/or the formation of new marital units and become invisible for research purposes in all but the most exceptional cases. In a U.S. study, 50% of single custodial fathers had married within a three year period (Grief, 1985).

Table 4-5:

*Type of Census Families in Private Households for Canada
1981 and 1986*

| | Total Families | | Lone Parent Families | | | | | |
| | | | Total | | Male Parent | | Female Parent | |
	1981	1986	1981	1986	1981	1986	1981	1986
Primary Families								
With additional persons	576,820	595,650	115,985	138,485	29,855	35,490	86,135	102,995
Without additional persons	5,556,385	5,938,715	537,450	647,425	82,600	102,050	454,850	545,380
Subtotal	6,133,205	6,534,365	653,435	785,915	112,455	137,540	540,985	648,370
Secondary Families	191,770	200,610	60,570	67,735	11,725	14,700	48,845	53,530
Total Families	6,324,975	6,734,980	714,010	853,645	124,180	151,740	589,830	701,900

Source: Table 2, Families Part 1, Statistics Canada, 93-106, 1987. ◆

Children in Lone Parent Families

A very large number of children are living in lone parent families in Canada. Table 4-4 shows that as of June 1, 1991, there were approximately 1.5 million children in this type of family. All but about 275,000 of these are resident with a mother. Low fertility rates have reduced family size overall; more than one half of all lone parent families have just one child (596,000 or 60% of the total).

Table 4-5 shows Census data from 1981 and 1986 to address the question of additional support within the *household* from non family members. Additional persons, who might be able to offer assistance, were in the household for about 18% of primary lone parent families in 1981 and 1986. In addition, lone parent families were the secondary family in the household for about 9% of affected households in 1981 and 8% in 1986.

Labour Force Participation

Males in all types of lone parent families have higher labour force participation rates than females. A possible exception is male parents with children less than three years of age where there are insufficient cases to provide an estimate. Table 4-6 shows male labour force participation rates are 20 percentage points higher than those for females in most instances. Unemployment rates are also higher for women. Consistent with the population as a whole, female lone parent labour force participation rates rose between 1989 and 1990 and then fell back in 1991, while those for comparable males fell slowly and continuously from 1989 to 1991. Unemployment rates are lowest for both male and female lone parents where there are no children less than 16 years of age. Similarly, the most pronounced effects occur for lone parents with very young children. The unemployment rate for lone parent mothers with children under three years of age was 25% for 1989, 27% for 1990 and 26% in 1991.

Income

There is also a major difference with respect to incomes. Census figures concerning incomes in 1980 and 1985 (in constant 1985 dollars) show lone parent fathers averaged $33,261 in 1980 and $31,252 in 1985 compared to incomes of $19,733 and $19,177 respectively for lone parent mothers. Lone parent fathers, though receiving incomes far lower than the average for all Census families, have a clear economic advantage in comparison to mothers. The disadvantage for lone parent mothers has long term cumulative effects as pension plan entitlements and other forms of equity are not built up. Burke and Spector found that "many lone parents, particularly women, enter a very vulnerable stage in their life as they approach age fifty-five. At this point, children leave the nest and child support, family allowance payments,

Table 4-6:

Lone Parents in the Labour Force, 1991 (000's)

	Pop. 15+ Years	Labour Force	Employment				Not in Labour Force	Partici-pation Rate	Unempl. Rate	Empl/ Pop. Ratio
		Total	Total	Full Time	Part Time	Unempl.				
Families with Female Head or Spouse, No Husband Present										
Total	**848**	**477**	**412**	**341**	**71**	**65**	**371**	**56.3**	**13.6**	**48.6**
With children less than 16 years	444	279	232	187	45	47	166	62.7	16.8	52.2
With pre-school children	190	95	74	55	19	22	95	50.1	22.6	38.8
With children less than 3 years	99	41	31	22	8	10	58	41.4	25.5	30.8
With youngest child 3-5 years	91	54	43	33	10	11	37	59.5	20.4	47.4
At least one child 6-15 years	254	183	158	132	26	25	71	72.1	13.8	62.2
Without children less than 16 years	404	199	180	155	26	18	205	49.2	9.2	44.7
Head less than 55 years	203	159	144	127	16	15	44	78.4	9.7	70.9
Head 55 years and over	201	40	37	27	10	n.a	162	19.7	n.a.	18.3
Families with Male Head, No Spouse Present										
Total	**241**	**172**	**149**	**141**	**8**	**23**	**69**	**71.3**	**13.2**	**61.8**
With children less than 16 years	65	55	46	45	n.a.	9	10	84.7	15.7	71.3
With pre-school children	15	13	9	9	n.a.	n.a.	n.a.	84.8	n.a.	63.1
With children less than 3 years	4	4	n.a.	n.a	n.a.	n.a.	n.a.	n.a.	n.a.	n.a.
With youngest child 3-5 years	11	9	7	6	n.a	n.a.	n.a.	80.2	n.a.	62.2
At least one child 6-15 years	50	42	37	36	n.a	5	8	84.6	12.8	73.8
Without children less than 16 years	176	117	103	96	6	14	59	66.3	12.1	58.3
Head less than 55 years	110	97	84	80	4	13	13	88.0	13.1	76.4
Head 55 years and over	65	20	18	16	n.a.	n.a.	46	29.9	n.a.	27.9

Source: Statistics Canada, Labour Force Annual Averages, 71-220, 1990. ◆

Table 4-7:

Incomes of Lone Parent Families in Constant 1985 Dollars
for 1980 and 1985 (Census Data)

| | All Familes | | Lone Parent Families | | | | Female/ Male Ratio | |
| | | | Males | | Females | | | |
	1980	1985	1980	1985	1980	1985	1980	1985
Median Income	$34,143	$33,434	$29,115	$27,405	$15,505	$15,005		
as % of all families figure	100%	100%	85.2%	81.9%	45.4%	44.8%	53.2%	54.7%
Average Income	$38,276	$37,827	$33,261	$31,252	$19,733	$19,177		
as % of all families figure	100%	100%	86.8%	82.6%	51.5%	50.6%	59.3%	61.3%

Source: Statistics Canada, 98-128, Table 2, 1989 (reproduced from Graves, 1991, Table 8). ◆

and, in many jurisdictions, eligibility for social housing programs cease for those between ages fifty-five and fifty-nine" (1991: 17). These mothers may also lack the financial resources to propel their children upwards on the socioeconomic ladder, thus adding a intergenerational element to a fully completed lone parenthood cycle.

Detailed income figures from Statistics Canada are only available for female lone parents with children under eighteen years of age; these show a long term decline in average family incomes for this group. The average family income of female lone parents in 1980 was $22,527 (in 1990 dollars) and stood at $21,961 in 1990. Average incomes actually rose from $10,325 in 1980 to $12,059 in 1990 for lone parent mothers who did not work for pay but these totals are so low as to minimize the impact of the increase.

Table 4-9 shows that a majority of lone parents live below the low income cutoffs; the proportion of all low income families below the low income cutoff rose from 54% in 1986 to 56% in 1990. The proportion of lone parent mothers who did not work for pay and who fell below the cutoffs rose from 93% in 1986 to 96% in 1990. The incidence of low income can also be expressed for all lone parent families (and not just those with children under eighteen years). These figures, while less stark than those in Tables 4-8 and 4-9, show the clear distinction in economic resources possessed by male-headed and female-headed lone parent families. Using the 1986 basis of calculation, 47% of female-headed lone parent families fell below the low income cutoffs in contrast to 19% of their male-headed counterparts. In 1990,

Table 4-8:

Average Family Incomes, Selected Years

	As Percentage of All Family Types		Average Family Income in Constant 1990 Dollars					
	1980	1990	1980	1986	1987	1988	1989	1990
Total lone parent family	4.2	4.7	24,234	23,231	24,338	23,872	25,923	24,020
Female lone parent family	3.6	4.0	22,527	21,085	21,687	21,717	23,687	21,961
No earner	0.9	1.1	10,325	12,192	11,707	12,052	12,338	12,059
One earner	1.8	2.2	22,176	22,791	22,439	22,717	24,464	23,200

Source: Statistics Canada, Income Distributions in Canada, 1990, 13-210, Text Table 1, p.21.♦

Table 4-9:

Incidence of Low Income, Selected Years

	As Percentage of All Family Types		Incidence of Low Income				
	1980	1990	1986	1987	1988	1989	1990
Total lone parent families	11.0	13.7	53.9	54.2	52.2	49.3	55.9
Female lone parent famiiies	10.2	12.8	58.8	59.0	56.7	52.9	60.6
No earner	4.7	5.7	93.1	96.5	94.7	95.4	95.6
One earner	4.5	6.0	48.7	50.6	48.7	44.2	51.6

Source: Statistics Canada, Income Distributions in Canada 1990, 13-210, Text Table 3, p.24.♦

female-headed lone parent families represent about 35% of all low income families and female-headed low income families are 8.6% of all families in total (Statistics Canada, 1990: 159, 164).

Occupation and Education

Lone parent fathers can also be distinguished from lone parent mothers by virtue of marginally superior educational attainment and higher occupational status. The 1984 Family History Survey found male lone parents to have both a higher proportion of professional and technical occupations (26% to 21% for female lone parents) and a much higher rate of semi-skilled and unskilled occupations as well (56% to 10%) leaving lone parent mothers clustered in the clerical, sales, and service middle ground (47%). This is a reflection of the nature of the Canadian occupational structure as it relates to men and women generally (Statistics Canada, 1986: Table 21). The 1986 Census data found 10% of lone parent fathers had received a university degree compared to 5% of lone parent mothers. The proportion of lone parent fathers with at least some university experience was 17% in comparison to 13% of the mothers. Twenty-two percent of lone parent mothers had less than grade nine education in comparison with 26% of lone parent fathers (Statistics Canada, 1989: Table 11).

Lone Parent Lifestyles and Stress

Parenthood is seldom easy especially when children are young. Instability added by the uncertainty of Canada's economic prospects, rapid change in general social conditions, and a technological revolution in the workplace have all contributed to the total burden of stress experienced by most Canadians. Lone parents face additional tests. Table 4-10 shows the time budget of female lone parents considering both labour force status and age of children. There is considerable pressure on free time and time for personal care including sleep. Female lone parents, employed with at least one child under five, report an average of only 1.3 hours per day for free time. The figure rises to 2 hours when the children are all over 5 years. If the mother does not work for pay, these figures rise to 2.9 hours and 3.2 hours respectively. Estimates of time spent on personal care, including sleeping, tend to be higher for mothers not in paid employment, although hours spent in social contacts are lower. Those not working for pay also tend to spend a much larger proportion of the average day in their homes.

There are few straightforward measures of stress but one survey bears directly on the topic. The 1990 Health Promotion Survey showed high levels of reported stress in the population. Reported levels of stress are related to marital status for families with children under fifteen years. Table 4-11 shows that the highest levels of stress (very high or somewhat high grouped together) were found for separated fathers (97%) and divorced mothers (83%). Divorced mothers also reported the most elevated levels of very high stress (36%), in contrast to 22% of divorced fathers. Widowed parents of both sexes generally had the lowest reported levels though these levels (32%

Table 4-10:

Average Time Spent in Hours by Female Lone Parents in 1986
(averaged per day* over 7 day period)

Activity	Female Lone Parents			
	Employed		Keeping House	
	At least one child under 5	All children over 5 years	At least one child under 5	All children over 5 years
Productive Activities				
Total	9.1	9.4	7.0	6.5
Paid work	5.6	5.9	0.3	0.4
Domestic work	1.8	2.1	3.3	3.8
Primary childcare	1.1	0.4	2.2	0.7
Shopping & services	0.6	0.9	1.0	1.3
Education	n.a	0.2	2.9	3.2
Personal Care (including sleep)	10.9	10.2	10.6	11.1
Media and Communication	2.7	2.5	3.4	3.2
Other Free Time	1.3	2.0	2.9	3.2
Social Contacts				
Others—total	11.6	10.4	11.1	9.0
Partner	0.3	0.4	0.5	0.3
Children of household	3.5	3.6	7.0	5.8
Other family	2.0	1.1	3.4	2.3
Friends	3.4	2.3	3.2	2.0
Others	5.1	5.0	0.8	1.4
Alone	2.6	4.1	3.8	5.5
At Various Locations				
Home	14.9	14.0	19.0	18.5
Work	5.0	4.3	0.1	0.1
Other places	2.2	2.1	3.0	3.6
In Transit				
Total	1.1	1.4	1.2	1.0
Car	0.5	0.9	0.7	0.5
Foot	0.1	0.1	0.2	0.3
Bus/Subway	0.4	0.3	0.1	0.1
Other	0.0	0.1	0.1	0.1

Source: Statistics Canada, GSS Analysis Series: Where Does Time Go?, 11-612E, Ottawa, 1991, Tables 19, 20, & 21.
* Note: Totals do not necessarily add to 24 hours because multiple responses were allowed.♦

Table 4-11:

Reported Stress by Current Marital Status with Children in the Home (%)

Would you describe your life as:	Men with Children under 15 Years at Home					Women with Children under 15 Years at Home				
	Single	*Married*	*Separated*	*Divorced*	*Widowed*	*Single*	*Married*	*Separated*	*Divorced*	*Widowed*
Very stressful	5.4	15.6	9.8	21.6	0	11.3	12.8	25.4	35.7	14.1
Somewhat stressful	43.4	58.6	87.6	26.4	32.0	48.9	55.9	52.3	47.2	46.3
Not very stressful	40.4	19.8	2.6	16.3	0	31.1	25.2	12.6	11.2	31.4
Not at all stressful	10.8	5.9	0	35.7	68.0	8.6	6.1	9.8	5.8	8.1
Not stated	0	0.1	0	0	0	0	0.1	0	0	-
Totals*	100	99.9	100	100	100	99.9	100	100.1	99.9	99.9
N	(522,119)	(2,682,567)	(48,605)	(30,158)	(581)	(567,184)	(2,692,504)	(99,812)	(146,180)	(46,180)

Source: Statistics Canada, Health Promotion Survey, 1990, special tabulations.

* Totals diverge from 100% due to rounding.♦

for fathers and 60% for mothers) are themselves quite high. The incidence of somewhat or very high stress is remarkable in every marital status where children are present. The measures indicate that parenthood exacts its price from everyone but lone parents bear a conspicuously greater burden in this respect.

These findings are consistent with a recently published study of suicides in Finland occurring in 1975 (Jarvanainen, 1991: 6). A suicide index was constructed in which the index (or probability of suicide) was set at 1.00 for both partners in father/mother couples (each sex taken separately). Higher indexes were found for all other family types. The index figures were 1.27 for fathers in couples with no children, 1.52 for mothers in couples with no children, 2.46 for male lone parents, 1.42 for female lone parents, 2.54 for other family types for men not alone, 1.67 for other family types for women not alone, 3.12 for men living alone, and 2.24 for women living alone. Lone parenthood in Finland seems to heighten the probability of suicide for both lone parent mothers and fathers though more markedly for the lone parent fathers. Solitary forms of living still retain higher risks of suicide.

Some of the actual sources of unhappiness in the lone parent state were explored by Moore and McKie (1990: Tables 9 and 10) by examining the average satisfaction levels of both male and female lone parents with a number of aspects of life measured in standard deviations from overall sample mean scores in the 1986 General Social Survey. The transition from an unhappy and/or violent marital union to lone parenthood must represent an improvement in quality of life for some former spouses. However, relative dissatisfaction is the norm over the longer run, even when the frame of reference is rooted in the present rather than the discarded marital union. Responses fall above sample average levels on only two of twenty satisfaction scores of lone parent fathers and mothers (taken separately). Male lone parents registered above average satisfaction with respect to finances and relations with other family members. In no case did the responses of female lone parents fall above sample means. Thus, female lone parents were more unhappy on average than were male lone parents. Lone parents registered more negatively than did the entire sample on virtually all the dimensions considered including finances, housing, friends, self-esteem, job or main activity, and life as a whole. Further, lone parents of both sexes spent much more time alone than did their counterparts who were living as couples.

Familial Polymorphism in the 1990s

As recently as November 1986, a Royal Society of Canada conference on the family in crisis paid little attention to lone parent families, either as a source or as a product of the crisis (Balakrishnan and Beaujot, 1989). Perhaps lone parent families were assumed to be temporary, impermanent, or transitory. But lone parent families have arrived as a permanent, visible, and growing structural element in the range of Canadian families, at least some proportion of which is the result of personal choice. As Conway has written, "materially, people have more choices, and, ideologically, people are more willing to exercise them … Fewer and fewer people, men and women, are willing to compromise too extensively if a marriage or family relationship is fundamentally dissatisfying and unhappy" (1990: 36, 31).

These families can no longer be dismissed as a passing abberation. Canadian society must now come to terms with their reality and the reality in which their members live. Lone parent families formed principally because of the death of one parental partner have been an integral part of humanity from time immemorial. But in the last 50 years the phenomenon has increased greatly in prevalence by virtue of the growing impermanence of marital partnerships. The reassignment of the sum of family responsibilities is both a significant departure from traditional models of the family and a source of tension in that the current body of law does not fully take this alteration into account. Structural disadvantage associated with this type of family is a reflection of well-entrenched earnings differentials between men and women.

How do marital partners readjust their lives to produce a robust and forward-looking equilibrated marital union when high rates of unemployment and slow growth (or actual decline) in real disposable incomes offer a compelling reason to increase total family hours of paid work? It clearly cannot be rooted in traditional sex roles, common nostrums, or glib formulas for life. Marital partnerships lived without a script must inevitably sap the will in many. But does exhaustion of the will to change necessarily demand solitude, relative reductions in standard of living, and the assumption of full parental responsibilities by one person as the sole alternative? The convenient fiction that lone parent families are a transient, peripheral part of social reality must be discarded. Their permanent and growing presence is everywhere to be seen, while the institutional matrix for fully taking this new reality into account is nowhere to be seen.

What is the current reality facing lone parents today? For all but a lucky few, the prospect includes a stressful life lived in social isolation, bound by limitations in an unreconstructed labour market, poverty if not destitution, and knowledge that intergenerational transfers of status will afflict many of their children with low social standing. Lone parents in Canada today face a complex set of life problems, in many cases bereft of help and assistance that might conceivably be focused on their lives. The long-term social consequences of this situation are incalculable.

5

Growing Up with a Single Parent, A Transitional Experience? Some Demographic Measurements

Nicole Marcil-Gratton

Single parenthood is not a new phenomenon. Families built around the enduring relationship of a man and a woman have been disintegrating from the beginnings of time, leaving one parent to take responsibility for leading the remaining flock into the safe harbour of adulthood; the culprit was death, which spared neither rich nor poor, and thus pushed great numbers of children into orphanhood, often by mother right from birth, or by either parent sometime later in childhood (Légaré and Desjardins, 1991). As late as 1960, although this abominable face of death had been reduced to a minimum, single parent families were still mainly a consequence of mortality. Research and policy have shown increasing interest on the fate of these families and their brood since marital disruptions have replaced widowhood as their main initiator.

The switch from one to the other created several outcomes. In the last thirty years, a growing number of families were involved, with an increased proportion of children who experience life with a single parent. Moreover, single parenthood covers a different reality. The former meant a shrinking of the family environment; even though replacement of the dead parent was common and especially fast when the mother was gone, the definite loss of one parent was recognized, with mourning being the only possible way of keeping contact. The latter made family networks more complex; from the children's point of view, not only are relations to be maintained with the absent parent and family, but often new ones are to be created with the step-parent and his or her own network. Life as a single person is not any more popular today than previously, now that death does not as often impede the course of marriages but marital breakups are experienced by more and more couples.

Two points may strike demographers as inconclusive in the growing body of knowledge about single parent families. First, a longitudinal perspective, which is necessary to understand how single parenthood is part of a process rather than a fixed state, is rarely adopted in most studies, largely due to the difficulties involved in getting the appropriate data. In the absence of prospective longitudinal surveys, only retrospective surveys with good information on marital histories will provide what sources like censuses or vital statistics on marriage and divorce can only approximate. For example, the 1986 Canadian Census reports that 16% of families with children at home are headed by a single mother; that information hides the more compelling fact that an estimated 34% of mothers will have known such an experience through their lifetime, as calculated from Statistics Canada's 1984 Family History Survey (Desrosiers et al., 1992). One of the demographer's main contributions is to provide other researchers and policy makers with adequate measures of different life events. Demographers must not shy away from the arduous job of seeking longitudinal indicators which might show the single parent family's transitional nature within the life course (Festy, 1991).

Second, analysis of single parenthood are usually conducted on a population of adults. Most social science studies adopt an approach in which adults concerned by the changes in their conjugal trajectories remain the units of observation. Children intervene as influential characteristics of their parents, rather than persons in their own right, whose life course is as much modified by complex marital behaviours as that of their mothers and fathers. Psychology and psychiatry have studied the links between family context of children and their development (Wallerstein, 1991); this came mainly as a result of a clinical increase in several behavioral problems in children, which could be linked to a disturbed family background including the parents' breakup. However, very little information could be gathered until fairly recently about the extent to which these "problem children" were representative of all children involved with disintegrating families, nor about the proportion of children who would experience their parents' separation before reaching adulthood. The lack of appropriate data may explain the relative silence of social sciences in general, and demography in particular.

The 1980s have seen several initiatives by social scientists to develop a demography of childhood that would yield a good statistical portrait of the effects on children of their parents' marital behaviours (Bumpass, 1981, 1984a, 1984b; Sweet and Bumpass, 1987, and Hernandez and Myers, 1986 in the USA; Ferri, 1976 and Haskey, 1983 in Great Britain; Bourguignon et al., 1985; Leridon and Villeneuve-Gokalp, 1988 and Norvez, 1990 in France). Childhood has become the focus of attention of a number of initiatives both politically and at the research level; for example, the European Centre for Social Welfare launched an international research project in which sixteen countries, including Canada (Pence et al., 1990), produced national reports covering several aspects of children's lives. Otherwise, apart from Wargon's attempt to draw attention on childhood (Wargon, 1979), little demographic analysis of the children's population and their life course has been produced in Canada.

Canadian data and a longitudinal approach is used in this chapter to understand the extent of children's experience of parental marital mobility. Questions to be addressed include: How many children experience their parents' separation before becoming adults? How soon does that occur in the children's lives? Is there an increase in intensity or precociousness of single parent family life for younger cohorts of children born in the 1980s? After the separation, does life with a single parent go on for the remainder of childhood or is it only a transitory experience, before a new family unit is reconstituted? Have recent cohorts of children experienced a multiplication of family contexts at younger ages? Answering these questions requires an evaluation of the links between changes experienced by children and the evolution of their parents' attitude towards legal marriage and the formation of families.

Some attention will be given to regional disparities in those new trends.

Methodology

The results presented in this chapter come from two consecutive studies done for the Review of Demography and its Implication on Social And Economic Policy, Health and Welfare Canada. The first study (Marcil-Gratton and Lapierre-Adamcyk, 1988) used data from Statistics Canada's 1984 Family History Survey. Representative samples of children were derived from the 7256 female respondents' declared offspring; this yielded some 1000 children for each of three cohorts born in the early 1960s, 1970s, and 1980s. Detailed information on the mothers' reproductive behaviour, lifetime labour force participation, and marital history were transposed to become events in the lives of the children. Thus the departure from the traditional family could be examined as to how it had affected the family context in which new generations of Canadians were being born and raised.

The second study (Marcil-Gratton and Lapierre-Adamcyk, 1992) was an update of the first. Statistics Canada's 1990 General Social Survey Cycle 5 (GSS 90) provided data for an analysis of the family context at birth of children born in the late 1980s; it was also possible to follow the early childhood of children born in the early 1980s and to compare family disruption and reconstitution for these youngsters and for their older peers six years after the first study. The second study presented two methodological challenges. First, the same indicators were measured on the same cohorts of children with a different data bank; the analysis was pursued for the six years between both surveys. Second, data was incorporated as reported in the mothers' file (6895 respondents) and in the fathers' file (6600 respondents); this could not be done in the first study due to differences in question formulation. The slight discrepancies resulting in lower frequency of marital disruptions experienced by children as measured with the GSS 90 did not refute any of the major findings, and could have been related to this first-time use of both female and male responses concerning their children and their marital life. Interesting knowledge was gained about the outcome of family life after the separation, whether the children remained with their father or their mother.

Non-Marital Cohabitation and Family Context at Birth

The dismissal of legal marriage as a sacred and indissoluble institution seems to be the most significant trend of the last twenty years concerning the evolution of family life. In Canada, this was first observed in the 1970s with a remarkable increase in marital disruptions following the 1968 law liberalizing access to divorce. The divorce rate decreased towards the middle of the 1980s, before further liberalizing of the law in 1985 (Dumas, 1990), due in part to the end of a catching up period. But at the same time, young people were backing off from the risk of marriage, preferring a less rigid form of setting for their life as couples. This new attitude became evident with the 1984 Canadian Fertility Survey, which showed that a majority of first unions formed in the early 1980s were made of young cohabitating couples. Greater marital instability can be linked to this initial manifestation of reserve towards a permanent engagement whether or not these first unions eventually lead to a legal marriage. In the late 1980s, cohabitation moved beyond use as a form of trial wedding or a flexible type of union for childless couples and became a chosen context in which to form a family and have children.

The proportion of children born to at least one parent who has ever lived in cohabitation has risen dramatically in the last thirty years. The phenomena barely existed in the early 1960s (2.5% of 1961–63 birth cohorts), increased to 9% for children born in 1971–73, climbed to 32% for those born in 1981–83, and reached 43% for those born in 1987–89. Figure 5-1 draws the attention to the fact that this trend was specially strong in Quebec, where 58% of 1987–89 birth cohorts were born to such parents. Cohabitation in Quebec is rapidly becoming a replacement of legal marriage, both as first unions' settings and as the context to give birth to children, and it may be considered a preview of things to come elsewhere in Canada. Our results show that even though cohabitating couples may eventually legalize their union, their initial reserve towards marriage translates into a greater propensity to end their union.

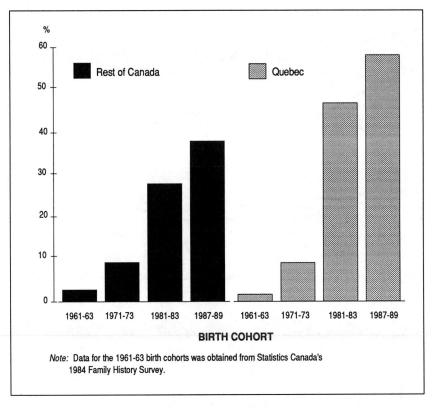

Figure 5-1:
*Percentage of Children from Various Birth Cohorts Born to at
Least One Parent Who Had Ever Lived in a Common Law
Union. Quebec, and the Rest of Canada.
General Social Survey 1990*

Born Out-of-Wedlock, But Within a Family

The first and most traditional form of single parenthood is that into which single parents (only a non-sexist attitude may prevent us to specify single mothers!) give birth to a child. Canadian vital statistics have long provided data on "illegitimate" births, which since 1974 are designated more neutrally as "out-of-wedlock;" these births totalled little more than 5% of all births up to the middle 1960s. There followed an upward trend, which doubled the proportion to 10% in the early 1970s, and again doubled to over 20% by 1988. Such a surge was in part due to the outbreak of out-of-wedlock births in Quebec; in 1975 the proportion of out-of-wedlock births in Quebec was lower than elsewhere in Canada, but the proportion boomed to 19% in 1980, climbed to 33% in 1988, and reached an astounding 38% of all births in 1990.

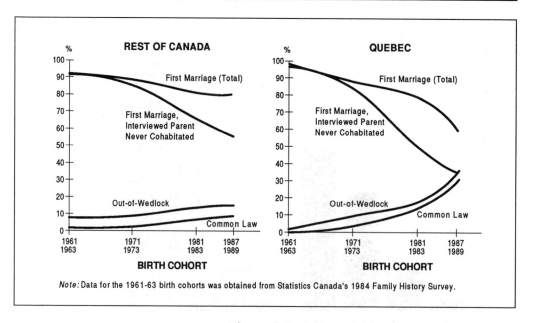

Figure 5-2:

Family Context at Birth for Various Cohorts of Children. Quebec, and the Rest of Canada. General Social Survey 1990

However, the large majority of these children cannot anymore be categorized as being born within a single parent family; although not legally married, their two parents often cohabitate.

Figure 5-2 shows how the family context of children has evolved in Quebec and the rest of Canada. In the early 1960s, children were still born into monolithic traditional family contexts. Over 90% were born within the first marriage of their parents, who had not been cohabiting either together or with someone else; this was true in Quebec as well as in the rest of Canada. The situation started to change in the 1970s but at a different pace in both regions. Cohabitation (common-law unions) became a preferred environment for a growing proportion of would-be parents, specially in Quebec where it reached its highest level for children born in the late 1980s. Figure 5-2 confirms that, for both regions of Canada, the single parent family did not get a growing share of the baby market with barely more than 5% of births being truly out-of-wedlock.

A majority of Canadian children are born within a first marriage; but there are differences between Quebec and the rest of Canada — 60% of Quebec cohorts born in 1987–89, against 80% in the rest of Canada. Quebec parents have shown a greater reserve about traditional marriage, since only 35% of those same cohorts of children had first time married parents who had never cohabitated before their birth. Cohabitation has not yet had the same impact in the rest of Canada, where 56% of children are still born within first marriages not preceded by any common law union. Diversification of family context at birth has become the rule in Quebec, much less so in the rest of Canada where 9% of the 1987–89 cohorts were born to a cohabitating couple compared to 31% of young Quebecers. The main finding is that the proportion of children who are born into families with both their biological parents present has remained as high as ever, even though the formal framework of their parents' union has changed.

Life With a Single Parent: An Increasingly Common Experience

Young generations of Canadian children may still have their two parents around when they are born, but growing proportions are losing daily coexistence with one and this is happening earlier in life. Figure 5-3 shows that marital instability has been experienced at different ages by different cohorts of children born since the 1960s. The slope of the curves reflects the 1968 law on divorce but not the slowdown of divorce rates in the 1980s. The impact of the first is visible for the 1961–63 cohorts, who were six years old on average when it was adopted; before that age, only 8% of these children had experienced life in a single parent family. Subsequently the proportion grew steadily, as the popularity of the newly accessible divorce procedures touched them through their school age years; by age twenty, one out of four children born in 1961–63 had known single parenthood.

Canadian divorce rates, which showed a slowdown in the middle 1980s, provide only a partial measure of marital disruptions, i.e. those sanctioned by law. Surveys such as the GSS 90 which provide detailed data on all separations, whether the union was legal or not and whether legal divorce was ever pronounced, indicate that a slowdown of marital breakups has not occurred. On the contrary, more children live through it and they do so at ever younger ages. By age twenty, one out of four children from the 1961–63 cohort had experienced life in a single parent family; that proportion was reached at age fifteen for the 1971–73 cohort. By age fifteen, 18% of the 1961–63 cohort had experienced single parenthood; the same proportion was reached at age six for the 1981–83 cohort. What will be the intensity of parental breakup for children born in 1981–83 by the time they reach age twenty taking into account their parents' attitudes towards cohabitation and the greater frailty of their unions?

Cohabitation and the Propensity to Separate

Backing off from marriage and choosing flexible forms of matrimony reflects a desire to be able to easily end a union that has become unsatisfying

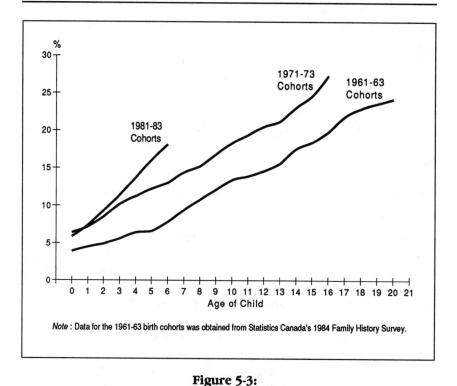

Figure 5-3:

*Cumulative Percentage of Canadian Children who were Born
to a Lone Parent or Have Lived Through the Separation of
Their Parents, from Birth to Last Birthday before Survey, for
Various Birth Cohorts. General Social Survey 1990*

to one or both partners. Children born to such parents are more at risk of
experiencing their parents' separation. The data did not yield sufficient
numbers of cases to isolate systematically those children born into common
law unions. But comparisons could be made between children whose
interviewed parent had ever lived in cohabitation before their birth, with
children whose parent had never done so. Figure 5-4 shows that children
from both the 1971–73 and 1981–83 cohorts, with both parents present at
birth, are two to three times more likely to experience single parenthood
before reaching school age if one of their parents has at one point lived in
a common law union. The intensity has remained the same at a ten years
time interval.

What has changed considerably is the proportion of children born to
parents who have cohabited. Only 9% of Canadian children from the
1971–73 cohorts were born in two-parent families in which at least one
parent had previously cohabited; the proportion was up to 33% for chil-

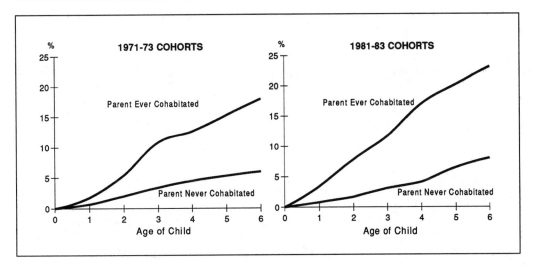

Figure 5-4:

*Cumulative Percentage of Canadian Children Born in a Two-Parent Family,
Who Have Lived through Their Parents' Separation before Age 6, Whether or
Not the Interviewed Parent Had Ever Cohabited before the Child's Birth. Birth
Cohorts 1971-73 and 1981-83, General Social Survey 1990*

dren born ten years later. What may we expect for the babies born in 1987–89
for whom the proportion born to cohabiting parents has risen to 44% (61%
in Quebec)? And what would be found by analyzing separately data for
those children born to a cohabiting couple? Data is only available for the
1981–83 cohort and reveals an even greater vulnerability to parental
separation for children born to cohabiting couples; 43% had seen their
parents break up before they were six years old. What does the near future
hold concerning the intensity of parental separation for children? Figure 5-5
leaves little optimism of any immediate slowdown; when last observed at
age sixteen, 53% of children from the 1971–73 cohort born to the group
whose parents had cohabited had seen their parents part.

After the Separation: Life With Mom, Dad, … and Someone Else?

There is more than one way to go for life after separation. Cross-sectional
analysis of Canadian families indicate that most single parent families are
headed by a lone mother. To find out what really happens to the children
requires collecting information on the destiny of those who stay with their
mother and those, indeed less numerous, who remain with their father. Does
life with a single parent become a quasi-permanent state, or does it evolve

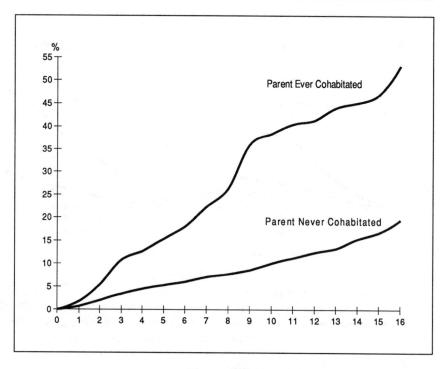

Figure 5-5:

*Cumulative Percentage of Canadian Children Born in a
Two-Parent Family, Who Have Lived through Their Parents'
Separation before Age 16, Whether or Not the Interviewed
Parent Had Ever Cohabitated before the Child's Birth. Birth
Cohorts 1971-73, General Social Survey 1990*

into a reconstitution of a two-adult household integrating the guardian
parent's new partner? Does this process unfold in a similar fashion when
Dad or Mom is in charge? What about when the two parents share equal
responsibility of the child on a time-sharing agreement? Is the multiplication
of family networks and relationships, almost inevitable for children of
separated parents, still reinforced by multiple episodes of family life
following the initial breakup of the parents? A source such as the GSS 90
cannot yield all the answers, but it does lift the veil to the most visible impacts
of parental separation and the unfolding of the remainder of childhood.

Children usually remain with their mother after the separation (McKie et
al., 1983). Figure 5-6 shows that nearly twice as many children remain with
their mother; the ratio does not diminish with the age of the child. Moreover,
even in the 1980s, fathers have not increased their participation in sharing
living arrangements with their children, 18% of children born in 1981–83
have seen their parents separate, but at age six only 4% live with their father.

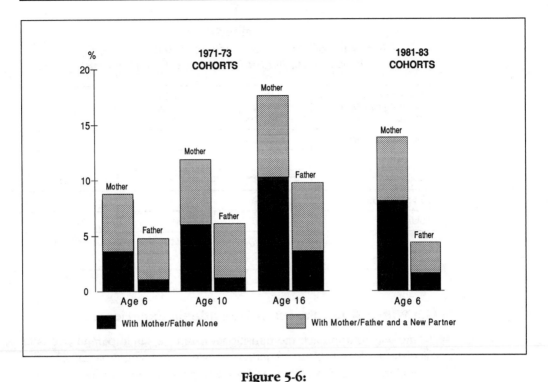

Figure 5-6:

Percentage of Canadian Children Who Have Ever Lived within a Single Parent Family, Whether They Live with Their Mother or Father, Alone or with a New Partner. Various Birth Cohorts, at Different Ages, General Social Survey 1990

Figure 5-6 also yields indications that children do not necessarily live for extended periods of time with a single parent. At any age, the proportion of those still living in a single-mother household is almost equalled by the proportion living with their mother and her new partner. The trend is even more pronounced for children who stayed with their father. Fathers do not assume single parenthood for long; at whatever the age of the children, the proportion of those living with a father and his new partner is often twice that of those living with a lone father. Father absence may be exaggerated in most single parenthood evaluation; the single fathers' haste to engage in a new relationship after a first failure results in their "disappearance" within reconstituted two-parent households. Thus the reduced visibility of single fathers who, even when their children have reached sixteen, seldom take charge of the children alone. In the 1971–73 cohort, only 4% of all children or 14% of children from broken unions lived with a single father at age sixteen, whereas the corresponding proportions were 10% and 38% who lived with a single mother.

Table 5-1:

Distribution of Children According to Number of Years Spent before Age 16, in First Episode with A Single Parent

Number of Years Spent Before Age 16 in 1st Episode	With Single Mother	With Single Father	With Either
Less than 5 years	64.0	87.3	71.9
5-7 years	15.3	2.2	10.9
8-9 years	6.8	4.5	6.0
10 years plus	13.9	5.9	11.2
Total	100.0	100.0	100.0
(N)	(245)	(125)	(370)

Life With a Single Parent: A Transitional Experience

One way to approach the transitional nature of single parenthood is to calculate the length of time children remain with a single parent after the separation and before Mom or Dad engage in a new relationship that modifies the living arrangements of the family.

There are measurement pitfalls because at the time of the survey children in the cohorts may still be experiencing their first episode of single parent family life. For the 1971–73 cohort, 61% of all first episodes experienced by the children were ended at time of survey; 72% of episodes spent with a father compared to 56% of episodes spent with a mother. Thus the measure is not the true mean number of years of the first episode, except for those for which this episode is already ended; the figure will represent the mean number of years from birth to age sixteen passed in a first episode of single parenthood.

The aggregate measure for children from the 1971–73 cohorts who have experienced life in a single parent family shows that this first episode lasted on the average 4.2 years between birth and age sixteen. The figure hides a noticeable difference between episodes spent with a lone mother (4.9 years on the average) and a lone father (2.7 years on the average). On-going episodes with the mothers show an average duration of 7.0 years, against only 3.2 years for on-going episodes with the fathers; this is consistent with the tendency of faster family reconstitutions for single fathers.

The distribution of the episodes by length (Table 5-1) confirms that very long periods of first-time single parenthood are experienced by relatively few children. This is especially true of children who have remained with their father; only one out of ten have spent half or more of their childhood up to age sixteen with their lone father, compared to one out of five of those who stayed with a lone mother.

These figures include data for both children born in a two-parent family and children who experienced single parenthood right from birth. Except for a very few (1 in 10) whose single parent never married or engaged in cohabitation, the latter quickly experienced life in a reconstituted family; their first episode of single parenthood lasted an average of only three years. For the 1971–73 and 1981–83 cohorts, 42% of children born to a single parent had experienced that parent entering marriage or cohabitation within 1.5 years; the percentage was up to 77% at age six, 85% at age ten, and 91% at age sixteen (1971–73 cohorts).

Cohabitation and the Multiplication of Family Life Experiences

Growing proportions of Canadian children experience life in a single parent family; this is happening earlier in their childhood but it does not necessarily last for a very long time. Single parenthood is not stable and the parental search for a satisfying union translates into a greater propensity for the children to experience several successive family contexts before they reach adulthood. Figure 5-7 confirms that the proportion of children who live within several family contexts as they grow up is on the rise and accelerating for younger generations. The first episode of single parenthood will remain the family context for a minority of children from broken unions; the others will experience at least a two-adult household reconstitution if not a second episode of single parenthood. For example, for the 27% of children born in 1971–73 whose parents parted, only thirty-nine out of a hundred were still within a first-time single parent family at age sixteen; sixty-one had known life within a family reconstituted with their guardian parent's new partner, twenty-two had seen this second two-parent family disintegrate propelling them a second time into single parenthood, twelve had experienced a second reconstitution, and five had experienced a third episode of single parenthood.

These eventful life courses do not yet involve large proportions of children, but the pattern is accelerating and may be linked to the parents' new behaviour towards cohabitation.

At age six, children from the 1981–83 cohorts not only have known single parenthood more frequently than their elders born ten years earlier, but they show a greater propensity to multiple family life experiences. Already ten out of a hundred children of broken unions had lived a second time within a single parent family before reaching school age, whereas only four out of a hundred of their elders from the 1971–73 cohorts had done so by the same age. The younger cohorts' greater likelihood of experiencing multiple family

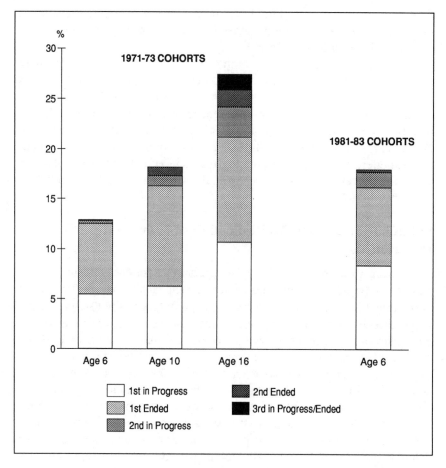

Figure 5-7:

The Multiplication of Family Contexts: Percentage of Canadian Children Who Have Lived with a Single Parent, According to Number of Periods Lived within a Single Parent Family. Various Birth Cohorts, at Different Ages, General Social Survey 1990

contexts appears linked to their parents' conception of the flexibility of conjugal bonds.

Figure 5-8 yields fairly convincing evidence that children born to parents having lived in a common law union are more likely to experience several family contexts while they are growing up. The cohorts analyzed were all born into two-parent families but their destiny greatly differed according to the parents' behaviour towards cohabitation. Children with parents having ever lived in a common law union experienced separation in greater

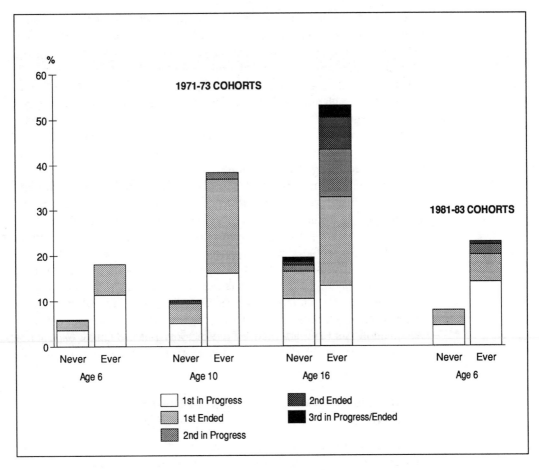

Figure 5-8:

Cohabitation and the Multiplication of Family Contexts: Percentage of Canadian Children Born in a Two-Parent Family Who Have Lived with a Single Parent, According to the Number of Periods Spent within a Single Parent Family, Whether or Not the Interviewed Parent Had Ever Cohabited before the Child's Birth. Various Birth Cohorts, at Different Ages, General Social Survey 1990

proportions (53% against 20% at age sixteen for 1971–73 cohorts), and change was a determining characteristic of their family environment thereafter. More than half of the children from broken unions whose parents have always refrained from cohabiting are still experiencing their first episode of single parenthood at age sixteen; three-quarters of the children from broken unions whose parents have ever engaged in cohabitation have at age sixteen experienced at least one new two-parent family and the integration of the new partner. The family life of children born to parents having ever cohabitated appears particularly unstable. Forty percent of them will have seen their family environment change at least twice before celebrating their sixteenth birthday; this includes 20% who have first lived with a single parent and then with his or her new partner; another 18% who have been through a second episode of single parenthood which four times out of ten ended with the arrival of a second other partner; and 3% who had time to live through a third single parenthood episode and a third new household reconstitution. The multiplication of family contexts has become a fact of life for that group of children.

The meaning of these figures becomes more significant when considering the rapid increase in the proportion of children born to parents having cohabitated, not to mention those born to cohabiting parents. Only 9% of children in the 1971–73 cohorts were born to such parents; the proportion climbed to 43% in the 1987–89 cohort and to 58% of the same cohort in Quebec. Does this not foresee an increase in family mobility in the coming years? Some may argue that cohabitation in the early 1970s was a marginal behaviour with its own characteristics, including instability, whereas today it shows greater resemblance to marriage as it was known twenty years ago. Cohabitation has been adopted by the majority but the family experience of children born in the early 1980s indicate that cohabitation is as unstable as ever.

Cohabitation and the Elusiveness of Family Reconstitution

Measuring the extent of family reconstitution is difficult because of limitation of the data usually available and the fluidity of the new forms of conjugal bonds. The rise in single parenthood is sometimes explained as resulting from a reduced tendency for men and women to engage in a second marriage after the failure of a previous commitment. Such an interpretation is largely due to the available data on divorces and remarriages. The results presented here confirm that legal marriage is not the majority choice to begin life as a couple in Canada; in Quebec, marriage is even getting to be a minority choice for giving birth to a first child. Those who have never married can also be expected not to do so the second time around. Others, who have married when such was the norm, may tend not to do so after going through the ordeal of a legal separation and divorce, at a time when less rigid forms of matrimony have become the rule. Such second unions escape the official accounting; only sources like the GSS 90 have the necessary versatility to grasp those new realities.

Single parenthood seems here to stay. But it too has evolved over time. In the early 1970s, the only issue was marriage or at best cohabitation that eventually lead to marriage. Such was the early experience of children born in 1971–73; at age six, eight times out of ten the first single parenthood episodes ended with the parent's remarriage, although that included almost a third whose parent and new partner had first tried living together before tying the knot; only two times out of ten did the episode end with cohabitation only. In the eighties the proportions have shifted; for children in the 1981–83 cohorts who experienced single parenthood by age six, only four times out of ten did the first episode end with a direct marriage; three times out of ten it ended by a marriage preceded by cohabitation; and four times out of ten it ended with cohabitation only.

Discussion

Marital trajectories become very hard to follow. And the lack of proper vocabulary, in French even more than English, reflects this sense of inadequacy that confronts research (Lefaucheur, 1985): how are we to understand what is going on if we can't even find the words to say it? Efforts to collect and analyze data have improved knowledge, but much remains to be done in view of the intensity and rapidity of the changes. For example, only unions in which the partners were co-residing have been included in most typologies. Little is known about stable relationships of people not living in the same households (Le Gall and Martin, 1988). Are these becoming a significant alternative to avoid problems when children from former unions are involved in the reconstitution of the marital life of their parents? Or do they reflect a further step allowing for ever more flexibility in conjugal relations? Do they represent the ultimate symbol of new marital freedom, where personal autonomy becomes a higher priority than the creation of a new family unit? Only further research into the motivations behind individual choices will bring answer to these questions.

Non-marital cohabitation has clearly lost its marginal character and is not confined to the role of an initiation ritual or trial marriage to permit young couples to make an adequate and viable long term choice. Cohabitation is replacing marriage as the framework to begin life as a couple, to give birth to children and start a family, and to reconstitute another unit when the first one has failed. That a majority now chooses cohabitation does not however mean a mere substitution to the institution of marriage with the engagement between the spouses remaining the same. Cohabitation and marriage represent different values, underlying priorities, and consequences for family life.

One may also question the everlasting relevance of certain characteristics traditionally associated with the individuals choosing cohabitation on one part, and experiencing single parent family life on the other. In particular, women whose life course included cohabitation and single parenthood have been overly represented in the undereducated, poor and generally depen-dant segment of the population. We are not to contest the truth of such observations until recent times. But the generalization of cohabitation as the standard way of union formation and the increasing instability of conjugal life are quickly changing the portrait of single parents, even more so now that women have access to better education, hold jobs in the workplace as never before and are taught the virtues of autonomy that were not so long ago considered as male prerogatives. Some might add that men are also making some of the necessary steps in acknowledging their responsibility as fathers even after they have parted with the mother of their children.

The main characteristic of cohabitation is flexibility in the management of conjugal relations. Cohabitation facilitates ending of unsatisfactory unions. The process of questioning conjugal commitment between two consenting adults can be difficult, but the repercussions can be limited when confined to personal interactions by the couple. But the presence of children may alter the virtue of flexibility for family life. Flexibility may constitute an adequate answer for adults in their search for an environment that will permit them to develop fully their personality in a world that values highly such a goal. Flexibility of family life for children may take the less appealing shape of instability. Not all children, however, suffer equally from their parents' conjugal tribulations; some might even find in a new family context good ground for development, which had been limited in their disintegrating initial family. Both research and policy should concentrate on identifying circumstances that permit families in transition to respond to the children's needs. The agenda could include those who succeed rather than only report on the negative effects of the new forms of family life (Tuzlak and Hillcock, 1991). The answer will not necessarily come from a return to old forms of unions, where stability did not guarantee either the personal development of individuals or the successful socialization of children. Mechanisms are required that will yield some of the required flexibility in conjugal relations, without compromising the development of children who remain entirely dependent on the adults who take charge of them.

6

Single Parent Families in Canada: A Closer Look

Donna S. Lero and Lois M. Brockman

Single parent families are not a new phenomenon in Canada. The number of single parent families, however, is increasing at a rapid rate, and these families comprise a large and growing segment of adults and children whose present and future well-being is frequently at risk. Knowledge and understanding of single parent families generally derive from large population-based studies (such as the census and other household surveys) and smaller-scale studies of single parent families (often selected or sampled as clients, welfare recipients, or members of a self-help group). Large population-based studies offer reliable statistical data and the opportunity to see trends over time, but often do not provide much detail. The smaller-scale studies can provide rich information about single parents' lives, but may reinforce stereotypes and not be generalizable due to sampling procedures and the tendency to focus mostly on dysfunctions and difficulties. Both researchers and policy makers are increasingly concerned about single parent families as a distinct population. Understanding the characteristics of single parents, the nature of life in single parent families, both for the adults and the children, and how factors (including social policies) influence daily life and longer-term outcomes is of key importance for developing policies to support the economic and social well-being of single parents and their children.

This chapter is organized into five main sections. The first section includes a brief review of what is known about single parent families from a demographic perspective and identifies the need for greater methodological rigour and consistency in research on this population. The second section presents new information about single parent families with children younger than thirteen years of age. The third section discusses single parents' involvement in the labour force and in educational activities in the context of demographic and family characteristics; information is also presented on single parents' reasons for not wanting or not being able to take a job. The fourth section of this chapter examines single parents' experiences in managing both work and family responsibilities and helps identify which factors contribute most significantly to work-family conflict for this group. Finally, we present recent data on child care arrangements used in single and two-parent families and discuss some of the implications of those findings.

Readers may note that the language used to describe single parents and their families reflects common attitudes and expectations. The term "lone parent" suggests that single parents are solitary, perhaps lonely persons who are bereft of social support. Other terms such as "broken homes," as opposed to "intact" families, suggest that single parent families, by definition, are dysfunctional aberrations, rather than alternate family forms that can function well, despite the fact that a greater burden is placed on a single person. The terms "single parent" and "lone parent" have been used interchangeably in this chapter because the literature that is cited uses the term lone parent as a general classification under which single, never married parents are subsumed; however none of the previous pejorative implications are intended.

Single Parent Families in Canada

The most reliable information about single parent families in Canada is based on census data, much of it reviewed by Craig McKie in Chapter 4. The rate of growth in single parent families has been particularly noticeable in the last three decades. The number of single parent families in Canada almost tripled between 1961 and 1991 from 347,000 to over 1,000,000. According to 1991 census data, 14% of census families were classified as lone parent families (Statistics Canada, 1991).

The incidence of child and family poverty among lone parent families is very high, especially in families headed by women. In 1986, 56% of lone parent families headed by women had annual incomes that fell below Statistics Canada's low-income cut-off points (often referred to as poverty lines), making lone parent, female-headed families the group with the highest incidence of family poverty in Canada (Ross and Shillington, 1989). The Economic Council of Canada confirms that lone parents, particularly women, not only enter poverty at a very high rate, but also exit more slowly than two-parent families: "lone parents tended to stay poor for much longer periods of time than other poor families" (1992: 47). McKie (1993) has noted that the effects of poverty for lone parents are long-lasting, with significant ramifications for future earning potential, lifetime savings, and pension entitlements.

The costs of being poor for lone parents are substantial indeed and are shared by their children. According to the National Council of Welfare (1991), the poverty rate among children being raised in single parent families led by women was 65% in 1988.

A lot more poor children live in one-parent families today than in the past, which is not surprising given the rising rate of single parenthood and the high risk of poverty among female-led one-parent families. In 1970, 79.3% of poor children had two parents, 17.9% were being raised by a single mother and 2.8% by a single father. In 1988, 55.1% of poor children were in two-parent families, 39.1% in one-parent families led by women, and 5.8% in male-headed one-parent families. In other words, the percentage of poor children being raised in single parent families more than doubled between 1979 (20.7%) and 1988 (44.9%) (National Council of Welfare, 1991, p.3).

The increase in the number of single parent families has been accompanied by changes in the characteristics of lone parents. The proportions of single parents who are separated or divorced or who never married have increased over time, while the proportion who are widowed has decreased (McKie, 1993). Never-married mothers made up 15% of all female lone parents in 1986, up from just 1% in 1951; while the proportion of women who were separated or divorced was 57% in 1986 compared to 33% in 1951 (Moore, 1990: 122). Census data indicate an increasing proportion of lone parents fall into younger age categories. In 1951, only 14% of lone parents were younger than 35 years old, but in 1986, 28% of lone parents were younger than 35, including 6% aged 15–24 years (Pool and Moore, 1991). This change in the age distribution of lone parents is correlated with the higher proportions who never married or are separated or divorced. Further, the proportion of female lone parents is much higher among younger age groups, and younger parents are likely to have younger children at home.

Historically, male-headed lone parent families have generally accounted for less than 2% of all census families and a minority of all lone parent families. In 1986, approximately 82% of all lone parent families were headed by women; however, women made up 94% of all lone parents aged 15–24 and 85% of those 25–44 years of age (Moore, 1990: 122). Published analyses of census data have not profiled changes in the age of the youngest child in lone parent families. If they did, they would probably demonstrate that a larger proportion of lone parent families now consist of women with young children — a population much more likely to experience difficulties maintaining an adequate family income while coping with the responsibilities of raising children. The 1991 postcensal estimates indicate that as of June, 1991, there were 211,000 lone parent families with at least one child under 6 years of age.

Research indicates that the majority of single parent mothers have participated in the labour force and, until recently, at a higher rate than married mothers. Dooley (1991, 1993) has explored some of the factors behind the converging market work patterns of married mothers and lone mothers using data obtained from the Canadian Survey of Consumer Finances for the years 1973, 1979, and 1988 for women with children younger than 18. Those analyses revealed interesting differences over time in the proportion of single parent mothers who participated in the labour force among different age groups. "In 1973, lone mothers in each age group were more likely to work in the market. By 1988, married mothers were equally or more likely to work in the market. This change was most dramatic for mothers less than 25" (Dooley, 1991: 10).

Statistics Canada's annual labour force averages provide another, perhaps more telling, story of important differences among married and lone mothers. These data can be analyzed to illustrate changes over time in married and lone mothers' annual participation rates among those whose youngest child is preschool age (under 6 years old) and those whose youngest child is 6–15 years of age. As shown in Figure 6–1, labour force participation rates have risen for all groups of mothers in the last 15 years, but most dramatically among married women, especially those with pre-school-age children. Among lone mothers with at least one child younger than 16, those whose youngest child is school age (6–15) increased from an average participation rate of 59% in 1976 to 72% in 1991. In contrast, lone mothers with preschool age children increased their labour force participation only marginally compared to other groups (from 44% in 1976 to 50% in 1991); the pattern suggests a plateau since 1980. These data suggest diverging labour force patterns among married mothers and lone mothers with preschool age children — a pattern that is masked when the age of children in the home is not considered.

The factors that might explain this differential pattern among lone mothers with young children require further investigation. However, the most likely explanations include:

- a greater proportion of lone mothers with preschool age children who are young themselves, often with limited education and/or job skills;
- single mothers' beliefs that their children need them at home and require their support and nurturance;
- difficulties managing a full-time job along with family responsibilities (part-time work being a less viable option for single parents);
- difficulties finding and maintaining affordable, suitable child care;
- limited income, which in turn increases the relative cost of working (transportation, clothing, child care); and
- social assistance policies that foster dependency, lower self-esteem, and discourage mothers from seeking work, as well as other policies that act as systemic barriers to their involvement in the work force (such as the limited availability of retraining programs).

Differences among married and lone mothers are greatest among mothers whose youngest child is under 3 years of age. The 1991 annual average

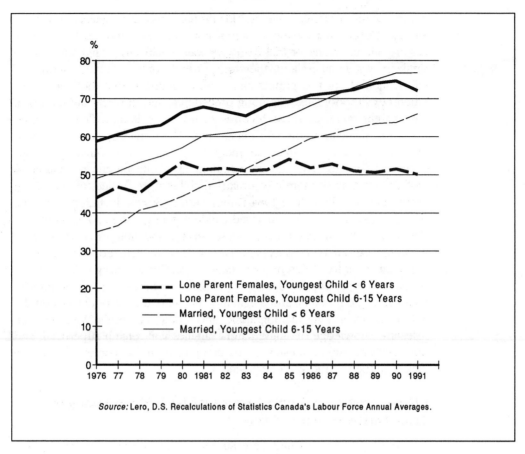

Figure 6-1:
Women's Labour Force Participation Rates by Marital Status and Age of Youngest Child, Canada, 1976-1991

labour force participation rates for mothers whose youngest child was an infant or toddler (0–2 years) was 64% for married mothers, but only 41% among lone mothers. The participation rate of mothers whose youngest child was 3–5 years old was 70% for married mothers and 60% for lone mothers (Statistics Canada, 1992). These data suggest that the presence of children younger than 3 years old acts as a stronger constraint on single mothers' labour force participation than is the case for married mothers.

In summary, single parents have been increasing in number, and in 1991 accounted for approximately one in seven census families in Canada. The typical single parent in 1986 was a single or divorced mother, 25–44 years old who, while employed or looking for work, lives with her children on an income considerably below the level conventionally considered adequate to provide for her family's needs. This profile is based on Statistics Canada's Survey of Consumer Finances, Labour Force Surveys, and the 1984 Family History Survey. None of these surveys was specifically designed to study single parent families, and, therefore, provide only a limited amount of information about this population. More troubling is that the studies use different methodologies, sampling procedures, and different definitions of lone parent families. These inconsistencies make it difficult to compare results or maintain a common perspective. The Canadian census is based on census families, while the monthly Labour Force Survey samples economic families. The census definition of a lone parent is a father or mother with one or more never-married children, regardless of age, living in the same dwelling. The 1984 Family History Survey included only lone parents aged 18–65 with unmarried children younger than 25 years of age. The Survey of Consumer Finances also sets the age limit for children at 24, while the Labour Force Survey of labour force participation rates uses an upper age limit for children of 16 years of age. Considerably more research is needed on subpopulations of single parent families (e.g., single fathers, younger single mothers, and single mothers who are not poor) and on the inter-relations among demographic and other variables. Without such research, knowledge of single parent families will remain superficial, and policies that could be sensitive to different needs and circumstances will be limited in their scope and effectiveness.

Characteristics of Single Parents with Children Younger Than Thirteen Years of Age

The 1988 National Child Care Survey (NCCS) provides more detailed information about single parent families with children younger than 13 years of age (Lero, Pence, Shields, Brockman & Goelman, 1992). The NCCS is one component of a larger study of child care in Canada, the Canadian National Child Care Study, a collaborative project involving members of the National Day Care Research Network and the Special Surveys Division of Statistics Canada. The main focus of the survey was child care needs, use patterns, and preferences, but a considerable amount of data was collected about parents' work involvement and family characteristics. The NCCS was conducted as a supplement to the monthly Labour Force Survey in September and October of 1988 and employed stratified, multi-stage cluster sampling techniques. Eligible households were comprised of economic families with at least one child younger than 13. The final sample consisted of 24,155 families, based on a response rate of 84%. Weighted population estimates describe 2,724,300 families with children younger than 13, including almost 400,000 single parent families. The findings described in the remainder of this chapter are weighted population estimates rounded to the nearest hundred.

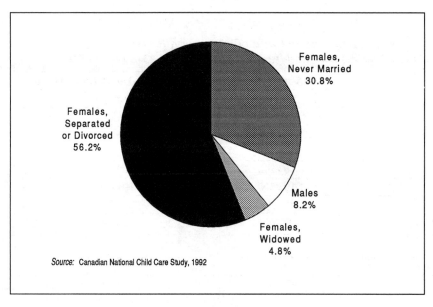

Figure 6-2:
Characteristics of Single Parents with At Least One Child
Younger Than 13, Canada, 1988

A Profile of Single Parents With Children Younger Than Thirteen

Almost 15% of NCCS families were defined as one-parent families. The gender and marital status of single parents in this population are shown in Figure 6–2. These families consist of a parent or person acting in the role of a parent to at least one child younger than 13 who did not reside with a spouse or partner. Families in which a married parent did not usually reside with her/his spouse were also considered one-parent families. The proportion of single parent families within each province ranged from 13% in Newfoundland to 18% in Manitoba. Ontario and Quebec together accounted for 60% of all one-parent families. Almost 92% of the single parent families were headed by women. Only 8% of one-parent families were headed by a single male. Further, the vast majority of single, father-led families contained only older children, generally at least school-age. Almost 95% of families with preschool-age children (0–5 years old) were headed by women.

The parent self-identified as most directly involved in making child care arrangements was interviewed and is the reference person for many questions in the NCCS. In single parent families, the interviewed parent was the lone parent; in two-parent families, 96% of interviewed parents were female. Characteristics of the interviewed parent (IP) in one- and two-parent

Table 6-1:

Age, Education, and Employment Status of Interviewed Parent* in One- and Two-Parent Families with Children Younger Than 13, Canada, 1988

	IP in Two-Parent Families		IP in One-Parent Families	
	Number	%	*Number*	%
Total	**2,324,800**	**100.0**	399,500	**100.0**
Age				
< 25 years	163,200	7.0	60,100	15.0
25-34 years	1,196,500	51.5	194,800	48.8
35-44 years	868,900	37.4	120,500	30.2
≥ 45 years	96,200	4.1	24,100	6.0
Education				
Less than grade 9	149,900	6.4	39,200	9.8
Grade 9-11	526,700	22.7	128,300	32.1
Grade 12 or 13; no post-secondary	696,600	30.0	98,600	24.7
Some post-secondary	216,100	9.3	45,000	11.3
Post-secondary certificate/diploma	417,600	18.0	54,000	13.5
University degree	317,700	13.7	34,500	8.6
Employment Status				
Full time	986,300	42.4	181,800	45.5
Part time	429,900	18.5	36,100	9.0
Unemployed	133,200	5.7	31,000	7.8
Not in the labour force	775,400	33.4	150,600	37.7

* The interviewed parent (IP) was the parent considered to have primary responsibility for making child care arrangements. In two-parent families 96.1% of IPs were female; in one-parent families, 91.8% of IPs were female.

Source: Canadian National Child Study, 1992.◆

families are shown in Table 6–1. Single parents tended to be somewhat younger and less well-educated in comparison to IPs in two-parent families. Forty-two percent of the single parents did not complete high school, while 22% had a post-secondary diploma or degree. In contrast, 29% of IPs in two-parent families did not complete high school, and 32% had a college diploma or university degree. In both populations, the majority of interviewed parents (62–66%) were in the labour force during the week preceding the NCCS interview (reference week), however, 30% of employed IPs in two-parent families worked part time, compared to less than 17% of employed parents in one-parent families.

Table 6-2:

1987 Parental Income and Poverty Status in One- and Two-Parent Families with Children Younger Than 13, Canada

	Two-Parent Families		One-Parent Families	
	Number	%	*Number*	%
Total	2,324,800	100.0	399,500	100.0
1987 Parental Income[1]				
Less than $10,000	87,400	3.8	176,800	44.2
$10,001-20,000	195,000	8.4	111,000	27.8
$20,001-30,000	361,800	15.6	64,100	16.1
$30,001-40,000	517,500	22.3	26,500	6.6
$40,001-50,000	442,400	19.0	13,000	3.3
$50,001-60,000	308,200	13.3	q 5,500	q 1.4
More than $60,000	412,600	17.7	...	...
Families Below 1987 Low-Income Cut-off Point[2,3]	278,100	12.6	225,400	65.3

[1] Total 1987 income reported received by both parents in a two-parent family and by the IP only in one-parent families. Income consists of all money received during the calender year from gross wages and salaries, net income from self-employment, investment income, government payments, pensions, and miscellaneous income. No correction was made in cases in which 1987 income was affected by the death of a partner, marriage or its dissolution, or other circumstances.

[2] Low-income cut-off points are set by Statistics Canada annually and include adjustments for family size and population density. These cut-off points may be interpreted as the relevant "poverty line" to which each family may be compared.

[3] Since low-income cut-off points are based on census family income, percentages were based on the number of families for whom such comparisons were appropriate (roughly 95.2% of two-parent families and 86.4% of one-parent families represented in the National Child Care Survey population).

...   Estimate too small to be reliable.
q   Estimate is subject to unreliability and should be treated with caution.

Source: Canadian National Child Care Study, 1992.◆

The measure of family income used in the NCCS was defined as total annual income received by parents in 1987 from all sources. The proportion of two-parent and single parent families in different income groups is shown in Table 6–2. The vast majority of single parent families with children younger than 13 can be described as low-income families. About 72% had a 1987 income of $20,000 or less and more often than not, single parents reported incomes of $10,000 or less. Average 1987 income for both parents combined was $44,097 in two-parent families. The average 1987 income for single fathers was $27,080; single mothers' average income was $14,302. Almost two-thirds of the single parent families that also qualified as census

Table 6-3:

Number and Ages of Children in One- and Two-Parent Families with Children Younger Than 13, Canada, 1988

	Two-Parent Families		One-Parent Families	
	Number	%	*Number*	%
Total	**2,324,800**	**100.0**	**399,500**	**100.0**
Number of Children < 13 Years				
1 child < 13	1,007,700	43.3	253,400	63.4
2 children < 13	971,300	41.8	114,100	28.6
≥ 3 children < 13	345,800	14.9	32,000	8.0
Number of Preschool Children 0-5 Years				
None	932,900	40.1	204,700	51.2
1 child < 6	915,300	39.4	158,900	39.8
≥ 2 children < 6	476,600	20.5	36,000	9.0
Age of Youngest Child				
0-17 months	499,000	21.5	48,700	12.2
18-35 months	378,900	16.3	48,700	12.2
3-5 years	514,000	22.1	97,500	24.4
6-9 years	551,900	23.7	121,100	30.3
10-12 years	381,000	16.4	83,500	20.9
Preschool and School-Age Children				
With preschool-age children only	805,300	34.6	129,700	32.5
With preschool and school-age children	586,600	25.2	65,100	16.3
With school-age children only	932,900	40.1	204,700	51.2

Source: Canadian National Child Care Study, 1992.♦

families fell below Statistics Canada's low-income cut-off points and would be classified as poor. In comparison, 13% of two-parent families were classified as poor.

Number and Ages of Children

The nature of family life is very much affected by the number and ages of children in the family. How time and money are allocated, whether parents seek employment, and the tasks involved in balancing work and family responsibilities are all affected by family composition. Our under-standing of single and two-parent families is enhanced when information is available to describe the nature of child-rearing demands in each group. Detailed information about children is included in Table 6–3. By design, all families in this population have at least one child younger than 13. Table 6–3 indicates that most single parents had only one child younger than 13. In contrast, two-parent families were more likely to have two or more children younger than 13 years. Almost 49% of one-parent families and close to 60% of two-parent families included preschool-age children. In fact, 21% of two-parent families had two or more preschoolers, compared to only 9% of single parent families. Approximately 25% of single parents had at least one child younger than 3 years.

Factors Affecting Single Parents' Employment and Involvement in Educational Activities

Parents can help ensure their family's economic well-being by earning sufficient income and by completing or continuing their education. Both activities require managing time and resources and arranging for or purchas-ing child care. What factors help and which frustrate parents' efforts to support their families? Information about parents' involvement in the labour force and in educational activities was obtained through use of standard Labour Force Survey questions and procedures. Parents were classified as employed full-time, employed part-time, unemployed but looking for work, or not in the labour force. Respondents were also asked if they were enroled as a full- or part-time student at a school, college, or university. Parents were classified as serious students if they were enroled on a full-time basis or, if part-time, stated that their main reason for studying was to improve job opportunities, for career development, or to increase their earnings (as opposed to those whose main reason for studying was personal interest). This information is presented in Table 6–4. In total, 55% of all single parents with children younger than 13 were employed and 14% were classified as serious students; 8% studied on a full-time basis and 6% were enroled part-time. Fewer than 4% of single parents were both employed and enroled as serious students.

Gender Differences

Single fathers, while only a small proportion of all single parents in this population, display a different pattern of labour force involvement than single mothers. Almost 81% of single fathers were employed, compared to 52% of single mothers. For these reasons, most of the analyses presented in the following sections pertain primarily to single mothers.

Table 6-4:

Employment and Student Status Among Single Parent Fathers and Single Parent Mothers, by Presence of Preschool Children (0-5 Years), Canada, 1988

	Number	% Employed	% Employed or Serious Student*
All Single Parents	399,500	54.5	64.5
Single Parent Fathers	32,600	80.6	82.8
Single Parent Mothers	366,900	52.2	62.9
With preschool children	184,900	41.2	54.4
Full-time		32.8	43.5
Part-time		8.4	10.9
With no preschool children	182,200	63.5	71.5
Full-time		52.7	59.2
Part-time		10.8	12.2

* A serious student was defined as one who was enroled in a high school, college or university on a full-time basis or, if part-time, stated that their main reason for studying was to improve job opportunities or to increase earnings.
Source: Canadian National Child Care Study, 1992. ◆

Number and Ages of Children

Examination of the data presented in Tables 6–4 and 6–5 confirms that single mothers with preschool age children (0–5 years old) were less likely to be employed or enroled as a serious student than mothers whose youngest child was school-aged. The difference is about 20%. The effect of having younger children at home appears to have a general suppressing effect, reducing the likelihood that the parent will be employed or enroled at all, rather than merely limiting the extent of her participation to part-time status. The data in Table 6–5 suggest that the younger the child, the less likely single mothers are to be employed or enroled as a serious student in an educational institution. Only 34% of single mothers with a child younger than three were employed, although 49% were classified as employed or enroled as a serious student. Similarly, single mothers with two or more children were less likely to be employed or a student than were mothers with only one child. Nevertheless, 55% of all single mothers with two or more children younger than 13 were either employed or attempting to continue their education in 1988.

Table 6-5:
Employment and Student Status among Single Parent Mothers, by Age,
Education, Number and Ages of Children, Canada, 1988

	Number	% Employed	% Employed or Serious Student*
Total	**366,900**	**52.2**	**62.8**
Age			
< 25 years	59,600	8.9	11.9
25-34 years	183,100	50.2	50.7
35-44 years	106,400	36.5	33.5
≥ 45 years	18,000	q 4.4	q 3.8
Education			
Less than grade 9	36,400	q 23.3	36.1
Grade 9-11	118,500	37.3	49.4
Grade 12 or 13; no post-secondary	91,400	60.0	66.4
Some post-secondary	42,200	60.9	75.1
Post-secondary certificate/diploma	49,300	70.6	81.8
University degree	29,100	81.0	90.2
Number of Children < 13 Years			
1 child < 13	231,300	56.9	67.3
2 children < 13	105,700	47.2	58.2
≥ 3 children < 13	29,900	q 33.5	45.5
Age of Youngest Child			
0-35 months	95,300	33.7	49.0
3-5 years	89,600	49.1	60.1
6-9 years	108,900	61.6	70.6
10-12 years	73,100	66.2	72.7

* A serious student was defined as one who was enroled in a high school, college or university on a full-time basis or, if part-time, stated that their main reason for studying was to improve job opportunities or to increase earnings.

q Estimate is subject to unreliability and should be treated with caution.

Source: Canadian National Child Care Study, 1992.♦

Mother's Age and Education

Table 6–5 also demonstrates the relationships among single mothers' age, previous educational attainment, and the likelihood of employment or participation in an educational institution. Mothers younger than 25 years of age were the least likely to be employed or studying; those 25–34 years of age were most likely to participate. Mothers with more limited educational backgrounds were less likely to be employed or enroled in educational institutions, while those with higher education, particularly mothers with at least some post-secondary schooling, were most likely to be employed or students. Discriminant analysis revealed that prior educational attainment was the most significant predictor of single mothers' employment status. These findings are not surprising and, of course, the variables are inter-related. Younger mothers are likely to have young children at home and are more likely to have had their education interrupted by child-bearing. The combination of these factors constrain opportunities for employment and educational upgrading, especially among those who have little social support or assistance to facilitate their involvement in these activities.

Reasons for Not Wanting/Taking A Job

Parents who were not employed at the time of the study were asked directly whether they wanted a job, and their main reason for not wanting a job or not being able to take a job in the reference week. Table 6–6 shows that 36% of single mothers who were not employed stated they wanted a job. The most common reason given for not wanting a job, or not being able to take a job (given by 30% of those who responded), was that the mother wanted to stay home to look after her children. Almost 19% said the main reason they did not work or did not want to was because they were going to school. Approximately 10% of single mothers said the main reason they did not want or could not take a job was difficulty finding or paying for suitable child care arrangements.

How Single Mothers Manage Work or Study and Family Responsibilities

What is the social, as well as the economic impact, of combining work and family responsibilities in single parent families? The literature on work-family conflict and role strain supports the contention that parents faced with heavy child-rearing demands (such as single parents, parents with infants, and parents with two or more preschool age children) face serious challenges managing work and family responsibilities and coordinating the practical demands associated with multiple roles (Emlen and Koren, 1984; Lero and Kyle, 1991). Work-family conflict is being recognized as a serious concern that potentially affects employees' physical health, emotional

Table 6-6:

Reason Single Mothers Did Not Want A Job or Could Not Take A Job in Families with At Least One Child Younger Than 13, Canada, 1988

	Number	**Percent**
Total Not Employed[1]	**175,300**	**100.0**
Wanted A Job In Reference Week		
Yes	62,300	35.7
No	112,300	64.3
Not Stated	...	...
Reason Did Not Want/Could Not Take A Job in Reference Week[2,3]		
Wanted to stay home to look after children	52,700	30.2
Going to school	32,700	18.7
Could not make suitable child care arrangements; available child care too expensive	17,700	10.1
Other personal or family responsibilities	12,500	7.1
Own illness or disability	11,100	6.4
Other reason	13,300	7.6
No reason	34,700	19.9

[1] Single mothers who were either unemployed or not in the labour force during the reference week (September - October, 1988). This number represents approximately 47.8% of all single mothers with at least one child younger than 13.

[2] Answers are combined from two separate questions.

[3] Respondents were permitted to state only one reason.

... Estimate too small to be reliable.

Source: Canadian National Child Care Study, 1992.♦

well-being, and family relationships, as well as worker productivity and costs to employers in the form of absenteeism, tardiness, and staff turnover. Work-family conflict may also affect children's health and the quality of parent-child relationships, although little research has addressed the issue. Current research recognizes the bi-directional nature of work-family conflict and reciprocal interactions between the effects of work-related problems and parental role performance (Frone, Russell and Cooper, 1992). Work-family conflict is considered to result from the relative effects of family-related stressors, family involvement, job stressors, and job involvement. Single parents with limited financial resources, few child care choices, and limited

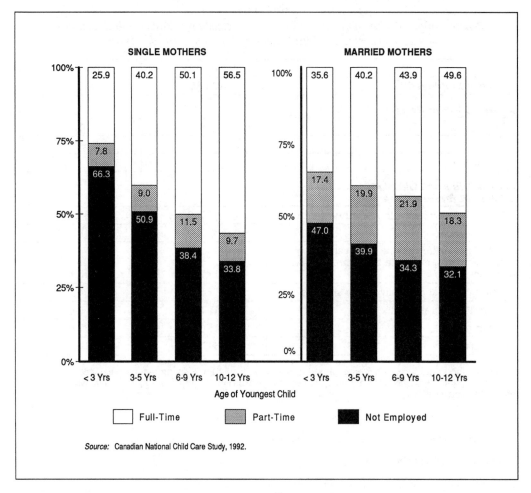

Figure 6-3:

*Married and Single Mothers' Employment Status, by Age of Youngest
Child in the Family, Canada, 1988*

social support would be classified as high on the family stress dimension
and highly involved in family tasks (i.e., a high parental workload).

One of the ways some mothers cope with strong family demands is by
limiting their work involvement to part-time status, at least while their
children are very young. Analyses of NCCS data, presented in Figure 6–3,
reveal that few single mothers enjoyed this option. One part-time wage is
not sufficient to maintain a single parent and her child(ren). As a result,
full-time job involvement tends to be the norm among employed single
parents.

Job related stressors include the nature of work, the degree of autonomy over the nature and timing of work tasks, and the quality of co-worker and employee-supervisor relations. Unfortunately, limited data were collected about the nature of parents' jobs and job-related circumstances in the NCCS. Analyses revealed few differences between married and lone parents' work schedules, other than the difference in full- versus part-time employment. Approximately 28% of single parents worked at least one weekend day, which is similar to their married counterparts. Slightly fewer single than married parents worked a fixed evening or night shift. Overall, 60% of interviewed parents in single parent families and 55% of interviewed parents in two-parent families worked a standard work week consisting of fixed daytime hours with no weekend work (Lero, Goelman, Pence, Brockman & Nuttall, 1992). Few differences are also evident in married and single parents' access to a variety of workplace benefits and practices that might facilitate the management of dual roles. A large majority of employed parents do not have flexible work schedules, or paid family responsibility leave when children are sick or care arrangements break down (Lero, Brockman, Pence, Goelman & Johnson, in press).

Work-Family-Child Care Tension

One of the sections in the NCCS interview was designed to capture the extent to which parents reported feeling tension on a daily basis as a result of juggling work, family, and child care responsibilities. Questions were asked only of interviewed parents who worked and who utilized some form of non-parental child care while they were working. Parents' perceptions of the amount of tension they experience were obtained; respondents were also asked to indicate how much tension they attributed to each of fifteen factors associated either with their work hours or work schedule, their spouse's work hours or work schedules, child care arrangements, or the logistics of balancing work and family life. The general level of work-family-child care tension was rated on a scale of 1–10. A rating of 1 signified no tension, while 10 indicated a great deal of tension. Single mothers had a significantly higher average score on general work-family tension. Single mothers had a mean score of 4.8; married mothers had a mean score of 4.2. The majority of both single and married working mothers who utilized non-parental child care described themselves as generally experiencing moderate or severe tension in managing work and family roles. Approximately 18% of married mothers rated their general level of work-family-child care tension as severe, as did 27% of single mothers.

Average ratings of factors that might contribute to tension are shown in Table 6–7. Naturally, some differences occurred because items such as "your spouse's work schedule" dropped out for single mothers. Nonetheless, several observations can be made:

Table 6-7:

Factors Perceived to Contribute Most Strongly to Work-Family-Child Care Tension by Working Mothers Using Non-Parental Care, by Presence of Spouse/Partner, Canada, 1988

Item Rank	Mothers with Spouse/Partner		Item Rank	Mothers with No Spouse/Partner	
	Item	Mean Rating*		Item	Mean Rating*
1	Feeling tired, overloaded	5.1	1	Feeling tired, overloaded	5.6
2	Maintaining a balance between work and family	5.1	2	Maintaining a balance between work and family	5.5
3	Time pressures re: daycare use	3.7	3	Child care costs	4.4
4	Number of hours mother works	3.6	4	Time pressures re: daycare use	4.2
5	Mother's work schedule	3.5	5	Mother's work schedule	4.0
6	Spouse's work schedule	3.4	6	Number of hours mother works	3.8
7	Number of hours spouse works	3.4	7	Concerns about child's safety and well-being	3.8
8	Concerns about child's safety and well-being	3.3	8	Lack of employer support	3.5
9	Child care costs	3.2	9	Worrying care may break down	3.4
10	Lack of employer support	3.0	10	Feeling job/career is being hampered	3.3

* Items were rated as contributions to work-family-child care tension on a scale of 1-10.

Source: Canadian National Child Care Study, 1992. ◆

- On average, the same items (e.g., "Feeling tired and overloaded;" "Difficulty maintaining a balance between work and family responsibilities") were rated as causing more tension for single mothers than married mothers.

- Several items were much more important contributors to work-family tension for single mothers than for married mothers. In particular, "Managing the costs of high quality child care" was rated as the third most significant source of work-family tension by single mothers, whose incomes certainly would be challenged by high child care costs. As well, single mothers rated "Concerns about your children's safety and well-being;" "Worries that your caregiver or care arrangement may break down or not be available much longer" and "Feeling that your job or career is being hampered" significantly higher as contributors to tension than did married mothers.

- Overall, the responses of single mothers to these questions suggest greater tension, more urgency, and more fragility in the balance they are maintaining.

These observations make sense when the various pieces of the puzzle are assembled. Often, single mothers work at a full-time job that does not pay enough to adequately sustain their family. Further, single mothers most often must cope with greater physical demands on their time and energy. Finally, there is a greater likelihood that single parents are relying on child care arrangements that may be barely affordable, provided by strangers, or ones that cause them considerable worry and concern, such as sibling or self-care arrangements. Such pressures are rarely diffused through workplace policies and practices that provide flexibility and support or by neighbourhoods that offer parents a variety of resources and services to support them in their role as parents.

Child Care Used for Work/Study Purposes

Among the kinds of support that are essential for parents who are employed or continuing their education is reliable, affordable child care that meets children's and parents' needs. Regular care arrangements are required, as are back-up arrangements when children, parents, or regular caregivers are ill; when care arrangements break down; and on occasions when extra time is needed for work, school, or personal reasons.

Many aspects of child care were investigated in the NCCS and descriptions of child care arrangements — the number of arrangements used, the purpose for which care is used, the number of hours children spend in care — are examined in detail in several of the reports emanating from the study. For the sake of brevity, this section describes the arrangement used during the

Table 6-8:

Primary Care Arrangement Used for Preschool Children (0-5 Years) While IP Worked or Studied in One-Parent and Two-Parent Families, Canada, 1988

Primary Care Arrangement Other Than School [1]	Children in Two-Parent Families		Children in One-Parent Families	
	Number	*%*	*Number*	*%*
Total	**948,700**	**100.0**	**114,400**	**100.0**
Regulated group care arrangement or regulated home care	164,100	17.3	40,800	35.7
Care by parent(s) [2]	302,400	31.9	...	...
Care by a relative, in the child's home or relative's home	169,300	17.8	28,200	24.6
Care by unregulated caregiver (non-relative in child's home or other home)	289,900	30.6	38,200	33.4
Sibling or self-care	...	...	...	...
No arrangement [3]	18,900	2.0	...	...

[1] Care arrangement used for the largest number of hours while parent primarily responsible for making child care arrangements (usually the mother) was working or studying.

[2] Care provided by parents while working and care provided by spouse while IP was working in a two-parent family.

[3] "No arrangement" category includes time spent in lessons, sports and recreational activities; in transit to and from school; and in medical or dental appointments. These were not considered to be child care arrangements for the purposes of the study.

... Estimate too small to be reliable.

Source: Canadian National Child Care Study, 1992.♦

reference week for the largest number of hours for each child while the IP worked or studied. The time spent in school has been excluded from these analyses, since school does not have to be arranged, unlike other supplementary care arrangements. Data are presented separately for preschool and school-age children.

Types of Care Arrangements Used

Significant differences were evident in the extent to which children in single and two-parent families participated in several kinds of child care arrangements while the IP worked or studied (see Tables 6–8 and 6–9). Among children younger than 6, children in single parent families are considerably more likely to spend the bulk of time when care is needed in licensed or regulated child care arrangements than children in two-parent

families. These regulated arrangements include half-day preschool programs, daycare centres, kindergarten programs, before and after school
programs, and licensed family home day care. Almost 36% of preschool
children in single parent families were enroled in a licensed/regulated
arrangement as the primary method of care used while the IP worked or
studied, compared to 17% of children in two-parent families. Children in
two-parent families were much more likely to be cared for by the IP's partner
while the IP worked or studied or by one of the parents while at work. Care
by other relatives was the primary arrangement for 18% of children in
two-parent families and 25% of children in single parent families, while
unrelated caregivers (paid baby sitters, friends and "nannies") were utilized
for 31–33% of the children in both groups.

Differences were also evident in patterns of care used for school-age
children. The most common primary care arrangement used for children in
two-parent families while the IP worked or studied was care by a parent
(usually the IP's partner). Regulated care arrangements for school-age
children (before and after school programs) are in short supply in Canada
and were used by a small minority of children; however, proportionately
more children from one-parent families participated in them. Care provided
by relatives and by unrelated caregivers were more common among children
in single parent families than those in two-parent families. Another important
finding pertains to the use of sibling and self-care arrangements as the
primary method used to supplement time in school. Almost one in three
children in single parent families and one in five children in two-parent
families were described as having spent the largest number of hours (outside
of school hours) in a sibling or self-care arrangement while the parent most
responsible for child care in the family worked or studied.

Effects of Child Care Arrangements on Families

What effects do child care arrangements have on children and their
parents? The answer to this question depends on many factors: the age of
the child; characteristics of the caregiver or child care program; how many
hours the child spends in care; how parents feel about the care arrangement;
and whether or not the care method that is being used is a preferred option
chosen for its ability to support parents and children in a positive way or is
a default used because other options were not available or affordable. A full
examination of these issues is beyond the scope of the present chapter.
However, analyses were conducted to determine whether or not parents
who used sibling and self care arrangements had reservations about their
child's care.

Analyses revealed that parents of 21% of the children in sibling care had
at least minor reservations about care by an older brother or sister;
furthermore, parents of 50% of the children in self-care arrangements said

Table 6-9:

Primary Care Arrangement Used for School-Age Children (6-12 Years) While IP Worked or Studied in One- and Two-Parent Families, Canada, 1988

Primary Care Arrangement Other Than School [1]	Children in Two-Parent Families		Children in One-Parent Families	
	Number	*%*	*Number*	*%*
Total	**1,328,600**	**100.0**	**221,200**	**100.0**
Regulated group care arrangement or regulated home care	46,400	3.5	23,400	10.6
Care by parent(s) [2]	521,600	39.3	q 8,600	q 1.6
Care by a relative, in the child's home or relative's home	118,800	8.9	44,100	20.0
Care by unregulated caregiver (non-relative in child's home or other home)	161,600	12.2	49,300	22.3
Sibling or self-care	256,700	19.3	71,200	32.2
No arrangement[3]	223,400	16.8	24,500	11.1

[1] Care arrangement used for the largest number of hours while parent primarily responsible for making child care arrangements (usually the mother) was working or studying.

[2] Care provided by parents while working and care provided by spouse while IP was working in a two-parent family.

[3] "No arrangement" category includes time spent in lessons, sports and recreational activities; in transit to and from school; and in medical or dental appointments. These were not considered to be child care arrangements for the purposes of the study.

q Estimate is subject to unreliability and should be treated with caution.

Source: Canadian National Child Care Study, 1992. ♦

they had at least minor reservations about the use of self care as a primary care method. The most common concerns expressed by parents using sibling care arrangements were concerns about children's safety (worries about accidents, fire, and lack of supervision) and concerns that the older sibling was not as mature or reliable as they would like. Parents also suggested that sibling care restricted the older child's free time and/or put too much responsibility on his or her shoulders. The most common concerns expressed about self-care were for the child's well-being (concerns about children being alone, perhaps getting into trouble), as well as general expressions that conveyed worry and guilt about children being left unsupervised.

These findings raise some interesting questions. On the one hand, a larger proportion of children from single parent families (but still, the minority) are cared for in licensed child care settings by caregivers who are trained in child development or are at least supervised in order to ensure adequate quality care. On the other hand, more children in single parent families than in two-parent families are cared for by someone who is unregulated and unrelated to the child; and more children from single parent homes spend considerable time in sibling and self-care arrangements. Under these circumstances, single parents may feel insecure — or at the least ambivalent — about the kinds of arrangements used while they work or study to provide for their children's needs.

Summary and Policy Implications

Single parent families, i.e., women and children who are put in the position of having to function without adequate physical, financial, and social resources, are at risk in a number of ways. Rhetoric in the form of statements, principles, and policy objectives can be found in such diverse areas as employment equity, affordable housing, harmonization of work and family responsibilities, gender equality, social welfare reform, and the desire to eliminate child poverty. But action towards these ends is woefully lacking. Existing social assistance policies appear to humiliate lone parents and, inadvertently, frustrate parents' efforts to become economically self-sufficient through capricious, and arbitrary policies that are inconsistent from one province to the next (National Council of Welfare, 1991). At the most basic level, sufficient resources must be provided to ensure that single parent families have the necessities of adequate food, clothing, shelter, access to educational and training programs, and affordable high quality child care. Social assistance benefits and tax policies must be restructured, and stronger efforts directed to ensure that awards for alimony and child support are enforced. Incentives and supports must replace barriers.

Some of the needed policy initiatives flow directly out of concerns for social justice. Others will be based on the economic benefits to government, employers, and Canadian society of reducing welfare dependency and strengthening the capabilities of current and future labour force participants. Still other policies will be justified by renewed and growing concern about the effects of poverty on children's health, school performance, and emotional well-being.

Nancy Fraser (1989) and others have begun to write about the coming welfare wars, which will be largely wars about or even against women. Her view stems from the recognition that, by and large, the role of caring for family members is not valued as productive work, and hence those who care for others rather than participating in waged work are counted among the dependents in society. The role of dependent wife has been acceptable but the role of a single caregiver who is dependent on public funds is increasingly less acceptable. Hence, single parenthood is now viewed as a significant problem. Current initiatives are focused on efforts to ameliorate single parents' economic distress through efforts to enforce child support and a new spate of workfare policies designed to encourage single mothers (including those with children as young as one year old) to enter or re-enter the labour force or a training program. Correlated changes in social assistance policies will have to address the limited supply of subsidized child care and recognize other systemic inequities and barriers than can work to frustrate positive outcomes. Such efforts, while laudable in their intentions, may require further thought, however. Is it necessarily in the best interests of parents, children, or the state to require or propel single mothers into full-time work in jobs that fail to pay a family wage, without adequate child care, and with little flexibility or support to help them manage their double load? Should efforts to encourage single parents to continue their education be predicated and evaluated exclusively on the basis that additional schooling is important for and will lead to later employment?

What are the short and long-term consequences for single parents and their children of current policies and experiences? What will be the intended and unintended effects of new welfare/workfare policies for both parents and children? Are there model policies already in place in other countries that would be applicable to the Canadian context? These questions, and others, are both empirical and political. Clearly, policy makers should be informed about single parent families and the factors that influence their well-being, both positively and negatively. Often such information is best obtained through rigorous program evaluations and planned variation, as well as longitudinal and strategic studies that can assess both the short- and long-term consequences of interventions. Consequently, establishing a healthy dialogue between researchers and policy makers in full view of an informed public is an important step towards truly addressing the pressing needs of single parent families.

Most of the statistical analyses presented in this chapter are based on data from the 1988 National Child Care Survey. The survey was conducted as one element in the Canadian National Child Care Study, a collaborative project involving four researchers affiliated with the National Day Care Research Network (Donna Lero, University of Guelph; Alan Pence, University of Victoria; Hillel Goelman, University of British Columbia; and Lois Brockman, University of Manitoba) and Statistics Canada. Funding for the study was provided by the Child Care Initiatives Fund of Health and Welfare Canada, by the Social Sciences and Humanities Research Council, and by the governments of Ontario and New Brunswick. Their support is gratefully acknowledged.

7

Recent Changes in the Economic Welfare of Lone Mother Families in Canada: The Roles of Market Work, Earnings and Transfers

Martin D. Dooley

My recent research has focused on two related topics in which lone mothers figure prominently. The first concerns the relationship among poverty, age and gender in Canada (Dooley 1992a). The second is the converging market work patterns of lone mothers and married women with children under eighteen (Dooley 1992b). This chapter will summarize findings that link the two topics together and are of greatest policy relevance.

Poverty trends are examined from two perspectives. First, changes in the incidence of low income among lone parent and two-parent families between 1973 and 1988 are presented. Second, changes in distribution of the low income population are considered, including why the proportion of lone mothers who are poor has been constant or falling while the proportion of poor families with children headed by lone mothers has been rising. An analysis is presented of the sources of income growth among one-parent and two-parent families with children. Families headed by lone mothers under thirty-five have had falling (or constant) market earnings and rising transfers. In contrast, the major source of income growth among younger couples has been the rapidly growing earnings of wives.

The principal reason for the convergence in the earnings levels of lone mothers and married mothers is the convergence in their rates of employment in market work. Brief consideration is given to other time uses of young mothers, most importantly job search and schooling. Multivariate analysis is used to investigate the association between the propensity of mothers to work in the market and such variables as level of education, number and ages of children, the earnings of other family members and the vailable level of welfare income. The most policy relevant inference is that these data offer no strong support for the hypothesis that the available level of welfare income markedly alters the probability of market work among lone mothers.

Data and Measurement

The data used in this study are for economic families with at least one child under the age of eighteen and are from the Survey of Consumer Finances (SCF) for the income years 1973, 1979, and 1988. All computations were performed by the author with data from the public use samples. The term couple refers to both legal and common law unions. A lone mother or lone father family refers to any family with a child under eighteen not headed by a couple. In most cases, the lone head is the parent of the child. The incidence of low income or poverty rate refers to the proportion of families in which total economic family income is below one of two poverty lines. The 1986 set of Statistics Canada Low Income Cutoffs (LICO) are used to measure moderate poverty and the 1969 LICO's measure severe poverty. These are absolute poverty lines in the sense that both are adjusted only for inflation over time. Wolfson and Evans (1989) argue persuasively that poverty is both a relative and an absolute concept. The measure of relative poverty used in this paper is to compare the incidence of severe poverty in 1973 with the incidence of moderate poverty in 1988.

The analysis emphasizes trends rather than levels at a point in time. One reason for this is that transfer income appears to be seriously under reported in the SCF. In particular, estimates of aggregate unemployment compensation and social assistance transfers from the SCF are much lower than reported provincial payments. However, the degree of under reporting appears to be relatively constant over time. Hence, even though the estimated poverty rates may be biased at one point in time, the estimated changes in such rates over time may not be.

Poverty Trends

Table 7-1 contains the incidence of moderate and severe low income. The basic trends are similar for both measures. The most obvious feature of this table is the difference between the poverty rates of lone mothers and couples. The rates for lone fathers are far closer to those of married couples than to those of lone mothers. Most types of families experienced a decline in the incidence of low income. The youngest lone female heads and couples (<25) are the only families which show an increase in the rate of poverty between 1973 and 1988. There is no apparent strong trend in the difference between lone mothers and couples. Between 1973 and 1988, these differences decreased in absolute size (percentage points), but increased in

Table 7-1:

Poverty Rate among Families with Children

Age	1973	1979	1988	1973	1979	1988
	1969 Low Income Cutoff			1986 Low Income Cutoff		
Lone Mother						
< 25	80.4	67.4	80.1	89.7	75.5	93.3
25-34	66.2	58.7	58.2	75.1	66.4	63.6
35-44	57.6	39.1	31.7	67.2	51.3	41.3
45-54	38.3	40.1	26.6	50.8	47.7	40.4
55-64	-	-	-	-	-	-
Subtotal	56.5	49.8	45.2	66.6	59.1	53.9
Lone Father						
	13.8	14.6	17.9	21.3	17.9	22.4
Couples						
< 25	13.1	16.9	21.7	23.2	15.2	31.3
25-34	10.0	7.7	7.1	15.8	12.0	11.1
35-44	10.0	6.7	4.5	15.5	10.0	7.4
45-54	9.3	6.5	4.9	13.3	18.6	7.2
55-64	13.3	9.0	10.1	18.6	12.8	11.5
Subtotal	10.4	7.6	6.0	15.9	11.3	9.3
Total	14.3	12.2	11.3	20.3	16.5	15.3♦

relative size (ratio). Consider the measure of relative poverty proposed in the previous section. A comparison of the first column of Table 7-1 with the final column indicates that relative poverty increased substantially for the youngest families. The incidence of relative poverty was constant for those age 25-34 and it decreased for most families with parents of age 35 and over. The most striking thing about Table 7-1 is the perseverance of severe poverty among lone mothers. Over the sample period, the incidence of severe low income did decline substantially for lone female heads over age 35. As of 1988, however, the problem of severe poverty among families remained a common phenomenon primarily among mothers living alone with their young children.

Table 7-1 provides one view of the relationship between poverty and family type, i.e., the relative incidence of low income in different families. An alternative is to examine changes in the composition of the total and low income populations by family type which is done in Table 7-2. The top

Table 7-2:

Distribution of Families with Children

All Families

		1973		1979		1988
Lone Mother		8.4		9.1		11.0
Lone Father		1.6		2.8		3.3
Couples		90.0		87.0		85.7

Poor Families

	1973	1979	1988	1973	1979	1988
	1969 Low Income Cutoff			*1986 Low Income Cutoff*		
Lone Mother	33.2	43.1	51.5	27.7	37.9	45.2
Lone Father	1.5	2.3	3.5	1.7	2.1	3.5
Couples	65.3	54.6	45.1	70.7	60.1	51.6♦

panel of Table 7-2 indicates a modest reduction in the proportion of all families with children which are headed by couples. The lower panel presents the distribution of low income among families with children. Changes in the lower panel reflect both the changes in the distribution of all families in the top panel of Table 7-2 and the changes the incidence of low income across different types of families in Table 7-1. The lower panel of Table 7-2 reveals a marked increase in the proportion of poor families with children which are headed by a lone mother. This occurred despite the evidence in Table 7-1 of decline in the incidence of both moderate and severe poverty among most lone mother families.

The concurrent decrease in the poverty rate among lone mother families and increase in the proportion of poor families headed by a lone mother reflects two phenomena: (1) the growing proportion of all families with children that are headed by a lone mother and (2) the fact that the poverty rate among lone mother families usually did not decline, and in some cases grew, relative to the poverty rate among other types of families. Tables 7-1 and 7–2 demonstrate the value of a multidimensional view of poverty. The rate of absolute poverty (either moderate or severe) was falling among most lone mother families, but not rapidly enough to keep the population of low income families from becoming even more disproportionately populated by lone mothers and their children. Both facts are important for policy.

Table 7-3:

Levels and Change in Sources of Income for Families with Children (1986$)

	1973	1988	Change	% Change
Lone Parent				
Total Income	19,345	22,328	2,983	14.4%
Head's Earnings	9,394	12,187	2,793	26.0%
Transfers	4,203	5,129	926	20.0%
Lone Parent < 25				
Total Income	10,445	11,230	785	7.2%
Head's Earnings	6,060	3,320	-2,739	-60.1%
Transfers	2,641	6,376	3,735	88.0%
Lone Parent 25-34				
Total Income	14,690	16,864	2,174	13.8%
Head's Earnings	9,279	9,503	224	2.4%
Transfers	2,642	5,412	1,827	41.0%
Couples				
Total Income	38,152	46,980	8,828	21.0%
Wife's Earnings	4,105	10,505	6,400	94.0%
Husband's Earnings	28,372	29,406	1,034	3.6%
Transfers	1,820	3,021	1,201	50.6%
Couples < 25				
Total Income	25,342	27,188	1,846	7.0%
Wife's Earnings	3,153	6,590	3,437	73.7%
Husband's Earnings	20,077	16,098	-3,979	-22.1%
Transfers	1,666	3,864	2,198	84.1%
Couples 25-34				
Total Income	34,356	39,919	5,563	15.0%
Wife's Earnings	4,001	9,278	5,277	84.1%
Husband's Earnings	27,926	26,437	-1,489	-5.5%
Transfers	1,461	3,048	1,587	73.5%♦

Sources of Changes in Family Income

While there has been no major change in the poverty rates of lone mother families relative to those of two-parent families, there has been a large change in the sources of income for these two types of families. The top panel of Table 7-3 shows that the youngest lone heads (mostly mothers) with children experienced a large decline in earnings and a large increase in transfers. Lone parents age 25–34 experienced stagnant earnings and a correspondingly smaller increase in transfers. Lone parents over age 35 experienced substantial earnings growth as can be seen by contrasting the top panel with the second and third. Most of these age differences also characterize couples with children. The additional factor which stands out for couples is the contrast between the earnings of wives and husbands. Married women increased their level of market earnings quite rapidly especially in comparison with the stagnant earnings of their husbands. This contrast was particularly marked in the case of couples under the age of 35. Table 7-3 provides the link between my research on poverty and that on market work. Note the large changes in the relative earnings of lone parents (mostly mothers) and married women with children. In 1973, lone parents age <25 with children earned almost twice as much as did similarly aged married mothers. By 1988, the reverse was true. The principal reason for this was the change in the relative propensity of lone mothers and married mothers to work in the market.

Market Work Among Lone Mothers and Married Mothers

Table 7-4 presents the proportion of lone and married mothers who performed any market work in 1973, 1979, and 1988. This labour supply measure is referred to as the employment rate (ER). The ER among all married women with children grew from 40% to 73%. This dramatic rate of increase was true of most age groups in each decade. In the span of fifteen years, full-time home workers went from the status of clear majority to that of clear minority. The experience of lone mothers was quite different. Their overall ER increased by 10 percentage points from 57% to 67%. However, both the magnitude and sign of the change varied greatly by age of lone mother. The proportion of the youngest lone mothers who worked in the market dropped from 63% to 48%. The ER of lone mothers age 25–34 changed little and the rate for lone mothers age 35–54 increased at a pace slower than that of comparably aged married mothers. The bottom panel of Table 7-4 indicates the change in the relative ER's of these two groups of women. In 1973, lone mothers in each age group were much more likely to work in the market. By 1988, married mothers were equally or more likely to work in the market. This change was most dramatic for mothers less than 25.

Table 7-5 provides some additional information about the time use of the mothers in my sample. The left hand side panel presents estimates of mean weeks of market work among all mothers. This measure behaves in a pattern similar to that of the ER's in Table 7-4. The right hand side panel presents a more comprehensive measure of time use. The SCF tapes do provide data on uses of time other than market work. One such variable is the number

Table 7-4:

Proportion of Lone Mothers and Married Mothers with
Children Who Worked in the Market

Age	1973	1979	1988
Lone Mothers			
< 25	63.4	50.8	47.8
25-34	59.7	65.8	63.5
35-44	54.2	72.4	76.9
45-54	56.6	56.3	68.5
55-64	-	-	-
Total	56.6	62.3	67.0
Married Mothers			
< 25	44.3	60.3	64.9
25-34	39.2	54.3	73.2
35-44	42.6	58.7	76.7
45-54	37.5	48.0	66.6
55-64	22.7	34.4	41.3
Total	40.0	54.9	73.2
Ratio of Married Mothers to Lone Mothers			
< 25	0.70	1.19	1.36
25-34	0.66	0.83	1.15
35-44	0.78	0.81	1.00
45-54	0.66	0.87	0.97
55-64	-	-	-
Total	0.71	0.88	1.09♦

of weeks without a job and looking for work, i.e., unemployed. A second variable is one's main activity during weeks without a job and not searching for one, i.e., when out of the labour force. One of the responses to this latter question is "at school." These two variables are used to ascertain more about changing the time allocation of the women in the sample. The right hand side panel of Table 7-5 presents an estimate of mean weeks devoted to the sum of weeks spent in market work, in job search when not employed, and in schooling when not in the labour force. This variable can be constructed for married women only in 1979 and 1988.

Note the top two rows of Table 7-5. Just as with the ER's, the mean weeks of market work decline among the youngest lone mothers and are stable

Table 7-5:

*Means Weeks of Market Work and Total of Weeks of Market Work,
Unemployment and Schooling* among Married Women and
Lone Mothers with Children*

Age	Weeks of Market Work			Weeks of Market Work, Unemployment and Schooling		
	1973	1979	1988	1973	1979	1988
Lone Mothers						
< 25	19.9	18.0	12.7	24.7	23.3	23.8
25-34	23.3	25.3	24.5	26.3	31.9	33.6
35-44	22.8	32.2	35.1	24.4	37.2	40.8
45-54	25.5	23.8	31.3	27.4	26.4	35.2
55-64	-	-	-	-	-	-
Total	23.0	25.4	27.8	25.4	30.5	35.2
Married Mothers						
< 25	12.4	19.8	23.9	-	24.9	30.3
25-34	13.6	21.5	30.8	-	24.7	35.6
35-44	17.4	25.2	34.4	-	27.1	37.7
45-54	15.2	20.3	30.1	-	22.2	32.2
55-64	8.9	15.8	16.0	-	16.8	19.4
Total	14.9	22.3	31.7	-	25.0	35.6
Ratio of Married Mothers to Lone Mothers						
< 25	0.62	1.10	1.88	-	1.07	1.27
25-34	0.58	0.85	1.26	-	0.77	1.06
35-44	0.76	0.78	0.98	-	0.73	0.92
45-54	0.60	0.85	0.96	-	0.84	0.92
55-64	-	-	-	-	-	-
Total	0.65	0.85	1.14	-	0.82	1.01

* Weeks neither performing nor looking for market work in which schooling is listed as primary activity.♦

for those age 25–34. However, combined weeks allocated to market work, search and school are stable for the lone mothers <25 and increasing for lone mothers age 25-34. The implication is that mean weeks of search and schooling increased by about six weeks for lone mothers less than 35. The left hand side of the bottom panel presents the ratio of mean weeks of market work for married to lone mothers. The magnitude of the increases over time are even greater than for the ER's in Table 7-4. The ratios for combined weeks of market work, search, and schooling also increase within each age category, but the magnitude of the change is much smaller than when only weeks of market work are considered. These data raise some interesting questions concerning the broader time allocation decisions of the youngest lone mothers which deserve further research.

What are the possible causes of these marked changes in the market work patterns of lone and married mothers? Table 7-6 shows the changes over the sample period in several variables which are commonly associated with variation in ER's in the literature. The period between 1973 and 1988 witnessed only small changes in the age distribution of married women, but the average age of lone mothers decreased substantially. There was a noticeable drop in the average number of children <18 which reflects the lagged effect of pre–1973 declines in childbearing. The proportion of women with a preschooler did go up for lone mothers due largely to the decline in the average age of this group. There were major increases in the schooling levels. One further significant demographic change for lone mothers is the doubling of the proportion who are never married. A small and decreasing proportion of lone mothers are married. Statistics Canada classifies a woman as a married, lone mother if her husband has a prolonged absence due to work or institutionalization.

Table 7-6 contains the means of a variable titled other income. This is defined as total family income minus the sum of the mother's earnings and government transfer income. Hence, other income includes all sources of income not as directly linked to the mother's market work as are her own earnings and transfers. The most important component of other income is the earnings of adult children in the case of lone mothers and the earnings of husbands in the case of married women. The trend in other income for married women reflects the declining earnings of husbands <35 and slightly increasing earnings of husbands age 35 and over. Other income is quite small and unchanged for the lone mothers under age 35. Other income is declining for older lone mothers which may reflect both fewer older children and their poor earnings prospects.

The final variable in Table 7-6 is welfare income. The value for 1988 is the population weighted mean of the figures published in National Council of Welfare (1990) for a lone mother with one child. This variable is defined as the sum of social assistance payments, family allowances, federal and provincial tax credits, and additional benefits in certain provinces (National Council of Welfare, 1987). The values for 1973 and 1979 are the most comparable ones available. These figures are based on Lalonde (1973), Banting (1982), Federal-Provincial Working Party on Income Maintenance (1979), and benefit schedules kindly provided to me by provincial and

Table 7-6:

Distribution of Lone Mothers and Married Mothers with Children
by Selected Characteristics

	Married Mothers			Lone Mothers		
	1973	1979	1988	1973	1979	1988
Age						
< 25	9.7	8.3	4.9	9.1	13.2	11.1
25-34	37.8	42.9	41.0	30.2	32.9	37.2
35-44	31.6	32.4	42.5	32.0	31.1	38.8
45-54	18.1	14.3	10.3	24.3	17.9	11.2
55-64	2.8	2.1	1.3	4.4	5.0	1.7
Number Children < 18						
1	31.2	36.1	37.9	39.7	54.1	54.9
2	35.9	40.7	44.1	30.8	32.7	32.7
3+	32.9	23.2	18.0	29.5	13.2	12.4
With Child < 7	48.7	51.2	51.5	35.3	37.1	44.7
Education						
Elementary	25.5	17.2	8.5	28.1	23.6	11.8
HS	55.7	57.0	52.3	55.2	56.4	55.1
Some Post-HS	15.5	19.3	26.5	13.6	15.8	24.6
Univ. Degree	3.3	6.5	12.7	3.0	4.2	8.5
Marital Status						
Married	100.0	100.0	100.0	13.7	5.6	4.2
Never Married	-	-	-	10.0	13.2	25.8
Other	-	-	-	76.3	81.2	70.0
Other Income[+]						
25	22,218	23,159	19,657	242	583	244
25-34	29,866	31,837	28,761	1,167	1,347	1,313
35-44	35,139	38,219	36,973	4,135	4,596	3,775
45-54	37,503	42,116	40,989	10,743	7,748	6,710
55-64	30,957	33,161	32,650	-	-	-
Total	32,206	34,688	33,109	4,680	3,704	2,903
Welfare Income for Lone Parent with One Child [†]	-	-	-	7,482	8,476	9,659

[+] Other income is total family income minus mother's earnings and government transfers.
[†] Includes Social Assistance Payments, Child Tax Credits and Family Allowance Payments.

Sources: include Lalonde (1973), Banting (1982), Federal-Provincial Working Party on Income Maintenance (1979), National Council of Welfare (1987, 1990) and figures received by the author from provincial and municipal officials. ◆

municipal officials. Two things should be noted about welfare income. First, real welfare income increased by 25% between 1973 and 1988. Second, this 25% increase raised the mean level of welfare income from 53% to 69% of the 1986 LICO for a two-person family and from 66% to 85% of the 1969 LICO. A lone mother and child reliant solely on welfare income are still severely poor as of 1988.

Multivariate Analysis of Market Work

Multivariate analysis (Dooley 1992b) is used to estimate the association between the probability of market work and the various observable characteristics of married women and lone mothers presented in Table 7-6. Multivariate analysis was done for two reasons. Nakamura and Nakamura (1985) assert that the explanatory variables traditionally included in models of the market work of women, such as education, fertility and wage rates, may not explain most of the increase in the market work of married women after the early 1970s. This claim has also been made in Canada by Ciuriak and Sims (1980) and by Blau and Ferber (1986) and Fuchs (1988) in the U.S. Multivariate analysis of SCF data is used to evaluate this claim.

The second reason derives from a recent working paper by Allen (1991). Allen uses data from the 1986 Census Public Microdata File to evaluate the association between various characteristics of low income women and the parameters of provincial welfare programs. Many of the low income women in Allen's sample are lone mothers, but he also includes unattached individuals and married women. The parameters of the welfare programs that he uses are the level of welfare income and the exemption levels for liquid assets as specified for all ten provinces by the National Council of Welfare (1987). Allen estimates a negative relationship between the probability of labour force participation and the level of both welfare benefits and the exemption levels for liquid assets. However, the magnitude of the relationship is not large. His estimates imply that an increase of $1,000 in either welfare benefits or liquid asset exemption levels would lead to a 2% decrease in the probability of labour force participation rate for low income women. Furthermore, Allen correctly describes his findings as tentative and in need of verification with richer data from different sources and time periods.

Why would the policy analyst be interested in Allen's question? One reason is to improve ability to forecast the cost of changes in income support programs. Such forecasts of necessity include an assumption about the response of current and potential participants. Work such as Allen's provides one means of evaluating assumptions. A second reason is interest in how time use changes in response to social assistance programs. For example, the data in Table 7-5 implies that there has been an increase in school attendance by young lone mothers. A policy analyst might very well wish to have some sense of the association between the adequacy of social assistance payments and the schooling decisions of lone mothers.

SCF data from 1973, 1979, and 1988 are used to estimate a series of models in which the dependent variable is whether or not the individual worked in the market at any time during the year. The independent variables include all of those in Table 7-6. These data have some advantages and disadvantages compared to Allen's. Allen's data are from a single cross section from the 1986 Census. The only source of variation in welfare income or asset exemption levels is that between the provinces in one year. Inter-provincial differences in welfare income may be proxying for many other variables which differ across provinces and which are associated with market work. The value of welfare income in the data used for this paper varies across provinces and over three time periods. In addition, a single set of dummy variables are introduced for each province. My data do not include liquid asset exemption levels in years before 1986. Further, the value of welfare income for a lone mother and one child is not a perfect proxy for the welfare income available to various types of lone mother families. Finally, neither Allen nor I have the exemption level for earned income in our models.

Probit analysis is the method of estimation. The probit estimates themselves are not easily interpretable. Table 7-7, therefore, presents the probabilities of market work which are implied by one set of probit estimates. The models were estimated with data from all three years, but separate estimates were obtained for married women and lone mothers. Although a dummy variable was included for each province, the coefficients are not reported in Table 7-7. The first row contains probabilities for the base case — a woman age 25–34 from Ontario with a secondary education and two children at least one of whom is a preschooler. Other income is assigned the value at the sample mean. The base case further assumes that a lone mother is previously married and has the mean value of welfare income. The probabilities in the other rows of Table 7-7 are obtained by altering the characteristics of the base case one at a time.

The cross-sectional pattern of probabilities for married women in 1973 is generally what one would expect. The probability of market work declines with the number of children and the presence of a preschooler. Schooling has a large positive effect and the age profile is fairly flat up to age 45. A 10% increase in other income is associated with only a 1% point decline in the probability of participation. These cross-sectional differences are generally the same for married women in 1979 and 1988.

One of the goals for this study was to assess the extent to which readily observed variables such as family size and education could account for much of the increase in the market work of married women since the early 1970s. The first row shows that the increase in the probability of market work for the base case was 32 percentage points. This is almost as large as the increase

Table 7-7:

Predicted Probability of Market Work for Lone Mothers and Married Mothers with Children

	Married Women			Lone Mothers		
	1973	1979	1988	1973	1979	1988
Base Case[1]	34	52	66	56	60	62
Mean Other[2] Income + 10%	33	51	66	56	60	62
Mean Welfare Income + 10%	-	-	-	52	59	60
Age						
< 25	38	53	57	62	57	56
35-44	32	50	64	47	64	60
45-54	20	33	56	38	43	49
55-64	8	19	23	-	-	-
Children <18						
1	44	63	72	65	72	71
3	28	44	56	44	47	50
No Child < 7	59	71	79	73	75	78
Education						
Elementary	23	37	45	27	35	38
Some Post-HS	56	63	78	82	79	79
Univ. Degree	60	71	85	70	85	89
Marital Status						
Never Married	-	-	-	44	46	53
Sample Mean	40	55	73	57	62	67

[1] The base case is age 25-34, secondary education, Ontario, two children, preschooler, and mean other income. The base case for a lone mother assumes mean welfare benefits and a previous marriage. A dummy variable was also included for each of the other provinces.

[2] See Table 7-6 for a definition of other income and welfare income. ♦

in the sample ER of 33 percentage points. A comparison of columns 1 and 3 in Table 7-7 indicates that the increase in each of the probabilities of market work was often 25 percentage points or more. This implies that changes in unobserved characteristics can account for a large portion of the observed change in the ER of married women. A formal statistical decomposition shows that only 25% of the observed change in the ER for married women can be accounted for by changes in observed characteristics of the sample, such as family size and schooling. This supports the claims of Nakamura and Nakamura and Ciuriak and Sims concerning the sources of the growth in market work for married women over the sample period. Unmeasured factors appear to account for most of the increase.

The cross sectional pattern of estimates for lone mothers is similar to that for married women in a number of ways. Large numbers of children, the presence of a preschooler, and low education are all associated with relatively low levels of market work. The status never married is associated with a decrease of 9 to 14 percentage points in the probability of market work. Hence, this characteristic appears to be more than just a proxy for low age and education. The age pattern of conditional probabilities for lone mothers undergoes the same changes over time as in Table 7-4. In 1973, the probability of market work is greatest for lone mothers under 25. By 1988, the youngest lone mothers are less likely to work in the market than are lone mothers age 25–44. Note, however, that the probability of market work for lone mothers under age 25 declines by only 6 percentage points in Table 7-7 whereas the ER for this group declined by almost 16 percentage points in Table 7-4. An increase of 10% in other income has virtually no association with market work of lone mothers in any year. An increase of 10% in welfare income is associated with declines of 4, 1 and 2 percentage points in each successive year of the sample.

The last row of Table 7-7 indicates an increase of 10 percentage points in the sample ER for lone mothers. About 50% of this change can be accounted for by changes in the observed characteristics of the sample, such as family size and schooling. Hence, the measured variables have better explanatory power for lone mothers than for married women. Nevertheless, the observed characteristics are unable to account for most of the change in the relative ER's of married women and lone mothers. The bottom row of Table 7-7 shows that the ratio of the ER of married women to that for lone mothers was 0.70 in 1973 and 1.09 in 1988. The other rows show that the ratio of the conditional probabilities of market work was in the neighbourhood of 0.5 to 0.8 in 1973. By 1988, these same ratios had grown to a value of 1.0 or more in all cases save women with post-secondary education. The change in this ratio was greatest for young women and those with more than one child.

The second goal in this section is to evaluate Allen's finding of a mildly negative association between the level of welfare income and the likelihood of market work for lone mothers. The estimate in Table 7-7 for 1988 is numerically identical to Allen's estimate for 1986. Several additional specifications were estimated to check on the robustness of the estimates (Dooley, 1992b). One alternative specification was to exclude the dummy variables for each province. The effect was to make the association between welfare and market work a positive one in 1979 and 1988. A second alternative specification was to interact welfare income with age of lone mother in light of the very different changes over time in the ER's of lone mothers of different ages in Table 7-4. The most interesting age-specific result is that the association between welfare income and the probability of market work is either positive or virtually zero for lone mothers under 25. This is the only age group that exhibited a declining ER in Table 7-4. A third alternative specification was to include a measure of potential market wages (weekly full time earnings) in the model. This specification is of particular interest from a policy perspective since it offers an opportunity to assess how lone mothers would respond to an increase in their net wage. In the past few years, several provinces have done just this by reducing the rate at which social assistance payments are reduced as the earnings of the mother rises. A positive association was found between potential wages and the probability of market work, but the magnitude of the effect is not large. A 10% increase in potential earnings power would lead to an estimated increase in the ER of between two and five percentage points for lone mothers and even less for married mothers. The model specification with wages yields the same inference as in Table 7-7 of a weak, negative association between the level of welfare income and the probability of market work among lone mothers. In this specification, as in virtually all specifications, the association between other income and the probability of market work is virtually zero for either married women or lone mothers.

Finally, Allen included the provincial value of both welfare income and the exemption level for liquid assets. I did the same using only 1988 data. Unlike Allen, I estimate that a 10% increase in the liquid assets exemption level is associated with only a 1% decrease in the probability of market work and that a 10% increase in welfare income is associated with a 4% increase in the probability of market work.

What do the multivariate estimates indicate about the relationship between social assistance policy and market work? The SCF data do not offer support for the hypothesis that the impact of moderately higher welfare payments would be to lower greatly the probability of market work for lone mothers. But the conclusion is a weak claim since that is all that the SCF data can support. Estimates for the effect of welfare income invariably have large standard errors since there is relatively small variation in this variable. Hence, standard tests of statistical significance are quite weak. One can not reject the hypothesis that the coefficient estimate for welfare income is equal to a wide range of numbers only one of which is zero. Thus, the search for a robust pattern of estimates across different models rather than just a single test of statistical significance. It would be improper to state that these data prove that there is no association between the level of welfare income and the probability of market work. Rather, the available data do not clearly favour those who argue that higher welfare payments will alter the employment rates of lone mothers.

There are several reasons for this conclusion. First, the only consistently negative estimates for welfare income across all age groups are for 1973. This is the smallest of the samples and measures behaviour of almost two decades ago. Second, the welfare income estimates for 1988 are at or close to zero in all estimated models save one. Third, the welfare income estimates are never strongly negative for the one group of lone mothers who actually had a declining ER over the sample period, those under age 25. Fourth, the estimates for other income are uniformly zero for lone mothers. In principal, these estimates should offer some insight concerning the market work response of lone mothers to an increase in income from any source other than her earnings. However, there may well be several indirect links between the value of other income for a family and a mother's market work decisions. Hence, only the negative conclusion of no support is drawn from the estimates for other income.

Summary

This research has focused on two related themes involving lone parent families. One theme is the relationship of poverty and family type in Canada. The second is the converging market work patterns of lone mothers and married mothers with children under 18. The incidence of low income among both lone mother and two-parent families has been falling. However, the proportion of low income families with children headed by a lone mother has been rising. The latter phenomenon has occurred because of the growing proportion of all families with children headed by a lone mother and the fact that the poverty rate among lone mother families usually did not decline, and in some cases grew, relative to the poverty rate among two-parent families.

Poverty trends for lone parent and two-parent families have been similar, but the sources of income growth have differed greatly. Families headed by lone mothers under 35 have been characterized by falling (or constant) market earnings and rising transfers. In contrast, the major source of income growth among younger couples with children has been the rapidly growing earnings of married mothers. The principal reason for the convergence in the earnings levels of lone mothers and married mothers is the convergence in their rates of market employment.

Multivariate analysis was used to investigate the association between the propensity of lone and married mothers to work in the market and such variables as level of education, number and ages of children, the earnings of other family members, and the available level of welfare income. The observed characteristics of the women in the data can not account for most of the convergence in employment rates of lone mothers and married women with children. Finally, the data do not offer support for the hypothesis that an increase in the level of welfare benefits will lead to marked reduction in market work among lone mothers.

8

Demographic Trends: Summary, Policy Implications, and Research Agenda

Fran McIninch and Maryanne Pentick

Lone parent families are now a fact of life in Canadian society. Over the past thirty years, the dissolution of marriages and custodial retention of children by single mothers have replaced widowhood as the primary precipitating cause of lone parent families. Craig McKie notes that the number of these families now exceeds one million, is predominantly female, and is growing at least three times as fast as husband/wife families. Nicole Marcil-Gratton similarly points out that according to the 1986 census, 16% of families with children at home are headed by single mothers. However, the cross-sectional nature of official statistics do not adequately reflect the transitional nature of the single family state. For example, the retrospective Family History Survey reveals that an estimated 34% of mothers will have experienced single parenting at some point in their life times.

McKie states that lone parenthood is associated with low income, poor quality of life, constrained choices, and high levels of stress. Martin D. Dooley finds that, while the incidence of low income among lone mother families has been falling, the major source of income growth for this group has been rising transfer payments and not market earnings. He concludes, however, that there is no evidence that increasing income support alters market work behaviour of lone parents. Donna Lero focuses on the urgent need for policy makers to come to an understanding of the effects of current social and economic policies on the well-being of lone parent families.

Policy makers must be aware of the diversity within these family structures. The needs of a professional, single father with an adolescent son are enormously different from those of a young, single mother with little education. Nicole Marcil-Gratton finds that cohabitation is replacing marriage as the choice of union and child bearing. But families created through cohabitation are prone to disruption resulting in increasing numbers of children experiencing single parenthood, reconstitution of new two-adult families often through cohabitation, and frequent break-up of these unions. She stresses that more knowledge is needed on the long-term effects of lone parenthood on children, and Lero urges policy makers to consider factors affecting family needs and circumstances, such as single parents' marital status, age, education, income sources, and number and ages of children.

So why is this group important? Why have international research and policy focus on single parent families? The importance of today's children for the future of Canadian society is undisputed. Large numbers of children growing up disadvantaged will have a significant social and economic impact on Canada's future. Lone parents who remain out of the work force for long periods of time, or who have had only low-paying jobs, will reach retirement age with few pension entitlements and minimal home equity. Investment in children is necessary so that when they grow up, they can sustain themselves, their families, and their society, including the rapidly aging population.

Social Policy Implications

Policy-relevant questions must be built into demographic research, bearing in mind the political context and constraints, if research findings are to have an impact on policy and program development. As well, policy makers must be clear on the questions they want answered by the research community, be willing to wait for the answers, and be able to act on them.

Legislation and programs must be adjusted to more equitably meet the needs of lone parent families. Despite growing evidence to the contrary, much of current Canadian social policy is based on the two-parent family, with one income earner and one parent at home caring for the 2.2 children. Public policy related to housing, need for supervised daycare, and taxation seems determined to punish rather than support the lone parent family. Short-sighted thinking such as this can only result in the continued impoverishment of generations of children and their parents. There is an imbalance in the attitudes of Canadian society towards seniors, who appear to be deserving of public support such as the Guaranteed Income Supplement, and children, especially those in lone parent families, who must in some way earn whatever support they can pull from a reluctant society. There are over one million lone parent families in Canada, 1.5 million children are part of these families, and many of these adults and children are poor. Their current needs must be met, not only for their own sakes, but also for the future of this country. A demographic crisis is looming. A declining working population, coupled with the growing number of elderly, will result in a shortage of labour and a weakened economic base. These factors have major implications for social, economic, and labour-market policy development.

What kinds of policies are needed to support lone parents and their children? Short-term approaches include work-related benefits such as extended parental leave and pay equity. The awarding and enforcement of child-support orders must become an integral part of a coherent family law policy in Canada. In the longer term, the issue of child care needs to be re-opened and addressed.

Research Agenda

Any approach to future research addressing the lone parent population must take into account not only structure, but also context and supports. Researchers must be more sensitive to the diversity and fluidity of lone parent families, the context in which they live their lives, the resources and supports available to them, and the outcomes experienced by both children and adults in these families.

What are some of the gaps in current single parent family research? There is need for more longitudinal or panel-study data in Canada, similar to Britain's National Child Development study. Existing data sources could also be exploited more fully, given sufficient funding and personnel. Available sources of data include the Labour Force Survey, Census data, Surveys of Consumer Finance, General Social Surveys, and Family Expenditure Data. Lack of ready access to various types of provincial data, such as social assistance statistics, has been a barrier to full use. Data collection strategies should be constructed to allow extrapolation of data on children. Current data on single parent families seldom allows conclusions on the children of those families, particularly with regard to life experiences and outcomes. This may be difficult, since the frequent formation and dissolution of a one-parent family is not always evident in the data. Single parenthood is a fluid process, and differs from family to family. A related problem is the lack of common terminology, measures, and definitions, such as family, household, child, out-of-wedlock, cohabitation, and marriage.

An emerging research agenda would include addressing policy relevant questions such as:

(1) What factors contribute to some lone parent families having more positive life experiences than others, both for parents and children?

(2) Precisely what are the social, health, and emotional outcomes for children and adults in lone parent families?

(3) How can we spell out more clearly the long term societal and economic costs of not dealing with the problems experienced by lone parent families?

(4) What are the impacts of current social and fiscal policies, such as the cap on CAP, on these families?

(5) How do countries such as Britain, France, and the United States compare with Canada in their approaches to these social policy issues?

(6) How do the provinces differ in their approaches?

While policy makers and researchers have a responsibility to attend carefully to one another, both must also invest in and nurture the shrinking social research infrastructure in Canada. The potential cost of not doing research, policy development, and experimentation is enormous.

PART III

CANADIAN PUBLIC POLICY IMPACT

9

Lone Parent Families: An Instable Category in Search of Stable Policies

Margrit Eichler

L ooking at lone parent families is like looking at a hologram picture: holding it one way, you see one thing, holding it another way, you see another thing. This can be profoundly disorienting. In order to avoid vertigo, I shall start by looking at the picture from different angles, turning it slowly, noting the shifting patterns. All of these angles are informed by the basic lens used here: what are meaningful concepts for social policy formation?

It is dangerous to identify problems — and thereby possible solutions — on the basis of a structural factor (the presence of one rather than two parents) when upon examination this factor does not turn out to be the crucial variable. Consequently, the first question is, in what way are lone parent families the same or different from two-parent families and from each other? What is the connection between poverty and lone parent families? What is the connection between household membership and family membership in lone parent and two-parent families? Underlying these questions will be another question: What are appropriate terms with which to label the various types of families?

I shall proceed from there to explore models of the family underlying various types of policies and their implications for lone parent families, and identify problems in the currently prevailing model as well as suggest a possible alternative model. I shall be using the term lone parent rather than one-parent or single parent family, since the latter terms provide an inaccurate description of most of the families under consideration.

Characteristics of Lone Parent and Two-Parent Families

The Origin of Lone Parent Families

There are five pathways by which lone parent families may come into existence. Three of them are subsequent to union dissolution, and two are through acquisition of a child by an unmarried parent. A lone parent family may come into existence

(1) through the death of a married parent,

(2) through separation or divorce of a married parent,

(3) through union dissolution of a parent living common-law,

(4) through birth to an unmarried woman (i.e., neither legally married nor cohabiting), or

(5) through adoption of a child by a single adult.

In three of these scenarios (#2, #3, and #4) there are, in fact, two parents alive and potentially available — they are simply not living within the same household. Only one parent is available in the other two cases (#1 and #5). These different pathways have different consequences for social policy. I shall refer to scenarios 1 and 5 as *simple lone parent families* (i.e., true one-parent families) and to scenarios 2 to 4 as *complex lone parent families*.

By contrast, two-parent families come into existence in only two ways:

(1) couple marry and subsequently have children through birth or adoption,

(2) person (with or without own children) marries a parent. This couple may have joint subsequent children as well.

Sex and Economic Position

Lone parents may be either female or male. The vast majority are female, but a small minority of them are male. The economic and social situations of female and male lone parents tend to be quite different, reflecting the differential economic and social positions of women and men in general (McKie, 1993).

Lone parenthood is quite often identified with poverty. There is a strong likelihood that lone parent families will be poor, especially if the parent is female (Dooley, 1993), but in absolute terms there are more husband-wife families in Canada who are poor than there are poor lone parent families. A full 60% of all poor families in Canada involve a married couple (Statistics Canada, 1988: t. B+C). Poverty is unfortunately a characteristic that is typical of both husband-wife as well as lone parent families (as well as unattached individuals).

The In/Stability of Lone Parent Families

Adopting the angle of the child — the participant who makes the lone parent family a family — we can see major differences in the existence of this family form. A child may live in a lone parent family during his/her entire childhood. Alternatively, living in a lone parent family may be preceded by living in a two-parent family, and/or this may be succeeded by living in a two-parent family, or there may be a repeated pattern of living in a lone parent/two-parent situation (Marcil-Gratton, 1993). This observation is premised on a very common slight of hand. It equates a spouse of a parent with a parent. In most cases we will be dealing with different adults who move in and out of family households; two-parent families that form subsequent to a period of lone parenthood constitute, in reality, a husband-wife family with dependent children. We have currently no terms at our disposal that allow us to distinguish between husband-wife families that are also two-parent families and husband-wife families in which only one parent is a biological parent. In other contexts, such families are described as remarriage families. This term defines the family structure from the perspective of the adults involved but is ambiguous with respect to the implied parental relationship.

Consider two instances. Two people (or one of them) may have been previously married, divorced, and then marry each other. If no children were involved in the first set of marriages, the marriage is a remarriage for the adults, but not in any real sense for any ensuing children. Alternatively, if a woman who had a child outside of marriage subsequently marries a man other than the father of her child, it is a first marriage for both of them, therefore not a remarriage, yet it shares the most important aspect of what is commonly designated a remarriage family, namely the presence of a dependent child who is the biological child of only one of the spouses. In remarriage families, the relationship of the parent's spouse to the children is legally and socially ambiguous, unless the children are formally adopted by the spouse.

Current terms are clearly inadequate when looking at the family structure from the perspective of the children involved. A lack of clear terminology confuses the issues considerably. I shall therefore designate husband-wife families in which all children are the biological children of both spouses as *biological two-parent families*, and husband-wife families in which the children are the biological children of only one parent *social two-parent families*. I shall refer to adoption of an unrelated child as an *adoptive family* and adoption by the non-related spouse as a *step-adoptive family*. In addition, various mixes of these four types are possible, which can be designated by using several adjectives, such as a *biological-social two-parent family*, and so forth. This allows us to look at a phenomenon that is often incorrectly attributed only to lone parent families, namely the lack of congruence between family and household membership.

In/Congruence between Household and Family Membership

There is an incongruence between household and family membership in many lone parent families. However, this is only true in the case of complex lone parent families; no incongruity exists in the case of simple lone parent

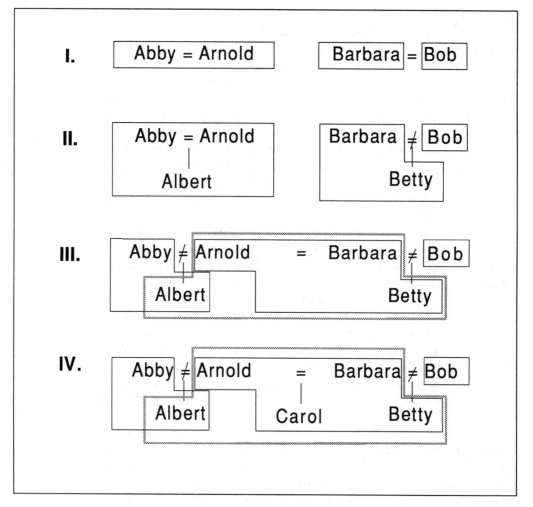

Figure 9-1:

Schematic Representation of Lone-Parent Family Reformation

families. Similarly, spouses in husband-wife families may or may not be biological or social parents, thus experiencing their own forms of in/congruity.

Let us consider an example illustrated in Figure 9-1. Let us assume that Abby and Arnold marry. At approximately the same time, Barbara and Bob are involved in a sexual relationship without getting married or forming a joint household. Abby and Arnold have a child Albert, while Barbara and Bob have a child Betty. At this point, Abby, Arnold and Albert constitute a biological two-parent family, while Barbara and Betty constitute a complex lone parent family with Bob as the external member. Researchers and policy-makers often forget about Bob at this point, and consequently he tends to drop out of the picture.

In our next snapshot, Arnold and Barbara have met, fallen in love, Abby and Arnold divorce, and Arnold moves in with Barbara and Betty. Now the nature of the family has shifted for everybody. Abby and Albert now constitute a complex lone parent family with Arnold as the external member, while Arnold, Barbara and Betty become a social two-parent family. Arnold is one of the rare fathers who keeps in regular touch with his son Albert. Albert visits Arnold, Barbara, and Betty regularly. Arnold is also one of the small number of fathers who pays regular child support to Abby. Albert is thus simultaneously a member of a lone parent family household, as well as an intermittent resident and family member of a social two-parent family. In the course of time, Arnold and Barbara have a child together, Carol. They have now moved from a social two-parent family to a mixed social-biological two-parent family. Figure 9-1 is a schematic representation of the various family and household relationships.

This is a severely simplified picture of familial and household relationships. For instance, we have ignored whether Bob or Abby also marry. Arnold and Barbara might divorce, and so forth. We cannot make the assumption that family and household memberships are congruent for either two-parent or lone parent families. This requires a re-thinking of the basic unit of administration appropriate for social policies, as well as a re-thinking of the responsibilities of the various parents involved, including Bob, who tends to be forgotten.

Differences between Lone Parent and Two-Parent Families

Looking now once more at the holographic picture of lone parent families as well as two-parent families (biological as well as social), we find that the differences within the category of lone parent families and between the categories of lone parent and two-parent families are as large as the similarities. Both lone parent and two-parent families may involve a parent who is not living with his (occasionally her) children. Household membership for children in lone parent, as well as two-parent, families may or not be congruous with family membership. Both types of families may be above or below the poverty threshold (although the likelihood of being located above or below the line differs dramatically by family structure). Lone parenthood may be a permanent or impermanent state, which is also true for membership in a two-parent family.

None of these characteristics differentiate lone parent families from two-parent families. Thus, for social policy purposes, the category of a lone parent family may so far not be a meaningful one. There is, however, one difference that is invariable. In a lone parent family only one parent resides with dependent children. This parent will be solely responsible for the day-to-day care and upbringing of the children, while in a husband-wife family (whether legally married or common law, whether a first union or a subsequent union) there are two spouses, who tend to be regarded as parents, living with dependent children. *This is the only structural difference which is in all cases associated with lone parenthood and that distinguishes it from biological as well as social two-parent families.* Appropriate policies for lone parent families must necessarily be located in the larger context of policies for families as a whole since lone parenthood is neither a stable category nor clear in its social and economic consequences. To do this, it is useful to identify various models of families that have historically underlain our family policy and that can be deduced to underlie our present policies affecting families.

Models of the Family Underlying Various Policies

Canada has never had a consistent explicit family policy (Eichler, 1988). The models presented here are heuristic devices, developed through asking the question "What model of the family would have to be adopted to explain a given policy?" (Eichler, 1987, 1990, and 1991). We can distinguish between at least three models of the family (and various hybrid forms) that have very different consequences: the patriarchal model, the individual responsibility model, and the social responsibility model. I shall examine a constant set of questions and see how they are answered according to all three models of the family. The questions with respect to each model are:

(1) What is the ideology concerning sex equality?

(2) What are assumptions about household/family membership in/congruence?

(3) What is the appropriate unit of administration?

(4) What are the assumptions concerning economic responsibility/dependency?

(5) What are the assumptions about care and service provision for family members in need of care?

(6) What is seen as the appropriate private-public division of responsibilities?

The Patriarchal Model of the Family

Characteristics of this model of the family are:

(1) The ideology is one of sex differentiation.

(2) Household and family membership are treated as congruous. This being so, a spouse is equated with a parent. Conversely, an external parent is treated as a non-parent.

(3) The family household is treated as the unit of administration.

(4) The husband is responsible for the economic well-being of the family household. The wife/children are treated as economic dependents of the husband.

(5) The wife-mother is seen as responsible for the provision of care and services to family members in need of care.

(6) The public has no responsibility for the economic well-being of a family where there is a husband/father present, and no responsibility for the care provision where there is a wife/mother present. If one of the spouses is missing or incapacitated, and children are present, the public will pick up the function left unfulfilled through absence or incapacity of one of the parents.

The Individual Responsibility Model of the Family

The individual responsibility model of the family shares some of the characteristics with the patriarchal family, and diverges on others.

(1) The ideology is one of sex equality.

(2) Household and family membership are treated as congruous. This being so, a spouse is equated with a parent. Conversely, an external parent is treated as a non-parent.

(3) The family household is treated as the unit of administration.

(4) Husband and wife are equally responsible for the economic well-being of themselves, each other, and any dependent children. Children are considered dependents of both their parents.

(5) Fathers and mothers are equally responsible for the provision of care and services to family members in need of care.

(6) The public has no responsibility for the economic well-being of a family or for the provision of care where there is either a husband-father or wife-mother. Temporary help will be provided in the case of absence or incapacity of one of them, but the assumption is that a parent-spouse is responsible for both the economic well-being as well as the care provision for dependent children.

Part of the attraction of the individual responsibility model is that it is ideologically premised on the notion of sex equality. However, the individual responsibility model of the family can serve as the ideological basis for a *decrease* in societal contributions to families when we ask about the policy implications for lone parent families of either model. Where, in the patriarchal model, the state would have replaced the financial contributions of the husband-father, in case he cannot or does not make them, it will not do so if an individual responsibility model of the family is used. The same applies to the service contributions of the wife-mother. In such a case, the expectations on the lone parent suddenly double — all in the name of equality.

The Social Responsibility Model of the Family

The third alternative model of the family can be described as:

(1) The ideology is one of sex equality.

(2) There is no assumption that household and family membership must be congruent. Consequently, a person can be a parent without being a spouse and household member.

(3) There is a recognition of potentially overlapping and varying sets of financial and care responsibilities, which may run across as well as within households, and there is no assumption that family membership of all household members is necessarily the same.

(4) Every adult is considered responsible for his or her own economic well-being. Where this is impossible, the support obligation shifts to the state, not to a family member. Children are considered to be the joint responsibility of both parents and the state. The parental responsibility remains independent of whether the parents are married or not and living in the same household or not.

(5) The state (not a family member) is responsible to pay for the cost of care for an adult in need of care, whether because of a permanent or temporary illness or handicap. A family member may still wish to *deliver* the care but she (or he) would receive compensation for the work done by the state, proportionate to the amount of time required. In effect, this would be a wage or wage replacement for delivering care to a person in need of care who would otherwise be cared for by the state. The cost of raising children is shared by the father, the mother, and the state, irrespective of the marital status of the parents.

(6) The public is responsible for the cost of care of adults who cannot care for themselves, and shares the responsibility for the cost of care of dependent children with both parents. If only one parent is available or capable, the public takes over the financial contributions of the unavailable parent.

Figure 9-2 summarizes the differences among these three models of the family for each of the questions.

	Patriarchal Model of Family	*Individual Responsibility Model of Family*	*Social Responsibility Model of Family*
Ideology	Sex Differentiation	Sex Equality	Sex Equality
Household/ Family Members	Assumed Congruent	Assumed Congruent	Incongruent/ Congruent
Unit of Administration	Family Household	Family Household	Family Across Households
Economic Responsibility/ Dependency	Husband/Father Breadwinner Wife/Children Dependents	Husband/Father & Wife/Mother Economically Responsible for Each Other and for Dependent Children	Husbands and Wife Individually Economically Responsible, Father and Mother and Society Responsible for Children
Care Provision	Wife/Mother	Wife/Mother & Husband/Father	Wife/Mother and Husband/Father and Society
Public/Private Responsibility	Care Responsibilities All Private	Care Responsibilities All Private	Care Responsibilities Private and Publically Shared ♦

Figure 9-2:

Schematic Representation of Three Family Models

Policy Consequences of Each Model of the Family

The policy consequences of each model of the family are inherent in the descriptions, but can be spelled out explicitly, particularly with respect to

(1) The constitutional and legal treatment of the sexes;

(2) Labour market policy;

(3) The tax structure;

(4) Social welfare legislation;

(5) The unit of administration; and

(6) The provision of social services.

The Constitutional and Legal Treatment of the Sexes

The patriarchal model of the family is premised on the notion of sex differentiation, while both the individual and the social responsibility model of the family proceed from the assumption of sex equality. An ideology of sex differentiation implies differential rights and responsibilities for each sex, with protective legislation for both sexes, but primarily for males, for instance through preventing women from entering male domains, different pay scales, different treatment under family laws, and so forth. By contrast, an ideology of sex equality implies formally equal treatment, often, however, with no guarantees that the consequences be equal as well.

Labour Market Policies

Labour market policies will differ dramatically, depending on whether they are premised on a notion of sex equality or differentiation. In the case of differentiation, we will find a strictly gendered labour market in which the gendering is bolstered by formal laws and policies that give preference to men in terms of hiring, promotion, eligibility for training programs, pay scales, and so forth. Women will be considered secondary wage earners, to be hired and trained only if no men apply, with legally lower pay scales, and so forth. In the case of sex equality, we will find formal sex equality with respect to eligibility to all occupations, equal pay for equal work or equal pay for work of equal value, equal eligibility to all training possibilities, but no true equality in the labour market as long as family care remains an exclusively private responsibility (Abella, 1984).

The Tax Structure

A wife and children are regarded as dependents of a husband-father under a patriarchal model of the family. This means that he can declare them as dependents on his income tax form. Under the individual responsibility model, a spouse can declare her or his spouse as an economic dependent if such is the case. Under the social responsibility model, neither spouse would be regarded as a dependent by virtue of being a spouse. The individual responsibility model sees children as dependents of the parent with whom they live. In the case of a complex lone parent family, this means that children are not seen as dependents of the non-co-residential parent. Tax benefits are therefore attributed only to the lone parent as income, rather than split between the parents; support payments are seen as an expense to the payer and as income to the recipient, rather than as an intrafamilial support that has no tax consequences (Revenue Canada, 1991).

Under a social responsibility model, children would be seen as the joint responsibility of the father, mother and society at large, irrespective of household membership. Tax benefits for children would be attributed to both parents, and support payments of fathers would not be tax deductible for the payer father nor would they need to be declared as income by the recipient mother. All statements may, of course, apply to either parent but at present it is mostly mothers who are lone parents and fathers who are non-co-residential parents; it is inappropriate to hide this fact under gender neutral language. The equivalent-to-married amount can be seen as grounded in a social responsibility model, since it constitutes a tax benefit for lone parents.

Social Welfare Legislation

Under the patriarchal model of the family, a family with an incapacitated husband-father would be eligible for social welfare payments irrespective of the labour force capacity of the wife/mother, and eligible for replacement care in the case of the absence or incapacity of the wife-mother irrespective of the care capacity of the husband-father. This becomes more complicated under the individual responsibility model. Both the wife/husband and mother/father are presumed capable and responsible for the economic well-being of the other spouse and dependent children and the care provision of dependent children. We may thus be faced with policies that presume that the presence of *one* capable adult parent is sufficient for both the provision of care and the economic provision of the family. This implies a lack of recognition that it is impossible to simultaneously be a full-time care provider and full-time earner without easily accessible affordable day care and other services. This is where we run into almost insurmountable difficulties.

The cost for the care of children is shared by both parents and society under the social responsibility model of the family. This means that all non-co-residential parents would be partially responsible for absorbing the cost of child care and child support; society would share some of this cost — either through provision of direct services (e.g. free or subsidized day care, school lunches, before and after school supervision, lunch time supervision, etc.) and/or other direct transfers.

Under the patriarchal and individual responsibility models, male partners of welfare mothers would be automatically assumed to be responsible for the financial well-being of the mother and her children, since a spouse is equated with a parent. Such would not be the case under a social responsibility model, where an unmarried woman with children who is eligible for social support, would retain this support even when a man resides in the household. Disentitling her from support might actually prevent the formation of a social two-parent family, which many policy makers uphold as the desirable ideal, due to the fact that the man may be either unwilling or unable to take over financial responsibility for both the woman and for another man's children. On the other hand, if the woman continues to be entitled to support, and assuming that her new partner earns a decent wage, this family would get public support while their neighbours, who also have two children and where the man has an identical income, do not get public support because the children happen to be his. The second family is therefore penalized for not having divorced. This is a matter of equity that needs to be carefully considered.

The Unit of Administration

Eligibility to family-based benefits depends on family household membership under both the patriarchal and individual responsibility models. Children living within a social two-parent or lone parent household would be considered members of this household only, rather than as belonging partially to the family of a non-co-residential parent. One of the ways in which this might surface would be if judges give preference to the well-being of a father as an individual man or to his second family (including non-biological children brought into the new union by the wife) at the expense of his first set of children. By contrast, under a social responsibility model, the obligations of a non-co-residential parent would be comparable to those of a co-residential parent, and children would be eligible to benefits via two parents, no matter what their family structure.

The Provision of Social Services

Care for children is seen as an exclusive parental responsibility under both the patriarchal and individual responsibility models. Under the social responsibility model, care is seen as a joint parental and societal responsibility. Child care would be provided by the public as a right to parents and children under the latter model, but not under the former models. Likewise, care in the case of illness of care providers or children would be available as a right under the social responsibility model, but would have to be managed as best as possible under the other two models.

The Current Canadian Situation

Canada does not have a coherent policy with respect to families in general. It follows that there is no coherent policy with respect to lone parents. (Coherent policies should not necessarily be equated with adequate or appropriate policies — they may be coherently awful!) Canada has moved from a predominantly patriarchal model of the family underlying its policies to a predominantly individual responsibility model of the family, with a few aspects of a social responsibility model interspersed. While the passing of the patriarchal family as a basis for policy formation is not lamented, the shift to an individual responsibly model is highly problematic. Nowhere does this become more obvious than in the case of lone parent families. One parent cannot at one and the same time be solely responsible for the economic well-being of herself and her children, as well as a being a full-time care-taker of the children.

Nevertheless, we have clearly moved to the individual responsibility model. Our policies are constitutionally required to be based on the notion of sex equality. Family laws attribute equal responsibility to spouses for their economic well-being and declare spouses mutually dependent on each other, while children are declared to be the dependents of both parents (Eichler, 1990) as long as the parents share one household with each other and the children. If one parent leaves the family household, official attention focuses on the lone parent, meanwhile largely treating the non-co-residential parent as a non-parent. Support payments of fathers are generally low and insufficient, generally defaulted upon, do not constitute a serious division of financial costs between the two parents, and do not sufficiently recognize that cost for the support and care of children are two separate needs each of which must be met (Canada Department of Justice, 1990: 81–98).

The tax structure treats the lone parent as a beneficiary of child support payments rather than as manager of an intrafamilial transfer of benefits to children, and treats support payments for non-co-residential parents as if they constituted an external expense rather than the fulfilment of an on-going parental obligation. Lone parents are in a mixed situation with respect to tax liability for child-related benefits. On the one hand, they have, as sole parents, a tax liability comparable to that of two parents, although there is only adult per household. An example in the 1991 tax guide reads:

> Tony and Lola separated in September 1991 … Lola has to report the Family Allowance payments she received from September to the end of the year. Tony has to report the Family Allowance payments for January to August, since his net income for the year was higher than Lola's (Revenue Canada, 1991: l. 118, 11).

Lola's income is lower after her separation, yet she has to report the Family Allowance as income in spite of the fact that she received it before her separation without having to report it. Tony, who is still the father and the higher income earner, is no longer considered a beneficiary of the Family Allowance. His tax liability drops and shifts to the economically weaker Lola who has to support herself and her children on her income. On the other hand, Lola does receive some societal support by being able to claim the equivalent-to-married amount, that can be seen as a societal contribution to lone parent families. Zweibel (1993) found that the interaction of the various tax provisions results in the non-co-residential father receiving a greater tax benefit than the co-residential mother. In general, poorer women are subsidizing the richer men not only directly, by carrying a disproportionate share of the direct costs associated with raising children, but also indirectly through the tax system.

Policies governing present provision of social services are squarely located within the individual responsibility paradigm. This poses problems for both lone parent families and two-earner two-parent families. The realization of our constitutionally mandated sex equality is impossible as long as all family care functions are regarded as a private responsibility of parents, be they lone parents or not. Some of the major limitations of this model include an inappropriate identification of a spouse with a parent, thus treating the external parent in many instances as a non-parent in terms of sharing financial responsibilities. There is a serious lack of public support services, and an implicit equation of the capacities of two parents with those of one parent, thus creating an intolerable burden on the lone parent. One of the consequences of being a lone parent is that the social and economic safety net is much more constricted than that for two-parent families. Crises loom more imminently, since there is less give in the system. If a lone parent loses a job, there is no spouse who may be still employed and/or able to find employment. If a lone parent or a child falls ill, there is usually no other adult who can share the caring. If a financial problem occurs (e.g. the car that is needed for transportation to the day-care centre and one's job breaks down) there is neither a second car nor a second source of income, and so on. Moving towards the social responsibility model of the family is a necessary change, for lone parent families, for two-parent families in which both parents are in the labour force, and for creation of a society that actually implements, rather than simply proclaims, sex equality.

Moving Towards a Social Responsibility Model of the Family

A move towards this model would benefit all families with dependent children or with adult members in need of care, such as elderly parents or a disabled spouse. But there are some issues specific to lone parent families that deserve attention. These include (1) reconsideration of the various obligations of fathers who are not living with their biological children, including income splitting of parents and access to the family residence, (2) consideration of the relationship between obligations and rights of non-co-residential fathers, (3) reconsideration of the interface between individual and social responsibilities, and (4) reconsideration of our tax structure as an instrument of social policy affecting families.

Obligations of Non-Co-Residential Fathers Towards (All) Their Children

Canadian law has a very confused attitude towards fathers. The term "father" is sometimes used for biological fatherhood and sometimes for social fatherhood; the various obligations and rights are unclear, conflicting, and inconsistent (Eichler and McCall, 1991). Social policies and laws both reflect as well as contribute to this overall image of rampant confusion. We do not any longer know who or what is a father. We are rapidly moving in the same direction for mothers through the new reproductive technologies and other related developments (Lippman, 1991; Overall, 1987).

A useful start to bring some clarity into this picture is to postulate, as a desirable policy goal, that all fathers maintain an equal responsibility towards the support and care of their children irrespective of whether they (a) live with them or not, (b) whether they are married to the mother or not, (c) whether the mother is married to another man or not, and (d) whether they are married to another woman or not. Applying this principle would result in some difficult issues of equity between the entitlement of first and subsequent families. Such difficulties should not be regarded as prohibitive. They exist now and are currently weighted against first families. This proposed principle would equalize the position of children from first and subsequent unions. Universal knowledge that the financial responsibility of a father was equal for all his children would send a clear message that the father has an unnegotiable responsibility towards his existing children for as long as they are dependent. Such a message would be considered by any woman contemplating entering into a union with a man who is already a parent with another woman. Such is usually the case for a man who marries a single mother. It would simply equalize the situation all around.

The Connection between Fathers' Rights and Fathers' Obligations

Quite often a connection is made between fathers' rights and fathers' obligations. I submit that such connection is inappropriate (Lamb, 1987). The obligations of a parent towards a dependent child are absolute, while rights of parents must be seen in the context of their effects on children and other affected people. If a father is, for instance, abusive to either his children or his ex-wife, this should effectively end any access he has to the child, while not affecting his responsibilities. It is the well-being of the child, as well as of the primary care-taker, that is the most important aspect here, not a presumed symmetry between support payments and access. The whole debate around fathers' rights is misplaced. The most frequently cited problem for complex lone parent families is not that unmarried fathers are prohibited from access to their children, but that they do not avail themselves sufficiently of the opportunities for interaction with their children, and that children suffer because their non-co-residential fathers neglect them. Nor should an ex-husband be capable of blocking an ex-wife in her residential mobility and, consequently, in her capacity to either form a new relationship, and/or upgrade her training or improve her employment possibilities.

The Interface between Father's Responsibilities and Public Responsibilities

Several provinces in Canada have moved towards a sightly more effective means of collecting income support than used to be the case. But, the system is still highly defective. A more efficient system would be to set minimum amounts of support payable to lone parents across the board. These payments would then be made automatically from public funds, and recouped from fathers according to their capacity to pay. This would mean that enforcement would be entirely a state responsibility and would be highly effective because the state is very skilled at collecting money from its citizens. This scheme differs from the child support assurance system as proposed by McLanahan and Garfinkel (1993) in so far as it would be applicable to all children, whether or not there was a court order for support and whether or not one of the parents was dead. Payments would never fall below a certain minimum, they would arrive with guaranteed regularity, and fathers would pay according to their capacity. To avoid inequities between biological and social two-parent families and lone parent families, two-parent families who fall below the income level set for a lone parent family, would also be eligible for the same child support as the lone parent family. Judges would still set levels of payment that are higher than the minimum for complex lone parent families, in cases where sufficient money is available to go beyond these minima. Similarly, family assets would still need to be divided in the case of a divorce. A special consideration is necessary with respect to the family dwelling. Often, a divorce means that the family home is sold and the lone parent has to move with her children to a less desirable residence. Here Lenore Weitzman's proposals on treating the family residence as the children's residence until they are no longer dependent seems a useful solution to the problem (Weitzman, 1985: 384–387).

Implications for the Tax Structure

The social responsibility model of the family assigns equal responsibility to both parents for a child. This would imply a partial restructuring of our tax system. One should study the potential effects of such a restructuring by calculating the effects of treating child support payments as an intrafamilial, non-taxable exchange and attributing any public transfers received by the lone parent to both parents when calculating tax liability. In the case of child support payments, the recipient parent would not have to report the payment as income and the payee would not report it as an expense. As for public transfers, the family allowance would be attributed 50% to the lone parent, and 50% to the non-co-residential parent, or forgiven in the case of simple lone parent families. The same would apply to the refundable child tax credit and any other transfers. We could shift to such a system if no unanticipated negative social consequences can be found after such calculations have been made.

Necessary Social Services for Lone Parent Families and Two-Parent Families

The social responsibility model of the family assumes a shared parental and societal responsibility towards dependent children. To some degree, this is already a reality in Canada, for instance in our medical and primary and secondary educational systems. But it is not yet implemented with respect to day care or post-secondary education. Day care is needed by both two-parent and lone parent families (Friendly et al., 1991). Making day care available to everybody, as has long been requested and promised by various Canadian governments, would have a number of beneficial effects beyond its impact on families. Universally available day care would create significant numbers of jobs for care providers that would be environmentally non-harmful. We also need some additional social services to support families. Needed, but not yet provided, social services include substitute care in the case of illness of either parent or child, a statutory right to a certain number of days off work for family reasons, respite for overworked lone parents, and others.

Conclusion

This view of lone parent families has revealed substantial similarities between some two-parent and some lone parent families, as well as differences and similarities in the situation of different lone parent families. Lone parent families constitute an increasing segment of our population. The problems experienced by lone parent families are urgent and must be addressed in a manner that is useful to them and without creating discrimination — positive or negative — on the basis of family status for the children. Trying to solve one type of problem should not result in the creation of new ones. Parents should discharge their parental obligations whether or not they live together with their children. Likewise, we must recognize, as a society, that the principle of sex equality cannot be implemented, in theoretical or practical terms, unless care for dependent children is seen as a shared societal and parental responsibility. A woman cannot, at the same time, be full-time in the labour force and solely responsible for the care of family members, particularly small children. Unless we care for our children well, we will pay the price when they are older.

10

Canadian Income Tax Policy on Child Support Payments: Old Rationales Applied to New Realities

Ellen B. Zweibel

Federal tax policy on child support is stuck in time. The Income Tax Act's (ITA) basic treatment of periodic child support payments has remained essentially unchanged since 1944. Until 1942, support payments between separated parents had no income tax consequences. High wartime taxes and the concern that many men with alimony obligations would not be able to pay both taxes and their support payments led to the enactment of a tax credit in 1942, followed by the present deduction/inclusion scheme in 1944 (Krever, 1983: 657–662). Today, qualifying periodic child support payments are deductible from the payor-father's taxable income and must be included in the recipient-mother's taxable income.[1]

The original rationale stemmed from the perception that a specific group of taxpayers required tax relief because of an extraordinary and temporary circumstance. The provisions were not the product of a systematic consideration of the appropriate tax support required for divorced and separated couples or for children in single parent households (Krever, 1983: 673). Over the years, other policy rationales have been suggested to justify the provisions (Krever, 1983: 656ff; Moran, 1989). Today, the deduction/inclusion scheme is popularly viewed as providing a beneficial form of income splitting for couples who were either previously married or cohabited.[2]

---

[1] The deduction/inclusion provisions are written in gender neutral language. For ease of expression and in recognition of the fact that 85% of custodial parents are mothers, the terms payor and father and the terms recipient and mother will be used interchangeably.

[2] Parents who never lived together may also be affected. Many commentators ignore this group of parents, most likely because of their assumptions on the composition or definition of the normative/standard family. Undoubtedly, there is a general bias in tax policy formation towards a standard form of nuclear family.

Despite its limited original agenda, the basic deduction/inclusion scheme has survived essentially unchanged for almost fifty years.

Unchanged, but not unchallenged! Recommendations calling for abandonment of the deduction/inclusion provisions for child support were issued by the Canadian Advisory Council on the Status of Women (CACSW) in June 1977 and most recently by the National Association of Women and the Law (NAWL) in February 1991. On June 10, 1991, Susan Thibaudeau, of Montreal, filed for class action status in a case challenging the constitutionality of including child support payments in custodial mothers' taxable incomes. These actions punctuate the growing perception that the deduction/inclusion provisions exacerbate the significant disparity in standard of living between custodial and non-custodial households.

This is a particularly appropriate time to re-examine the tax treatment of child support. Inadequate and unpaid child support is generating significant interest within provincial and federal governments. Private child support payments are currently seen as an under-utilized resource. Reforms geared to increasing the amount, collection rate and consistency of child support awards have been implemented in the United States, Australia and New Zealand. Other countries, such as Sweden, have used support formulas in conjunction with advanced maintenance programs for a considerably longer time. In Canada, a Federal/Provincial/Territorial Family Law Committee (1991 and 1992) is studying child support guidelines as one solution to the current problems of inadequacy, inconsistency and inequity in child support determinations. The Committee explicitly recognized that any Canadian guidelines must take income tax effects into account.

This chapter takes a critical look at the current income tax policy on support. Hypothetical examples constructed from data in the Department of Justice's *Evaluation of the Divorce Act* (1990) are used to test the validity of the Department of Finance's current justifications. The relative tax recognition given to the custodial and non-custodial parents for supporting children is analyzed, as is the extent to which the income tax treatment of support contributes to a disparity in the standard of living between the custodial and non-custodial households. Other equity issues, such as the relative tax recognition given to two-parent families compared to non-custodial parents, the bias in favour of high income earning non-custodial fathers, the significant tax burden on support payments received by custodial parents in the middle and high income tax brackets, and the tax disincentives for remarriage by custodial parents are considered. As well, design flaws which inhibit flexibility, discriminate against certain types of families, increase control by the non-custodial parent over the expenditure decisions of the custodial parent, and overcomplicate the provisions are discussed.

Views on the appropriate relationship between the family, the individual and the state, and views on the ideology of the family and on women's work, as well as fiscal constraints and priorities, underlie any reform initiative. The income tax system should also reflect these considerations. This point is often missed with respect to child support payments because family lawyers, concentrating on the bottom line support amount, tend to view income taxation only as an add-on computational adjustment. Policy makers, however, should not ignore the impact and interaction of the *Income Tax Act*'s revenue-raising and income-redistribution functions on family law policy and public income security programs. The same critical scrutiny should apply to all three regimes and proposals for changes to one should be accompanied by a re-examination of the effects on the others. At the very least, child support taxation and other child related tax measures should produce results that are consistent with and do not undermine government policies in other areas.

Background: Overview of the Income Tax Provisions

This chapter focuses on the income tax consequences of child support and isolates child support from spousal support. Although the distinction is irrelevant for income tax purposes, it is becoming very important from a policy perspective. The *Divorce Act, 1985* provides different criteria or objectives for spousal and child support. While spousal and child support are both determined based on needs, means and ability to pay, the four objectives for spousal support in subsection 15(7) are different from the standard for child support in subsection 15(8). The Federal/Provincial/Territorial Family Law Committee is reviewing the effect of these criteria and is currently considering the implementation of detailed guidelines relating only to child support. Both the CACSW and NAWL resolutions would result in separate treatment of child and spousal support. Furthermore, Susan Thibaudeau's constitutional challenge to the tax treatment of child support payments takes the position that child support is her children's income and not hers. This has stirred the imagination and political will of many custodial mothers. In Quebec, centres have been set up to advise women on preparing their income tax returns consistent with Ms. Thibaudeau's position. Momentum is building for separating the income tax treatment of child and spousal support.

The *Income Tax Act*'s treatment of periodic child support payments is relatively simple to state. Qualifying periodic child support payments can be deducted from the payor-father's taxable income and must be included in the recipient-mother's taxable income (*ITA* ss. 56(1)(b), (c), (c.1), 60(b), (c), and (c.1)). In addition, eligibility for child related tax benefits changes when parents live apart. Although the basic income tax consequences for parents living apart are easy to outline, the details have become quite complex for several reasons. First, Revenue Canada restrictively construes the technical criteria of the deduction/inclusion provisions resulting in considerable litigation and complicated amendments. Second, in recent years, the scheme's coverage has expanded to include more types of payments under detailed and sometimes complicated conditions. Third, in the first year of separation different rules apply to family allowances and child tax credits which sometimes create unanticipated problems for custodial parents.

The February 25, 1992, Federal Budget proposes to substitute a new child benefit scheme for some of the components discussed below. As discussed at the end of this chapter, the effect of that proposal parallels the effect of the present child related benefits.

Non-Refundable Dependant Child Tax Credit (ITA s. 118(1)(d))[3]

The *Income Tax Act* has always recognized that parents with dependant children have greater, non-discretionary financial demands on their income than other taxpayers. However, the amount of tax recognition given to parents has been decreasing. For instance, in 1984, the phased in reduction of the $710 per child deduction began and the larger deduction for older children was eliminated.[4] In 1988, the deduction was converted to a credit of $69 for each of the first two children and $138 for each additional child (1991 values). The conversion from a deduction to a credit effectively reduced the amount because a low conversion rate was used.[5] Since 1985, the credit (a deduction at the time) has been partially instead of fully indexed for inflation. Because of this, the value of this credit and all the credits discussed in this chapter continually erode.

The non-refundable dependant child tax credit is available to the person who includes the family allowance in their income. In a two-parent household, although the mother actually receives the family allowance, the *Income Tax Act* deems it to be included in the taxable income of the higher income earning parent (*ITA* s. 56(6)). Thus, it is generally the father who reports the family allowance as income and claims the non-refundable dependant child tax credit. When parents live apart, the mother reports the

---

[3] ITA s. 118(1)(d) is commonly referred to as the dependant child tax credit, but it is available for a broader range of dependants as defined in s. 118(6).

[4] S.C. 1983–84, c. 1, ss. 48(1) to (4). It is interesting to compare the $69 credit for children with the $890 credit for a dependent spouse. Although children require care and services and are the most economically vulnerable member of the family, their costs are minimally recognized. In contrast, the dependent spouse, who increases the household's standard of living by production of household services, generates a significant tax credit. Brigitte Kitchen (1986) notes that the deductions "are clearly wrongly apportioned in size and purpose for the higher value is attached to the wife, who provides services to the family, instead of the child, who requires service."

[5] The credit was converted at a 14% rate which is less than the lowest federal marginal tax rate of 17%. Other credits were converted at higher rates. This effectively reduced the tax benefit for most families with two or less children. Not all families were affected the same. Families with more than two children receive a larger credit for the third and subsequent children, which in many instances compensated for the loss in tax savings caused by the low conversion rate.

family allowance and claims the credit. The father is specifically precluded from claiming any dependency credit for a child for whom he makes deductible child support payments (*ITA* s. 118(5)).

Non-Refundable Equivalent to Married Tax Credit (ITA s. 118(1)(b)) [6]

Single custodial parents are entitled to a non-refundable, equivalent to married tax credit for one child. This credit was $850 in 1991. Because it is a non-refundable credit, it provides no extra benefit to single mothers without taxable income, for example those receiving non-taxable social assistance or those whose tax liability has already been eliminated by their own personal tax credit. It ceases to be available if the custodial parent remarries, and has evoked criticism as a disincentive to remarriage because of this.

Family Allowance

A direct family allowance payment for every child under age 18 is made monthly, generally to the child's mother. The annual payment per child was approximately $407 in 1991. The family allowance is taxable income to the higher income earning parent, generally the father, in a two-parent household. When parents live apart, the family allowance is paid to the custodial mother and included in her taxable income. Because the family allowance is treated as taxable income, most families pay back a portion of it through the income tax system.[7] Beginning in 1989, a special tax, popularly referred to as the clawback, took effect (*ITA* s.180.2(1)). It requires full or partial repayment of the family allowance once either parent with whom the child lives has net income over $51,765. The repayment rate is set at 15% of net income over the threshold. A family with one child will repay the full family allowance when a parent living in the household has income over $52,666. With two children full repayment will occur when income reaches $55,240.[8]

The threshold itself is only indexed for inflation over 3% so that it will effectively require repayment from an increasing number of middle income families. It has been estimated that by 1995 the clawback repayment

---

[6] *ITA* s. 118(1)(b) The credit for a wholly dependent person is commonly referred to as the equivalent to married credit. It is available to all lone parents, including persons who were never married, widows and widowers. It is also available for persons supporting their parents or other relatives in their households.

[7] Only the poorest families, who have no tax liability, actually keep the full family allowance payment. For example, working poor families earning about $20,000 pay back approximately 26% of the allowance, while middle income families earning about $50,000 pay back approximately 40%. Prior to 1989, when the clawback became effective, high income earning families, those with net incomes above $70,000, would have repaid up to 45% of their family allowance through the income tax system (Battle, 1990).

[8] The clawback is not effectively targeted at just high income earners. Average (mean) family income in 1989 was $47,310, which is very close to the initial $50,000 clawback threshold. As well, affluent, two income earning families will escape the clawback as long as neither parent's individual income exceeds the $50,000 threshold. Thus, not one cent of family allowance will be clawed back in a household with two income earning parents when each person earns $49,000, and the total family income is $98,000.

threshold will be the equivalent of $41,886 in 1990 constant dollars (Battle, 1990). Since single mothers have relatively low wage and support income, initially very few will be affected by the clawback. But this will change as the real value of the threshold declines due to inflation.

Refundable Child Tax Credit (ITA s. 122.2)

Low and modest income families receive additional assistance with the cost of raising children through the refundable child tax credit. This is a refundable, diminishing credit paid to the parent, generally the mother, who actually receives the family allowance payment. Because it is a refundable credit, persons with incomes so low that they do not owe any tax still receive the full benefit, provided that they apply by filing an income tax return. Although the mother receives the credit, entitlement is based on family income so that the credit amount starts to diminish when the family income rises above a stated income threshold. It eventually disappears once family income rises outside the target income level.

The basic credit for 1991 was $585 per child. The credit starts to diminish at the rate of 5% once net family income exceeds $25,215.[9] Since 1988, there is an additional supplemental credit of up to $207 per child under age seven, available only if neither parent claims more than $800 in work-related child care expenses under *ITA* section 63 (1991 values).[10]

The refundable child tax credit is not specifically targeted for single custodial parents. However, after separation or divorce many single parents become entitled to a portion of this credit because the non-custodial parent's income is no longer included when determining eligibility. Upon remarriage, the new marriage partner's income is included, regardless of whether he supports the children.

In summary, when parents live apart the father can deduct his child support payments from his taxable income. Family allowance payments will no longer be included in his taxable income and he will not be entitled to the non-refundable child tax credit. The mother is required to include the child support payment in her taxable income. She can then claim the non-refundable equivalent to married tax credit for one child and the non-refundable child tax credit for any other children. Family allowance payments will be included in her taxable income. Also, the mother is more

---

9 The refundable child tax credit has been increased several times since its inception in 1979. However, partial indexation of the credit amount and income eligibility threshold is eroding both the credit value, and its availability to middle income earners. By 1995, it is estimated that the maximum benefit for a family with two children, one under and one over age seven, will decline from its 1990 value of $1,353 to $1,102 and that the threshold will decline from its 1990 value of $24,769 to $20,184 (Battle, 1990).

10 The additional supplemental credit was phased in beginning in 1988 at $100 and increasing to $200 in 1989. The supplemental credit is reduced by 25% of the child care expense deduction claimed. The additional credit was primarily targeted for mothers who are not in the paid work force. It may also useful to working mothers who cannot take full advantage of the child care expense deduction in *ITA* s. 63.

likely to qualify for the income tested refundable child tax credit, as well as the goods and services tax credit, since the income threshold for eligibility will be applied solely to her individual income.

Tax Policy Critique

The *Income Tax Act* serves two major purposes. First, it provides government with a reliable and predictable source of revenue. Second, it is an instrument for implementing diverse economic and social policies ranging from encouraging investments in particular regions or industries to a redistribution of wealth. Tax expenditure provisions are frequently used to achieve the non-revenue producing goals. These provisions are intended to either influence private economic behaviour or assist persons in certain disadvantaged categories. The government indirectly supports the economic activity or assists the particular category of persons by foregoing taxes rather than spending money directly. The deductibility of support payments was included as a tax expenditure item in the Department of Finance's *Account of the Cost of Selective Tax Measures* (1985).[11]

In achieving its two main purposes the *Income Tax Act* balances three, often conflicting objectives:[12] equity,[13] economic efficiency (neutrality),[14] and simplicity.[15] Ultimately, tax policy is concerned with balancing competing

---

[11] A familiar example of the first type of tax expenditure is the deduction for Registered Retirement Savings Plan (RRSP) contributions which encourages individuals to accumulate private retirement savings. The special credit for the elderly is an example of the second type.

[12] Maureen Maloney (1987: 2) suggests a fourth objective, "substantive" or "result equality," which is not generally discussed in standard economic analysis, but which she views as "an independently desired objective" and perhaps "a required one" since enactment of the *Charter*. Result-oriented equality requires "removal of systemic discriminatory provisions and, potentially, affirmative action."

[13] Equity or fairness has two components, vertical and horizontal. Both reflect a foundation principle that taxes should be based on a person's ability to pay. *Vertical equity* addresses the distribution of the tax burden among persons with different economic power and opportunities. Vertical equity is often measured by the degree of progressivity in the tax burden. A tax system or tax provision is progressive, and vertical equity is enhanced, if persons with higher income levels, who presumably have greater discretionary spending power, pay a greater proportion of their income in taxes. Vertical equity is diminished when taxes are regressive and lower income earners pay a relatively greater proportion of their income in taxes than high income earners. *Horizontal equity* seeks to tax persons with the same economic power at the same level. For instance, a tax system meets the criteria of horizontal equity if all persons with the same amount of income, regardless of how it was earned, pay the same amount of tax. Despite this easy sounding example, horizontal equity can be a difficult concept to apply. Determining which taxpayers have the same economic power and, therefore, should be taxed alike, becomes a complicated issue. It is a central problem in evaluating both the existing income tax treatment of child support as well as any proposed reforms.

[14] Economists view taxation as a potentially distorting factor in economic behaviour. People will conform their business or other economic arrangements to minimize taxation and will choose tax wise strategies over more sound business strategies. The goal of economic neutrality is to minimize this distortion. For example, an economically neutral tax system should avoid creating disincentives for women to enter the paid work force.

[15] The tax system should be simple enough for people to understand the tax consequences of their economic plans. Simplicity enhances collection and enforcement, decreases the cost of compliance and increases respect for the system. Ironically, the objectives of horizontal and vertical equity most often conflict with

fiscal and non-fiscal objectives in a way which produces fair results among persons with different economic power.

Child Support Deduction/Inclusion Provision

The deduction/inclusion provisions represent a particular resolution to a specific problem. It is only one of many possible resolutions. There is an assumption that the provisions soften the financial hardship of family dissolution by providing an overall tax saving. Since taxable income is shifted from the father, who is presumed to be in a relatively high marginal tax bracket, to the mother, who is presumed to be in a relatively low marginal tax bracket, there is an anticipated tax saving that is now available to increase the amount of support and promote compliance.

These assumptions were reiterated by the Finance Department in a letter by former Finance Minister Michael Wilson responding to criticism put forward by the CACSW:

> Under the Income Tax Act, alimony and maintenance payments are deductible for the payor and taxable in the hands of the recipient. This tax treatment provides several benefits to separated and divorced couples.
>
> First, it recognizes that the payor has a reduced ability to pay tax as compared to someone who, except for this obligation, has the same income. Second, the tax assistance offered by the deduction provides an incentive for the payor to make regular and complete payments.
>
> Third, and most important, making payments deductible to the payor encourages higher levels of support payments. This happens because the tax saving to the payor exceed the tax liabilities on the support payments since, typically, the payor is in a higher tax bracket than the recipient. Indeed, almost 40 per cent of recipients are non-taxable. Thus, the existing tax treatment of alimony and maintenance payments is not only fair and appropriate but provides real benefits to separated and divorced couples (Wilson, 1991).

The assumption that significant income shifting actually takes place and that it in fact benefits custodial parents is debatable. The fact that "almost 40% of recipients are non-taxable" is more likely linked to low support awards, non-compliance with support awards, and the significant percentage of single mothers who rely on non-taxable social assistance. The Department's justifications have not been re-examined in light of the contemporary realities facing single mothers, the disparity in economic wealth between the custodial mother and her dependent children and the father,[16] and the effect of the Department's own major tax reforms.

---

simplicity.

[16] The Department of Justice's *Evaluation of the Divorce Act* (1990) compares the relative well-being of fathers with that of custodial mothers: 11% of fathers had income below the low income cut of line after paying child support, compared to 58% of the mothers after receiving child support. After paying support, on average, a father's income was $13,500 above the low income cut off line.

The deduction/inclusion provisions illustrate a general failure in tax policy formation — the failure to analyze the impact of tax provisions on women as a distinct constituency. Does the taxation of child support leave custodial mothers with sufficient income to support their children? Does the tax system create or maintain a disparity in the standard of living between the custodial mother's and the non-custodial father's households? Current family law policy seeks to apportion the child support responsibility between parents based on their relative ability to pay. Does the *Income Tax Act* countermand this by disproportionately subsidizing the non-custodial parent's support obligation? These are the questions crucial to a women-centred analysis.

There are two difficulties in proceeding with this analysis. First, because the *Income Tax Act* does not distinguish between spousal and child support, there is no published income tax data specifically related to child support. Second, information is needed on the relative income levels of payors and recipients of child support to gage whether and to what extent the deduction/inclusion provisions create or maintain economic disparities between custodial and non-custodial households. Published tax data does not provide this link. The only recent data which had the potential for providing this type of information was collected by the Department of Justice (1990) in its study of divorced and separated couples from four Canadian cities. The research team analyzed court files and conducted interviews with separated couples in two time frames, just prior to the effective date of the *Divorce Act* in 1986 and again in 1988.

The study separated child support awards from spousal support and attempted to ascertain the incomes of the parties. The study discusses the difficulties that occurred in gathering complete financial data (Department of Justice, 1990: 21–26). Of the 1,478 data records in the 1988 phase, 223 had the information required to analyze the relative effects of the income tax provisions. These 223 cases are used in this research to design 14 hypothetical fact patterns. The Department of Justice (1990) data provides a more realistic set of hypothetical examples than otherwise might have been constructed. The hypothetical examples are set out in Table 10-1 together with notes explaining how they were derived from the Department of Justice data. The income tax analysis applies the 1991 *Income Tax Act* and an average provincial tax rate of .546 of basic federal income tax. The Department of Justice data based on income support payments in 1988 has been converted to 1991 values.[17]

---

[17] The Department of Justice is currently conducting another study on support awards from which more complete data may be available for a follow-up analysis.

Table 10-1:

Hypothetical Examples

Family Number	Number of Children	Non-Custodial Parent's Income	Custodial Parent's Income	Child Support Payment
1	1	$18,757	$15,280	$2,335
2	2	$19,705	$16,714	$4,073
3	1	$44,041	$21,653	$4,315
4	2	$43,385	$19,684	$6,974
5	1	$45,401	$36,785	$4,772
6	2	$43,282	$41,037	$7,656
7	1	$76,734	$41,315	$6,148
8	2	$76,734	$41,315	$12,296
9	1	$75,521	$74,465	$5,186
10	2	$75,521	$74,465	$9,909
11	1	$78,170	$25,246	$5,011
12	2	$78,170	$25,246	$10,022
13	1	$28,727	$37,375	$2,871
14	2	$21,379	$36,897	$3,798

The 223 cases in the Evaluation data were divided into income sub-groups based on federal tax rate brackets of the non-custodial payers and custodial recipients: Families 1 and 2 both in the 17% bracket; Families 3 and 4 payer 26%, recipient 17%; Families 5 and 6 both 26%; Families 7 and 8 payer 29%, recipient 26%; Families 9 and 10 both 29%; Families 11 and 12 payer 29%, recipient 17%; and Families 13 and 14 payer 17%, recipient 26%. The income and support amounts are the average amounts for families in that income sub-group with the number of children indicated. However, there were an insufficient number of cases to provide averages for family types 7, 8, 9 and 10, so a global average of income for families in those brackets was used.♦

According to the Finance Department, the deduction/inclusion scheme has important tax expenditure goals and provides horizontal equity between particular groups of taxpayers. The three rationales are:

(1) *Incentive for Payment.* The tax assistance offered by the deduction provides an incentive for the payor to make regular and complete payments.

(2) *Providing Higher Payments.* By permitting a form of income shifting, the scheme encourages higher levels of support payments because the tax saving to the payor exceeds the recipient's tax liability on the support payment.

(3) *Horizontal Equity.* The deduction merely recognizes the father's reduced ability to pay tax in comparison with an identical income earner without the support obligation.

Incentive for Payment

There is a very tenuous connection between the deduction and preventing default in payment. First, default rates remain significant despite efforts to strengthen enforcement mechanisms. The Department of Justice (1990) found that even after a relatively short period of time, 12 to 15 months after the divorce was finalized, only 71% of women were able to state that they always received their support payment and only 51% received the amount on time. Of those who reported not receiving regular payments, nearly half had not received any payment in six months (Department of Justice, 1990: 89; Canadian Institute for Research, 1981; Baar and Moore, 1981: 100–101).

Second, default is not a simple function of ability to pay. A 1981 study by the Canadian Institute for Research attributes non-compliance to several factors, including resentment towards former partner, dissatisfaction with access and child custody, and a general sense of having been mistreated by the legal system (1981: 22 and Marcus, 1983: 31–32). Other research indicates that over time there is a gradual process of disengagement from the family by the non-custodial parent, which is linked to an increase in non-compliance with their support obligations. The system of enforcement is far more important in encouraging payment than is the size of the order (Chambers, 1979: 114–121).[18]

Encouraging Higher Payments

The tax subsidy to fathers is unlikely to produce higher child support payments. In theory, shifting income from a higher income earner to a lower income earner should free up disposable income which could then be made available to the custodial parent. Family lawyers have assumed for a long time that they can use the tax saving to their clients' advantage. But research suggests there is a very weak connection between the current tax treatment and obtaining higher support payments. Researchers in Canada report very low child support payments relative to the cost of raising children. In most cases, a consistent dollar amount is ordered, regardless of the father's income (Burtch, Pitcher-LaPrairie and Wachtel, 1980:10). Research in the United States and Australia, where there is no tax deduction for child support, showed the same pattern prior to the introduction of child support guidelines (*Development of Guidelines*, 1987: II–2–3; Edwards, 1986; Harrison, Snider and Milo, 1990; Harrison et al., 1991). The Department of Justice study (1990) reported that when inflation was taken into account, the average child

---

[18] Chambers' study is based on U.S. data, where child support payments are not tax deductible. One of his major conclusions is that the size of the support order is not a major factor influencing payment until the order is more than 50% of the obligor's income.

support awards were actually decreasing. The 1988 awards were about $30 lower in value than the 1986 awards.[19]

There are several possible reasons why the father's favourable tax treatment does not result in higher awards. First, there is no obligation for the father to pass along the tax saving. The potential for increased payments depends on the expertise and negotiating skills of the mother's lawyer or the judge's comprehension of the tax effects. Although many lawyers publicly state that family practitioners always consider the income tax consequences, the following remarks by Judge R. James Williams of the Family Court of Nova Scotia are sobering:

> Disclosure (at least to the court) should include income tax calculations (re maintenance). Counsel *frequently* fail to provide such information. It is critical (especially where *both* parents are working) — not only to determine the actual cost of the maintenance but to determine what will be received for the child. These calculations cannot be undertaken if counsel are not prepared to present a range within which they believe an order should be made. I experience more than a little frustration when as a judge I inquire as to a party's position and am told "whatever you think is just, fair reasonable … etc." I can get *that* from the statutes [Emphasis is the court's](1988: 240).[20]

Second, the idea that there are significant tax savings which can be passed along through higher support payments has always been based on the paradigm of the high income earning father making payments to the unemployed housewife. One tax specialist noted

> There is always this sense, when you are talking to your opponent, that there is a 50-cent dollar being paid by the husband, and there is only a 25-cent cost to the wife. That seems to be the range (Evlyn McGivney quoted in Schmitz, 1989: 6).

However, this assumption has been relatively outdated for some time. Most single mothers are in the paid work force and most fathers making support payments are not high income earners. Both the custodial mother and non-custodial father were in the lowest income tax bracket in 54% of the 223 Department of Justice (1990) files used in constructing the hypothetical examples.

Further, the income tax reform of 1987 increased the likelihood that there will be very little difference in the tax rates of custodial and non-custodial parents. Replacing the former ten marginal tax brackets with three expanded ones has substantially increased the possibility that more ex-spouses will be

---

[19] Average support awards also decreased as a percentage of the father's pre-tax income. In 1988, support awards represented an average of 16% of father's pre-tax income, down from 18% of pre-tax income in 1986. Support represented 35% of mother's total income in 1986 and 24% in 1988. The mother's decreased reliance on support was linked to a general increase in paid employment.

[20] *See* Grassby (1991), who notes the limited degree to which income tax is taken into account in setting awards. *But see* Krever (1983: 692–93), who suggests that there is adequate information available to lawyers and judges.

taxed at the same rate. In addition, aside from any surtaxes, there is only a 3% difference in the middle and high federal income tax brackets. In many instances there will not be a significant tax saving to pass along. Family tax practitioners are beginning to notice this effect. One family tax specialist has suggested that the impact of bracket changes was an "inadvertent disadvantage of tax reform" and that he doesn't

> ... believe that the government addressed it, or thought about it, or even as yet has stopped to recognize, just how devastating that is to the vast majority of tax-paying Canadians who are separated (Douglas C. Campbell quoted in Schmitz, 1989: 6).

There are two ways to measure the tax savings generated by the deduction/inclusion provisions. First, the combined taxes that would have been paid by the family if the parents had not decided to live apart can be compared with their combined tax liability after separation. This comparison is done in Table 10-2.

Second, and of more practical value, the tax saving generated for the father by the deduction can be compared with the mother's tax liability on the support payment and an overall combined tax saving can be determined. As suggested by the Finance Department (Wilson, 1991), if the father's tax saving exceeds the mother's tax liability there is a net tax saving which could promote higher payments. This analysis is provided in Table 10-3. The *Combined Tax Saving* column shows the net tax saving which could be used to make higher support payments. The non-custodial parent's tax saving and the custodial mother's tax liability were calculated by comparing each one's tax liability with and without the application of the deduction/inclusion provisions. In this way the tax effect of the support provision is isolated from other factors.

In Table 10-3 the greatest overall savings occur in examples 3 and 4 when there is a significant spread between the father and mother's income tax rates. These examples involve a father in the middle rate bracket (26%) paying support to a mother in the lowest bracket (17%). But even in these examples, the overall savings, $504 and $782 respectively, are modest. Examples 11 and 12, involving a father in the highest rate bracket (29%) paying to a mother in the lowest (17%), produced lower overall savings, $261 and $79, because the support payment moved the mother into the middle bracket (26%). In eight of the fourteen examples, the overall tax savings predicted by the Finance Department did not materialize.

Since family law practitioners are aware of the income tax consequences, it is sometimes argued that the support award must already include the mother's additional tax liability: that the original child support amount agreed upon has been increased, or "grossed-up," by the mother's additional taxes, that in effect she has already been indemnified. A critical perspective on this position is gained through the last two columns of Table 10-3,

Table 10-2:

Taxes Paid as a Family Compared with Taxes Paid when Living Apart

Family Number	Combined Taxes Paid if Living Together	Combined Taxes if Parents Are Living Apart			Difference: Living Together vs. Apart
		Non-Custodial Parent's Taxes	Custodial Parent's Taxes	Total	
1	$5,307	$2,241	$625	$2,866	$2,441
2	$5,478	$2,015	$783	$2,797	$2,681
3	$15,995	$10,232	$2,926	$13,158	$2,837
4	$15,263	$8,857	$2,550	$11,407	$3,865
5	$21,661	$10,607	$9,744	$20,351	$1,310
6	$22,602	$8,531	$12,761	$21,292	$1,310
7	$37,897	$23,778	$12,192	$35,970	$1,928
8	$38,191	$20,843	$20,843	$35,878	$2,313
9	$52,056	$23,658	$27,048	$50,705	$1,351
10	$52,349	$21,403	$29,595	$50,999	$1,351
11	$32,534	$25,006	$4,743	$29,749	$2,785
12	$32,827	$22,614	$6,675	$29,288	$3,539
13	$15,058	$4,706	$9,197	$13,903	$1,155
14	$13,021	$2,522	$9,089	$11,611	$1,409 ♦

comparing the support award with its value after taxes have been paid. Under the indemnification argument, the *After Tax Value of Support Payment* in the last column would correspond to the originally agreed upon child support award, and the *Child Support Payment* column would correspond to the "grossed-up" or tax-inclusive amount. Most of the after-tax support amounts in these examples would be relatively small considering the non-custodial father's income and the cost of raising children.

Whether custodial mothers are actually being fully indemnified for their tax liability, as suggested by some family lawyers, or whether the estimated income tax consequences are only loosely considered in the negotiated settlements or court orders, is quite speculative. In any event, the *Combined Tax Saving* in Table 10-3, indicates a small or non-existent overall tax saving is potentially available to parents living apart. The calculation necessary to arrive at the proper "grossed-up" support payment is complicated because the additional indemnification amount will itself be taxed and will effect the availability of the income tested tax credits. The effect on those who do not

Table 10-3:

Taxes Saved by the Non-Custodial Parent and the Taxes Paid by the Custodial Parent on the Support Payment

Family Number	Non-Custodial Parent's Taxes Saved	Custodial Parent's Taxes Paid	Combined Tax Saving	Child Support Payment	After Tax Value of Support Payment
1	$634	$634	0	$2,335	$1,702
2	$1,105	$1,103	$2	$4,073	$2,970
3	$1,791	$1,287	$504	$4,315	$3,028
4	$2,894	$2,112	$782	$6,974	$4,862
5	$1,980	$1,980	0	$4,772	$2,792
6	$3,177	$3,513	($336)	$7,656	$4,143
7	$2,935	$2,551	$384	$6,148	$3,597
8	$5,869	$5,658	$211	$12,296	$6,638
9	$2,476	$2,476	0	$5,186	$2,711
10	$4,730	$4,728	$2	$9,909	$5,181
11	$2,392	$2,131	$261	$5,011	$2,880
12	$4,784	$4,705	$79	$10,022	$5,318
13	$923	$1,191	($269)	$2,871	$1,680
14	$1,030	$1,764	($734)	$3,798	$2,034♦

have lawyers or accountants to assist them is significant. There is very little to be gained through the deduction/inclusion provision and considering the diminished after tax value of support payments, there is a lot to be lost by any custodial mother whose support payments are not properly "grossed-up."

Tax Equity or Father's Ability to Pay Tax

Giving recognition to the extra burden on a father paying child support in comparison to other persons with the same income but no child support obligation reflects tax equity considerations. The Finance Department's position appears sensible until it is put into the broader context of the small recognition of the cost of raising children given to other families, the current low level of child support payments, the relative recognition given to the custodial parent, and the relatively poorer standard of living experienced by custodial mothers and their children as compared to the non-custodial fathers. As well, providing non-custodial fathers with a tax deduction, rather

Table 10-4:

*Child Related Tax Recognition Given to Families Living Together Compared
with the Tax Recognition Given to Non-Custodial Parents*

Family Number	Non- Custodial Parent's Taxes Saved	Parents Living Together		
		Refundable Child Tax Credit	Non-Refundable Child Tax Credit	Total Family Tax Recognition
1	$634	$125	$107	$232
2	$1,105	$569	$213	$782
3	$1,791	$0	$107	$107
4	$2,894	$0	$213	$213
5	$1,980	$0	$107	$107
6	$3,177	$0	$213	$213
7	$2,935	$0	$107	$107
8	$5,869	$0	$213	$213
9	$2,476	$0	$107	$107
10	$4,730	$0	$213	$213
11	$2,392	$0	$107	$107
12	$4,784	$0	$213	$213
13	$923	$0	$107	$107
14	$1,030	$0	$213	$213♦

than a tax credit, introduces vertical equity issues between fathers in different
income tax brackets.

Equity comparisons are difficult and there can be disagreement as to the
appropriate comparators. Certainly, a father making child support payments
has more non-discretionary financial demands on his income than the single
man with the same income.[21] But, this is true for all parents when they are
compared to other persons without children. Horizontal equity between
parents and non-parents in the present tax system has diminished to an all
time low by the reduction in the value of the non-refundable tax credit, the
introduction of partial indexation, and the clawback of family allowances.
This is particularly true for parents with net family incomes outside the range
of the refundable child tax credit (approximately $37,000 for one child over

---

[21] Krever (1983: 694), discusses this point in the context of spousal support. He notes that although some
recognition may be appropriate, an "unlimited deduction" is not warranted because it overcompensates
the support payment relative to persons who have lost economic control over income for other reasons.
Further, to the extent that the payment represents an obligation based on consumption choices, total tax
relief is inappropriate.

Table 10-5:

Child Related Tax Recognition Given to Non-Custodial Parents Compared with the Tax Recognition Given to Custodial Parents

Family Number	Non-Custodial Parent's Taxes Saved	Custodial Parent's Child Related Tax Recognition			
		Taxes Paid on Child Support	Refundable Child Tax Credit	Non-Refundable Tax Credits	Custodial Parent's Total Tax Recognition
1	$634	$634	$585	$1,375	$1,327
2	$1,105	$1,103	$1,170	$1,482	$1,549
3	$1,791	$1,287	$527	$1,375	$616
4	$2,894	$2,112	$1,059	$1,482	$429
5	$1,980	$1,980	$0	$1,375	($605)
6	$3,177	$3,531	$0	$1,482	($2,031)
7	$2,935	$2,551	$0	$1,375	($1,176)
8	$5,869	$5,658	$0	$1,482	($4,176)
9	$2,476	$2,476	$0	$1,375	($1,100)
10	$4,730	$4,728	$0	$1,482	($3,246)
11	$2,392	$2,131	$313	$1,375	($443)
12	$4,784	$4,705	$627	$1,482	($2,596)
13	$923	$1,191	$0	$1,375	$184
14	$1,030	$1,764	$355	$1,482	$73♦

the age of seven, $40,329 for one child under age seven, and $51,828 with two children, one over seven and one under).

Table 10-4 compares the value of the child related tax recognition given to the fourteen hypothetical families prior to the parents' separation with the tax saving available to the non-custodial parent through the child support deduction. Table 10-5 compares the value of the child related tax recognition available to the custodial and non-custodial parents when they live apart. The last column in Table 10-5 calculates the total value of the custodial parent's child related tax recognition by adding her refundable child tax credit, equivalent to married tax credit and non-refundable dependent child tax credits and then reducing this total by the additional taxes she owes because she must include the support payment in her income. The fourth column of Table 10-5 combines the non-refundable dependent child tax credit and the equivalent to married tax credit. In both Tables 10-4 and 10–5, the credit values include the additional provincial tax savings.

Some preliminary observations are possible from these tables. Only in Table 10-5, examples 1 and 2, does the custodial parent receive greater tax recognition of the cost of raising the children than the non-custodial parent. This occurs in those examples because the custodial parents' incomes, including support, are below the income threshold for receiving the full refundable child tax credit. In all other examples the maximum recognition is given to the non-custodial fathers. Middle and high income custodial mothers effectively receive no recognition of the cost of raising children because of the taxes owed on the support payment. They bear the full tax cost of the father's support obligation and receive no recognition of their own separate monetary contribution. Yet, under the *Divorce Act*, both parents are assumed to make contributions based on their relative abilities to pay. In Table 10-4, families with two adults receive a tax saving of $107 for one child and $213 for two, as compared to the tax savings available to the non-custodial parent which ranged from $634 to $2,935 for one child and $1,030 to $5,869 for two children.[22]

These comparisons raise many questions.[23] What is the justification for providing a greater subsidy to fathers who are supporting children outside their household than to parents in a two-adult family? Because of the low level of support awards, the father making support payments is probably spending less on the children now than he was before the family unit broke up. But, the most important issue is the relative position of the custodial mother to the non-custodial father. Is the tax system delivering the appropriate tax relief to the group with the diminished ability to pay tax?

The hypothetical situations suggest that, except where the mother qualified for the full refundable child tax credit, the tax recognition given to the mother is considerably less than that given to the father. The more children she has, the greater the disparity. This is because the non-refundable child tax credit for each additional child is relatively small compared to the tax liability on the additional support received for her additional children. Also, the higher her employment income, the less tax recognition she gets

---

[22] In most of the hypothetical examples, the two-adult family had income outside the range of the refundable child tax credit. This is because the examples assume that the pre-separation family income was equal to the parent's combined post separation incomes. In fact, their incomes may have changed for any number of reasons, including the mothers entry into the work force. A more complete comparison of these two groups would look at a wider range of incomes for two-adult families.

[23] Although it would be interesting to compare the benefits available to different categories of lone parents, i.e. separated, widowed, never-married, it is not possible without further data. In this regard, it should be noted that although a widow must include as taxable income any federal or provincial survivor benefits she receives on her own behalf, the benefits her children receive under these same statutes are not taxable to her, nor do they effect her eligibility for the refundable child tax credit. They could impact on her eligibility for the full equivalent to married and dependant child tax credits which are reduced to the extent that the child's taxable income exceeds $500 and $2,500 respectively. The maximum Canada Pension Orphans Benefit payable to a child is $114.13 per month or $1,369 annually. The impact, if any, on the mother's non-refundable credit will be slight, unless the child has income from other sources. The current tax treatment of a child's survivor benefit could suggest an analogous treatment for child support payments.

Table 10-6:

Tax Consequences of the Custodial Parent's Remarriage

Family Number	Custodial Parent's Disposable Income after Separation	Custodial Parent's Disposable Income after Remarriage*	Decrease in Disposable Income
1	$17,397	$15,166	$2,231
2	$20,819	$18,130	$2,689
3	$23,449	$21,290	$2,159
4	$24,886	$22,140	$2,738
5	$32,220	$30,910	$1,310
6	$36,746	$35,436	$1,310
7	$35,678	$34,368	$1,310
8	$39,389	$38,080	$1,310
9	$53,011	$51,660	$1,351
10	$55,593	$54,236	$1,357
11	$25,921	$24,192	$1,730
12	$29,408	$27,472	$1,936
13	$31,456	$30,146	$1,310
14	$32,420	$30,755	$1,665

* The refundable child tax credit was calculated with the assumption that the custodial parent's new spouse's income equalled hers. ♦

because she will be outside the range of the refundable child tax credit. Providing the greatest subsidy to the father is a distortion of both vertical and horizontal equity given the disparity between men and women's earning potentials, the added childrearing responsibilities of the custodial mother and the known effect of the demands of single parenting on the mother's earning potential.[24]

A further problem is the effect of remarriage on the relative subsidy given to the custodial parent. The equivalent to married credit is no longer available. In most of the examples this credit provided the primary cushion for the additional tax liability owed on the support payments. As well, her refundable child tax credit will likely be significantly reduced since her new marriage partner's income will be included in her family income for purposes

---

[24] In *Brockie* v. *Brockie* (1987), 5 R.F.L.(3d) 440 at 447–448 (Man. Q.B.), *aff'd* (1987), 8 R.F.L. (3d) 302 (Man. C.A.), the court recognized the lifestyle burdens of being the custodial parent, including limitations with respect to accommodation, shift work, sickness, night courses, and career development opportunities.

Table 10-7:

*Effect of Support Deduction/Inclusion on Non-Custodial and
Custodial Parents' Disposable Income Expressed as the
Percentage Change Attributable to the Tax
Treatment of Support*

Family Number	Non-Custodial Parent's Percentage Increase in Disposable Income	Custodial Parent's Percentage Decrease in Disposable Income
1	4%	4%
2	8%	5%
3	6%	5%
4	11%	8%
5	7%	6%
6	12%	10%
7	6%	7%
8	13%	14%
9	5%	5%
10	11%	9%
11	5%	8%
12	11%	16%
13	4%	4%
14	7%	5%♦

of the income threshold. Table 10-6 illustrates the additional tax liability and the drop in disposable income experienced after remarriage.

Finally, Table 10-7 suggests that the Finance Department has not reviewed the vertical equity issues inherent in the present subsidy scheme. The first column in Table 10-7 indicates the percentage increase in the non-custodial father's disposable income attributed to the child support deduction. Because the subsidy is in the form of a deduction, high income earning fathers have the highest percentage increase in their disposable incomes. The upside-down nature and class bias of this aspect of the provisions has been noted by other writers (Krever, 1983: 694; Maloney, 1989: 209).

The Income Tax Act's Effects on Relative Standard of Living

There are generally more downward pressures on the custodial family's standard of living than on the non-custodial parent. Does the tax treatment of support contribute to the disparity in their living standards? Tables 10-7 and 10–8 provide a basis for answering this question.

Table 10-8:

The Effects of the Tax Treatment of Child Support on Relative Standards of Living

Family Number	Pre-Separation Family Income /LICO	Non-Custodial Parent's Disposable Income / LICO	Custodial Parent's Disposable Income / LICO	Non-Custodial Parent's Income / LICO Support Not Deducted	Custodial Parent's Income / LICO Support Untaxed
1	1.16	1.09	.90	1.04	.93
2	1.08	1.04	.85	.96	.90
3	2.00	2.26	1.21	2.12	1.28
4	1.65	2.11	1.02	1.84	1.11
5	2.43	2.30	1.66	2.15	1.77
6	2.13	2.08	1.50	1.83	1.65
7	3.21	3.59	1.84	3.36	1.97
8	2.75	3.34	1.61	2.89	1.85
9	3.92	3.58	2.74	3.39	2.87
10	3.35	3.39	2.28	3.03	2.47
11	2.84	3.69	1.34	3.51	1.45
12	2.43	3.49	1.20	3.12	1.40
13	2.05	1.62	1.62	1.55	1.69
14	1.59	1.15	1.33	1.08	1.40♦

Table 10-8 compares the relative standard of living of the non-custodial and custodial households to each other and to their standard of living when they lived together. The disposable income of each household was compared to the low income cut off line (LICO) for that household's size.[25]

For the purposes of this research, the low income cut off lines (LICOS) for urban cities with populations over 500,000 was used. LICOS are reported based on gross income levels for different size households without regard to the composition of the family. Because this research is comparing the net after tax income of different groups, for consistency it was decided to convert the LICOS from a gross income to a net after-tax amount. This was not done by the Massachussets child support project which compared child support guidelines based on net after tax income to U.S. LICOS based on gross income.

---

[25] This method of comparing post-separation standards of living was used in the development of Massachusetts' child support guidelines (Smith and Laramore, 1986).

Converting LICO incomes to after-tax incomes required making certain assumptions in the calculation of the LICOS for the two-adult family. The original LICO income level had to be apportioned between the adults. A 60:40 ratio was used, assuming both were in the paid work force. As a check on the validity of using an after-tax LICO, another version of Table 10-8 was calculated using the original LICO amounts. Although the specific ratios were different, the relative positions of the custodial and non-custodial parents were similar to those presented in Table 10-8. The first column of Table 10-8 is the ratio of the family's disposable after-tax income prior to separation. The second and third columns are the ratios of the non-custodial and custodial household's post-separation disposable incomes to the LICO for their respective family sizes. The custodial parent's disposable income is her income with support and less all taxes. The non-custodial parents' disposable income is his income less both taxes and his support payment.

The custodial parent's standard of living always declines relative to the family's former standard of living but, in some examples, the non-custodial parents' standard of living improves, even after taxes and support payments are taken into account. The primary reasons for the disparity in standard of living is unequal earning power and the relatively small child support payments. However, the fifth and sixth columns of Table 10-8 and Table 10-7 provide insight into the tax system's contribution to the disparity. Table 10-7 shows the percentage increase in the non-custodial parent's disposable income attributable to the child support deduction, while column 5 of Table 10-8 indicates what the father's standard of living relative to the LICO would be if child support was not deducted. In Table 10-7, the increase in his disposable income attributed to the child support deduction ranges from a modest 4% to a significant 13%. Likewise, Table 10-7 shows the percentage decrease for the custodial parent and Table 10-8, column 6, indicates how the mother's standard of living would increase if support was not taxable. The decrease in her disposable income attributable to the taxation of child support ranges from 4% to 16%.

Overall the research and analysis in this chapter supports a revamping of the income tax treatment of child support. There are, however, additional design problems with the present provisions.

Other Design Flaws in the Present Provisions

Limitations on Negotiating Tax Consequences

Although the *ITA* support provisions contain identical criteria for deduction and inclusion, they are not strictly speaking reciprocal. It is mandatory for the mother to include qualifying periodic payments in her income, regardless of whether the father chooses to deduct the payments. There is no flexibility under the *ITA* for the father to agree to forego the deduction in order to spare the mother from including the payments. The father can, of course, agree to pay the mother's tax liability on the support payment. However, the additional amount may itself be taxed as a periodic support payment. Sometimes tax indemnification clauses are used. This is an awkward solution since it necessitates an annual disclosure of the mother's private financial information to the father. In addition, the interpretation of indemnification clauses can be problematic.[26]

Gaps in the Relationships Covered

Not all parents living apart come within the statutory scheme. The following relationships are excluded:

(1) A step-parent supporting a step child may only deduct support payments made during separation, but not once the divorce is finalized.

(2) Parents who have never married, but who have either co-habited or are the common natural parents of a child, can come within the scheme, but only if they apply for court ordered support. Support arrangements contained in written agreements between unmarried parents do not qualify.[27]

(3) Payments made on behalf of an adopted child of unmarried parents will not qualify, regardless of whether there is court ordered support.[28]

(4) Payments made between same sex couples are expressly excluded.[29]

Lump Sum Payment of Arrears

Revenue Canada has a long-standing administrative practice of allowing a full deduction and requiring a full inclusion of lump sum payment of support arrears. This interpretation was upheld by the Federal Court of Appeal in *R. v. Sills*, [1985] 1 C.T.C. 49, 85 D.T.C. 5096 (appeal to S.C. dismissed on 26 May 1986) and has important practical and policy ramifications. The amount agreed upon would have been calculated to provide her with a sufficient amount to met her needs net of taxes, assuming that the mother, her attorney and the judge all understood the tax consequences of

---

26 See *Letchford* v. *Letchford* (27 April 1990), Lond 5245/90 (Ont. S.C.) where the court calculated the man's liability for his former wife's increased taxes on the basis that the support payments were her only source of income. Not surprising, under this interpretation no indemnification payment was required.

27 Unmarried mothers can obtain support for their children in any province or territory. However, only six provinces and the Yukon will order support on behalf of the unmarried person herself.

28 *ITA* ss. 56(1)(c.1)(iii)(B) and 60(c.1)(iii)(B) require the payor to be the "natural parent of the child."

29 *ITA* ss. 56(1)(c.1)(iii) and 60(c.1)(iii) specifically refer to "individuals of the opposite sex."

the support arrangement. Now, instead of the bargained for amount, she receives a lump sum in a different tax year, which could easily result in higher taxes and less after-tax support dollars. These unanticipated tax consequences are in addition to the hardship caused by non-payment of the support in the first place (Zweibel, 1986: E85–86).

Complexity

Several complicated sections were added in response to perceived gaps in coverage and to case law. Each new amendment added its own specific conditions and fine points for drafting agreements.[30] For example, since 1984, under *ITA* subsections 60.1(3) and 56.1(3), payments made prior to a judicial order or written agreement can be brought within the deduction/inclusion provisions if they are specifically designated as having been "paid and received pursuant to the order or agreement." The amendment was intended to remove a disincentive for the husband to voluntarily assist with support prior to formal legal action between the parties. Taking advantage of the provision requires specific wording and the deduction is restricted to voluntary payments made within a specified time limit.[31]

Expanding Support to Include Earmarked Funds

Income Tax Act subsections 60.1(2) and 56.1(2) expand support to include funds earmarked for specific items such as mortgage payments, medical, and educational expenses. This provision has a double edge. On the one hand it provides a potential bargaining tool to increase support. The father might now be persuaded to pay for these specific extras. However, the father might just as easily determine that he can afford to contribute a set amount of money for support and will now insist that he control how that money is spent. The section provides no guarantee that a basic amount of non-earmarked support will also be provided. It can become the father's means of asserting control over both the mother's decisions on expenditures and the child's activities, rather than a vehicle for increasing support.

---

[30] For instance, in *Gagnon* v. *R.*, [1986] 1 C.T.C. 410, 86 D.T.C. 6179, the Supreme Court's interpretation of "allowance" enlarged the availability of deductions for certain earmarked payments. It exposed some women who had received these payments on a non-taxed basis to new tax liability. *ITA* ss. 56.1(2) and 60.1(2), which had been enacted while *Gagnon* was pending, were arguably made partially ineffective. As a result, *ITA* s. 56(12), enacted in 1988, overrides *Gagnon* for both the payor and the recipient in post–1987 tax years. It also reinstates the pre-*Gagnon* standard of inclusion for recipients who would otherwise have been adversely affected by the case.

[31] Only payments made in the year in which the order or agreement is made or in the immediately preceding taxation year will qualify. There is thus a limit on deducting pre-agreement and pre-order voluntary payments, although in some circumstances up to 24 months of prior payments could be deducted. This would be the case if the parties separated in January 1990 and payments were made until an agreement was signed in December 1991.

Problems Related to the Deduction Provision and the Availability of Tax Credits in the Year of Separation

The distribution of child related tax credits in the year of separation is not always straightforward. Revenue Canada has a long standing policy of allowing the father to claim either the child support deduction or the dependency credits, whichever is most beneficial to him in the year of separation.[32] The custodial parent's eligibility for the refundable child tax credit will be affected if the non-custodial father opts for the dependent child tax credit.[33] Under paragraph 122.2(2)(b), his income will be automatically added to the custodial mother's income for purposes of calculating the refundable child tax credit. The mother may either completely loose or suffer a significant reduction in her refundable child tax credit for all her children, not just the child for whom the father claims the dependent child tax credit.

Proposed Federal Child Benefit

The February 25, 1992, Federal Budget announced the release of a Health and Welfare White Paper proposing a new child benefit system beginning in 1993. The proposed child benefit will replace the existing family allowance, dependent child tax credit, and refundable child tax credit with a single, non-taxable monthly child benefit payment. The maximum child benefit of $1,020 per child will diminish at the rate of 2.5% for one child and 5% for two or more children once family income exceeds $25,215. There will also be an earned income supplement. This component of the child benefit system is new. It would provide a maximum benefit of $500 per family for those families with earned income between $3,750 and $20,921. The earned income supplement will diminish at a rate of 10% as family income rises above $20,921 and will disappear completely once family income exceeds $25,215.

The effect of the proposed child benefit and earned income supplement varies with family, income size, and income source. Low income families qualifying for the earned income supplement will receive an increase under the new system. Some families will loose benefits because their incomes will be outside the range of eligibility for the new child benefit and they

---

[32] *See IT-118R3*, paragraph 20 and *Interpretation Bulletin 513: Personal Tax Credits* (3 February 1989), paragraph 11.

[33] The problem does not arise if there is only one child. The custodial parent is entitled to the equivalent to married tax credit for that child under *ITA* paragraph 118(1)(b). Once she claims the equivalent to married tax credit, *ITA* paragraph 56(7)(a) deems her to be the only supporting person for that year and, hence, she includes the entire family allowance in her taxable income. She is also the only person whose income is taken into account for purposes of calculating the refundable child tax credit.

Table 10-9:

Comparison of the Custodial Parent's Pre- and Post-Budget Disposable Income

Family Number	Pre-Budget Disposable Income	Post-Budget Disposable Income	Increase (Decrease)
1	$17,397	$17,992	$595
2	$20,819	$21,368	$549
3	$23,449	$23,617	$168
4	$24,886	$25,075	$189
5	$32,220	$32,564	$344
6	$36,746	$36,967	$221
7	$35,678	$35,874	$196
8	$39,389	$39,598	$208
9	$53,011	$53,011	$0
10	$55,593	$55,479	($114)
11	$25,921	$26,256	$334
12	$29,408	$29,673	$265
13	$31,456	$31,832	$377
14	$32,420	$32,685	$265♦

will no longer receive any income tax recognition of the cost of raising children through the dependent child tax credit.

These points are illustrated by Table 10-9 which compares the custodial mothers' disposable incomes under the present system with their disposable incomes if the child benefit and earned income supplement become effective. The child benefit and earned income supplement are in 1991 dollars. The increase in disposable income ranges from $0 to $595, with the largest increases going to custodial parents who qualify for the earned income supplement. Because child benefits will now be paid directly, outside of the tax system, the comparison between the non-custodial and custodial parent originally presented in Table 10-5 must be reoriented to compare the relative government support given to each parent both directly through monthly payments and indirectly through tax recognition. This analysis is presented in Table 10-10.

In Table 10-5, the custodial parent's child related tax recognition was greater than the non-custodial parent's only in examples 1 and 2. This remains the same in Table 10-10. In all the other examples, the father's child related tax saving exceeds the mother's benefits under both the existing tax system (Table 10-5) and the proposed child benefit system (Table 10-10). Under the proposed system non-custodial parents will still be favoured over

Table 10-10:

Child Related Tax Recognition Given to Non-Custodial Parents Compared with the Tax Recognition and Child Benefit Given to Custodial Parents under the White Paper on Child Benefits

Family Number	Non-Custodial Parent's Taxes Saved	Custodial Parent's Child Related Tax Recognition and Child Benefit				
		Taxes Paid on Child Support	Basic Child Benefit	Low Income Supplement on Earned Income	Equivalent to Married Tax Credit	Custodial Parent Total
1	$634	$634	$991	$486	$1,343	$2,219
2	$1,105	$1,103	$1,982	$441	$1,343	$2,694
3	$1,791	$1,208	$972	$0	$1,343	$1,139
4	$2,894	$1,963	$1,911	$0	$1,343	$1,324
5	$1,980	$1,980	$582	$0	$1,343	($22)
6	$3,177	$3,177	$807	$0	$1,343	($994)
7	$2,935	$2,551	$434	$0	$1,343	($741)
8	$5,869	$5,102	$561	$0	$1,343	($3,165)
9	$2,476	$2,476	$0	$0	$1,343	($1,100)
10	$4,730	$4,730	$0	$0	$1,343	($3,354)
11	$2,392	$1,822	$864	$0	$1,343	($49)
12	$4,784	$4,129	$1,478	$0	$1,343	($1,275)
13	$923	$1,191	$615	$0	$1,343	$799
14	$1,030	$1,576	$1,207	$0	$1,343	$1,007 ♦

custodial parents. But the degree of disparity will diminish slightly in most examples. The exception is example 10 where the disparity between the non-custodial father and custodial mother increases because her overall tax recognition is less under the proposed child benefit.

The 1992 Budget also proposes to broaden the definition of spouse to include common law spouses effective in 1993. The broader definition will apply for both income tax purposes and the calculation of family income for computing the proposed child benefit. One of the effects of this change is to decrease the custodial mother's child related benefits when she enters into a new relationship, regardless of whether her new partner has assumed any responsibility for her children. The "marriage penalty" illustrated in Table 10-4 will now apply to a broader set of living arrangements.

Social policy commentators are responding to the government's White Paper and the developing critique may influence the design or even the eventual implementation of the proposed child benefit system. However, assuming it is enacted, it would not change the basic conclusion in this chapter that the *Income Tax Act* treatment of child support payments inappropriately distributes the economic consequences of divorce and separation between parents.

Getting Unstuck: Designing a Better System

Current tax policy is based on outmoded concepts of incomes and inadequate recognition of the cost of raising children both generally and where children have roots in two households. Rather than fostering women's economic independence, when custodial mother's obtain middle and upper income earning jobs, they effectively receive no tax recognition of child-rearing costs. All women, but particularly those relying on the refundable child tax credit, are discouraged from remarrying. The inevitability that the 1987 bracket reduction would diminish the potential subsidy for parents living apart was not addressed. There is also discrimination against non-traditional households, both same sex couples and families where the step-father retains a commitment to his step-children after divorce.

Getting unstuck requires integrating what is known about the economic barriers for women generally, and single mothers in particular, into the policy formation process. Income tax reforms must be co-ordinated with reforms in the area of family law and with income support programs to ensure that any changes in these three areas actually advance the economic well-being of custodial parents and their children. Specific research testing new child support taxation models is required. Reforms are clearly necessary and they must not maintain the status quo of inadequate support for custodial families and disparity in living standards between custodial and non-custodial households.

This paper was supported by a grant from the Policy Research Centre on Children, Youth and Families. Richard Shillington, Tristat Resources, provided a valuable contribution to the analysis of the data from the Department of Justice, *Evaluation of the Divorce Act* (1990). Research assistance from Karen Cooper (LL.B. 1992) is gratefully acknowledged.

11

Family Law and Policy in Canada: Economic Implications for Single Custodial Mothers and Their Children

E. Diane Pask

amily law deals with legal relationships among individual family members. A discussion of family law policy in Canada implies that such an entity exists. It implies that there is a coherent consistent approach which informs the drafting of legislation affecting the relationships among family members, provides the judiciary with a basis for interpreting and applying legislation, and permits the impact of law to be monitored with respect to specific goals. In fact, there is no such policy in this sense. This has occurred, in part, because of jurisdictional divisions and judicial diversity. There has been a simplistic fragmentation of what are intertwined and complex issues. This chapter summarizes recent legal research on selected current issues in family law relevant to the economic circumstances of single custodial mothers and their children, together with limited reference to case law. Concerns about the economic future of single custodial mothers within Canada's aging population are raised. Proposals for reform of the law in this area form part of the concluding portion.

The Impact of Jurisdictional Divisions and Judicial Diversity on the Development of Family Law

Family law is an area of divided jurisdiction in Canada. First, legislative authority is divided between the federal and provincial governments: exclusive jurisdiction over divorce and essential capacity to marry falls into the federal sphere whereas the province has jurisdiction over property and civil rights, solemnization of marriage, and the administration of justice. In practice this has resulted in overlapping legislative jurisdiction, as for example, in the area of custody.[1] Second, judicial jurisdiction is divided.

Judges appointed pursuant to s.96 of the *Constitution Act*[2] have certain broad inherent powers which permit them to act without specific statutory authority whereas provincially appointed judges are confined to the provisions in the statute pursuant to which they act. These jurisdictional divisions form a structural impediment to the implementation of coherent consistent national family law policies since: (1) provincial legislative policies affecting families do not extend to the situation of divorce; (2) federal legislative policy applicable to divorce does not directly affect cohabiting couples and their children or married couples and their children where divorce is not in issue; and (3) legislation on subjects within provincial jurisdiction can vary greatly from province to province.

Intergovernmental agreement on principles to guide the overall development of legislation has been relatively rare. Further, there is little agreement among judges as to the meaning and application of statutory provisions. In family law, the facts of the case in question are crucial to the decision and the facts always differ in some respect from case to case. Further, relatively little precedential authority has developed because few clients can afford to appeal family law decisions. This means that most decisions are made on the basis of motions or at trial and are based primarily on the trial judges' perception of the facts. This results in a situation of uncertainty as to result, which is more conducive to dispute and litigation rather than to settlement since each spouse may be perceived to have some chance for success. Such litigation is largely limited only by the available finances, existing anger or bitterness, and by whatever client control is exercised by legal counsel. This process has an immediate impact on women. Women can be as bitter as men but they often lack the financial resources necessary to litigate; further, many women will give up everything else in order to retain a strong role in the parenting of their children. Physical or psychological abuse may result in an unwillingness to be self-assertive or to claim entitlements. These factors result in a power imbalance between the parties with women often at a disadvantage during the negotiations which restructure the legal obligations among family members.

Current Research on Child Support

The economic consequences of divorce or relationship breakdown are important issues for custodial mothers. Women received sole custody in over 70% of cases (Department of Justice, 1990: Table 4.18; Statistics Canada, 1990) and all or some portion of custody in 92% of cases (Statistics Canada, 1990). Since women earn 67% of the income of men in all occupational

---

[1] *Papp* v. *Papp* (1970), 8 D.L.R. (3d) 389 (Ont. C.A.).

[2] *Constitution Act, 1982*, being Schedule B of the *Canada Act, 1982* (U.K.), 1982, c. 11.

groups (Statistics Canada, 1992) this generally means that a formerly married or separated woman is supporting two or more people on a salary less than that which supports her former husband or cohabiter. A primary consequence of divorce or family break-up, besides emotional trauma and pain, is the development of a serious disparity in economic circumstances between the two units of the now divided family: men largely maintain the same standard of living as they had before the marriage whereas the women and children live in poverty (Eichler, 1990; Rogerson, 1991b).

The Weitzman study of California families found that one year after divorce the standard of living of the custodial parent and children had declined by an average of 73% while that of the non-custodial parent had gone up by 42% with an even greater disparity in upper income families (Weitzman, 1985). This study has not been replicated in Canada, but a recent national study of divorced persons reported average gross monthly incomes of $2,343.00 for men and $1,505.00 for women (Department of Justice, 1987). The average income of divorced women rises from 64% to 77% of the earnings of divorced men if maintenance is assumed to be paid. The proportion of men below the poverty line after paying support was 18% in 1986 and 16% in 1988 compared to the roughly two-thirds of women and children whose total income, including support, was below the 1988 poverty line (Department of Justice, 1990). Where support is excluded, for example, where it is not paid, approximately three-quarters of divorced women and children live below the poverty line (Department of Justice, 1990). If men were to uniformly pay one-third, instead of less than one-fifth, of their gross income as support, the percentage of women and children in poverty would be reduced from 58% to 26%. Non-custodial fathers would still have an average annual gross income, after paying support, of $8,000 above the poverty line (Department of Justice, 1990). That national study found that 71% of the divorced women always received the full amount of maintenance, whereas only 51% received it on time (Department of Justice, 1987). Some 36% of women reported irregular payment and over 20% received no payment or less than that ordered (Department of Justice, 1987). Another study concluded that more than half of support orders are never paid (McCall, Hornick, and Wallace, 1988). In a Winnipeg study, single custodial women reported a 41% drop in income after divorce while the single custodial males reported a drop of 26% (Steward and Steel, 1990). That study compared pre-and post-divorce incomes, assets and debts for 134 women and men having $40,000 to $49,000 pre-divorce median household incomes. That study found that single custodial women had the lowest gross household income of the groups compared (single or unmarried, custodial or non-custodial women or men) and experienced the greatest change and drop in income and assets. These studies are as close as any Canadian study has yet come to comparing post-divorce standards of living and provide evidence that support payments have a substantial impact on the poverty status of post-divorce women and children.

Principles Affecting Child Support Awards

The *Divorce Act, 1985*[3] (hereafter the *Divorce Act*) provides in ss. 15(8) that both parents have an equal responsibility toward their children and should contribute in accordance with their own means to the needs of the children. Ss.15(7) also requires that the costs of child raising be taken into account in making orders for spousal support in that such an order should apportion between the spouses any financial consequences arising from the care of any child of the marriage over and above amounts assessed as child support. The formula most frequently used for establishing child support has been stated in *Paras* v. *Paras*,[4] to, as far as possible, continue availability to the children of the same standard of living as that which they would have enjoyed had the family break-up not occurred. The necessary sum should be divided between the parents in proportion to their respective incomes and resources with payment to be made by the non-custodial parent, notwithstanding that some indirect benefit may accrue to the custodial parent. The possibility of such an indirect benefit should not be a reason for limiting the scale of children's maintenance. However, serious disparity of income and of standards of living between the custodial and non-custodial household has resulted (Rogerson, 1991b; Department of Justice, 1991). Rogerson concluded that the household of the single custodial mother (one adult and one or more children) has an income of between 40 to 80% of that of the non-custodial father (Rogerson, 1991b). Child support orders are irrelevant for some families because of payor poverty but there are many other families where resources exist but are not being shared. The failure to fairly share resources has been attributed to the method of determining and allocating the costs of child raising between parents (Department of Justice, 1991).

Quantum of Child Support

Canadian studies completed between 1980–1987 showed child support figures of between $50 to $145 per month per child (McCall and Pask, 1990). A national survey compared 1985–1986 child support awards with 1988 data and found that the average amount of total child support awarded per family was less in 1988 than in 1986 when adjusted for inflation (Department of Justice, 1990). Such awards have been strongly criticized as inadequate and as resulting from the failure by judges, lawyers, and parents to recognize

---

[3] *Divorce Act*, R.S.C. 1985, c. 3 (2nd Supp.).

[4] (1971), 2 R.F.L. 328 (Ont. C.A.) at 331–32.

the real costs of raising children and to confront the grossly unequal impact of this failure on custodial mothers. The Report of the Federal/Provincial/Territorial Family Law Committee contains the results of studies intended to determine average estimates of expenditures on children in Canada (Department of Justice, 1992). These estimates have been criticized as low (Advisory Council on the Status of Women, 1992). Studies estimating such expenditures have been used in the U.S. and in Australia to provide the basis for the development of child support guidelines. The 1991 Report of the Federal/Provincial/Territorial Family Law Committee has raised the question of the development of child support guidelines for Canada (Department of Justice, 1992). Some judges have taken the criticisms to heart and have taken steps to set out guidelines of their own. The case of *Kienitz* v. *Kienitz*,[5] stated that child support in the amount of at least $300 to $400 per month per child is the minimum necessary to meet the requirement that adequate provision must be made for children of the marriage.

There is a developing belief among lawyers that child support awards have risen substantially over the past few years and concern has been expressed that child support guidelines may be proposed for Canada which result in awards lower than those that are currently being obtained in many cases. This concern is based on questions about the data which may be used to underpin guidelines as well as on the methodology used to develop a guideline formula. The results of a study examining current levels of child support in six Canadian locations have not yet been released by the federal Department of Justice.

The Glass Ceiling and the Self-Support Reserve: Impact on Child Support

Under the present method of determining child support, the costs are purportedly accurately determined and divided between parents in proportion to their income. Two further difficulties exist even where this is done. First, a glass ceiling may be applied to costs even when they are accurately determined, and, second, the question of calculation of a self-support reserve for both parents and the impact of such a calculation on child support awards needs to be considered.

Glass ceiling is the term applied by Miriam Grassby, a Quebec lawyer, to the moment in an application for child support where the judge decides, after having applied the tax tables, that it is impossible for the wife to be required to pay as much tax as the tables indicate, that it really cannot cost that much to raise these children, or that the resulting order would be more than is generally ordered. "A glass ceiling glides invisibly into the courtroom" (Grassby, 1991b: 390) and the judge orders some lesser amount. Abella

---

[5] (1991), 79 Alta. L.R. (2d) 270 (Q.B.).

describes this ceiling as judicial protection of the non-custodial spouse (Abella, 1981). The refusal to recognize evidence of the real costs of raising children means that a disproportionate burden falls on the custodial parent by virtue of the fact that those costs are part of the implicit order made against the custodial parent. In other words, the custodial parent absorbs the difference (Pask and McCall, 1989). Grassby points out that the glass ceiling, combined with the failure to recognize that two orders for child support are always made has a long-term impact on the single custodial mother whose needs for current health care and future retirement security are not met (Grassby, 1991b).

The costs of raising children, assuming that they have been determined, may be divided between parents in proportion to their income. This approach is often applied without recognizing that a proportional share of the children's costs can have a disproportionate impact on the lower incomes of most women. This is because a greater proportion of a lower income goes for basic necessities than is the case when the same necessities are purchased by a higher income. One result is that often the custodial mother ends up devoting almost the entirety of her income to the children's needs whereas the non-custodial and more highly paid father is allowed funds for a vehicle, entertainment, and retirement security. This situation may leave the custodial mother with no ability to similarly provide for herself (Grassby, 1991b). Some judges are now considering whether parental income is sufficient to sustain the parent at a basic level before being required to contribute proportionally to the costs of raising children. Two recent Alberta cases, *Murray* v. *Murray* [6] and *Levesque* v. *Levesque*, [7] adopted a self-support reserve in the range of $1,000 to $1,500 per month. In *Levesque* the reserve amount was set with explicit reference to minimum wage levels:

> In determining the amount the father reasonably needs to live, I do not simply look at his budget and his monthly living costs. The budget in this case shows the father, if he were to continue his present pattern of spending, would not have sufficient monies left at the end of the month to pay the support ... the non-custodial parent spends all of his income and more on himself and then says he does not have enough left to pay child support. To allow that type of argument would be to allow parents to arrange their affairs to defeat their obligations to their children. Therefore, in determining what amount a parent should be entitled to retain before obligated to pay child support, one looks not at actual debts except those of equal priority to child support such as obligations to support other children of prior or current relationships. Absent such obligations of equal priority, the court should allow the parent to retain that which the government expects many Albertans to live on, the income slightly over that earned at current minimum wage levels and then award the sum over and above that to any child support up to the proper amount of the

---

[6] (June, 1991) Decision #4803–77799 (Alta. Q.B., Trussler J.).

[7] (December 10, 1991) Decision #4803–78496 (Alta. Q.B., Bielby J.).

award as calculated above (*Levesque* v. *Levesque* (1991) Alta. Q.B. decision #4803–78496, p.2).

Concerns have been raised about the impact of a self-support reserve applied equally to low-income parents, if costs are not fairly determined and shared. The use of an unequal self-support reserve is one means of ensuring that non-budgeted costs of raising children are recognized (Zweibel, 1992). The report of the Federal/Provincial/Territorial Family Law Committee applies an annual self-support reserve equal to the federal personal income tax exemption of $6,280 to the incomes of both parents (Department of Justice, 1992).

Impact of Multiple Families

The problems of inadequate levels and non-payment of child support are exacerbated by serial marriage and its concomitant financial obligations. This situation frequently arises when new obligations are used as the basis for an application to vary downward a previous support order. Most support orders are for child support; thus, such applications place the children of the first marriage or relationship in competition with the subsequent children or spouse. Historically, courts took the view that first-family obligations took clear precedence over subsequent familial obligations based on the public interest in encouraging responsibility for previous commitments.[8] Movement away from this position occurred throughout the 1960s and early 1970s. Courts increasingly noted that the second family was a factor to be considered and could warrant a reduction in a prior support order to enable the payor spouse (usually the father) to support a second wife or subsequent children or both.[9] The extreme result of this view is found in those cases that have denied any support to the first family on the ground that it is in the public interest that the second family be given every opportunity to succeed and prosper.[10]

Either extreme approach is unacceptable in law or in policy. It has been held that the *Divorce Act* requirement that a grant of divorce is contingent upon satisfactory child care arrangements constitutes a legislative preference for the first family.[11] But any priority either way could be construed as a denial of a child's right to equal protection under the law, pursuant to s.15(1) of the Charter of Rights and Freedoms *Charter of Rights and Freedoms.*[12]

---

[8] E.g., *Moody* v. *Moody* (1924), 34 B.C.R. 49 (B.C.S.C.); *Edwards* v. *Edwards*, [1938] 1 W.W.R. 880 (Alta. S.C.).

[9] E.g., *Kingborn* v. *Kingborn* (1960), 34 W.W.R. 123 (Sask. Q.B.); *Armich* v. *Armich* (1970), 3 R.F.L. 207 (B.C.C.A.); *McQuilkin* v. *Dawson* (1975), 62 D.L.R. (2d) 381 (Que. C.A.); *McKellar* v. *McKellar* (1972), 7 R.F.L. 207 (Ont. C.A.); *Oldborn* v. *King* (1986), 5 R.F.L. (3d) 220 (Man. C.A.).

[10] E.g., *Turner* v. *Turner* (1972), 8 R.F.L. 15 (Man. Q.B.).

[11] *Doole* v. *Doole* (1991), 32 R.F.L. (3d) 283 (Alta. Q.B.).

A policy which discriminated between children solely on the basis of birth order or which required a parent to see children, with whom that parent lives on a daily basis, in real need and to direct money away from them, notwithstanding irresponsibility on the part of the parent, is difficult to justify.

The question concerns the method whereby the children's interests will be balanced while parental responsibility and accountability are clearly maintained as values. Canadian judges and lawyers have been accused of gender bias in analyzing and comparing standards of living since caselaw shows that a higher standard of living is often seen as necessary for men as opposed to the lower standard which women may be judicially perceived to require (Grassby, 1991b: 370; Wachtel and Bustch, 1981). These are difficult cases with insufficient funds to go around. In essence, the court is asked to share the poverty or to divide a limited amount of freedom from stress. However, there is often little or no judicial discussion of the reality of the situation, of the impact of the order, or of the underlying complex issues involved.

Current Research on Spousal Support

The shift in philosophy regarding the basis of entitlement for spousal support is a move away from the factors of fault, sex, and the right to be supported and towards an emphasis on self-sufficiency, need, and equality (Davies, 1985). This shift, in the context of a high divorce rate, has been more extensive than law reformers contemplated, resulting in a narrow focus on self-sufficiency leading to a clean break between the spouses.[13] The language of the *Divorce Act* does not obviously lead to that narrow focus. The Act in ss. 15(5)(7) lists a number of factors to be taken into account in providing for spousal support and identifies four explicit objectives, only one of which relates to self-sufficiency. The Department of Justice recently examined whether and to what extent the *Divorce Act* in Canada had been full-time homemakers. The Department of Justice surveyed four cities (Department of Justice, 1987, 1990), surveyed lawyers, and requested a review of reported cases dealing with original spousal support applications or variation applications (Rogerson, 1991a, 1991b). Phase I of national survey collected data on 1,310 divorce cases in 1987 at St. John's, Montreal, Ottawa and Saskatoon and interviewed 617 divorced persons. Phase II reviewed 1,478 divorce files and interviewed 599 divorced or divorcing persons at the same sites in 1988. In Phase I, 58% of women had incomes below the poverty line for various family sizes. In Phase II, 46% of women interviewed had

---

[12] *Canadian Charter of Rights and Freedoms*, Part I of the *Constitution Act, 1982*, being Schedule B of the *Canada Act* 1982 (U.K.), 1982, c.11.

[13] See caselaw subsequent to the "trilogy": *Pelech* v. *Pelech* [1987] 1 S.C.R. 801; *Richardson* v. *Richardson* [1987] 1 S.C.R. 857; *Caron* v. *Caron* [1987] 1 S.C.R. 892.

total incomes below the poverty line whereas only 11% of men in Phase I and 13% of men in Phase II were found to have incomes below the poverty line for one-person households.

The case review and the Phase II study both concluded that women over fifty leaving very long traditional marriages were not being disentitled to support because of the objective of self-sufficiency, since courts have recognized the need for permanent support in those cases (Department of Justice, 1990; Rogerson, 1991a: 163). However, the level of support awarded is far too low and provided an income to former wives significantly lower than that of former husbands (Rogerson, 1991a: 163). Women in their thirties and forties, who had ceased or reduced their work force participation during the marriage and who undertake post-divorce custodial responsibilities suffer from the unrealistic application of the concept of self-sufficiency through the use of time-limited orders or, more frequently, orders terminating a previous indefinite order to support. Rogerson saw the real problem as being the meaning attached to the concept of self-sufficiency, which has been seen by some courts as full-time employment or $20,000 per year (Rogerson, 1991a: 164).

Use of minimal income levels may mean self-sufficiency from the standpoint of eligibility for social assistance but does not properly recognize the other objectives of spousal support. The economic advantages to husbands and the economic disadvantages to wives of having given priority to marriage and children rather than to paid employment is not recognized by these orders. The Rogerson study also found an emphasis on segregating spousal support from child support resulting in an indirect deprivation of children and a failure to recognize the indirect costs of child-raising to the custodial parent, through the limitation on that parent's income-earning capacity (Rogerson, 1991a: 160–165). The lack of clear, normative standards in the *Divorce Act*, and the lack of appellate decisions developing a precedential jurisprudence were responsible for the great diversity in approach and in quantum which has resulted (Rogerson, 1991a: 161). The responsibility of the Bar in the financial burdening of women is found, in part, in the many contracts negotiated for wives which Rogerson sees as even less generous than the courts (Rogerson, 1991a: 164).

A further problem has been a restrictive interpretation of the causal connection test, a test requiring that a causal connection be shown between the entitlement to support and the marriage itself. Restrictive interpretations have ignored the direct connection between the functions undertaken in the marriage and the lack of job skills, seniority, other employment related job finding, and keeping advantage or the lack of medical and sick leave health benefits that are often available as a benefit of employment. All of these employment-related benefits are lost when women leave or reduce labour force participation because of marriage and child raising (Pask and McCall,

1989). More recently, beginning in British Columbia, courts have accepted the view that a primary purpose of the law of spousal support is to redress economic disadvantage flowing from the marriage.[14] The Ontario Court of Appeal has concluded that Parliament, in setting out a variety of factors and conditions without priority, intended to recognize the diversity of marriages:

> The objective of self-sufficiency must be assessed in the context of the marriage, particularly in a marriage involving a long period of cohabitation. To do otherwise is to recognize inadequately the economic value of the functions of child care and household management and the economic disadvantages accruing as a result of a long-term absence from the work force. Defining self-sufficiency in the context of a wife's employment some 24 years before separation does not adequately recognize the economic advantages accruing to the husband. Nor does that approach adequately recognize the economic disadvantages accruing to a wife who has been substantially out of the work force while undertaking child care and household management responsibilities for an extended period (*Linton* v. *Linton* (1990) 30 R.F.L. (3d) 1 (Ont. C. A.) at 35).

Unfortunately the impact of many earlier cases is likely to be found in a developing population of divorced senior women living in poverty.

The Impact of Variation Orders

Recent research has related the contribution of low or non-existent spousal support and low levels of child support to the poverty stricken elder years of single custodial women (Grassby, 1991a, 1991b). This research concluded that the early years of a marriage are spending years in the sense that the children are young and costly, mortgage payments are high, and there is little money available. During the middle years costs go up but savings may start to develop through increased home equity and increased salary levels for those persons who have maintained full-time middle-class employment with increasing job skills. The main savings cycle, however, occurs in the later years when employment salaries are highest, the mortgage has been paid off, and teenagers are completing education. Where divorce intervenes, the single custodial mother never reaches a savings cycle because of inadequate spousal and child support together with an inability to acquire higher income through her own employment. Thus, no retirement savings are ever made (Grassby, 1991b).

This situation is compounded by applications to cancel or reduce spousal support that occur as the divorced population ages. We know that indefinite spousal support orders only exist with respect to women leaving long-term marriages who undertook traditional stay-at-home roles (Rogerson, 1991a; Department of Justice, 1990). Accordingly, applications to reduce or cancel

---

[14] *Story,* v. *Story* (1989), 23 R.F.L. (3d) 225 (B.C.C.A.) followed extensively; *Linton* v. *Linton* (1990), 30 R.F.L. (3d) 1 (Ont. C.A.).

support apply to women who have already established to their former spouse or a judge that they are unlikely to become self-supporting. Why then do courts grant these applications? The reasons may be a sympathy with the payor spouse who now has been paying spousal support for at least five to ten years or more and who is often not wealthy, the perception that the recipient spouse is a taker without recognizing that this spouse became dependent as a result of years of giving during a long-term marriage, the idea that employment outside the home is real work whereas work within the home is not, the view that the passage of time is itself a reason to reduce or cancel support, and because support is not to be a pension for life (Grassby, 1991b). As *Linton* v. *Linton*[15] points out, the choice by a couple to have one spouse not pursue his or her individual economic advancement has a major impact on that person's long-term financial situation. A fair and equitable application of the law will recognize and share that long-term effect between both parties (Grassby, 1991b: 22).

Moge v. Moge

The recent, unanimous, 78-page decision of the Supreme Court of Canada in *Moge* v. *Moge*[16] is expected to have a tremendous impact on the principles applied and the evidence accepted in future spousal support cases. The facts are as follows: The parties were married in Poland in the mid-50s and moved to Canada where the husband worked as a welder and the wife cared for the home and their three children by day and cleaned office by night. The parties separated and in 1974 the husband was ordered to pay $150 per month spousal and child support. This amount was continued upon divorce in 1980. In 1987 it was varied to $400 per month. In 1989, when the Manitoba Court of Queen's Bench terminated all support, she was earning $800 gross per month and he was earning $2,200 gross per month. He also had an RRSP, money in the bank, a car and a house. She had none of these economic security supports. The Court of Appeal reinstated $150 per month indefinite spousal support which decision was appealed.

The Supreme Court held that the trilogy, *supra*, was only to be applied to domestic agreements. The Court stated that the 1985 *Divorce Act* requires a fair and equitable distribution of resources to alleviate the economic consequences of divorce and recognizes the economic disadvantage suffered by women because of roles and functions undertaken during the marriage. The trial judge was wrong to have focused on self-sufficiency while failing to consider the disparity between the earning abilities of the parties and the fact that the wife was disadvantaged by the marriage. Five

---

15 *Supra,* note 15.

16 Unreported decision, file no. 21979, 17th December, 1992 (S.C.C.).

members of the Court said that expert evidence cannot reasonably be required of the parties in such cases but that the general economic impact of divorce on women should be amenable to judicial notice. Two of the judges also said that the causal connection between the economic disadvantage alleged and the marriage is a common-sense non-technical relationship which can be ascertained on the basis of the ordinary facts of a case.

The decision cites much of the previously-noted research in reaching these conclusions. It overturns the notion that all women can and should overcome the disabilities in obtaining and retaining employment arising from child birth, an unequal sharing of the obligations of childcare and home making, age and health. Further, the case may create rebuttable presumptions of economic disadvantage based on factual evidence of the particular roles and functions undertaken during the marriage and of a related disparity in earning abilities. *Moge* will go a long way to resolving the question of the principles applicable to issues of spousal support. However, it will have its greatest impact on the average party to divorce if it reduces the financial burden of adducing evidence in the ordinary case.

Property Division and Support

There has been little analysis of the extent to which there is consistency between jurisdictions as to the principles governing property division, their application, or how the legislation impacts on single custodial parents. The impact of the different definitions of divisible property, the criteria applied, and the results of the different methods of valuation, division, and distribution are not understood. Recent research is drawing connections between property division, support, and projected poverty for the aging group of single custodial women.

Retirement Security and Pension Division

The women whose marriages or cohabitational relationships have ended by divorce at forty to forty-five years of age or older are the most likely to encounter particularly difficult financial problems in old age. These women have forfeited job skills and career development in favour of child-rearing and homemaking. They will have no personal employment-based pension, either public or private, and little chance of acquiring one, and are likely to lose their right to any survivor's benefit arising under a pension plan of which their spouse is a member (Pask, 1989: 858).

Enforcement of division of pension benefits is a major problem under the authority of provincial matrimonial property statutes. The member of the pension plan in question does not always have sufficient other assets to satisfy the share of the pension to which the spouse is entitled after division. This is particularly likely where the marriage has been lengthy and pension benefits have been accumulating throughout the marriage. The only alternative is for the parties to share the pension when it matures and is paid.

The majority of Canadian provinces and the federal government have enacted legislation requiring plan administrators to divide the value of the pension benefit. The spouse is generally given some options as to the form in which to take the divided benefit; for example, by directing the fund into a Registered Retirement Savings Fund or by having a retirement annuity purchased with the amount of the benefit. This mechanism provides a means of division that separates the spousal interests and avoids the problems of enforcement.

These improvements are being accompanied by a substantial reduction in the value of the share assigned to the spouse. This occurs because the regulations provide that the value of the share is to be calculated by the termination method of valuation, under which the member is assumed to have terminated employment on the date of valuation of the pension benefit. The termination method of valuation does not operate fairly in regard to the defined benefit type of plan found among public employees, teachers, university professors, management, legislators and the judiciary. This benefit is defined by a formula which, most commonly, is based on the member's average salary over a specified number of his or her final or best earning years. These years usually are the years immediately prior to retirement. The formula, therefore, ensures that the member begins retirement with a pension which is level with inflation, since a certain component of most salary increases relates to inflation. This (or a hybrid of this type of plan) is the only type of plan providing protection from inflation in the plan or formula.

When the termination method of valuation is applied to this type of plan, value is calculated on the salary level the member is then receiving as if the member had terminated employment. Thus, the termination method of valuation makes no allowance for the protective aspect of the plan. In a plan of this type, the early years of employment and contribution establish the base upon which the ultimate value of the benefit rests. Courts ordering a distribution of the proceeds of the pension, if and when received, have often based the distribution on the actual salary at the time of retirement, rather than at the time of the breakdown of the marriage or of trial (Pask and Hass, 1990: chapters III and VII). Use of the termination method of valuation under the new legislative mechanism for dividing pensions will result in a much lower benefit being received by the spouse. This occurs because the benefit in a defined benefit plan increases sharply over the years immediately prior to retirement. An additional problem with the termination method of valuation is that there are different ways of calculating it. A number of Canadian cases have calculated termination value by deducting the value of certain benefits before calculating the shareable value of the pension benefit. This, again, results in a substantially lowered share of the value of the benefit being provided to the spouse. The member, however, retains for the benefit of his or her estate the value of the death benefit, enjoys the anti-inflationary effect of indexing and, upon retirement, receives the value of his share of the full benefit built up over the marriage. Improvements in the method of distribution between spouses of the divided pension may be accompanied by valuation methods that substantially reduce the amount of pension received by the spouse.

The Matrimonial Home

All provincial matrimonial property statutes now provide that the court may delay division and grant sole possession of the matrimonial home to a spouse after consideration of such factors as the means and needs of the spouses and the needs of the children. Only one study in Canada has examined the disposition of the matrimonial home. Steward and Steel (1990) studied Winnipeg families pre- and post-divorce who owned a home and who had at least one dependent child under eighteen years of age. That study focused on changes in housing and examined the pre- and post-divorce standards of living of the custodial and non-custodial parents. The marital home is one of the major assets that make up the standard of living. The median pre-divorce household income was $40,000 to $49,000 but after divorce, the women had a mean income of $33,000 and men had a mean income of $47,018. The study dealt with 134 persons (80 women, 54 men). The home was sold to third parties in 44% of cases, to the wife in 29% and to the husband in 21%. Possession of the home was granted to a spouse in only 6% of cases. Where the house was awarded or sold to a spouse, the spouse was the custodial parent in 81% of those cases (Steward and Steel, 1990: 1). The study found that 19% of non-custodial males obtained the home at time of divorce but that at the time of the survey only 9% of them were still living in the home. More single custodial women (40%) were still in the marital home than any other group. More single custodial women than men felt severely constrained in their choice of housing and 44% of the group of single custodial women said that custody affected their choice of home location. The monthly cost of housing was above 30% of income for 18% of single custodial women as compared to 9% of all men. Net income should not be the sole basis for calculating and comparing standards of living because of a need to take into account the direct and indirect costs of supporting children and the relative poverty of women (Steward and Steel, 1990: 104–105). Steward recommends legislative amendments to ensure that provision of a stable home environment is made a first priority in the division of matrimonial property to the extent necessary to keep custodial parent housing costs within 30% of income. The study is some confirmation of the view that possession of the matrimonial home is rarely provided and that most women and children must move after divorce. Questions concerning the long-term consequences of divorce on parents and children and, in particular, on the long-term ability of single custodial women to maintain a home environment for their children await further research.

Confusion Between Assets and Support

Property division payments carried out through instalment payments may be confused with support and subjected to downward variation or termination if their property asset division nature is not clear to the court. Assets of the parties are a factor to be considered in applications to cancel or reduce support. Courts often fail to recognize that a payor spouse may have apparently fewer assets than a recipient spouse because of a difference in spending habits. Divorced older women are often terrified of the possibility of cancellation of spousal support and deprive themselves while in receipt of support in order to prepare for disaster (Grassby, 1991a: 34). However, a view exists that support awards should not permit the recipient spouse to save. At the same time, many men feel that saving only subjects them to an application for payment of increased support (Grassby, 1991a). In light of an aging population, these issues need to be addressed with more sophistication based on knowledge of long-term economic needs.

Policy Issues and Approaches

Family law deals with rights and obligations as between partners to the former union. The argument is made that the majority of women and children or of single custodial women who live in poverty do so for reasons that cannot be remedied between the parties (Eichler, 1990). But is the fact that family law can affect relatively few people a reason not to enforce equal responsibility and accountability for the costs of child raising as between parents, not to recognize and enforce compensation for the economic disadvantages which accrue to individual women from child raising and homemaking, and not to ensure that individual women have access to retirement security equal to that of their former spouses where the pension was earned throughout the marriage? Is the alternative to concentrate societal resources on income security reform? Does family law reform interfere with that process? In fact, society is not about to jettison divorce, custody, support, and property division legislation. The answer to the challenge of the current inadequacy of income security policy is not to ignore or increase private law unfairness. Both areas involve elements of public policy and overall fairness requires that similar principles be applied in both areas. The independence and formal equality approach is rarely applicable at relationship breakdown because childraising and homemaking within marriage and cohabitational situations involve dependence and interdependence (Mossman and MacLean, 1986). It is necessary to take account of the actual economic circumstances of the parties and of the fact that former husbands and former wives are not, in actuality, similarly situated for family law to provide real and effective equality (Mossman and MacLean, 1986). In the *Andrews* case the majority of the Supreme Court of Canada held that whether a law violated s.15(1) depended on its impact not on its form.[17] A law which treated groups similarly might, in fact, have an unequal impact upon them. This decision was an important move away from the idea that equality means formal equality and suggested a willingness to look at how the law detracts from the real or actual equality of persons.[18]

Change in the area of income security may be unlikely to occur through the mechanism of *Charter* litigation (Hasson, 1989; Bakan, 1991). The *Charter* protects from state action. It does not require that the state act positively to remediate unequal social and economic relations. *Charter* litigation is extraordinarily costly and the judiciary is somewhat conservative with respect to issues of social struggle (Bakan, 1991). Therefore, efforts towards law reform must continue in both areas. The political will is at issue. Mobilization of political forces may currently appear unlikely but, nonetheless, may offer the greatest hope for overall social change.

A number of law reform proposals have been raised. These include ensuring that the care and support of children receives priority, the costs of child raising and the economic advantages and disadvantages flowing from the marriage or its breakdown are equally shared in light of the circumstances of the parents, and recognizing the need of each parent for adequate retirement security. Thus, let us presume that an entitlement to spousal support exists (unless it is shown otherwise) where children were born to the parties, where the spouse undertook a childrearing or homemaking role or both, or where the spouse changed employment because of the career changes of the other spouse. There is sufficient evidence as to the economic disadvantage accruing from those factors to justify such a presumption. Let us similarly presume that a spouse is not self-sufficient where that spouse is unable to provide for retirement security (based on a consideration of capacity, age, physical and mental health, the measures available, the length of time required and cost of the measures to become self-sufficient) and where the other spouse has the ability to provide retirement security. Any determination of self-sufficiency should at least include a consideration of the financial consequences arising from the care of children of the marriage

---

17 *Andrews* v. *Law Society of B.C.*, [1989] 1 S.C.R. 143 (S.C.C.).

18 As argued in the intervention of the Women's Legal Education and Action Fund in the appeal of *Moge* v. *Moge* (1990), 25 R.F.L. (3d) 396 (Man. C.A.), leave to appeal to S.C.C. granted 7th December 1990. 28 R.F.L. (3d) xxxiv; unreported decision, file no. 21979, 17th December 1992 (S.C.C.).

over and above the obligation apportioned as part of the direct costs of child raising and a consideration of the standard of living of the marriage.

Until such time as child support guidelines are developed which provide for a reasonable and adequate level of child support, a minimum level of child support payments in the amount of $300 to $400 per month per child should be presumed to be required unless the opposite is shown. The needs of a child for support are similarly presumed to require priority over any other debts. In calculating the costs of child raising, regard shall be had *inter alia* to the child's needs for housing, the child's needs for extra-curricular activities, and supervision outside of regular employment hours. The courts have long held that the child should be maintained at the standard of living of the unified family, insofar as this is possible: can we agree that the grave disparity in the standard of living between the two units of the divided family which presently exists in too many cases is presumed not to be in the child's interests? Finally, effective enforcement of support is essential. Society can no longer continue with a system in which the least financially-able parent bears the greatest share of the costs of divorce and the costs of child-raising.

12

Single Parenthood: Policy Apartheid in Canada

Susan A. McDaniel

What is known about single parent families in Canada? A great deal as is evident from the other chapters in this volume. The overwhelming majority of single parents (82.0% in the 1986 Census) are women, so it is single mothers that are important to policy. Single parents, both male and female, are known to be at greater financial risk than two-parent families, with single parents averaging an annual income of $21,321 in 1985, compared to $40,222 for two-parent families (Statistics Canada, 1989: 15). The risks of poverty are much higher for woman headed single parent families (57% in poverty in 1987) (National Council of Welfare, 1990:58) whose incomes average only $19,117, compared to $31,252 for man headed single parent families (Statistics Canada, 1989: 15). Single parenthood is increasing; from 1951 to 1986, the number of man headed single parent families increased 103%, woman headed, 180% (Statistics Canada, 1990:53). Many single mothers face economic and other struggles; some of the consequences are known for children (Dooley, 1991; Fuchs and Rechlis, 1992; United Nations Children's Fund, 1991), for women (Dooley, 1989; Grindstaff, 1988; National Council of Welfare, 1990; Status of Women Canada, 1985), and for society (Bassuk, 1991; McDaniel, 1990; Dooley, 1989 and 1991; Fuchs and Rechlis, 1992; United Nations Children's Fund, 1991; Grindstaff, 1988; National Council of Welfare, 1990; Status of Women Canada, 1985). A theoretical understanding is developing of the ways in which social policy and societal assumptions work through patriarchy and capitalism to shape the single mother family's experience, structure, opportunities, and disadvantages (Eichler, 1988; Fraser, 1987; Jones, Marsden and Tepperman, 1990; Pupo, 1988; Ursel, 1986).

But much remains to be known. The relation, for example, between the individual and the collective category of single mothers has not been much explored, with diversity and heterogeneity often hidden under the presumption of similarity. The actual experiences of single mothers, and notably their own voices and insights, are only beginning to be examined, in research like that of Clark (1992), McNaughton (1993), and Gorlick and Pomfret

(1993). Little is known about the current crisis in welfare state capitalism and how it affects single mothers as a group and shapes families and their experiences. There has been no exploration thus far of the consequences of population aging, and the greater embeddedness of women in generations, on single mothers. The remarkable recent growth in non-marital childbearing among women ages 30–39 (Statistics Canada, 1990) has not been adequately studied either theoretically or empirically.

Policy discussions regarding single parents often move to income maintenance issues. While the risk of poverty for single mothers with dependent children is high, attention devoted largely to the policy challenges of income maintenance for single mothers may have two unfortunate consequences. First, policy-makers and the public may become oblivious or impatient with the neediness of single mothers. Second, preoccupation with income maintenance might preclude attention to the many other policy considerations that impinge, directly and indirectly, on single mothers. This chapter provides a thematic look at the conundrum of social policies, broadly defined, that relate to single parents in Canada. The focus is on links, interconnections, and problems that might otherwise be invisible.

Single Mothers: The Fiscal Issue

Cost is the policy issue in Canada in the 1990s, cost to the society, to the public purse, and to future generations through the image of accumulating deficits. These images have come to form the guiding paradigm of public social policy since the mid–1980s. Although real and getting larger all the time, why the deficit has come to be seen as the ultimate evil, the threat to destroy us, the issue beside which all other problems shrink, is a political rather than an economic story. The deficit paradigm works for business and neo-conservative governments in bolstering public awareness of issues of costs. It convinces the public that spending in the public sector must be controlled and curtailed, not for any socially justifiable reason, but because of affordability. At first glance, affordability and debt are ideas to which the mythical everyperson can relate — we are taught that overspending for individuals is untenable in the long run. But what about indebtedness for mortgages, for Registered Retirement Savings Plans, for our children's educations? This sort of indebtedness is not perceived as bad. On the contrary, debt for some future gain is an indicator of postponed rewards and rational financial planning. Debt and interest on debt drive the economy. And why is deficit the problem, as opposed to poverty, homelessness, inadequate education for our children, or growing unemployment rates in Canada? The deficit has been sold to us as the number one public problem of the 1990s largely for ideological reasons.

What are the implications for single parents? The concepts of deficit and affordability, as ideological constructs, are used to justify cutbacks in income maintenance payments to single mothers with dependent children or to alter the eligibility requirements for social programs, including essential unemployment insurance benefits. The ideology of deficit, in conjunction with strongly held beliefs about public spending, have revealed some implicit aspects of policies on single parents. Three are immediately apparent. First, the family is essentially private and self-sufficient, i.e. not really entitled to state support, even in crisis. Second, gender differentials in the market economy are of little consequence to public policy on income maintenance. If these differences were accounted for, the enormous income gap between male headed and female headed single parent families would be smaller. Third, social policies on single parent families contain a large measure of moral reification, i.e. some kinds of families are really dispensable and not worthy of public support.

Research Focus and Remaining Questions

The intention here is to step behind research to look at the underlying conceptual frameworks that shape and guide the research questions and how they are asked. This will reveal some of what remains unanswered. Policy issues have a way of becoming policy problems because any policy discussion tends to be problem-oriented. The concept is of policy as ameliorative or as redistributive of some social resource (money, power, skills, etc.). Without a problem, there is no need for amelioration, no need for redistribution, and some might argue, no need for social policy. The difficulty with a problem approach to social policy is one of perspective. What is the problem of poverty to the rich may be the problem of riches to the poor.

Single parenthood, even without images of deficit, has been seen as a problem to society for some time. Single parenthood at the individual level is something to be avoided. It is seen as punishment for sin, a sign of moral character weakness, an indication of women's independence (seen as a negative attribute in this instance), or perhaps insufficient willingness to try to make marriages and relationships work. At the societal level, single parenthood is taken as an indicator of society in trouble, possibly dangerous for children (lack of male role models arguments), a reflection of gender roles changing (not necessarily for the better), and a drain on the public purse.

Single parenthood, viewed as a problem, is treated by social policy as solvable. Thus, social policy on single parents tends to be reinforcing of the incorrigible propositions of gender and family; the nuclear family is sacrosanct (despite mounting evidence to the contrary) and gender differentiation and heterosexuality are natural as well as essential to society. Social policy on single parents then is morally imperative, bolstering the privacy and supposed self-sufficiency of the nuclear family, premised on gender inequities. This interpretation fits well with the privatization of family troubles in the name of the deficit.

Social policy on single parents has several fundamental components. First, it is familized, in that single mothers are seen first and foremost as family members. Only rarely do men claim benefits on the basis of family status; instead, they more often make claims as individuals, such as for unemployment insurance. Social policy is categorizing single parents unequivocally as familial and is defining them, by default, as secondary wage earners who cannot receive benefits as individuals and so tumble into the family category. Second, social policy on single mothers creates dependency, both familial and economic. Mothers with dependent children who lack access to jobs with living equitable wages, to quality day-care programs, to educational opportunities — all of which act together for single mothers of every class to diminish life chances — are not autonomous human beings. Social policies at various levels construct single mothers as dependent. Labour market differentials are not considered a central part of the policy equation. Not surprisingly when research reports that women who have children early in life have the least life chances of all (Grindstaff, 1988). And third, social policy which translates experiences of single mothers into administrable categories of need misses the diversity of the realities single mothers face. This denies autonomy in that administrative creations become the means by which experiences are interpreted and acted on. "Facts are interpretations of reality which are real for the people in the situation, whether they are based on a wrong interpretation of the situation or not" (Brittan, 1973: 13). Few of these kinds of questions have been addressed, by research.

The issue and challenge of child care is illustrative of several dimensions of what research questions remain to be answered. Child care has been variously defined as a women's issue, a workplace challenge, and a family issue. The fundamental question of private versus public responsibility and entitlement is implicit, and sometimes explicit, in the debate about child care. That this question is very much gender-based has less often been explicitly acknowledged in all its ramifications. To the extent that child care is seen as a woman's responsibility, indeed a women's monopoly in that child care done for pay is also women's work, the incorrigible propositions of gender and family are maintained. This occurs in several ways. First, gender division of labour at home is mirrored in the workplace and used to justify paying women lower salaries than men. So, when marriages or "unions libres" (the French term for common-law unions) come apart, it is women who differentially face the brunt of inequities both at home, in child care responsibilities, and at work in their low earnings. Second, women are held accountable for childrearing in large measure in society, even as empirical studies reveal that many other forces impinge on children's lives as they mature. Mothers are often cited with contempt for their failures in the heightening of tensions between men and women illustrated by the Montreal massacre of 1989 and in numerous instances of child abuse and deviance. Whether these are real failures or, more likely women-blaming or blatant misogyny, is very important. But the fact of women's centrality in child care leaves women vulnerable to having the psychological fallout of identities gone awry linked to women's mothering. Some feminist psychoanalytic approaches have begun to consider these issues, but more could be done, especially in exploring at the macro level the implications for single mothers.

Social policy on single mothers builds on the contradictory notions of intentionality and victimization. The concept of intentionality relates to the idea that women are devious creatures who will stop at almost nothing to achieve their ends of lives of dependency, if not on a man, then on the public purse! A popular belief is that women lure men into situations, through either fantasy (the Thomas hearings) or diabolical manipulation (the Tyson trial), to block the man's ambition, gain access to his fortune, or simply to avenge some imagined or real injustices. Related is the notion that women, en masse, would deliberately use pregnancy as a means of obtaining welfare benefits. Intentionality is built into social policy on single mothers in the implicit, but sometimes explicit, assumption that single mothers are in need of support only until they locate another man on which they can become financially dependent. Intentionality is also assumed in today's prevalent idea of childbearing as choice — i.e., she had the choice to get pregnant or not, so she now must face the consequences of that choice. The rubric of choice can be illusory, particularly in light of gender structure and the non-choices it implies, not the least aspect of which would be difficult or non-existent access to abortion.

Victimization is the now stuffy idea that young women fall into difficult situations of unwanted pregnancy and abandonment in marriage as a result of their own inadequacies or those of the men they fall for. Missing in this quaint scenario, of course, is the all too real victimization that occurs to women when they are left with the responsibility for raising children on their own with limited child support from ex-partners, and with limited job prospects. The newer notion of empowering women with labels, such as survivor, although welcome in many ways, might diminish the dialectical relationship between socially structured opportunities and individual self-image. Can one be a survivor in psychological terms when one's job prospects remain so limited?

The tension between intentionality and victimization parallels the long established good girl/bad girl concept. The classical rational male or androcentric image of the man in charge is transposed to the woman in the case of intentionality. With the victimization lens, the single mother is stripped of all wilfulness and becomes the swooning maiden. The reality is somewhere in between, with both intentionality and victimization needing the intensive scrutiny of research. One way to approach this unanswered question would be to listen to single mother's voices on their own terms, to hear their perceptions as they see them, and their images of what social policy for them might be.

What seems most needed in policy research on single mothers is frames for the pictures. The pictures are clear enough: poverty, struggle, unlikelihood of recovering totally, tighter and tighter public purse strings, and tighter economic constraints with reduced employment and educational opportunities. What is needed is a framework that ties together the various ways in which social policy and structure work to create these pictures and leave them unaltered in essential terms for generations, despite the supposed changes society has experienced.

Moving Targets

Much of the background to social policy on single mothers is changing, and yet social policy and researchers act as if the picture were static. The image of the classical man as the guiding hand in the formulation of state policy is eroding slowly. In part, the extent and emotionality of the backlash of the 1990s against feminism, against welfare state policies of the past, and against public programs which essentially share wealth and resources more equitably might be measures of the insecurity of the classic man and his guiding hand. Victories are everywhere — in the growing public support among Canadians for aboriginal self-government, in the increasing likelihood that something of a social charter might be written into the new constitution of Canada, and in the increasing influence of Aboriginal and women's groups on the constitutional process. Father knows best as maker of social policy might be becoming something of the past.

And yet, there are new challenges quickly moving onto the horizon. Unemployment and the current economic crisis in Canada is one of the most powerful of the new moving targets (Smardon, 1991). Fine (1992) makes it clear that recession reconstructs families: women work while men look after the home and children, marriages fail more often, children are more often placed in foster care, violence against women and children increases. Unemployment might be the biggest threat to masculinity men face. Unemployment for men also calls into question the construction of the family as based on a breadwinner male and a dependent female (true whether or not the woman also works outside the home as well because of the differential earning power of men and women). It further calls into question the family as a private haven from work. The difficulties and enormous stresses families face in the current economic crisis allow social scientists a laboratory in which to examine the economic underpinnings of family life in Canada and to gain insights into what single mother families are in the larger picture of family and societal change.

Child poverty is another moving target, catching the attention of Parliamentarians of all parties in Canada and of the world through the United Nations report on children (United Nations, 1991). The House of Commons report on child poverty, tabled in December 1991, notes that child poverty is a "blight on society" (*Globe and Mail*, 16 December 1991: A18). Children, the report notes, are much more likely to live in poverty if they live in single parent woman headed families. And the report aims to eliminate child poverty in Canada by the turn of the century while vague on the essentials of how this might be done. It is not clear, whether there will be further initiatives on child poverty other than the 1992 Federal budget's child benefits proposal, intended to provide greater assistance to low income families. Whether it does this, in reality, is open to debate.

The United Nations report (1991) makes the compelling link of child poverty to gender inequities and uses the unequivocal term of "the apartheid of gender." Allocation of scarce resources, jobs, rights, property, health care, and so forth on the basis of gender is the undeniable cause of child poverty in the world, says the report, and the largest impediment to development. This seems to be an immense leap forward, shifting the paradigm from blaming women for having too many babies in many parts of the Third World to a contextual understanding of the interconnections between women's status and children's life chances. This, indeed, is a target which is moving rapidly and in the direction of improved understanding and more effective social policy development.

Population aging is another moving target with fundamental consequences for single mother families. Demographic changes over the past few decades have meant more generations in families (McDaniel, 1990; 1992a; Walker, 1991), greater proportions of our lives spent caring for older relatives (McDaniel, 1992a; 1992b), longer times spent as widows, and pensions that remain user-unfriendly to women for reasons that relate to women's job ghettoes with no benefits packages at all and to the privatization of pension responsibility and reform (Gee and McDaniel, 1991; National Council of Welfare, 1990). Family sizes have declined, resulting in fewer child-related responsibilities, but more generational responsibility falling to adult children who might be only children, or one of two. Family life today for Canadian women is a vastly different experience than it was one or two generations ago.

The implications of shifting demographic age structure for single mothers are many, all unexplored so far in research. The prospects for financial security in old age for women, who are barely scraping through raising children on their own today, are not bright. Women without partners remain normatively responsible as well for older relatives, including mothers, aunts, and sometimes former mothers-in-law. Walker (1991) found that women are the preferred helpers to older relatives. Women's imbeddedness in family does not decline with an increased divorce rate, or a lower birth rate, as some pundits might have us believe.

Caring is another moving target. For women, caring is something expected, something done for love rather than pay or extrinsic reward. Very little research has been done on caring and its central place in society (McDaniel 1990, Myles, 1991; Walker, 1991). Reitsma-Street (1991) reveals how caring and the societally reinforced compulsion to care constructs women's lives. Reitsma-Street looks at delinquent girls and how caring is policed into them by so-called caring professions and institutions such as the criminal justice system. She argues that girls, whether delinquent or not, are coerced into caring for others to the neglect of themselves, their future careers, and to bear the costs of caring with little complaint. The failure to care for others, according to Reitsma-Street, is the failure to be accepted as a good girl in our society. More research on these aspects of caring for women's lives, and in particular for single mothers, is needed.

Privatized caring, whether of dependent children or of older relatives, or indeed of bosses in the workplace, tends to make invisible the needs of both the cared for and the carer at the micro level. If caring is women's nature, women's reward for being good, and an intrinsic part of the gendered division of labour in the family as we construct it, then state policies will reflect this as a given. The consequence may be unintended, but it is to drive a wedge between the cared for and the carer. Women, particularly single mothers, cannot indefinitely bear the costs to themselves of having so much of the caring fall to them.

Changes are occurring at a faster pace than ever in the economy and in the ways in which family life is lived within the wider sweep of time. Social policy has been slow to reflect the new realities. Social research could beneficially examine some of the new trends and emergence of new collective understandings, and what implications these might have for understandings of single mothers in context.

Conclusion

The prevailing image today in Canada is one of retrenchment: job losses and plant closures, cuts to social programs, and talk about getting leaner and meaner. The direct and indirect consequences of this for single mothers are negative indeed. But there are other forces at work too — demographic changes, new political alliances, and perhaps most importantly, shifting conceptual frameworks and tools to enhance our understandings of single parenthood in both pictures and frames.

A few tendencies to be wary of include demographic determinism, substitution of the category for the individual, and emphasis on coping to the neglect of everything else. Demographic determinism is a growth industry in Canada — explaining everything from supposed lack of competitiveness, to women's demands for equal rights and opportunities, to problems with health care and pensions, to increasing numbers of single parents. The notion seems to be that social policy can only be reactive if any aspect of the cause of a phenomenon is demographic. An inertia, or perhaps cynical fatalism, runs through this kind of thinking. The substitution of the category for the person is similar. This is reinforced by administrative fiat, but the paradigm is used in other ways as well. The futility of giving a single mother a break in any way to enable her to get ahead because all single mothers are X, Y and Z, is but one example of using the category to the detriment of the individual. Coping takes various guises in today's era of retrenchment. The prevalent notion of belt-tightening is one form. The image is of people collectively cutting back on an extravagant lifestyle for the good of all. Those who belts are tightened most are forced to cope, without consent or recourse, and without the voice they require to articulate the other edge of coping or caring.

13

Canadian Public Policy Impacts: Summary, Policy Implications, and Research Agenda

Kim Clare and Robert Glossop

These chapters provide a thorough and often troubling portrait of the characteristics, circumstances, and needs of the steadily growing number of Canada's families comprised of unpartnered women and their dependent children. Time and again, thoughts are drawn to an acknowledgement of both the short and long term consequences of the poverty, financial insecurity, social isolation, vulnerability, and paucity of options and opportunities that characterize the lives of many unpartnered women and their sons and daughters.

The policy challenges are many and complex and cut across several domains of public policy including family law, income security, education and training, employment and labour, and housing. Yet, there is no explicit, coordinated, or coherent approach to family policy development in Canada. Families in general, and particularly lone parent families, do not escape the consequences of the often ill conceived and frequently conflicting aims embedded in the diverse range of public policies and programs that influence both directly and indirectly the formation and dissolution of families as well as their patterns of functioning. Nor are lone parent families sheltered from the fallout of the jurisdictional battles within which the kinds and levels of support provided by various levels of government are determined. Lone parent families, like many other families, tend to suffer when public policies are predicated on a stereotypical image or model of family life and, thereby, discriminate against those that do not fit the image. Too often, family relevant policies have been built upon a weak foundation of taken-for-granted assumptions about the structure of families, patterns of functioning, gender relations, and about the relationship between families and the state.

The Theme Papers

For Margrit Eichler, one structural variable distinguishes the lone parent family from all other forms of family, namely, one parent resides with dependent children. Beyond this single common aspect, however, there is tremendous and consequential variation among lone parent families that are created in different ways through the separation or divorce of a married couple, the dissolution of a common-law relationship involving children, the birth of a child to an unmarried woman, or the death of a spouse. Furthermore, the status of lone parent may be relatively permanent or impermanent. Great variations are experienced from lone parent family to lone parent family with respect to the social and economic consequences of their particular family status and circumstances. Eichler argues that policies to support the various forms and patterns of functioning within lone parent families must build consistently on policies in support of families in general.

Eichler proceeds to critically assess three implicit models of the family that have influenced the development of public policies. Different notions and assumptions about the relationships between men and women within families, about household and family membership, about the distribution of responsibilities and dependency, and about the role of the state and public authorities are embedded in what she characterizes as the patriarchal, individual responsibility, and social responsibility models of the family. Eichler contends that family policies predicated on the patriarchal model of the family have largely given way to policies and programs based on the assumption that individual men and women are equally responsible for their own economic and social well-being as well as that of their dependents. The challenge for family policy is to overcome the limitations and inequities that result from the model of individual responsibility by moving toward implementation of family policies that acknowledge that responsibility for the well-being of families and their members rests both with individuals and the larger society.

Susan A. McDaniel invites readers to assess the assumptions about families and about lone parent families that are built into the fabric of Canada's social policies. Single mothers are defined, above all else, by reference to their family role as mother. Accordingly, their role as principal wage-earner within a household is regarded as secondary. Not surprisingly, social policies directed specifically to single parents are often viewed as a form of public welfare involving income maintenance. Yet, other policies predicated on the notion of choice or on the assumption that family problems are private problems may be inconsistent with or contradictory to this assumption. Policies that respond to the lone parent family as nothing more than a problem in need of a solution can create dependency and constrict the human potential of single women and their children. McDaniel searches for an approach to policy for single parents as distinguished from policy on single parents. She identifies the consequences, both intended and unintended, of a broad range of government initiatives dealing with economic policies, workplace policies, child poverty initiatives, family-support policies and income security policies. Most of all, she calls for an approach to family policy development that listens to the voices of single mothers as they imagine what forms and types of public policy might best respond to their needs and aspirations.

Diane Pask and Ellen Zweibel each examine the impacts of particular public policies on custodial lone parents. Each study provides a concrete illustration of the problems that Eichler and McDaniel have warned of in their discussions of the principles and assumptions that have guided the formation of family policies in Canada. Pask draws attention to the fact that there is no consistent nor coherent body of public policy that guides the development of statutes and jurisprudence within family law. This becomes evident when consideration is given to such issues as the division of matrimonial property, spousal support, and child support which are too often treated in a fragmented fashion as distinct policy responses to distinct problems. She argues that topics that are distinct in law are, in fact, complexly interwoven in reality, intertwined and exercising considerable impact upon one another. She goes on to explore the long term consequences on women of episodes of lone parenting that increase the likelihood of poverty and financial insecurity for women, especially for those who have given priority to marriage and to child rearing rather than to paid employment. She notes that political forces must be marshalled to energize a movement towards the just and fair reform of both family law provisions and income security policies.

Ellen Zweibel examines Canada's income tax policies and calculates the differential impact on custodial and non-custodial parents of the way in which child support payments are treated as taxable income in the hands of the recipient and as a deduction for the non-custodial parent. The tax treatment of such support payments contributes to a significant disparity in the standard of living between the custodial parent's (usually the mother's) household and that of the non-custodial parent (usually the father's). Zweibel identifies other imperfections of the tax system that inhibit flexibility, discriminate against some types of families, and potentially increase the level of control that may be exercised by the non-custodial parent on the expenditure decisions of his former spouse. Like Pask, Zweibel's argument demonstrates that it is essential to assess the impact of any family policy provisions on the individual members of families and most especially on women and children.

Each of these papers reveal that public policies can be detrimental to the very group they are intended to serve. Challenges to be confronted in developing policies for the future are gender bias, inconsistencies and contradictions among policies, jurisdictional disputes, limitations of short-term solutions to immediate problems that can exacerbate the long-term risks encountered by lone parents and their children, and the competing and often contradictory demands of labour force participation and parenting.

A number of common themes, findings, and preoccupations are evident from these four research papers as well as the other papers in this volume. Research themes and policy issues relate to specific dimensions of family functioning including the material (or economic), nurturant (or care-giving) and educational (or socialization) roles carried out within lone parent families. These are roles or responsibilities assumed by lone parent families to the benefit of the individual members of the families and the larger society. Both Eichler and McDaniel pose questions about the assumptions and the philosophical and ideological foundations of both inquiry and intervention. These latter considerations may lead to a critical assessment of many of the fundamental principles that have guided and legitimated public policy responses to the circumstances, needs, problems, and potentials of families in general and of lone parent families in particular.

Policy Implications: Foundational Principles

Several foundational principles will lend coherence to public policies in support of families and might optimistically build the solidarity necessary to advance the interests of lone parents and their children.

(1) Public policy in Canada must be built upon a new balance in the distribution of private and public responsibilities, a proposition that challenges researchers and policy-makers alike to examine and to carry out research pertaining to the respective roles of the state, parents, and other kin in ensuring the well-being of families and their members.

(2) Public policies intended to influence the functioning of families may affect different members of families differently. To move toward a more equitable treatment of men and women will require more discriminating analyses of the differential impacts of real or proposed public policies on individuals.

(3) The emphasis on the heterogeneity of the population of lone parent families and of two-parent families as well, demands a greater degree of discrimination in the analysis of how different kinds of families are affected differently by public policies. Lone parent families, like families in general, are differentiated one from another by virtue of relationship histories, ages of members, heritage, structural and membership characteristics of the immediate family and kin networks, socio-economic status, geographical location, availability of resources, and patterns of family functioning and

distributions of household labour. While attending to the unique characteristics of the sub-groups, researchers and policy-makers must not lose sight of the strikingly apparent correlates of disadvantage that are all too commonly experienced by lone parents and their children.

(4) Vestiges of the image of the family as a static institutional foundation of social order must be discarded to build both research and policies on an appreciation of families as the embodiments of change — collections of interwoven biographies. This holds both conceptual and methodological consequences and implies the need to comprehend the evolution of family structures, family dynamics, and patterns of functioning over time.

(5) Detailed consideration of the interrelatedness of social and economic policies and the part they play in shaping the life chances and opportunities of lone parents and their children is necessary to better understand families as dynamic and active organisms. Appreciation of families in context calls for analyses of how the roles and experiences of men and women are moulded differently in both the public and private spheres of activity.

(6) The goal of coherence for both research endeavours and public policies will continue to be elusive until the definitional confusion that surrounds even official sources of data is resolved. Agreement should be secured on the age at which individuals are no longer characterized as children. More difficult will be coming to terms with when it is appropriate and when it is inappropriate to use the notion of family as a unit of analysis in research or as an administrative category.

(7) The metaphor of need and dependency that has guided much of the research and public policy with regard to lone parent families is profoundly limited, potentially dehumanizing, and ultimately counter-productive. The metaphor of social investment is preferred and calls upon researchers to more seriously probe questions about the potential of lone parents and their children.

Toward a Research Agenda

These principles will guide a search for alternative approaches to developing a coherent strategy of public investment oriented toward enhancing the well-being of lone parent families and their children. Topics for applied public policy research of both short-term and long-term significance can be classified into three high priority areas.

Public Policies and the Material, Financial and Economic Insecurity of Lone parent Families

The most pressing research topics within this category are those related to child and spousal support. Specific topics in need of exploration include:

- the nature of support orders and the factors associated with the determination of levels of support.

- models of private and public responsibility in response to the economic consequences of separation and divorce.

- the distribution of pension benefits and the tax treatment of corollary relief.

- gender bias as manifest in the administration of family law.

Specifically, pilot studies should be carried out with regard to alternative models for the determination and provision of child support before any one approach is implemented. The economic insecurity of lone parent families calls also for further examination of the consequences of labour market dynamics on lone parent families and, equally, of the consequences of family changes on labour markets and their evolution. Within this broad domain of research, there is a need for studies pertaining to the:

- determination of the wage-earning capacities of lone parents and an assessment of the potential to significantly enhance that capacity, a topic that requires, in turn, the examination of the impact of gender-based wage inequities on the economic circumstances of lone parent families.

- possible disincentives to education, training, and employment opportunities that may be built into the social assistance systems or expressed through inconsistencies between the objectives of social service and other government departments.

- the aspirations of lone parents and the relationship of those aspirations to such recent policy approaches as opportunity planning.

- apparent contradictions between the reproductive and productive roles and responsibilities of women with a view to understanding better the short-term and long-term costs of motherhood and the potential of policies for employees with family responsibilities to reduce the tension between these roles.

An aging society, in which the well-being and security of the older members of the population becomes a more visible policy objective, increases the importance of examining the consequences that episodes of lone parenting have on the long term financial security of women. Research must examine the potential limitations of short-term responses to immediate issues that may, in the long run, contribute to the creation of trajectories of long-term disadvantage.

Public Policies and the Nurturant and Care Provider Roles of Families and Family Members

Child care is identified as a crucial example of how public policies can supplement the capacities of families to carry out responsibilities on behalf of their members and the larger society. Child care is an essential step towards the realization of the broad societal objective of gender equity. The role of affordable, accessible, and high-quality child care as a key element in the creation of a structure of choice and opportunity for unpartnered mothers needs to be better understood.

Violence as perpetrated against women and children in families is the opposite of the nurturant role of families and often leads women and their children into their experiences as members of lone parent families. This suggests the need for inquiries into the part played by fathers in the creation of lone parent families and in the determination of the economic, social, and psychological consequences associated with this particular family structure. Other antecedents of family breakdown should be studied to explore options that might prevent family violence and family disruption.

Public Policies and the Educational and Socialization Roles of Families

Research with regard to the impact of public policies on the educational and socialization roles of families will include studies of the efficacy of supplementary educational programs for children-at-risk, parenting programs and, in recognition of the growing numbers of young never-married women who are raising children alone, sex education programs. There is a need to address through both research and programs the fact that lone parents lack sufficient information and knowledge about their rights, and the resources, programs and services available to them. There is insufficient Canadian data on the ethno-cultural differences among families and among lone parent families particularly.

Enhancing the Utility of Research

Finally, a number of suggestions are intended to enhance the utility of the research initiatives including:

- effort should be devoted to the development of user-friendly and accessible information-sharing strategies and tools.
- research reports need to be widely distributed to the public and policy makers and need to be presented in an understandable format.

- the general public needs to be more aware of the findings and conclusions drawn from the research about lone parent families.

- research and policy workshops are an effective first step in establishing an on-going process of information sharing and communication among the members of the research and policy communities.

- comparative research about the variety of public policy responses to the characteristics, circumstances, and needs of lone parents and their children is needed.

- inquiries into the various administrative options that can be employed by governments as they attempt to develop coherent approaches to family policy issues would be beneficial.

PART IV

SUPPORT NEEDS

14

Support Needs of the Canadian Single Parent Family

Susan M. Clark

This paper presents information from a recently completed study in Nova Scotia (Clark et al., 1991). The data are drawn from interviews with women who started motherhood as single parents and examines the consequences of single motherhood over a ten year period in comparison with a comparable group of married mothers. The study was initiated in order to gain a better understanding of the circumstances of unmarried mothers, particularly young or teenaged unmarried mothers (MacDonnell, 1981). A distinct shift occurred in the 1970s as the majority of mothers raised their children themselves rather than placing them for adoption. In Nova Scotia social service agencies were not organized to assist young unmarried mothers and their children. Anecdotal reports from medical and social service personnel questioned the capacity of young unmarried mothers to look after their children. This research was prompted, therefore, by concerns about the well-being of the children and the future of women who entered motherhood at a very early stage of their lives.

There were few Canadian studies of unmarried mothers in the 1970s (Statistics Canada, 1984). Findings from studies in the United States were not easily transferable to the Canadian situation (Furstenburg et al., 1987). Many United States' studies were based on small samples of unmarried mothers, often accessed through public health facilities, and frequently dealt with the most disadvantaged, urban minorities. Policy responses to these women would also be different given the way in which basic services are organized and accessed in the two countries. In addition, virtually all of the available studies reported only on unmarried mothers, which made it very difficult to know how different the needs and experiences of unmarried mothers were in comparison to their married counterparts. Consequently, the Nova Scotia study included unmarried mothers from urban and rural areas of the province as well as married mothers who were at the same stage in their lives with respect to entering motherhood. Thus, the study addresses the circumstances of Canadian unmarried mothers and does so in a more comprehensive manner than previous studies.

The mothers included in the study gave birth to their first child between July 1978 and February 1979. All unmarried mothers giving birth from July to November 1978 were asked to participate in the study. Proportional selection by county based on a ten year average of the number of births occurring in each county was used to secure a sample of married mothers. The married mothers' children were born between July 1978 and February 1979. The objective was to have an equal number of unmarried mothers, and the first interviews included 347 unmarried and 325 married mothers.

The mothers were interviewed three times in the first phase of the study — when the children were 3–6 weeks old, 9 months, and 18 months. Ten years later, mothers in the original study were again interviewed. The interviews focused on issues related to the economic and social well-being of the mothers as well as the well being of the children. Table 14-1 shows the response rates for each of the interviews. Analyses of the previous data on the mothers who could not be located for the fourth interview indicated that there were no significant differences between the mothers who were interviewed and those who were not. To facilitate the analysis and attempt to untangle the independent effects of age and marital status, an additional sample of 70 teenaged married women were added for the fourth interview as the number of women in this category in the original study had been very small. Most interviews were conducted in the mothers' home. For the fourth interview, however, a modified questionnaire was developed to allow phone interviews with mothers who had moved out of Nova Scotia.[1] Extensive psychological and educational assessments of their intellectual, social, and emotional development were compiled for 223 of the children. The tests used were the Wechsler Intelligence Scale for Children (WISC-R), the Peabody Picture Vocabulary Test-Revised, the Basic Achievement Skills Individual Screener, the Beery Visual Motor Integration Test, and the Piers-Harris Self Concept Scale. Teachers and mothers of the children also completed the Achenbach Behaviour Rating Profile which assesses the children's behaviour in the areas of social withdrawal, activity, and aggression. The assessments were conducted by psychometrists under the direction of a psychologist and were conducted in the schools attended by the children once the mothers and children had agreed to participate. These data were supplemented by an analysis of hospital records at the regional children's hospital in order to learn more about the circumstances of the children who had received some form of hospital care.

---

[1] The interview schedules for each set of interviews are available from the Nova Scotia Department of Community Services.

Table 14-1:

Response Rates for Each Data Collection

	Original Sample Size	*No. of Participants First Data Collection 3 to 6 Weeks*	*No. of Participants Second Data Collection / 9 Months (Percentage of Original Respondents)*
Married	403	325	308 (95%)
Unmarried	416	347	327 (94%)
Total	819	672	635 (94%)
		No. of Participants Third Data Collection 18 Months (Percentage of Original Respondents)	*No. of Original Participants Fourth Data Collection 9 to 10 Years (Percentage of Original Respondents)*
Married		295 (91%)	274 (84%)
Unmarried		299 (86%)	215 (62%)
Total		594 (88%)	489 (73%)
Additional sample			70
Total interviewed			559

Source: Mothers and Children, p.15.♦

This study permits an analysis of the needs of women who are single parents because they have chosen to keep a child born outside of marriage rather than single parents whose status results from the dissolution of a marriage. Comparisons between unmarried and married mothers also allows a study of how the needs of unmarried mothers may be different from the needs of any mother with young children. Further, the study permits comparisons between teenaged or young unmarried or married mothers and older unmarried and married mothers, i.e. those who were at least twenty years old when their first child was born.

Economic Support

Being an unmarried mother has discernable economic and social consequences ten years after the birth of the child. Comparisons on a number of economic indicators are presented in Table 14-2.

Differences occur despite the fact that 81% of the unmarried mothers do marry (87% of younger unmarried mothers, 69% of older unmarried mothers). While having a child prior to marriage does not effect the chances for marriage for the great majority of the young unmarried mothers, the old unmarried mothers are considerably less likely to marry. The disadvantaged position of this latter group will be apparent on a number of occasions. The

Table 14-2:

Economic Indicators by Age and Marital Status at First Birth

	Younger Unmarried Mothers	Older Unmarried Mothers	Younger Married Mothers	Older Married Mothers
1. Percent living below Statistics Canada's low income cutoffs (1988)	52%	54%	29%	16%
2. Average monthly income (1987)	$1,948	$2,011	$2,327	$3,184
3. Percent of income spent on housing	33%	34%	24%	11%
4. Dependence on social assistance: - percent received - average duration	69% 38 months	58% 48 months	43% 18 months	10% 26 months♦

overall poverty rate of 32.8 % for the respondents was more than double the provincial poverty rate of 14.5% and the national rate of 12.3%. The unmarried mothers were considerably more likely to be living below the Statistics Canada low income cut-offs in 1988 than the married mothers. But, it should be noted that even the older married mothers, the most advantaged group in the study, had a poverty rate in excess of the provincial average. The difficult economic circumstances of many families with young children, irrespective of the marital status of the parents, are confirmed by such figures. Average monthly incomes for each group of mothers in 1987 varied from $1,948 for the younger unmarried mother to $3,184 for the older married mother. In addition young mothers and unmarried mothers had high levels of dependence on social assistance programs as a source of income. With respect to housing, a third of the unmarried mothers spent more than 30% of their income on housing. These indicators of the mothers' economic situation show the very straightened circumstances in which many families cope and reinforce the very real need for greater financial assistance to families (MacKay, 1983; Moore, 1987; Pool and Moore, 1986, Trussell, 1976).

The study allowed for exploration of reasons for the low economic status of many of the families. The economic circumstances of the unmarried mothers are related to relatively low levels of education and limited opportunities for employment (MacKay, 1983). The younger unmarried mothers had the lowest educational attainment of all the mothers in 1978; some were still in school but, despite their best intentions, many were unable to continue school because of the competing demands on their time. The 1988 results are despite the fact that 54% of the unmarried mothers and 32%

Table 14-3:

Percentage of Mothers with Completed High School by Age and Marital Status at First Birth

	1978	*1988*
Young unmarried mothers	11%	34%
Old unmarried mothers	34%	44%
Young married mothers	24%	41%
Old married mothers	70%	78% ♦

of the married mothers indicated immediately after child birth that they intended to continue their education; further, 50% of the unmarried mothers and 27% of the married mothers had participated in some type of training or educational program by the time their first child was 10 years old. Despite the good intentions, and some action, the overall educational level of the younger mothers (married and unmarried) and older unmarried mothers is very low (see Table 14-3). Whether a mother planned to continue her education depended on whether she was in school at the time she became pregnant and her age. Mothers who had left school prior to becoming pregnant were less likely to consider continuing their education than mothers still in the educational system. The older a woman was when she gave birth, the higher the probability that she would not consider further education. Women who planned their pregnancies were also less likely to consider going back to school. Younger women appear more receptive to pursuing an education particularly if they are in school when they become pregnant. While many do so, their level of achievement is still low and has significant consequences for their participation in the work force.

The discrepancy between the labour force participation rates of the married and unmarried mothers decreased over time. In 1978, 34% of the unmarried mothers and 71% of the married mothers were in the work force but, by 1988, 50% of the unmarried mothers and 62% of the married mothers were in paid employment. This is to be expected as the very young mothers leave the educational system and become eligible to enter the work force. Although a smaller percentage of the unmarried than married mothers were employed, those who did work had very similar time in the labour force. Unmarried mothers who had held a job averaged 5 years and 2 months in the work force and married mothers averaged 5 years and 7 months. Involuntary unemployment was more characteristic of the unmarried mothers and the young mothers. Only 17% of the old married mothers had experienced involuntary unemployment between 1978–88. By comparison, 40% of the young married mothers had done so, 36% of the young unmarried mothers, and 46% of the old unmarried mothers.

Table 14-4:

Percentage of Mothers in the Labour Force by Marital Status at First Birth

	Unmarried Mothers	Married Mothers
1978	34%	71%
1988	50%	62%♦

Information from the mothers' employment history indicates that unmarried mothers experienced substantially more employment-related problems than the married mothers. Mothers most frequently report difficulties with combining a job with child rearing responsibilities, difficulty finding someone to look after the children, unavailability of jobs, and the expense of child care. Unmarried mothers are more likely to experience these disadvantages than married mothers (with the exception of combining paid work with child rearing) and the differences are particularly noticeable for mothers who report that they need more education or more work experience. Age and marital status have independent effects with respect to education and work experience resulting in the younger unmarried mothers seeing themselves as the least prepared for employment. Unmarried mothers are also more likely to live in communities where jobs are scarce and transportation difficult. Scarcity of jobs is particularly noticeable for the older women since 58% of the older unmarried mothers report this difficulty compared to 37% of the older married mothers. In addition, unmarried mothers report more concern about losing other forms of support such as social assistance and child support. Unmarried mothers are more dependent on sources of income other than wages; thus, the loss of this income has to be carefully weighed against the wages and other benefits of working.

Factors such as educational attainment and availability of jobs explain in part the different types of work undertaken by the mothers and the resulting differences in salary levels. A dual labour market approach was used to classify the occupations the mothers held as primary or secondary sector jobs (Piore, 1971). The disadvantage of the younger mothers and the older unmarried mothers compared to the older married mothers is striking. Considering just the last position held by those mothers who had been in the labour force, 60% of young unmarried and young married mothers held secondary sector jobs and 46% of the older unmarried mothers. These figures contrast with those of the older married mothers where 24% of them held secondary sector jobs. Not surprisingly, the job sector relates to wages. For the last job held, only 7% of the unmarried mothers earned $12.50 or more an hour compared with 39% of the married mothers; 46% of the unmarried

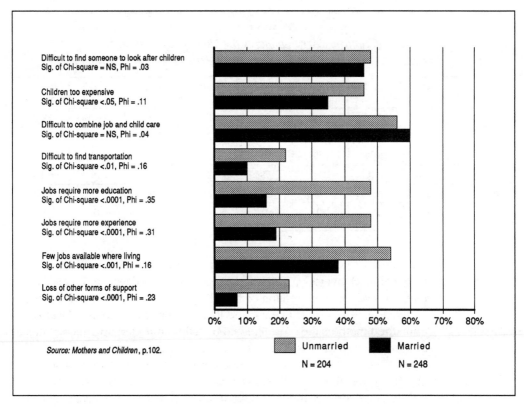

Figure 14-1:

Percentage of Mothers Who Experience Various Obstacles to Employment after Childbirth by Marital Status

mothers and 22% of the married mothers earned less than $6.50 an hour in 1988.

Housing

Securing adequate housing is a primary concern for low income families (Klodawsky et al., 1983; Klodawsky et al., 1985). In general, unmarried mothers are more likely than married mothers to rent urban apartments, spend a larger proportion of their income on housing-related expenses, share their accommodations with individuals outside the nuclear family, be dissatisfied with their housing, and move frequently.

Table 14-5 indicates that unmarried mothers have more variation in their housing arrangements than married mothers. Unmarried mothers increased their home ownership from virtually zero to 47% between 1978 and 1988, but this is still considerably less than the 87% home ownership figure for

Table 14-5:

*Types of Tenancy Arrangements for Mothers by Age and
Marital Status at First Birth*

	Younger Unmarried Mothers		Older Unmarried Mothers		Younger Married Mothers		Older Married Mothers	
	1978	1988	1978	1988	1978	1988	1978	1988
Own	1%	48%	9%	44%	27%	77%	60%	87%
Rent	22.8%	46%	35%	48%	39%	23%	34%	10%
Board	18.8%	4%	24%	7%	22%	0	2%	1%
Free	57.1%	2%	32%	1%	12%	0	4%	1%
Other	0	1%	0	0	0	0	0	1%♦

the married mothers and for Canadians (62.4%) and Nova Scotians (71.8%) in general. Conversely, 51% of the unmarried mothers and 12% of the married mothers were renting or boarding in 1988. By 1988, older married mothers were the most likely to be living in private residences and older unmarried mothers the most likely to be living in rented apartments. Rental accommodation increases the range of difficulties that mothers may experience. While 67% of unmarried mothers indicated that their housing had improved over the 10-year period, the unmarried mothers were slightly less satisfied than their married counterparts. The mothers who were dissatisfied (10%) had strong complaints, the most frequent being the small size of the accommodation and unsatisfactory neighbourhoods. Other problems were lack of basic amenities, lack of control over heating, dissatisfaction with lessors, rundown conditions, and inconvenient locations. Mothers reported being unable to find better accommodation because of lack of money. An interesting sidelight with regard to housing satisfaction relates to mothers on social assistance and those with the same level of income but not on assistance. For this latter group, satisfaction is considerably higher because they do not see themselves as constrained in their housing choices as mothers on social assistance.

Low incomes, unsuitable living arrangements and changing relationships come together to promote a high degree of mobility for unmarried mothers. Only 10% of the unmarried mothers, compared with 29% of the married mothers, remained at the same location between 1978 and 1988. Forty-eight percent of the unmarried mothers but only 15% of the married mothers moved more than three times. On average, the unmarried mothers moved 3.7 times in ten years and the married mothers 1.7 times.

Caring for the Children

Mothers in this study report difficulties in finding affordable, quality child care (Johnson and Dineen, 1981; Lero, 1985). The importance of family support is very striking in the total care given to children. Husbands and relatives constitute the major source of help with the children. Over the ten years, about 70% of the mothers received help from husbands, 14% from relatives, 13% from child care facilities, friends, or babysitters, and 3% from the child's father (not married) in each of the three stages of childhood — 0–2 years, 2 to starting school, and starting school to 10 years. This level of family support highlights the difficulties of women who are not married and who do not have relatives to assist. Assistance from relatives very rarely involves payment whereas depending on friends, baby sitters, or child care arrangements nearly always has a financial cost. Assistance from the family seems particularly important when the child is young as most mothers do not use babysitters for very young children both because of the costs associated with babysitters as well as the idea that one should not leave the care of a very young child to anyone but family. Use of babysitters increased from 43% to 59% to 74% over the three stages of the child's development.

Mothers also report greater assistance with caring for children as the child grows up. For instance, 72% of the mothers reported during the first interview that they were the sole caretaker of their child. Even many women who were married did not consider their husbands as partners in this early stage. Fifty seven percent of the mothers reported they were the sole caretaker in the second and third interviews and this figure reduced to 17% by the fourth survey. In 1988, the ten year follow-up, 19% of the younger unmarried mothers, 38% of the older unmarried mothers, 21% of the younger married mothers, and 9% of the older married mothers reported that they were the sole caretakers for their child. The networks of assistance do not appear to be extensive. For instance, 41% of the mothers indicated that they had only one person they could call on for assistance over an extended period of time, while 30% had only one person for assistance of a few hours. The most frequently mentioned source of assistance was the husband; a fact that again points to the difficulty for single mothers.

The nature and quality of the mother-child interactions was taken up in this study. Factor analysis of 70 items identified six factors — encouragement of the child's self-responsibility, consistency of the mother's actions, control of the child's inappropriate behaviour, caring, and reinforcing appropriate behaviour. There were very few differences by age and marital status in the ways in which mothers interacted with their children. Differences that were observed typically occurred between the older mothers. For instance, more older unmarried mothers reported controlling their children through guilt and through withdrawal of contact, being less consistent in their dealings with the children, and they appear less encouraging with respect to the child's sense of responsibility. They stand out from both the married older mothers on these items and from the younger mothers. Overall the results suggest that the children are experiencing a caring home environment but effective and consistent discipline techniques are less evident for all mothers.

The older unmarried mothers are the most disadvantaged with respect to social support. This is illustrated by the fact that 38% of them indicated they were the sole caregiver of their child in 1988. Relative isolation is also seen with respect to the mothers' reports of loneliness. Between 26 and 31% of the younger and older married mothers indicate they are never lonely but only 19% of the older unmarried mothers describe themselves this way. Only a minority of the mothers are involved in activities outside the home with the exception of belonging to a church. The older married mothers are the most active group. Mothers indicate that making arrangements for the children to be looked after is a difficult task and one that hampers participation in activities outside the home. About 45% of each group of mothers reported this difficulty. For unmarried mothers, a lack of money for outside activities is also problematic. Twenty-one percent of married mothers report this difficulty compared to 38% of younger unmarried mothers and 42% of older unmarried mothers.

Children's Health

The relative lack of assistance with the children can also be inferred from the hospital data on the children that is presented in Table 14-6. While the reasons for emergency visits to the children's hospital did not vary significantly, for instance the majority were in the not very severe category, the average number of visits did vary. Children of unmarried mothers average more emergency hospital visits than those of married mothers. This may be indicative of a trend to use the hospital services because the mothers do not have alternative health care arrangements. With respect to hospital admissions, the children of unmarried mothers were more likely to be diagnosed as having moderately severe diagnoses than the children of the married mothers. For these latter children, the diagnoses were less severe. Children of the unmarried mothers also averaged longer stays. In addition to severity of the illnesses there is some indication that children remained in hospital longer for social reasons. Unmarried mothers had more difficulties in making arrangements to care for the children once they were released from hospital and hospital authorities were looking to ensure the children were well on the way to being fully recovered before discharging them. The children in this study have very similar experiences to children in the Halifax area. While the majority do not come into contact with the hospital, those who do generally have typical childhood accidents and complaints. There is, however, still some question about the health of the unmarried mothers' children which warrants further investigation. For mothers whose children are

Table 14-6:

*Indicators of Children's Health by Mother's Age
and Married Status at First Birth*

	Young Unmarried Mothers	Old Unmarried Mothers	Young Married Mothers	Old Married Mothers
Average number of visits to emergency ward	7.1	7.6	6.7	4.5
Average length of hospital stays (days)	4.5	5.2	1.9	2.8 ♦

chronically ill, there is virtually no alternative but to dedicate all their time to their children.

Children's Development

The great majority of the children were developing intellectually and socially at appropriate levels and the mothers reported being aware of appropriate parenting strategies. There were, however, some differences among the achievement levels and behaviour of the different groups of children. For instance, a significant difference on the IQ assessments occurred for the older mothers where the children of the unmarried mothers had a lower level of verbal comprehension than the children of married mothers. Other assessments, while not demonstrating significant differences, show that the older married mothers' children had the highest levels of achievement on each of the four areas of assessment. The children of the younger unmarried mothers had the lowest levels of achievement, with younger married mothers' and older unmarried mothers' children ranking second and third. But the differences between these categories of children were very slight. There are some indications that the children of younger unmarried mothers are not achieving at quite the level at which they might be capable. A similar finding occurs with respect to assessments on receptive vocabulary, reading, math and hand-eye coordination. Children of married mothers consistently perform better than children of unmarried mothers with children of younger unmarried mothers having the lowest levels of achievement on all measures except visual motor. On this measure the children of older unmarried mothers have the lowest attainment.

Behaviour assessments by teachers and mothers show significant differences among the four groups of children. Children of married mothers, regardless of age, were seen as less socially withdrawn, more attentive, and less hyperactive than children of unmarried mothers. Children of younger unmarried mothers were assessed as the most problematic.

The data indicated that children in rural communities had lower levels of achievement on math, verbal, and full scale IQ assessments than their urban counterparts. These differences may well be partially explained by the more restricted opportunities and services available in rural areas. There is also a relationship between the mothers' education and the level of performance of the children. The children of mothers with low levels of education (i.e., eleven years of schooling or less) had lower performance levels on reading, math, and hand-eye coordination and more problematic behaviour than children of better educated mothers.

Each group's assessment is within normal levels for the respective tests. Overall, the children can be said to be achieving and performing as expected. There are, however, consistent variations which lead to the conclusion that some children are disadvantaged because of the age, marital, and educational circumstances of their mothers and the location of their homes. There is cause for concern about the impact the behavioral characteristics of the children will have on their future school work and out of school activities. Inattentive and socially aggressive ten year olds may not be successful at school when the work becomes more rigorous and challenging. And children who do not have a good grasp on reading and comprehension at ten may find school work difficult in later years.

Policies and Programs of Assistance

What supports would be of assistance to these mothers and their children? The research suggests that many families would benefit from additional support regardless of the marital status of the head of the household. Many of the single parent households would be eligible for assistance made available to all families. Such an approach will avoid a need to categorize families before they can be eligible for assistance. Further, many of the supports which would be of assistance to single parent families are equally beneficial to other families. Few services are so specific that they should be targeted only at single parents. Support is needed for families so that they can be financially independent and look after their children as they would wish to do.

There is need for programs designed to prevent many women from becoming single mothers. The Nova Scotia data indicate that 68% of the unmarried mothers had not planned nor wanted to become pregnant. The younger the mother the less likely the pregnancy was wanted. National figures show that about half of the unmarried women under twenty who become pregnant terminate their pregnancies, again indicating that many women had not planned on motherhood at this time (Clark et al., 1991, Appendix A). The younger unmarried mothers in this study also indicated that they would caution other young women about the difficulties and advise against early motherhood. Ten years ago teenagers' knowledge of contraception was very incomplete. Contraceptive practices were intermittent and easy access to contraceptive devices or procedures was not common. The approach to contraceptive information is still less than wholehearted despite improvements in knowledge and access to contraception over the past ten years. School programs have been developed to teach students about sexuality and sexual relations. But whether programs are offered can depend on individual school boards and whether children attend the programs can depend on their parents' wishes. The Planned Parenthood Federation maintains that less than half of all Canadian schools offer any type of sex education. If we do not reach the young people while they are in school, we lose a valuable opportunity of reducing the risks of unwanted pregnancies. Although access to contraception has generally improved, access to abortion continues to vary by province and by region within the provinces. Rural and northern areas are less well served and require additional expenditures to access the services in urban areas. The right to abortion and access to abortion services continue to be important aspects of any approach which strives for secure and healthy families.

Single parent families will continue as a significant form of family; their requirements should be addressed in the delivery of services to families in need. A series of interrelated programs are required if the objective of support and assistance is the development of families that are economically secure, healthy, and able to give appropriate care to children. Many families, and a disproportionate number of single parent families, live in very straitened financial circumstances. Economic policies must address the issue of job creation and the lack of job opportunities. The rapid growth in service sector jobs which have low wages and are often part-time results in available positions yielding less than a living wage. Further, most part-time jobs do not give access to such benefits as extended health care coverage or private pension plans; thus, many women are financially disadvantaged now and will be disadvantaged in later life. Labour force policies including employment equity, pay equity, and minimum wages must be expanded to allow women better access to positions and fair remuneration for the jobs they do.

The results of the Nova Scotia study, however, point to the fact that even if secure jobs were available, many women could not take advantage of the situation because they lack the necessary education or job training. Educational programs must address the needs of those who did not complete high school and who require adult education courses as well as the needs of young people still in school. Steps are necessary to ensure that as many young people as possible complete a high school education. Some children may need special assistance since low levels of achievement in basic skills will lead to leaving school at an early age. Education must be coupled with job training programs as women enter and re-enter the labour force.

Figure 14-2:

Areas of Assistance to Families

Economic Development

- secure jobs

Labour Force Policies

- economic benefits for all jobs
- employment equity
- pay equity
- adequate minimum wage
- realistic jobs training programs

Education

- adult education upgrading programs universally available
- programs to encourage young people to complete high school or further
- supplementary programs for children at risk
- sex education and personal living skills courses for all children and in each level of schooling

Child Care

- affordable quality child care for all children

Housing

- increased supply of affordable housing

Health

- access to family planning and abortion services
- coverage for all health services and special needs irrespective of labour force or social assistance participation
- extended assistance to families with chronically ill children

Taxation

- less regressive tax system
- integration of transfer payments

Social Assistance

- increased financial support from social assistance programs
- improved integration and transition from family benefits programs to education/training programs and to the labour force
- development of parenting skills
- assistance with child care; e.g., during illness♦

The major barrier for women seeking to upgrade their education or enter the labour force is the competition between the demands of raising children and the demands of a job. These competing demands are made more acute by the lack of affordable, accessible, quality child care facilities. Without access to child care, many mothers are simply unable to take advantage of education programs, job training, or paid work.

There are further difficulties for mothers and families whose income comes from social assistance programs. Levels of assistance are inadequate, especially when other supports such as subsidized housing or day care are very limited. There are also disincentives built into these programs which deter mothers from entering the labour force. Social assistance payments and benefits need to be maintained at a sufficient level during transition to the labour force. Special benefits such as extended health and dental care programs should be extended to families other than those on social assistance.

Assistance with children is an area in which services are limited. Mothers who can call on the assistance of other family members find life manageable. For mothers without this support, life is very precarious. One unexpected event, such as an illness, will put the family in a very difficult position. Single mothers have less support than their married counterparts and are particularly vulnerable because of a lack of support with parenting or with family emergencies.

The supports that families in need require are probably available in some form in each of the provinces. But the services are not equally available to all mothers, there are too few spaces or programs, and there is a lack of coordination and integration of services (Social Assistance Review Committee, 1988). The longer term problems have not been addressed by recognizing that some mothers are going to take several years to become economically independent. The economic prospects for some communities are so bleak that it is difficult to envisage economic independence for some families. There are programs or pilot projects available that address every family need which has been identified. The imagination to design the programs is present; what is lacking is the will or the capacity to make support programs available to all families who are in need.

15

The Housing Needs of Single Parent Families in Canada: A Dilemma for the 1990s

Aron N. Spector and Fran Klodawsky

This chapter begins with a discussion of key demographic, income, and expenditure characteristics of the single parent family population linked to issues of housing need. Second, an overview of the Canadian housing market and housing policy issues that have implications for single parents is presented. Finally, social welfare criteria are used to examine the housing situations of single parents and to assess some of the ways in which their housing needs are presently being met (Klodawsky and Spector, 1988; Klodawsky, Spector, and Rose, 1985).

Extant research indicates that the housing, income and demographic situations of single parent families without young children are radically different than those with children (Klodawsky, Spector and Hendrix, 1983). Thus, this discussion is restricted to census families containing a single adult with one or more unmarried children eighteen or under living at home; roughly two-thirds of the approximately one million single parent census families now living in Canada.

Data on the demographic, income, labour force, tenure and income of single parent families are derived from the 1986 Census Public Use Microdata Files, the 1990 Household Income, Facilities and Equipment Microdata File, the 1990 Survey of Consumer Finance Microdata file and the 1986 Survey of Family Expenditures Microdata File (Statistics Canada, 1988; 1990a; 1990b; 1991a; 1991b).

The Heterogeneity of the Single Parent Group

The last quarter century has seen a major shift in the families and households that make up the Canadian mosaic. One of the most dramatic changes has been the growth in the number of families headed by a single parent. In 1966 roughly 4% of families with children eighteen or under were headed by a single parent; this percentage had grown to approximately 11%

by 1990. There are now roughly 700,000 single parent families with at least one child eighteen or under.

Two distinctions among single parent families stand out as pre-requisites in understanding their housing needs. First, over 85% of single parent families are headed by women. Income differences are highly correlated with gender. Most single parent families headed by women are poor, with family incomes on average just over 43% that of two-parent families with children. Over 53% of these families had incomes below the Statistics Canada 1986 low income cutoff. In contrast, male headed single parent family incomes average approximately 75% that of their two-parent family counterparts. Just over 19% of these families had incomes below the 1986 cutoff.

These income variations can be partially traced to the degree and type of labour force participation of single mothers. Approximately 58% of female heads were in the work force in 1990. Among these women, 55% were employed in low paid service and clerical occupational groups. Like other women, single mothers experience discrimination in the work force. In 1986, within all major job classifications, full time employed women continued to earn approximately a third less than their male counterparts (Gunderson et al., 1990). Full time employed single mothers in 1986 earned less, on average, than did other women in the labour force holding occupational category and age constant. This may be related to the inability of single parents to exercise choice among job opportunities or to be flexible over work schedules due to the restrictions imposed by child rearing. Exacerbating wage issues is the greater number of single mothers who are employed part time. An important future concern is the implication of loss of experience and seniority in the job market. While generally income for both men and women increases with age, the gap between the sexes and between female single parents and others also dramatically increases. Many of these mothers have and will continue to face a prolonged period of low income, an important point for understanding housing need.

Single parent families, particularly those with younger children, have the disadvantage of having only a single adult to undertake child rearing and household upkeep. While female headed single parent families are resource poor, they still require the housing and community resources important to rearing children. Single parent families tend to spend much higher percentages of their income on shelter than do other family types. Without access to economic resources, affordability is a major and long term problem for most female single parent families.

How single parenthood was initiated is a second distinction important in understanding the housing needs of single parents (Spain, 1990). A key historical event was the 1968 reform to divorce legislation which allowed marriage dissolution to become a real alternative for many. In 1966, the majority of single parent families was headed by widows or widowers.

Today, between a quarter and a third of husband/wife families with children end up divorcing, and approximately 66% of single parent families are either separated or divorced. Among the remaining 34% of single parent families, about 14% are widowed and 20% never married. Both income and access to assets are related to how single parenthood was initiated and is key in understanding the housing situation of single parents.

A large proportion of never married single parents are young, and direct recipients of very little income. In 1990, close to 95% of these single parents were women. While approximately a quarter of families belong to larger family units or economic families, and many may be recipients of interfamilial income or service transfers, the vast majority have very low incomes. In addition, very few have significant tangible assets. Of those living on their own, approximately 8% were home owners in 1990. Among this group, the duration of single parenthood tends to be short, ending in most cases as a result of marriage (Moore, 1988).

A significant, though gradually declining proportion of single parent families is made up of the widows and widowers. Most of these people are in their late forties and fifties. The vast majority of this group do not live with related persons, although the incidence of living with unrelated persons and having boarders is relatively high. This group remains income poor but is relatively asset rich. While the incidence of low income among this group is high, so too is the presence of a home. In 1986, over 68% of these single parents were home owners.

Most single parent families are formed as a result of separation and divorce. Many of them become single parents during their thirties and remain so into their forties and fifties. Klodawsky, Spector, and Rose (1985) estimated that the average length of single parent episodes until: (1) terminated by marriage, (2) all children leaving home/passing their nineteenth birthday, or (3) death, was over 10 years for women and 9.5 years for men. Single parenthood occurs for this group well after leaving the family home and in the midst of the onerous task of rearing young children. It is thus not surprising that over 83% of these families lived alone in 1986. The proportions of primary custody award of children to mothers has remained relatively static around 77% into the mid part of the 1980s, primarily contributing to the continued dominance of female heads. The situation of many of this group is in considerable flux. The initial years following divorce reform, when asset splits in divorce settlements often favoured male partners and the payment of child support and alimony payments were not well policed, witnessed the emergence of a major new group of very poor female led families (Wheeler, 1980). The degree to which reforms in child support, higher participation rates of women in the labour force, and pay equity initiatives may presently be affecting this group is unknown, although there is some evidence that home ownership rates have increased marginally during the 1980s. For many women, single parenthood will be a long and financially difficult part of their lives. Most will have little or no access to home ownership and will continue to allocate large proportions of their income to housing.

Single Parent Family Housing in the Urban Environment

Contemporary housing design and the fabric of the housing market are reflections of traditional views of the life cycle (Rossi, 1982). The majority of urban Canadian adults are assumed to move from the family home to a series of rental accommodations, then to a single family owner occupied home designed for child rearing, and possibly back to a condominium or rental unit (Social Planning Council of Metropolitan Toronto, 1979). The design of much of the Canadian urban housing product is predicated on the assumption that during the full extent of the life cycle, each household unit is occupied by either a single unattached individual or a single nuclear family, headed by a husband and wife. Extended family households, containing multiple unit families, are becoming far less common. In addition, older children have, within the last two decades, more frequently left the family home while older adults have joined separate communities away from younger adults raising children. An impact of all of these trends has been an increasing demand for separate housing units each occupied by a smaller number of people.

Households containing single parent families reflect these trends. Most single parent families are separate, nuclear families. Previous bulges of single parent families, which occurred during and following World War II, were more likely to be extensions of existing households. Thus, today, single parent families are part of a housing market characterized by increasing demand in a situation where only particular types of housing are geared towards child rearing (Social Planning Council of Metropolitan Toronto, 1979).

Implicit in this life cycle housing model is the central role of home ownership as an investment opportunity. The early part of the adult life cycle is a period of savings in the expectation of accumulating a sufficient down payment for entry into the home ownership market. The primary presence of the federal government in the housing market is through provision of mortgage insurance which encourages lending at relatively low interest rates to those purchasing homes with minimal downpayments (Canada Mortgage and Housing Corporation, 1991d). For example, 120,000 home mortgages were insured by CMHC in 1988 (roughly a quarter of all new residential mortgages). Paying off the home mortgage has represented the principal source of investment and savings for the great majority of Canadian families. The house is an asset useable by the mature family for such functions as financing higher education and sustaining an adequate standard of living during retirement (Goldberg, 1983). Present taxation practices, which exclude the taxation of imputed rent or of capital gains resulting from the sale of a principle dwelling, encourage and favour home ownership as an investment and as a tenure form (Fallis, 1983; Cooperative Housing Federation of Canada, 1991).

Single parent families, with income levels well below those of other family types, are faced with a number of problems in the housing market, primarily related to inability to enter or re-enter the market for owner-occupied homes. In 1990, approximately 68% rented in contrast to just over 26% of other families with children. Single parent families are, by and large, unable to take advantage of housing and neighbourhood forms designed for child rearing. They are also unable to simultaneously allocate housing expenditures to both shelter and tax sheltered savings. An exception is the widowed population where close to two-thirds were owners. Finally, they face the dual responsibility of maintaining and sustaining a family in a environment either not intended for these purposes (much of today's rental stock) or where these functions are presumed to be undertaken by two adults (much of today's owner occupied housing stock) (Brandwein, 1977).

Much of the housing occupied by female led single parent families is either directly subsidized or provided by provincial or federal governments. Social housing has its origins in the public housing programs which began following the second world war and reached their peak in the 1960s. These programs were developed to provide modest, temporary shelter for families most in need and who were not well served through private sector development. The housing was assumed to be temporary until circumstances changed and the families could afford to purchase homes.

By the late sixties, various changes were starting to affect housing policy. Central urban commercial facilities and adult-centred, high-rise apartments began replacing low-cost housing. Centrally located housing for the poor became costly and difficult to find. At the same time, the relative dominance of two-parent families with children began to wane and a surge occurred in the number of senior households, a large proportion of whom had low incomes. Housing policy focused on provision of social housing to seniors during the 1970s. At this point the single parent population began to grow.

Beginning in the mid seventies, the need for social housing was acknowledged to be diverse and broad based and the direction of housing programs was towards the encouragement of community input into design, development, and management. Some provinces initially experimented with supply provision through the private sector but most new social housing development has been undertaken through partnership with municipal and private non-profit entities and co-operative housing. The move in this direction provided diversity of housing and a shift towards provision and design of support services as part of a housing package. During this period, there was also a shift back towards the provision of more housing specifically designed for families.

Single parent families make up over 42% of all families with children below the 1986 Statistics Canada low income cutoff. Single parents have a significant presence in Canada's 700,000 units of social housing — roughly 8% of the total housing stock, because of allocation systems which favour those in deep poverty and those with children. In 1986, about 50,000 public housing units, and in 1989, 14,000 cooperative units were occupied by single parent families. This represents approximately a quarter of the units in these two portfolios (derived from CMHC, 1990a, 1990b, and additional information provided by CMHC). Evidence from Quebec indicates that approximately a third of units in their non-profit programs are occupied by single parent families. In each case, over 90% of single parent families are headed by women. Thus, more than one in four female led single parent families is likely to reside in social housing. Further, this housing support is unlikely to be temporary given the long term nature of poverty for female led single parent families.

Assessing the Housing Problems of Single Parent Families

How well do present housing and housing related policies address the needs of single parent families? A series of eleven criteria are drawn from literature on women and environments, discussions on contemporary families, and housing policy analyses (Klodawsky and Spector, 1988). The criteria incorporate the inter-relationships between housing and the dynamism of the family life cycle of single parents who are dominantly resource poor and often in transition. Emphasis is on providing for a nurturing environment to meet the physical and psychological requirements of family members.

Affordability

A primary concern in households maintained by a single parent is the relegation of the principal roles of family sustainer and income earner to a single person. Loss of income potential is often quite dramatic among female single headed parents, but is less extreme among male single parents. Male heads, because of their income position, are usually better able to go to the market to purchase household and child support services. Nevertheless, for all single parent families, the loss of a parent through death or divorce or the birth of a child, is a time of disruption and marked loss of income flow and may also be a time to involuntary use assets to finance current consumption. In 1986, two-parent family assets grew by an average of $700 while female single parent assets declined by an average of $1,400 and male single parent assets by $1,100.

Shelter is the single largest expenditure for single mothers and, in 1986, increased to 34% of household income. Expenditures vary by position in the life cycle and tenure, ranging in 1986 from an average of over 39% of total budget allocations for those under 35 to 21% for those over 55. Single mothers often have average incomes well below CMHC Core Need Income Thresholds in most markets (a measure based upon the ability to afford average rents in local housing markets). Affordability problems tend to be concentrated in the rental population where families allocated an average of 36% of expenditures to shelter. In contrast, among home owners without mortgages, such as among the widowed population, families allocated an average of 18%.

Affordability is a crucial issue, particularly since raising children requires both living and amenity space. The transition to home ownership is impossible for the majority of female single parent households. In Canada's twenty-seven largest housing markets during the last six months of 1991, between 12% and 51% of renting families could afford a starter home (CMHC, 1991c). Estimates of the income level of renting female led single parent families indicates averages in the second quintile of renting families. The supply of multi-bedroom single dwellings with access to play areas continues to be relatively limited within the private rental market. Thus, like other Canadian renters, most single parent families reside in multiple family dwellings. In 1986, reflecting the need for space and access to play areas, a greater proportion of single parent renters rented row housing or detached dwellings than did other renters. Cooperative housing, which has had the goal of providing modest, family housing, and which offers the possibility of a housing subsidy (CMHC, 1991b) has been heavily populated by female led single parent families.

The option of home sharing for those with income flow problems who own their own home has been explored as a solution to the affordability problem (Pettit, 1987). Within Ontario, where home sharing programs have been established, very few single parents owning homes have been attracted to this option and single parents with children have not been seen as attractive partners by the primarily senior population of home providers.

Access

Mother led single parent families spend, on average, roughly one third less of their income on transportation than do other families because they are less likely to have access to a motor vehicle. In 1990, roughly 40% had no access to an auto, in comparison to 4% of two-parent households. Mobility loss may be both a cause and an effect of low income, since lack of access to an automobile may adversely affect job choice and access to other services. The task of ferrying children to school and reaching work on time without an automobile is very difficult for many parents. Choices for single parents in the labour market are limited by lack of capital for purchasing and the cash flow for maintaining a car. In turn, these tend to limit residential choices to relatively expensive, but accessible and service-rich downtown locations in large and mid-size Canadian cities. Thus, a strong relationship exists between need for access and affordability problems (Hayden 1981; Hayden 1984; Michelson 1988; Robertson, 1984).

Availability

In 1986, mother-led single parent families allocated close to twice as much of their incomes to housing as did two-parent families, but spent somewhat less ($434 compared to $460 per month). Therefore, supply of low and moderate income housing is especially important to this population.

The provision of modest cost family housing is becoming the domain of non-profit housing. Availability is related to activity in this sector, which in turn is linked to the vagaries of public policy. A dramatic decline in federal participation in the provision of new social and market housing has occurred recently, and only some provinces have taken up the slack. The impacts have been particularly negative for single parent families with income problems (Cooperative Housing Federation of Canada, 1991). Evidence of continuing discrimination against female single parents in rental units further compounds the problem. Audits of a number of housing providers in the Montreal area and the consistent presence of case loads involving single parents have indicated that women with children have more difficulty obtaining accommodations than do other household types (Gurstein and Hood, 1975; Aubin and Paquin, 1986; CERA, 1992). In many cases, single parents who are also members of visible minority groups have been especially open to discriminatory behaviour (Aubin and Paquin, 1986; Bernéche, 1991).

Capacity for Maintenance

In 1986, mother led families spent, on average, about 70% more of their incomes on household maintenance, excluding child care, than did their two-parent counterparts. At the same time, a marginally higher proportion of single parents lived in housing requiring major repairs. The loss of a parent provides an additional onus on the remaining adult, and sometimes on other family members, to provide the missing services, either through market substitution or additional effort. Neither time nor income for home maintenance is usually available for mothers in these families. There has been little work in the area of housing design and maintainability for single parent families (Sprague, 1991; Pettit, 1987). Shared living arrangements that permit the pooling of maintenance tasks among groups of single parents or between single parents and others has been one suggested solution. It is noteworthy that this type of arrangement is a requirement in the existing federal and provincial cooperative housing programs where volunteer labour is an often an important input to daily operation and maintenance.

Opportunities for Sharing and Support

Some of the responsibilities of an absent parent, such as child care, transportation, or simply information sharing, can be taken up by the extended family, neighbours, or other community members. In some cases, the complementary skills and needs of single parents can be met through cooperative activity (Simon, 1982; Soper, 1980). Young, never married, single parents may return to their parents' home, becoming part of extended families. In many cases, this situation leads to conflicts over issues such as privacy and child rearing (Anderson-Khleif, 1981) but being part of an extended family does often have the benefit of aiding short term adjustment to single parenthood (MacKay and Austin, 1983).

The provision of collective child care and car pooling are examples of activities that are easily organized when single parent housing is clustered. Collective child care, though, may require common neighbourhood space. Shared housing experiments have been beneficial in reducing housing cost, spreading various household responsibilities such as maintenance and child rearing, and providing emotional support from empathetic peers. The design of such housing with appropriate private, public, and collective space, is important to the success of such experiments (Leavitt, 1984; Simon, 1986).

Single parent housing is also often emergency housing. The initial stages of single parenthood for women fleeing abusive and violent relationships are traumatic and may require the provision of both peer and institutional support. Movement away from abusive relationships and the re-establishment of lives involves transition, often requiring support, counselling, and protection as part of a housing package.

Suitability for Transition and Empowerment

The period of single parenthood is a time of transition, adjustment, and often trauma. For most, transition and adjustment is tied to tenure change. The need for transition varies with circumstances. At one end of the spectrum is need for emergency shelter on a very short term basis. Somewhere in the middle is a need for taking stock and starting again without the encumbrance of long term commitments. At this stage, rental accommodation often provides the advantage of flexibility. At the other end is need for a long-term housing environment necessary to establish a stable nurturing environment. The concept of transition is integral to a number of single parent housing models. In the United States emphasis has been placed on religious and community involvement in the development of single parent communities designed to facilitate and encourage a transition towards independent living through provision of child care, job training, and counselling. The model of Warren Village in Denver is a good example (Wireman, 1984; Sprague, 1991). In Canada, the co-operative and non-profit sector have also been significant in providing options with an the emphasis on training in cooperative living and decision making as well as the development of internal, community support mechanisms (Wekerle, 1988). An additional emphasis has been on longer stage transition with movement from emergency to second stage to more standard housing arrangements within the housing community. The process is one of empowerment by moving towards a greater capacity to function independently or as a constructive member of a group.

There are examples where the concept of empowerment has been extended to include community economic development in conjunction with social support. Within the City of Ottawa, for example, community development officers have encouraged both job training and entrepreneurial activity ranging from establishing word processing pools to a resource group coordinating the development of non-profit housing. These community economic development activities largely involve single parents within public housing communities. Similar efforts have been undertaken in the United States (Leavitt and Saeggert, 1990).

The housing decisions of many widowed single parents have not been congruent with most transition models. These parents often have accumulated assets in the form of a home with little or no mortgage. These are significant as savings for retirement and as replacements of earnings from investment income. Income flow loss may provide problems, particularly where investment is primarily in an owner occupied home. Initiatives that encourage mutual support, ranging from introduction of other single parents as boarders to the establishment of mini cooperatives, have had little success. The investment required in producing successful matches has proven to be considerable as has been the case in most home sharing schemes. There is often reticence to move away from the privacy, comfort, and sanctity of the home which symbolically still belongs to the family. Mobility rates for this group have continued to remain much lower than for the population of families at large.

Secure Tenure

Single mothers are predominantly low and moderate income renters, and thus prone to the vagaries of tight housing markets and their own economic circumstances. Conversions to luxury apartments and condominiums have affected the security of tenure for this group. For many single parents, the capacity to be assured of a stable, secure place of residence is of special importance particularly for those who have recently adjusted to such traumatic situations as marriage dissolution, death of a spouse, or the responsibility of a new born child (Anderson-Khlief, 1981; Schorr and Moen, 1979; Weiss, 1984; Wheeler, 1980).

Threats to security of tenure due to economic eviction are less the case where public assistance through rent geared to income programs are available. Here, rental or housing charge payments remain a constant proportion of income, as long as income remains below an upper threshold. Publicly funded housing, however, is geared towards providing relatively short term relief for the poorest of families. There may be a requirement to increase rent and eventually to vacate once a single parent increases her income through employment and/or through the earnings of teenage children. In Ontario this is also the case where children are out of school or are over eighteen years of age. The cooperative and non-profit sectors often provide a buffer, where incomes fall temporarily and where income supplements are unavailable, through a common security or tenure fund (CMHC, 1991c).

Appropriate Facilities for Children

With the notable exceptions of the work of Hayden (1984) and Leavitt (1984), there is very little evaluative work done on the general adequacy of the present stock of low income housing for child rearing, let alone the situation of single parent families. In contrast, British policy is to allocate families eligible for council housing to row housing or the first floors of multistorey buildings (Henderson and Karn, 1987). Approximately 45% of Canadian single parent families with female heads under thirty-four lived in multiple unit apartment complexes in 1990. Policy on the adequacy of housing for child rearing is difficult to find in Canada outside of the design parameters set by some non-profit and co-operative housing groups. Policy evaluation could be done using available National Housing Act design guidelines for play spaces and unit design appropriate for children of all ages in various types of housing units. Simon and Werkele's work to encourage provision of visual access from inside the home to neighbourhood play areas was a major step in this direction (Simon and Wekerle, 1985). A related issue is access and provision of child care facilities. A number of non-profits and cooperatives have made these services available on site or nearby. This has been a boon to single parents with young children who want access to the labour market; job opportunities to others in the community have been generated at the same time (Wekerle, 1988).

Privacy

The concentration of the Canadian single parent population in modest, social housing and in rental accommodations has, on occasion, produced tensions. Experiments in the development of shared family living areas have met with limited success, particularly for the divorced population (Ahrentzen and Franck, 1989). Such families may wish and require enhanced supports from the community and from neighbours, but the continuing presence of others, and the necessity for confining rules and restrictions in modest, affordable housing can be stifling (Wekerle, 1988). Single parents' communities can provide both considerable support and considerable tensions. A study of a sample of Nova Scotia cooperatives found a high incidence of conflict among single parents who were not provided with adequate support and training (Nasdasdi, 1988). In one case, the viability of a co-operative under study was completely undermined. Single parents have children and children often are noisy; thus, adequate sound proofing is required, a detail which has often been inadequately addressed. While easily addressable at the design stage, this remains an aggravation to many who have rented in both the private and non-profit sectors (Ontario Standing Committee on the Administration of Justice, 1982).

Safety

Many women heading single families are extremely vulnerable.

For example, there are a number of cases where, because of their disadvantaged situation, single parents, particularly those belonging to visible minority groups, have been targeted for sexual harassment by landlords (Aubin and Paquin, 1986; Garon 1988). Women have been victims of abusive relationships where the partner continues to threaten violence (Mellett, 1983). Appropriate housing can be part of the alternative to an abusive relationship. Protection and anonymity are prime requisites to allow for the adjustment and healing process often required in these circumstances.

More globally, there is a need for assure that living and neighbourhood environments are safe and secure. The presence of good lighting, visibility of one's surroundings, and common spaces which are both used and supervised, are requisites for the design of housing and neighbourhoods addressing the needs of women raising children. Two recent case studies indicate a high correlation between residential and neighbourhood satisfaction and perceptions of single mothers that housing and the surrounding neighbourhood were safe (Anthony et al., 1990; Cook, 1989).

Cost-Effective Use of Public and Private Funds

Cost effectiveness is a strong emphasis in social housing evaluations (CMHC, 1991a, 1991b). The literature in this area has not, however, considered the costs imposed on Canadian society of neglect in providing adequate support to those raising children alone. Low income and onerous housing expenditures are major drains among female single parents. Pressure is imposed by the absence of a second adult member and is accentuated by the general wage prospects for women and the loss of experience in the labour force due to the requirements of child rearing. Support services such as accessible child care and job retraining are special needs. Cost effectiveness can be equated to net benefit of creating an environment where the human capital of single parents and their children can be developed. The capacity of single parents and their children to cope, adjust, and flourish can be enhanced by creating affordable, safe, secure, and nurturing environments. Community based initiatives can effectively and inexpensively provide appropriate and innovative housing options to single parents and other low and moderate income Canadians (CMHC, 1991b).

Life Cycle and the Single Parent Family

The onset of single parenthood is a period of transition, of adjustment and, sometimes, of loss. Loss occurs in present and future income earning capacity, both from a lost adult income earner and from the deferred time required for child raising. The period when children are being raised is also a time of savings and asset accumulation for many two-parent Canadian families (Frazer, 1981). The effect of lost income potential at this period has long term effects on single parents' ability to support themselves in their later life and to support children in furthering their education. In what situations is there a potentially useful role for public assistance? Are income supplement programs required? Or housing supplements? Or, possibly, more co-ordinated initiatives in housing and neighbourhood engineering and design?

The age of the single parent head is a major factor in assessing the relative situation of the family. Women under twenty-five, most of whom are never married parents, have the most complex set of problems since they have no income or asset base, have little earning potential or experience, and tend to have young children. The greatest breadth of short term social support is required for this group — ranging from child care to job training to the provision of adequate, affordable, housing. In contrast, women between twenty-five and forty-four, who now make up the major and fastest growing group of single parents, have income problems because of lost job experience, and differential access to jobs and seniority. Many in this group face the prospect of life long poverty for themselves and their children. Their supplementary support needs are job retraining, higher levels of mandatory child support by absentee parents, and environments that are more compatible with the needs of families who both work in the labour force and parent. Despite strides by government to better assure child support payments and the capacity to obtain and hold better paying jobs, the incidence of poverty and of major housing affordability problems remain high for this population.

Housing Policy and the Single Parent Family Housing Problems

Single parents' housing problems and housing solutions are tied to access to income and resources and these are related to the problems of a differentiated labour market where women's employment income is much less than men's. Moves towards alleviating income problems are also moves towards alleviating housing and most other problems for single parent families. The income problem is exacerbated by the opportunity costs of child rearing. Women lose experience and job opportunities in raising young children. When they do enter the labour market, they often are limited in the jobs they are able to take and the hours that they are able to work. Initial low income levels limit access to the mobility support of the private automobile in seeking and choosing jobs, housing, child care, shopping, and other opportunities. Continuing inability to secure adequate child support payments exacerbates these problems for many separated and divorced single parents. Housing for single parents must address this web of poverty through solutions that emphasize affordability, access, support, and empowerment.

There is also the problem of lost adult resources. The job of maintaining a household, of shopping, cleaning, and fixing is onerous when combined with the jobs of sustaining the family and earning a living. Housing, where tasks such as cooking and child supervision cannot be easily co-ordinated or which requires large amounts of maintenance, can make single parent-hood even more onerous. The single parent lives as one adult in a world designed for nuclear families. Housing options must be both supportive and maintainable. Housing for single parent families must be designed to provide secure, safe, and appropriate housing, and adequate facilities for child rearing.

Failure to address the housing and community needs of single parent families will lead to generations of women and children who have not achieved their skill and aptitude potentials. The number of older single women over fifty in poverty, many of whom were single parents, is growing at the same alarming rates that was evident for single parent families in the late 1970s and 1980s (Burke and Spector, 1991). The costs of an inadequate response to this problem are potentially enormous and threaten a movement away from the effective development of Canada's social capital, a theme which has been part of the country's rationale for social policy since the 1930s.

16

Hope and Circumstance: Single Mothers Exiting Social Assistance

Carolyne A. Gorlick and D. Alan Pomfret

Some circumstances are more stressful than others. Poverty is one, having children is another, and being alone, or relatively isolated, without much support from others is another. Single mothers on social assistance combine all three features. Consequently, they and their children are especially vulnerable. Much of the research has focused on the more pathological consequences of poverty for mothers and their children. What happens to their physical health and sense of mental well-being? Can effective social support networks alleviate some of the more negative aspects of their circumstances? These are important questions. Social support is one of the emphases in this paper. The main focus, however, is on the involvement in exit strategies by a group of single mothers on social assistance. The definition of exit strategies (Gorlick and Pomfret, 1991) is expanded to include social as well as documentable exit strategies. Social exit strategies consist of aspirations and satisfactions. Social support is examined in terms of its associations with parental involvement in exit strategies. Situational and personal factors are analyzed to clarify the relationships among various types of social support and exit strategies.

What emerges from the analysis is a portrait of persistent willingness and ability to deal with circumstances in a positive, active, and determined manner. The analysis, while not minimizing the difficulties and problems confronting these families, stresses the mothers' competencies rather than their dysfunction. Recognition of what mothers can and do, do for themselves focuses attention on what social policy makers may do to assist in their search for a way out of welfare. In addition, social support affects parental engagement in exit strategies in a way that has important social policy implications, especially for newer initiatives such as opportunity planning (Social Assistance Review Committee, 1988). These themes are developed in the paper's conclusion.

Sample Description and Research Design

In 1986 a sample of 150 female single parents on general welfare assistance (32%) and family benefits allowance (68%) was drawn from social service and educational client lists in London, Ontario. A double blind sampling technique was employed to assure respondents and institutional anonymity. The sample includes separated (51%), divorced (31%), widowed (4%), and never married (14%) female single parents who have at least one child under the age of sixteen years living at home. Three interviews were completed with the respondents. At the time of the first interview, 60% had separated in the past three years, and over half of the group had separated during the previous year. The average age of the respondents was 32.3 years and the mean number of children was 1.8; 67% of the children were under 12 years old. A follow-up interview occurred 1.5 to 2 years after the first interview. Eighty-five percent (n=125) of the original sample agreed to participate in the second interview.

The Two Faces of Exit Strategies

Single mothers on social assistance seek and engage in a range of activities with the hope of permanently ending their need for social assistance. The more observable activities, such as seeking various kinds of employment and additional education or training, are documentable exit strategies. These strategies are easily observed or verified, well known, comprehensible, and have a clearly defined and socially legitimated objective that is to increase a mother's employability and end her need for social assistance.

An additional social or hidden component of exit strategies consists of both the perspectives mothers construct concerning their aspirations for their children and themselves and their general satisfaction with themselves and their social environment. Both dimensions are social exit strategies. The aspirations dimension is more future oriented and goal directed than is the satisfaction dimension. The satisfaction dimension represents a more diffuse response to the parents' general social environment, a response that assists them in dealing with current everyday problems so as to facilitate planning for the future and acting on such plans. Recognition of the existence and nature of social exit strategies leads to a fuller appreciation of both the range of strategies parents use and their willingness and ability to persist in the pursuit of them.

Why are aspirations and satisfactions conceptualized as strategies analogous to formal documentable activities? A strategy exists when one deliberately or consciously selects a specific goal and corresponding course of action from a realistic range of alternative goals and courses of actions. Both choice and intentionality must be present. Yet, aspirations and satisfactions are typically portrayed as traits caused by a matrix of interacting biological, psychological, and sociological influences. This more deterministic view should not be ignored or summarily dismissed. At the same time, environmental and other factors constrain rather than determine people's responses. Moreover, these same factors may also be enablers. This suggests that parents confront a range of choices in terms of responding to the array of environmental and individual features that make up their lives. Within limits, they can choose to enrol in one program or another, or none at all. Within limits, they can choose to take this job or that, or none at all. Within limits, they can choose to be more or less satisfied with their situation. Within limits, they can choose to aspire to one goal or another. The choice may represent a second or third best alternative. But the possibility of making deliberate, conscious, and informed choices qualifies aspirations and satisfactions as strategies. The mothers appear to be aware of the choices confronting them; choosing to pursue documentable and social strategies is intended to help them exit social assistance.

What influences parents' adoption and use of exit strategies? Parents' involvement in exit strategies is influenced in part by the circumstances of their lives and in part by how they interpret and respond to these circumstances. This analysis focuses on the influence of social support on exit strategies. Also included in the analysis are the personal characteristics of age and education as well as the four situational factors — number of children, whether any are pre-school age, mother's time on Family Benefit Allowance, and time on General Welfare Assistance. These factors are especially helpful in clarifying the nature and importance of the connections among social support and exit strategies.

Documentable Exit Strategies

The documentable exit strategies consist of educational upgrading, completion of an educational program, and obtaining employment. Each main type is further sub-divided into three more specific strategies. Within the enrolment category, parents can upgrade educationally in a secondary school subject, enrol in a technical or training program, or enrol in a post-secondary program in a college or university. Educational completion involves completing a program in any of these three educational or training areas just mentioned. For employment, mothers can obtain seasonal, part-time, or full-time employment. This results in nine specific documentable exit strategies. Tables 16-1 and 16-2 show that only 18% (23) of the 125 parents did not engage in any kind of documentable exit strategy in the time between the two interviews. Employment was the most frequently strategy used by 55% (69) of the mothers; part-time employment was obtained by 33% (41), full-time employment by 22% (28), and 4% (5) obtained seasonal employment. Enrolment in an educational or training program was the second most favoured strategy used by 45% (56) of the parents. Approximately 18% (22) of the mothers enroled in each of the three areas or

Table 16-1:

Participation in Specific Exit Strategies
(Second Interview)

Exit Strategy	N	Percent
Enrolments		
Educational upgrading	24	(19.2)
Technical/training	20	(16.0)
Post-secondary	22	(17.6)
Total enrolments (Number of mothers)	66 (56)	(44.8)
Program Completions		
Educational upgrading	21	(16.9)
Technical/training	13	(10.4)
Post-secondary	12	(9.6)
Total completions (Number of mothers)	46 (39)	(31.2)
Employments		
Seasonal	5	(4.0)
Part-time	41	(32.8)
Full-time	28	(22.4)
Total employment (Number of mothers)	74 (69)	(55.2)♦

Table 16-2:

Participation in Main Types of Exit Strategies
(Second Interview)

			Main Type of Exit Strategy					
	Any Exit Strategy		Enrolment		Program Completion		Employment	
Number	N	Percent	N	Percent	N	Percent	N	Percent
0	23	(18.4)	69	(55.2)	86	(68.8)	56	(44.8)
1	47	(37.6)	47	(37.6)	34	(27.2)	65	(52.0)
2	34	(27.2)	8	(6.4)	3	(2.4)	3	(2.4)
3	17	(13.6)	1	(0.8)	2	(1.6)	1	(0.8)
4	1	(0.8)						
5	2	(1.6)						
6	1	(0.8)						
Total (1-6)	102	(81.6)	56	(44.8)	39	(31.2)	69	(55.2)
Total	125	(100.0)	125	(100.0)	125	(100.0)	125	(100.0)♦

Table 16-3:

*Participation in Combinations of Main Types of Exit Strategies
(Second Interview)*

Combination	N	Percent
No exit strategy	23	(18.4)
Single strategies		
Enrolment only	19	(15.2)
Program completion only	2	(1.6)
Employment only	32	(25.6)
Multiple strategies		
Enrolment + Completion	12	(9.6)
Enrolment + Employment	12	(9.6)
Completion + Employment	12	(9.6)
Enrolment + Completion + Employment	13	(10.4)
Totals	125	(100.0) ♦

upgrading, training, and post-secondary programs. Lowest in terms of participation was completion of an educational or upgrading program used by 45% (38) of the respondents. A post-secondary program was completed by 10% (12), another 21% (17) completed upgrading, and 10% (13) finished a training program.

There was a slight trend to engaging in multiple strategies across sub-categories within each of the main categories (e.g., seasonal with part-time employment or upgrading with training). There were 4 such multiple specific strategy parents in the employment area with 74 employment positions taken by 69 mothers; 9 mothers within the enrolment area with 66 enrolments by 56 parents; and 5 parents within the completion category resulting in 46 completions by 39 mothers. Four of the parents tried four or more specific strategies. Table 16-3, however, indicates a far stronger trend was to combine strategies across the main categories of enrolment, program completion, and employment. Thirty-nine percent (49) of parents combined two or more main types of exit strategies during the course of the year; 29% (36) combined two different main types of strategies (such as completing an educational program and obtaining employment) and 10% (13) of the mothers tried all three.

Social Exit Strategies

Aspirations and satisfaction are two general kinds of social exit strategies. The aspirations are for self and children. With respect to aspirations for self, mothers were asked: "Where do you feel you are likely to obtain your family

Table 16-4:

Mother's Educational Aspirations for Their Children
(Second Interview)

Degree of Education	Daughters (Percent)	Sons (Percent)
Other	16.7	11.5
Complete secondary school	5.1	11.5
Complete community college	15.4	13.8
Complete university	62.8	63.2
Totals	100	100
	(N = 78)	(N = 87) ♦

income next year (in the next five years)?" Forty-six percent of the parents cited employment as their main source of income next year, and 80% cited it as their main income source in five years. Close to half the parents aspired to be off social assistance within the year. Four out of five parents aspired to exit welfare within five years. Aspirations for their children refers to educational aspirations. Table 16-4 reports the parents' aspirations for daughters and sons. Most parents (about 2 out of 3) want their daughters and sons to go to university. About 80% aspire for their children to have post-secondary education. Both aspirations for self and aspirations for children are high.

The high aspirations for self and children are dwarfed by the even higher satisfaction scores. Table 16-5 reports the parents' mean satisfaction levels with the different kinds of social support. The highest possible score is six. Satisfaction increased between the two interviews and is very high for all categories. The remaining satisfaction exit strategies are self esteem, satisfaction with parents, and satisfaction with community groups. The mean for self-esteem is 5.45 on a 7 point scale with 57% of the parents scoring in the top two categories and 78% in the top three. Only 29% of the 111 mothers in contact with their parents assess the relationship as unsatisfactory. Of the 98 parents engaged with community groups, only one found the association unsatisfactory, 83% reporting satisfactory associations, and 14% rated their involvement in the groups as somewhat satisfactory.

The most notable characteristic of all the social exit strategy indicators is the consistently high scores, especially for the satisfaction strategies. The rate of parental participation in social exit strategies exceeds their previously noted high participation rates in the documentable exit strategies. This may partly reflect the opportunity to exercise choice. Social exit strategies, in comparison with documentable strategies, allow parents more control over

Table 16-5:

Mothers' Levels of Satisfaction with the Main Types of Social Support (Second Interview)

Type of Social Support	Satisfaction Levels (Means[1])	
	First Interview	Second Interview
Overall support	4.78	5.28
Close support	4.80	5.25
Esteem support	5.00	5.34
Information support	4.56	5.19
Instrumental support	5.00	5.30

[1] The satisfaction scale ranges from a low of 1 to a high of 6.♦

their willingness and ability to participate in such strategies. The high scores may indicate the parents' decisions to exercise this choice.

The Evolving World of Social Support

The mothers experienced a number of social support continuities and changes in the 18 to 24 months between the two interviews. Sarason's definition of social support " ... as the existence or availability of people on whom we can rely, people who let us know that they care about, value, and love us" (Sarason et al., 1983: 127) was used. The categories of social support providers and the types of support mothers feel they receive from these persons was examined (Gorlick and Pomfret, 1988: 3–8). Social support provider categories are daughters, sons, mothers, fathers, female relatives, male relatives, female friends, male friends, and counsellors. This classification of service providers permits an analysis by gender. The types of social support are overall support, close support, esteem support, informational support, and instrumental support. Overall support refers to Sarason's and others' (1983) definition of social support and is an aggregate of the four sub-categories. Close support involves " ... how deeply integrated with or tightly bound to another a parent feels" (Gorlick and Pomfret, 1988: 8). Esteem support is nominally defined as " ... information that a person is esteemed and accepted" (Cohen and Wills, 1985: 315). Informational support is " ... help in defining, understanding, and coping with problematic events" (Cohen and Wills, 1985: 315), Finally, instrumental support consists of " ... the provision of financial aid, material resources, and needed services" (Cohen and Wills, 1985: 315).

Table 16-6 reports the extensiveness of the social support provided to mothers at the time of each interview. The extensiveness of the support

Table 16-6:

Mother's Level of Social Support for the
Main Types of Social Support

Type of Social Support	Extensiveness (Index) of Social Support (Means)[1]	
	First Interview	*Second Interview*
Overall support	3.06	3.48
Close support	3.42	3.79
Esteem support	3.38	3.89
Information support	2.16	2.48
Instrumental support	3.02	3.52

[1] The Social Support Indexes can range in value from a low of 0 to a high of 9. ♦

provided is fairly stable and has even increased slightly for each social support category. In general, the mothers were receiving more social support by the time of the second interview than they were receiving at the time of the first.

Table 16-6 provides information on how much support mothers felt they were receiving from different support providers for the different kinds of social support at the time of each interview. Information in Table 16-6 is consistent with Table 16-5 and indicates that, other than for children, there has been an increase in the amount of support provided to the mothers by all persons on all support dimensions between the two interviews. Mothers receive all types of support from all types of support providers even though the extensiveness of support varies considerably within categories. Support is seldom evenly distributed. The means indicate that some social support is being provided within each social support category; but the medians indicate that, within specific types of social support categories, at least half the parents are receiving no social support from counsellors or fathers and no informational support from anyone other than female and male friends. Most of the support tends to come from females; female rather than male friends, mothers rather than fathers, and female rather than male relatives. Female friends are the main sources of social support for female single parents. Fathers and male relatives are least likely to provide support. The only exception to this gender pattern is children. Sons provide slightly more support to parents than do daughters. At the time of the second interview, 79 of the mothers reported daughters living at home, with two or more daughters in 25 of the families, and 89 of the mothers reported sons still living at home, with two or more sons in 26 of the families. Mothers see sons as providing as much support as daughters, especially close and esteem

Table 16-7:

Mothers' Levels of Social Support by Support Provider and
Main Types of Social Support

Type of Support Provider	Extensiveness (Index) of Social Support (Means[1])									
	Type of Social Support									
	Overall		Close		Esteem		Information		Instrumental	
	Interview		Interview		Interview		Interview		Interview	
	1st	2nd	1st	2nd	1st	2nd	1st	2nd	1st	2nd
Friend										
Female	.84	1.01	.96	1.08	.81	1.03	.68	.78	.90	1.19
(median)	.54	.85	.75	.75	.50	.75	.33	.67	1.00	1.00
Male	.43	.53	.47	.60	.44	.57	.36	.47	.44	.59
(median	.25	.46	.25	.50	.25	.50	.00	.33	.00	.50
Child	.59	.55	.69	.70	.92	.90	.15	.13	.21	.18
(median)	.50	.46	.50	.50	.75	.75	.00	.00	.00	.00
Daughter		.27		.34		.43		.07		.09
(median)		.15		.25		.25		.00		.00
Son		.29		.36		.48		.06		.09
(median)		.15		.25		.25		.00		.00
Parent	.43	.48	.46	.53	.41	.49	.33	.37	.66	.55
(median)	.33	.46	.50	.50	.25	.50	.00	.00	.00	.50
Mother		.32		.37		.33		.25		.20
(median)		.23		.25		.25		.00		.00
Father		.16		.16		.16		.12		.20
(median)		.00		.00		.00		.00		.00
Relative	.53	.61	.60	.62	.57	.66	.37	.43	.64	.34
(median)	.33	.31	.50	.25	.25	.25	.00	.00	.00	.50
Female		.47		.48		.51		.36		.58
(median)		.15		.25		.25		.00		.00
Male		.14		.14		.15		.08		.20
(median)		.00		.00		.00		.00		.00
Coun.[2]	.24	.26	.24	.25	.23	.25	.28	.30	.17	.24
(median)	.08	.00	.00	.00	.00	.00	.00	.00	.00	.00

[1] The Social Support Indexes can range in value from a low of 0 to a high of 9.
[2] Coun. refers to counsellors, priests, ministers, and other "professional" support providers.◆

Table 16-8:

Individual Changes in Levels of Social Support
(Between the Two Interviews)

	Direction of Change in Level of Social Support			
	Decreasing	No Change	Increasing	Totals (percent)
Type of Social Support				
Overall support	16.3	48.9	34.8	100.0
Close support	16.0	53.6	30.4	100.0
Esteem support	19.2	47.2	33.6	100.0
Information support	18.7	53.7	27.6	100.0
Instrumental support	18.4	46.4	35.2	100.0♦

support although much less informational and instrumental support. Mothers are least supported by anyone in the area of informational support. Yet, as will be seen, this type of social support has the strongest association with the mothers' participation in documentable exit strategies.

The pattern is even more complex at the individual level. The overall trend within the group is towards increasing support. However, a substantial proportion of the parents did not experience the increase in social support that characterized the parents as a group. Table 16-8 indicates the pattern of changes at the individual level. Within each social support category, the increases went to about a third of the parent group, with about a sixth experiencing a decrease, and the remaining half receiving the same level of support.

What Influences Social Exit Strategies?

Social Support

What are the associations between social support and social exit strategies? Does social support influence the aspiration and satisfaction dimensions of social exit strategies in similar ways? Table 16-9 displays the associations between the various types of social support and the corresponding levels of parental satisfaction. Actual levels of social support are good predictors of mothers' satisfaction. Changes in support levels are good predictors of changes in satisfaction levels but are not as good at predicting actual levels of satisfaction. Support levels, while good at predicting satisfaction levels, are only weak to moderate in strength. Depending on the type of support, support levels explain between 2% and 19% of variance in satisfaction levels. This suggests that parents' satisfaction with support is only partly influenced by the actual support received and by changes in such

Table 16-9:

Estimates of Selected Associations between Social Support and Satisfaction Levels

	Type of Association		
Type of Social Support	Levels of Social Support with Levels of Satisfaction at the Second Interviews	Changes in Levels of Social Support with Changes in Levels of Satisfaction between Interviews	Changes in Levels of Support between Interviews with Levels of Satisfaction at the Second Interview
	Gamma (r)	Gamma (r)	Gamma (r)
Overall support	.53 (.43)	.42 (.29)	.24 (.18)
Close support	.62 (.38)	.54 (.27)	.24 (.09)
Esteem support	.43 (.37)	.54 (.30)	.31 (.21)
Information support	.53 (.41)	.58 (.30)	.34 (.14)
Instrumental support	.45 (.38)	.35 (.27)	.14 (.14)♦

Table 16-10:

Association between Main Types of Social Support and Selected Social Exit Strategies (Gammas)

	Type of Social of Social Support				
Type of Social Exit Strategy	Overall	Close	Esteem	Information	Instrumental
Aspirations:					
Education of: Daughter	.37	.35	.31	.16	.46
Son	.09	-.01	-.09	.19	.24
Employed in:					
One year	.10	-.13	.00	.23	.16
Five years	.22	.08	.27	.22	.52
Satisfactions with:					
Self	.27	.33	.13	.08	-.07
Parents	.53	.42	.66	.22	.27
Community	.23	.12	-.03	-.14	.19 ♦

support. Put differently, at least some parents are choosing to view the support they receive much more positively than is warranted by that support or changes in that support.

Table 16-10 suggests that social support also has differing associations with the remaining satisfaction and aspirational strategies. Support is generally strongly associated with aspirations for daughter, with longer rather than shorter term aspirations for self, and with satisfaction with parents. Both informational and instrumental support have stronger associations with a much wider range of exit strategies than do esteem and close support. In general, social support has stronger impacts on aspirational than on satisfaction exit strategies other than actual satisfaction with support. Informational and instrumental support have more widespread consequences than esteem or close support, especially on parents' aspirations for self and children.

Situational and Personal Influences

Table 16-11 reports the associations among situational and personal factors and social exit strategies. There is a weak tendency for older and more educated respondents to report lower levels of satisfaction. Still, more educated persons are also more likely to adopt aspirational exit strategies, especially long term ones for themselves. Situational factors, except for the number of children, have relatively little impact on the satisfaction strategies. Parents with more children report higher levels of satisfaction with support than parents with fewer children. But the number of children discourages the adoption of aspirational exit strategies, although parents with no pre-school aged children are more likely than those with pre-school aged children to plan to exit social assistance within the year. Both length of time on Family Benefits Allowance and General Welfare Assistance tend to discourage the adoption of any kind of exit strategy, although the associations are generally weak.

The most notable feature of the information in Table 16-11 is the large number of relatively weak to, at best, moderate associations between the situational and personal factors and social exit strategies. Thus, the mothers are not letting the circumstances of their lives — the number of children they have, whether they have pre-school children, length of time they are on social assistance, their age, or educational level — have an overwhelming negative impact on them given that both the overall aspiration and satisfaction exit strategy levels tend to be quite high. These parents may be consciously fighting back against these circumstances by refusing to become too discouraged and giving up hope. They are maintaining high levels of satisfaction with their social environment and also high levels of aspirations. They are getting some help from their social support networks in this fight against these more material conditions. Social support tends to have stronger

Table 16-11:

Associations between Situational Factos, Personal Characteristics
and Social Exit Strategies (Gamma)

Type of Social Exit Strategy	Situational Factors				Personal Characteristics	
	Pre-Schoolers	Number of Children	Time on FBA	Time on GWA	Age	Education
Aspirations:						
Education of: Daughter	.13	.22	-.14	-.12	-.16	-.10
Son	.01	-.13	-.47	-.19	.03	.19
Employment in: One year	.40	-.35	-.11	.05	.06	.40
Five years	.07	-.09	-.25	-.12	.01	.26
Satisfactions with:						
Self	.08	.09	-.10	-.34	-.08	.03
Parents	-.36	-.09	.04	.21	-.18	-.03
Community	.07	.02	-.32	.02	-.15	.08
Social Support:						
Overall	.02	.35	-.05	.22	-.10	-.14
Close	.00	.30	-.09	.11	-.22	-.08
Esteem	.21	.29	-.14	.11	-.17	-.21
Information	.19	.24	-.12	.16	-.13	-.04
Instrumental	.00	.19	-.27	.05	-.07	-.16♦

associations than the situational and personal factors with exit strategies, especially with satisfaction with social support. This would suggest that the parents' social support environments are a crucial resource in the parents' fight to have hope triumph over circumstance. But the associations are far from overwhelming suggesting that, as crucial as the social support environments are, parents are drawing on additional resources to construct a definition of their lives that will allow them to carry on in the face of adversity. These additional resources may derive from or consist of memories of their pre-social assistance life, their concern for and sense of responsibility to their children, a belief in the openness and fairness of society, or certain moral or ethical orientations. The nature of the relationship between the social and personal resources, or between the enabling and constraining forces, in the parents lives has yet to be determined. But there is an extraordinary amount of motivation and ability within the parent group.

What are the factors that influence parents' social exit strategies? The short answer is the parents themselves. A longer answer must take into account the interrelated constraining and enabling features of the parents' social and material environments. The high levels of participation can be explained as the end product of conscious decisions by mothers to respond to their environment in as constructive and positive a manner as they possibly can. This explanation neither downgrades the importance of environmental factors nor does it romanticize the parents' virtue and freedom of choice.

What Influences Documentable Exit Strategies?

Table 16-12 reports associations between all of the previously mentioned factors and documentable exit strategies. The analysis attempts to answer three questions. First, what influences whether parents pursue or do not pursue any documentable exit strategy? Second, what affects the number of documentable exit strategies a parent pursues? Third, what influences the main kinds of exit strategies parents pursue? This analysis ignores the more specific strategies. The move from considering more specific strategies to more general levels of whether parents pursue any strategy involves a continuum of increasing choice. A mother's choice is most constrained at the specific level. For her to participate in a specific strategy, that strategy must be realistically present for her. The circumstances of her life must be such that if she desires a given choice she will be in a position to act on such a preference. Circumstances, however, may prevent a parent from acting on her first choice. For example, there may be no appropriate full-time employment available. Or the presence of pre-school age children may rule out certain desired courses of action. In such cases a parent may act on a second or third preference which may be more compatible with the environmental constraints and enablers than is her first preference. Subsequently she may take part-time employment or a training program. Thus in moving from the specific to the general strategies the movement is from more to less constraining levels of actions.

Social Exit Strategies

Aspirational social exit strategies are more potent predictors of documentable exit strategies than are satisfaction social exit strategies. This may not be too surprising in that aspirational measures are more goal oriented. Almost all the social exit strategies are better at predicting whether parents are engaging in any documentable exit strategies than predicting the number or type of strategy. This may be due to the fact that the number and type of documentable exit strategies one can engage in are more constrained by the environment than is the decision to engage or not engage in any strategy at all. If blocked in one direction, parents may pursue another. Completion of an educational or upgrading program is the documentable exit strategy

Table 16-12:

Associations between Social Support, Social Exit Strategies, Situational Factors, Personal Characteristics and Documentable Exit Strategies (Gammas)

Predictors	Any	Number	Enrolment	Program Completion	Employment
			Type of Documentable Exit Strategy		
Social Support:					
Overall	.39	.17	.21	.11	.38
Close	.15	.12	.08	.23	.27
Esteem	.34	.15	.18	.05	.29
Informational	.58	.28	.21	.18	.20
Instrumental	.20	.11	.06	-.03	.38
Social Exit Strategies:					
Satisfactions with:					
Social support Overall	.03	-.02	-.07	-.22	.05
Close	-.20	.02	-.16	-.02	.27
Esteem	.27	.14	.00	.13	.38
Informational	.31	.11	.20	-.02	.14
Instrumental	.08	.05	.08	-.07	-.13
Self	.20	.14	.07	.26	.41
Parents	.03	.19	-.25	.31	.45
Community	.23	.03	-.28	.50	.35
Aspirations:					
Education of					
Daughter	.36	.02	.44	.01	.53
Son	.17	.02	.12	-.08	.23
Employed in					
One year	.50	.24	.23	.10	.11
Five years	.65	.72	.21	.71	.68
Situational Factors:					
Pre-schoolers	-.04	.01	.17	-.12	.30
No. of Children	-.27	-.26	-.01	-.10	-.16
Time on FBA	-.10	-.13	.15	-.24	-.21
Time on GWA	-.47	-.28	-.13	-.10	.00
Personal Characteristics:					
Age	-.33	-.24	-.06	-.14	-.22
Education	.23	.31	.29	.02	.51 ♦

most affected by all social exit strategies and, along with employment, is most strongly affected by aspirational social exit strategies.

Social Support

Social support has a consistently stronger impact on documentable exit strategies than does satisfaction with social support, and information support, among the social supports, has the strongest impact on documentable exit strategies. Completion of an educational program is associated with all types of support. In short the concrete support provided by formal and informal means does have a demonstrable impact upon the mothers' exit strategy behaviour. These trends suggest that policy and program efforts should focus on increasing informational and instrumental support without interfering with close and esteem support.

Situational and Personal Influences

Virtually all of the situational factors act as constraints on parents' participation in exit strategies — especially the number of children and time on General Welfare Assistance. Whether one has children at home is relatively unimportant as is time on Family Benefit Allowance although in both case there tends to be small negative influences. The effects of personal characteristics are split, with older mothers being less likely to engage in documentable exit strategies while more educated mothers are more likely to do so, especially obtaining more educational upgrading. More educated mothers are also more likely to have fewer children, fewer pre-school age children, less likely to be longer on Family Benefits Allowance and General Welfare Assistance, but are also older. With the exception of age, all of these factors are positively (but weakly) associated with participation in documentable exit strategies. Time on General Welfare Assistance and number of children correlate negatively with documentable exit strategies but positively with satisfaction social exit strategies. This would suggest that, although both act as constraints in terms of documentable strategies, parents are using them as resources in social satisfaction strategies. Both time on General Assistance and number of children have weak negative associations with aspirational social exit strategies.

Conclusion

Parental involvement in any kind of documentable exit strategy is most strongly associated with social support, especially informational support, and the aspirations component of social exit strategies, especially parents' aspirations for themselves. These are also the main predictors of parents' employment. Satisfaction with the level of information support is the best social support predictor of documentable exit strategies. Other than parents' long term aspirations for self, the best predictors of parental participation in enrolment strategies are satisfaction with self, parents, and community. Completion of an educational program responds to a wide range of factors including social support and most of the social exit strategies. With the notable exception of long term aspirations for self, very few factors correlated strongly with the number of exit strategies in which parents engaged, although the social support factors played a larger than average role. With the single exception of education, the personal and situational factors acted as constraints rather than facilitators of parental involvement in any of the documentable exit strategies.

The relative importance of the role of information support is notable because this is the type of support mothers are least likely to receive and with which they are least satisfied. At least half the mothers receive no information support from anyone, including counsellors. Yet its pervasive influence on all the documentable exit strategies is surpassed only by parents' long term aspirations for self. Within the satisfaction with social support grouping, satisfaction with information is rivalled only by satisfaction with esteem support as a predictor of mothers' pursuit of exit strategies. However, each predicts different strategies and both are more weakly and less consistently associated than information support and long term aspirations with strategies.

The impact of social support, situational factors, and personal characteristics on social exit strategies is different than their impact on documentable exit strategies. Social support does influence parents' satisfaction with social support. Satisfaction levels increase as levels of support increase. This is slightly more likely for information support than for the other types of support. Aspirations for daughters and satisfactions with parents are affected by virtually all the types of social support, while aspirations for sons are affected by none. Still, information and instrumental support tend to influence aspirations, while close and esteem support tend to affect satisfaction with self, parents, and community.

The impact of situational and personal factors on social exit strategies is also less clearly demarcated than is their influence on documentable exit strategies. None act consistently as facilitators or constraints. Education is positively associated with parents' aspirations for self, but is generally unrelated or even negatively related to every other exit strategy. Nor are the remaining factors consistently associated negatively with social exit strategies in the same way they are with documentable exit strategies. For example, whereas the number of children tended to decrease mothers' documentable exit strategy behaviour, parents' satisfactions with every dimension of social support increases as the number of children increases. Although time on General Welfare Assistance was more of a constraint than time on Family Benefits Allowance for documentable exit strategies, the opposite is true for social exit strategies. The remaining situational and personal factors have only weak to non-existent impact on parental involvement in social exit strategies and alternate between enabling and constraining roles depending on the strategy.

The analysis clearly indicates the mothers' desire and commitment to exiting social assistance. Single mothers on social assistance actively involve themselves in an extensive range of social and documentable exit strategies. Parents enrol in, and complete, educational and training programs. They seek and obtain employment. They maintain as realistic and hopeful an orientation as possible towards themselves, their children, their parents, their friends, and their community as well as to the present and the future. They set goals, devise strategies, and act on them. They may not always do what they desire or prefer. But they do what they can rather than do nothing at all.

Although related, the two kinds of exit strategies play different kinds of roles in the mothers' lives and represent two different ways of keeping hope alive given difficult circumstances. When objective circumstances such as young children, lack of child care, or lack of money make participation in documentable exit strategies temporarily unrealistic, parents resort to social exit strategies as a way of giving a meaning to their lives that allows them to cope with the present and with the future in mind. In saying they are satisfied, the parents' are not saying that they are happy or content with their lot as social assistance recipients. If nothing else, their extensive involvement in documentable exit strategies should put that thought to rest. They are saying that they are probably doing as well as they can under the circumstances and that they are coping with the present in a way that at least does not destroy hope for either their own or their children's future. Social exit strategies will not necessarily lead in any predictable way to participation in documentable strategies but they do appear to be a necessary precondition for entering and remaining in documentable exit strategies.

Parents do much of this work themselves and draw on the environment to assist them. The pervasive influence of social support, especially information support, on parental involvement in exit strategies is notable. Investment in information (compared to monitoring or counselling) support would produce substantial returns in stimulating exit strategy behaviour. Information is not the only answer, but it is one that is often under emphasized or overlooked as other aspects of the social assistance phenomenon claim limited attention and resources. The circumstances of these parents lives are difficult. It is clear that the mothers have not given up hope. They continue in a multitude of ways to resist the more negative aspects of their environment. They are ready to help themselves. But they cannot do it all on their own.

17

Social Support Needs: Summary, Policy Implications and Research Agenda

Laura C. Johnson and Burt Galaway

For single parent families, as for the larger population of families, supports are needed in four primary areas: (1) public and private income maintenance programs, (2) human capital programs such as employment, training, and education, (3) housing, and (4) child care. In addition one can think of support in terms of social support which, in Sarason's words, means " … the existence or availability of people on whom we can rely, people who let us know that they care about, value, and love us" (Sarason et al., 1983). These supports can be provided to single parent families either through formal or informal systems. The chapters presented in this section address the support needs of single parent families in the areas of financial, child care, housing, and social support.

Susan M. Clark uses a panel design to follow, over a decade, a group of Canadian women who gave birth to their first child in late 1978 or early 1979. Independent variables were age at first birth (under/over age 20) and marital status at the time of first birth. After ten years, most of the unmarried mothers had married but their economic conditions tend to be worse than that of the women who were married when their first child was born. The unmarried mothers are more disadvantaged than the married mothers; 52% of the younger unmarried mothers and 54% of the older unmarried mothers were living below the low income cutoff line compared to 29% of the younger married mothers and 16% of the older married mothers. Unmarried mothers tend to spend a higher proportion of their income on housing, to receive social assistance and to be on social assistance for a longer period of time than the married mothers. The unmarried mothers are more likely to experience obstacles to employment such as lack of affordable child care, transportation problems, or lack of education and experience than are the married mothers. Many of the mothers reported difficulties finding affordable child care. Husbands and relatives constitute the major source of help with children; over the ten years, the husbands provided the major source of help for 70% of the mothers, relatives for an additional 14%. At follow up after ten years, 19% of the younger married mothers were the sole caretakers of children, as were 38% of the older unmarried mothers, 21% of the younger married mothers, and 9% of the older married mothers. Sixty-eight percent of the younger unmarried mothers had not planned or wanted to become pregnant.

Carolyne A. Gorlick and D. Alan Pomfret studied the relationship between social support and engaging in documentable exit strategies in a sample of single parent families. Documentable exit strategies are strategies that are designed to secure exit from social assistance and for which participation can be documented; examples include participation in educational and training programs and securing employment. Involvement in documentable exit strategies is associated with social support, especially informational support, and the aspirations which parents hold for themselves. Informational support is one of five types of social support and includes giving useful suggestions to avoid making mistakes, being told in a helpful manner when improvement is needed in some way, and providing support in major decisions. Female friends and relatives are the main source of all kinds of social support received by single parents.

In Chapter 6, Donna S. Lero and Lois M. Brockman report on their study of child care arrangements for a representative sample of Canadian families with children under the age of thirteen. Data were secured for a reference week in 1988 from the Canadian National Child Care Study, a national probability sample of 24,155 families. Minorities of both single parent and two-parent families make use of regulated group or individual child care; 36% of the children five years and younger in one-parent families are in regulated group or home care compared to 17% of the children in two-parent families; the percentages for children ages six to twelve are 11% for the children from one-parent families and 4% for children from two-parent families. The major differences are the children from two-parent families are more likely to be cared for by a parent (32% of the children ages 5 and under and 39% of the children ages 6 through 12) but this is not an option for the employed single parent. Children in one-parent families are more likely than children in two-parent families to be securing care from a relative, sibling or to be left unattended in self care. Twenty-five percent of the children five years of age or under in one-parent families receive care by a relative compared to 18% of those in two-parent families. Thirty-three percent of the children ages 5 and over from one-parent families receive unregulated care, as do 31% among those in two-parent families. Lero and Brockman found that 21% of parents with children in sibling care and 50% of the parents of children in self care expressed at least some minor reservations about the care. The researchers used a ten point scale to measure self reports of the tension that parents experienced in juggling work, family and child care responsibilities; there was a relatively small difference between the married and single mothers in this regard. Single mothers had a tension score of 4.8 compared to a score of 4.2 for the married mothers (1 represented no tension and 10 indicated a great deal of tension).

Housing needs of single parent families were analyzed by Aron Spector and Fran Klodawsky against eleven criteria. The single parent family represents a very heterogeneous group in terms of housing needs; these vary through the life cycles of these families and must take into consideration the transportation and employment needs of the family, suitable environments for raising children, and the resource deficiency of the single parent family. Resource deficiency occurs because one adult has all the responsibilities, including home maintenance, which in two-parent households are shared by two adults.

Themes

Several themes emerge from these chapters which are supported by the other chapters in this volume. The first is that the support needs of single parent families cannot be isolated and treated separately from those of the larger population of families. For example, the ability of the single parent family to enhance economic position is linked to the capability of securing employment at adequate salaries. This, in turn, is related to the availability of child care, affordable housing located close to employment, public transportation, and an informal support system to provide both encouragement and practical assistance to the single parent attempting to provide both parenting and economic supports to a family.

Second, single parent families are characterized by a condition of resource deficiency. A single parent often has sole responsibility for caring for children, housekeeping and home repair, providing economic support for the family, and maintaining links with a broader community. Both informal and formal supports need to be analyzed in terms of the extent to which they reduce resource deficiency. These chapters, as well as a number of others in this volume, note that single parent families are neither a homogeneous nor a stable family form. A great deal of heterogeneity is found within this group and some parents regularly move in and out of marriage or cohabitation and, thus, in and out of single family status. Support needs change as families move through a variety of stages.

Third, single parent families, as do all families, regularly draw on informal social supports. There is no particular indication that, as a group, they are isolated. Gorlick and Pomfret found that the mothers were satisfied with the level of social support they were receiving; over a period of ten years Clark found that the social support for children came primarily from husbands and relatives (in ten years, most of the sample of unmarried mothers had married), and Lero and Brockman note that single parent families tend to rely on family members and unregulated care givers for child care.

Finally, heterogeneity can also be noted in terms of formal supports. While 52% of Clark's younger unmarried mothers were below the poverty line three years after the birth of their child, 48% were above the poverty line; 48% were in the labour force, 52% were not. Differences within the group of single parent families may be as great as differences between single parent and other family forms.

Policy Implications

The chapters presented in this section suggest a number of policy considerations including focusing on resource deficiency, placing the single parent family in an overall family policy, relating policy to the integrated nature of the support needs, and recognition of the single parent family and informal support systems as active participants.

Resource deficiency was one of the central themes. Resource deficiency, in this context, does not refer to a deficiency within a person but rather to the recognition that one person is expected to carry responsibilities normally handled by two adults. Public policy could be directed towards remedying these deficiencies. But the research also suggests that the single parent family is a unit frequently in transition. Families and their members regularly move in and out of this status. This raises the question of whether the single parent family is an appropriate or useful unit development of public policy and design of programs to implement public policies. Perhaps the whole matter needs to be put into a broader context of family policy, realizing that all families have support needs, some of which can be met by formal programs, and that these needs will vary and change over the life cycle of the family.

Resource deficiencies of the single parent family are, nonetheless, real and the source of considerable strain. The formal supports necessary to meet these needs should be integrated into a system of supports. The presence of adequate child care, housing, and transportation are essential to the economic support provided by employment. Providing job training and employment assistance, for example, would be of relatively limited effectiveness unless supports relating to housing, transportation, and child care are available. Because responsibility for these various support services cut across different jurisdictions, public policies may be inconsistent and contradictory. There is a clear need to examine both the intent and effects to determine whether public policy is moving in a consistent, coherent direction.

There is also a need to agree upon and articulate common policy goals. Agreement may not exist on what these goals should be in relation to the single parent family or to families in general. Is the goal of policy to promote the healthy development of young children? Should the policies promote the economic independence of single mothers? Should policies permit parents to spend more time with their young children? Are policies to promote stability in the lives of young children? Public policies directed towards permitting parents to spend more time with children and to secure stability in the lives of children may not be consistent with the notion of promoting economic independence for single parents. Should any of these policies be targeted exclusively to single parents, or is it more appropriate that policy focus on the larger population of families?

Finally, single parents are not passive recipients of services. They are imbedded, to varying degrees, in informal support networks. How do public policies affect these networks? Do public policies and programs encourage or discourage participation and decision making by single parents? In what manner do policies encourage the development and use of informal support systems?

Research Agenda

The research agenda can be organized in two related areas. The first area relates to the need to develop a clearer understanding of the support needs, including the role of informal social support systems, of the single parent family at the various transitions through which this family moves. The second area has to do with the study of the impact of public policies and programs on the single parent family and on meeting support needs.

Families, Single Parent Families, and Transitions

Most of the research to date has been cross-sectional, examining the family at one point in time. The reality of family life includes movement through a variety of transitions. Research needs a longer term perspective on these transitions. Research approaches must be implemented to capture and understand these changes. Large scale, longitudinal studies are needed to collect information at multiple points in time for a cohort of the Canadian population. A carefully designed data base, with regular follow-ups, could be made available to policy makers and researchers to address a number of questions such as:

(1) What are the antecedents to separation and divorce?

(2) What are the short and long term economic and social consequences of divorce for men, women, and children in Canada?

(3) What is the relationship over time between family structure and poverty, including the income level of the parent, after the last child leaves the home?

(4) What are the intergenerational patterns of support within families?

(5) What are the effects of geographic mobility on supportive behaviour of family members?

(6) Under what conditions does the family, including the extended family, function as a safety net?

(7) What factors interfere with provision of informal support?

(8) How do public policies encourage or discourage such support?

(9) How do men and women perceive their familial obligations?

(10) What are the social support and the support needs of the single parent family at different stages in the life cycle? How are these supports being provided?

(11) What are the long term consequences of children's experiences in single parent families?

(12) What factors affect men's participation in domestic work?

Such a data base would permit the focus on the child as the unit of analysis, as well as the family, and would facilitate research using a variety of definitions of families and children.

Research on Effects of Policy and Programs

A data base assembled for a cohort of Canadian citizens may be used to test the effects of policy and programs on Canadian families, including the single parent family, to the extent that measures of program participation are included. Assembly of such a data base will, necessarily, be a long term undertaking and will not quickly provide information regarding the impacts of public policy and programs on Canadian single parent and other families.

There is an immediate need to move beyond simply counting participants in formal support services and to include assessments of program quality and outcomes. A prerequisite to doing this, however, is to conduct research to develop standards or criteria of program quality, acceptable program outcome criteria, and to develop methodologies for measuring both quality standards and outcome criteria. Once this is done, research on public policies and programs can be conducted in areas such as:

(1) The intended and unintended consequences of public policies.

(2) Connections between formal and informal social support systems.

(3) Given the existing variety of family-related public policies in various Canadian jurisdictions, assessment of the effects of these diverse policies on single parent families.

(4) Research on public policy implementation to assist in developing a long-term vision for family-related policy in Canada.

(5) Short-term research linked to program development. Ongoing research is needed to guide program development and policy implementation and to suggest program modifications as necessary.

(6) How single parent families perceive and experience public policies and programs.

PART V

SOCIALIZATION
EXPERIENCES OF CHILDREN

18

Socialization Experiences of Children in Lone Parent Families: Evidence from the British National Child Development Study

Elsa Ferri

The impact on children's welfare and development of being brought up by a lone parent is probably the most extensively researched aspect of life in this type of family. Yet it is also one of the most complex areas to investigate, and the body of available evidence requires careful assessment and interpretation. Lone parent families are a far-from-homogeneous group; the caring parent may be the mother or father, and the situation brought about by divorce, separation, bereavement, or birth outside marriage or a stable partnership. The sex of the children concerned is also likely to be of importance, as is their age at the time the family situation occurred, the point at which their development is assessed, and the duration of any measured effects.

Moreover, family structure is not a static condition; the dynamic nature of family formation and dissolution, which may involve a sequence of changes from two- to one-parent situations, further complicates the picture and the task of isolating the effects of particular family experiences. When all these points are added to the very diverse range of developmental outcomes which require investigation — cognitive functioning, social and emotional development, physical growth and health, attitudes and values — the complexity of the subject becomes increasingly clear, as does the corresponding need for carefully designed, conducted, and interpreted research. It also becomes easy to appreciate why the considerable number of studies undertaken in this field do not aggregate to a body of clear-cut, conclusive evidence.

The research requires large, representative samples given the number of variables which need to be taken into account. Early work on the subject was carried out using small, selective samples of children and families who had come to the attention of specialist services such as child guidance clinics. Such studies, while providing valuable information for diagnosis and treatment, were inadequate for producing evidence concerning the socialization of children from lone parent families in general.

The most productive source of data for such enquiry will be longitudinal studies of large, representative samples, in which the timing and sequence of key events, experiences and outcomes can be used to clarify causal relationships. Britain is fortunate in having three such data sources in the ongoing national birth cohort studies; the life course and development of all persons born in one week in 1946, 1958, and 1970 have been monitored by means of regular follow-up surveys. Information collected for the National Child Development Study, involving the 1958 cohort, has been exploited most fully in relation to the experiences and development of children in lone parent families.

The National Child Development Study

The National Child Development Study (NCDS) began as a Perinatal Mortality Survey involving more than 17,000 births in Britain in the week of March 3–9, 1958. The multidisciplinary, longitudinal study that began in 1965 was taken forward by the National Children's Bureau. Information was gathered from parents (interviewed by health visitors) and school staff, medical examinations were carried out by school health services, and ability and attainment tests and questionnaires were completed by the children themselves at ages seven, eleven, and sixteen. Considerable quantities of data were obtained concerning each child's family situation, parental employment, housing and other socio-economic circumstances, as well as his or her physical, educational, social, and psychological development. The first adult survey, for age twenty-three, collected information from the cohort members about their own social and economic circumstances and their transitions to adulthood.

In 1985, the study became the responsibility of the Social Statistics Research Unit at City University, London. The most recent follow-up, for age thirty-three, has, in addition to obtaining further information about the cohort members themselves covering all the major life domains, added similar data from their spouses or partners and, most importantly, developmental assessments of a one in three sample of their children. The assessments parallel those carried out for the National Longitudinal Survey of Youth in the United States, thus offering rich possibilities for cross-cultural comparisons. They considerably enhance the NCDS by creating a three-generation data set and the opportunity for investigating inter-generational transmission.

Extensive use has been made of NCDS by the research community indicated by the several hundred publications covering aspects of child health and development across the whole cohort (eg., Davie, Butler and Goldstein, 1972; Fogelman, 1983), or studies of specific sub-groups such as adopted children (Seglow et al., 1972), those born illegitimate (Crellin, Pringle and West, 1971), those from disadvantaged backgrounds (Wedge and Essen, 1982), and children from lone parent families (Ferri, 1976).

Development During the School Years

The first major investigation of children living in lone parent families used the data collected at the age of eleven to examine their school attainment, measured by tests of reading and mathematics, and behavioral adjustment, rated by both teachers and parents (Ferri, 1976). Those in the lone parent category were sub-divided according to the sex of the parent and the cause of the family situation (death of the absent parent, marital breakdown or illegitimate birth). Initial comparisons of average scores on each measure showed that children from the lone parent groups had lower attainment and poorer behavioral adjustment than those in two-parent homes. Measures of the relationship between development and family situation must, however, make allowance for background differences in view of the socio-economic disadvantages associated with lone parenthood. These are themselves independently related to developmental outcomes. Accordingly, a series of multivariate analyses were carried out to include social class, family size, income level, whether the child had ever been in care, standard of housing, number of schools attended and parental aspirations for the child's educational future as independent variables. In regard to parental aspirations, divorced/separated mothers held slightly lower aspirations for their daughters' school leaving age and further training, as did single mothers and widowed fathers in respect of children of both sexes.

The results of these analyses were complex in that the influence of living in a lone parent family varied according to the sex of the parent and the reason for the situation. The attainment and behaviour of children living with widowed mothers differed very little from that of their peers in intact homes when allowance was made for other factors. Similar findings emerged in relation to children who had been born illegitimate. Interestingly, maternal employment among this group was found to be positively related to school attainment and social adjustment. The position of children with lone fathers, and those whose lone mothers were divorced or separated, was rather different. There was a tendency for them to have done less well than children in two-parent homes, even after allowance was made for background differences. Only on the mathematics test, however, did the differences reach statistical significance. The differences attributable to family situation were much smaller in magnitude than those accounted for by socio-economic factors, in particular the financial hardship of so many lone parent families.

These findings were replicated when a similar set of analyses were undertaken of the school attainment scores at the next NCDS follow-up, when the cohort were aged sixteen (Essen, 1979). These compared the same sub-groups in terms of family situation, with the lone parent groups further sub-divided according to whether parental absence had been experienced before or after the age of seven. The findings revealed no differences in reading attainment after allowing for background factors. Only in mathematics was there a tendency for girls whose parents were divorced to do less well than those who had been bereaved. No consistent association was found between school attainment and the age at which the child had experienced a lone parent situation. These NCDS studies are consistent in showing that, whilst the development of children in lone parent families during their school years is less favourable than that of their peers in intact homes, the influence of the socio-economic disadvantage that accompanies lone parenthood is considerably greater than that of parental absence per se. A similar pattern of findings emerged from a study comparing the ability and social adjustment of five-year-old children in lone and two-parent families in the 1970 cohort (Osborn et al., 1984). Also, Wadsworth and Maclean (1986), using data from the 1946 cohort, found that economic and material disadvantage accounted for more of the difference in educational achievement at twenty-six than did the emotional disruption associated with divorce.

The NCDS school years surveys also provided information on the cohort members' aspirations and expectations concerning their future education, occupations, and family life. These areas are of considerable interest and importance in terms of well-being and long-term development, yet they have received rather less attention in the research literature. Ferri (1976) found that, at the age of eleven, boys from father-absent families, especially those living with divorced or separated mothers, were more likely than those with both parents to anticipate leaving school at the earliest opportunity, and that both the sons and the daughters of widowers echoed their fathers' relatively low aspirations in this area. Essen and Lambert (1977) discovered some slight differences at the age of sixteen in aspirations concerning marriage and a family of their own. A slightly higher proportion of boys living with lone mothers stated that they did not wish to marry, while more boys and girls in these families claimed not to want children of their own. Of those who did want children, more fatherless boys wanted them later in life, whilst girls anticipated earlier motherhood. It is important to stress, however, that the great majority of young people in lone parent families at sixteen held aspirations regarding their future family lives very similar to those of their peers who had not experienced family disruption.

Pre-Divorce Effects

Recent research using NCDS data has employed a rather different approach to investigating the effects of divorce. The studies referred to so far indicate that children in families that have experienced divorce show some, albeit relatively small, effects attributable to their family situation, even when other relevant factors have been taken into account. While research questions are conventionally framed in terms of the consequences, or aftermath, of divorce, more recent work in this area has exploited the longitudinal potential of the NCDS data by exploring the pre-divorce behaviour of children whose parents subsequently parted. Thus the focus switches to look at divorce itself as merely one stage in a process of family change that may have a measurable impact prior to the formal rupture.

Cherlin and others (1991) examined scores at ages seven and eleven, on tests of school attainment and social adjustment, of boys and girls whose parents had divorced by the time they were eleven, and compared them with a group whose families had remained intact. Their findings showed that, for boys, significant differences on all measures at eleven between the two family groups were no longer significant when allowance was made for the seven-year-old score. Thus, the difference between boys in divorced and intact families was present before the divorce occurred. A similar trend was apparent for girls, although significant differences remained on some measures at eleven, indicating some effect of the divorce itself. A similar approach was adopted by Elliott and Richards (1991) who found that children whose parents divorced displayed more disruptive and more unhappy and worried behaviour at sixteen than those whose parents remained together, but that they had also shown these differences at seven, prior to the divorce. The same pattern emerged on tests of attainment.

These adverse outcomes may thus be associated with marital conflict, change, and disruption in relationships rather than divorce. This does not, however, rule out the possibility that both child development *and* an increased chance of divorce may be influenced by a third factor or set of factors. The analyses undertaken included only father's social class at birth as a further independent variable. Other background factors, especially measures of socio-economic disadvantage, could have affected both development and the likelihood of divorce.

Outcomes in Early Adulthood

A major area of interest in relation to the impact of lone parent families on development concerns later life consequences and outcomes such as final educational achievement, training, occupational success, and the experience of adult partnerships and parenthood. Information collected for the NCDS survey at age twenty-three enables analyses of the relationship between family experience and key transitions in early adulthood. Elliott and Richards (1991) found that young people with divorced parents were more likely than those whose parents had remained together to have left school early, and less likely to have obtained any qualifications or to have received a university education.

Kiernan (1992) explored a number of outcomes in examining whether the timing of transitions into adult life varied for young people from different family situations. These included age at leaving full-time education, age at entering first job, at leaving home, entering first partnership, marriage, and parenthood. Although, in general, those from lone parent families differed from their peers who had grown up in intact homes, the pattern of findings showed variations according to the reason for the family situation and the sex of the cohort member. Those who had been bereaved differed little from the control group, especially those whose fathers had died. Young people whose parents had divorced were more likely to have left school at the earliest possible age and, linked to this, entered employment sooner, than those from intact homes. When ability and social class of origin were taken into account, however, the difference was significant only in the case of young men. This could reflect the pressure on those from the most economically disadvantaged lone parent group to begin earning and contributing to the family income.

A slightly different picture emerged when age at leaving home was examined. Here, controlling for background variables resulted in a significant difference only in the case of young women, with those from divorced families having left home earlier than their counterparts from unbroken families. There was also some indication that friction in the home was a more common reason for early leaving among all the lone parent groups, especially those whose parents had remarried. Young women whose parents had divorced were also more likely to have entered into teenage partnerships, to have had a first child before the age of twenty, and to have had an extra-marital birth. These relationships were weaker in the case of young men, although those with divorced mothers were also more likely to have formed early partnerships. The sex differences no doubt reflect the fact that, on average, women enter into partnerships and have children at younger ages than men. Only a minority of those from any family background had made these transitions by the age of twenty-three; future follow-up data will be needed to give a complete picture of the family formation behaviour of the cohort.

No conclusive evidence emerged in respect of any of the outcomes concerning the age at which the lone parent situation had come about. Findings from the 1946 cohort suggested that subjects whose parents had divorced or separated before they were five, were, by the age of twenty-six, more likely to display long-term emotional difficulties, to have committed a serious crime, or to have had an illegitimate birth (Wadsworth and Maclean, 1986). Such findings point to the importance of inter-cohort comparisons to throw light on the relative contribution of period effects and factors intrinsic to the situations being studied.

Wadsworth and Maclean (1986) also found that the downward social mobility traced in the families of origin of cohort members whose parents divorced was not compensated for by the social class status which they themselves achieved by the age of twenty-six. This trend also emerged in relation to the NCDS cohort; Fogelman, Power, and Fox (1987) found that, especially among young males from non-manual backgrounds, the absence of a father during childhood was associated with a general depression of the level of job obtained in early adulthood. However, they also examined a range of health indicators (including height, hospital admissions, scores on a malaise inventory, psychiatric morbidity and self-rated health) among twenty-three-year-olds from different family backgrounds and found little evidence of adverse effects related to father absence earlier in life (Fogelman, Power, and Fox, 1987). The only significant difference between this group and those from intact families was in the higher level of psychiatric morbidity among males from manual social class backgrounds.

Most of the research has employed multivariate analysis but studies on adult outcomes (in which most of the statistically significant differences have emerged) have included far fewer independent variables than those under-taken on the school-age data. Moreover, many of the adverse adult outcomes — such as early school leaving, lack of qualifications and relatively low employment status — could well be linked to social and economic disadvantage in earlier life rather than to direct influences of family experience. The adult outcomes studied so far have been recorded at age twenty-three; many important life transitions have still to be made for a large proportion of the sample. Further information collected when the cohort members were ten years older will provide greater insight into any long-term effects of lone parenthood.

Conclusion

Evidence from the most robust studies of the effects of the lone parent family on the development of its children is complex and requires careful interpretation. On the one hand, it offers considerable support for explana-tory theories of social disadvantage as the main determinant of poorer developmental outcomes of children in such families when compared with their counterparts raised by both natural parents. On the other hand, multivariate analyses have also revealed some significant residual effects due to the family situation itself especially when the cause has been marital breakdown, rather than bereavement, and when the caring lone parent is the father. Evidence concerning the effects of single motherhood upon child development is relatively sparse. In 1958, the NCDS cohort was born; this was a small group, both in absolute terms and as a proportion of all lone parent families.

The studies have thrown considerable light on the relative contribution of structural and behavioral factors in influencing developmental outcomes. Yet the necessarily general nature of large-scale survey data furnished by the NCDS and other cohort studies cannot adequately address the questions which next arise. These concern the actual processes and mechanisms whereby the circumstances and functioning of different family environments act to produce particular outcomes. Osborn and others (1984) sought to account for developmental differences attributed to family situation in the 1970 cohort in terms of curtailed parent-child interaction in families in which one parent was missing. Very little is known, however, about whether and how changes take place in the various roles and relationships involved in households that experience the transitions in and out of lone parenthood. The survey findings need to be complemented by more in-depth, qualitative data, which examine in detail the ways in which different family structures are linked to patterns of functioning, roles, and relationships. Such investigations should address the situation from the perspectives of all those involved, including children and the non-residential parent. Divorce is frequently conceptualized as a lost relationship; statistics on post-divorce contact between children and non-residential parents in British studies suggest that, for many, this may indeed be the case. However, there is also evidence (Richards and Dyson, 1982) that more favourable developmental outcomes in children following divorce are associated with a continuing positive relationship with the absent parent. Further investigation is needed into the nature of post-divorce relationships and the conditions which facilitate such positive interaction. A long-term perspective is also required to monitor further change in the situation such as the adjustments which occur when one or both of the parents enters a new partnership. Research could be fruitful by moving away from the conceptual approach that treats divorce simply as a static, categorizing variable, towards one which focuses on the processes and changes involved at various stages in the life of the divorcing family.

Studies of how parenting roles are undertaken in lone parent families need to consider parenting in the context of family life in general, and of the major changes which are taking place in this domain including the division of parental roles along gender lines. A qualitative study, based on a special follow-up interview with a sample of lone parents in the NCDS, highlighted the difficulties they experienced in undertaking what they saw as two incompatible roles — as the provider of affection and nurturance and as the source of discipline and control (Ferri and Robinson, 1976). This study, however, was carried out at a period in which parenting roles in the families concerned were likely to have been divided according to traditional divisions of paternal breadwinner and source of authority and maternal homemaker and provider of emotional support. There are important questions to be addressed concerning role allocation in the contemporary family and the implications this has for the socialization task facing those who undertake it singlehandedly.

In summary, research to date has shown that differences due to family status, as such, were small in magnitude. They were also average differences among large, representative groups. Many of those who had grown up in lone parent families had done as well, if not better, than their peers who had enjoyed more stable family lives. Future research is needed to examine the factors that promote successful outcomes for lone parent families. Perhaps the focus of past research has been overly concerned with identifying risk factors associated with problematic outcomes. Knowledge of what enables families to rear children successfully despite the pain, stress, and disadvantage that accompanies family dissolution would be of considerable value, not only to those who face this challenging task, but also to the policy-makers and practitioners who seek to provide sufficient and appropriate support for their efforts.

19

Adult Outcomes Associated with Childhood Family Structure: An Appraisal of Research and an Examination of Canadian Data

Ellen M. Gee

Alarge, generally U.S.-based, research literature examines effects of single parent family structure and marital disruption on children, usually pre-adolescent children (Demo and Acock, 1991; McLanahan and Booth, 1991). Fewer studies focus on adults who experienced a single parent family situation while growing up. The research emphasis on parents and dependent children may reflect an implicit assumption about the primacy of the nuclear family unit in western society, an ageist bias in intergenerational family research, mundane issues of data availability, or a combination of these factors. The research on adults shares theoretical perspectives and methodological limitations with the studies dealing with younger children. This chapter begins with a discussion of theoretical and methodological issues and then provides an overview of research findings along dimensions of educational attainment, socio-economic status, divorce proneness, other family-related variables, and adult adjustment and well-being. Finally, an analysis of data from the Canadian General Social Survey (GSS–2) allows for a comparative exploration of characteristics of adults who experienced varying family situations as children with regard to parent loss.

Theoretical and Methodological Issues

Theoretical Perspectives

The social learning/socialization model is a dominant perspective employed to explain the consequences of marital dissolution and single parent family structure although the research on younger children contains other less prominent theoretical perspectives, particularly family-stress theory. The social learning perspective is based on the notion that parents, as role models, play a critical role in determining how children will turn out. Two parents residing with the child are necessary for the transmission of the values and behaviours that produce well-functioning adults. This occurs through their reinforcement of the child's appropriate behaviours and through their own performance of socially expected behaviours. Anything less than two parents in-residence results in inadequately socialized children who will, as adults, be deficient in some way. Socialization agents other than parents, such as other adult relatives, siblings, friends, and media are downplayed.

The inadequate socialization for adulthood that occurs in one-parent families operates through three mechanisms. First, the custodial parent — usually the mother, who is often the only functional parent (Furstenberg et al., 1983) — is placed under considerable stress, resulting in low supervision (Hetherington, Cox, and Cox, 1978; Colletta, 1979; Astone and McLanahan, 1991), inconsistent discipline (Rickel and Langner, 1985), and emotional over-dependence on the child that shortens childhood and results in subsequent difficulty in reaching maturity (Wallerstein, 1991). Thus, the child as adult lacks the basic psychological and pragmatic tools to function in a mature fashion. Second, the less traditional attitudes of the custodial parent related to her willingness to leave an unsatisfactory marriage in the first place, to her choice not to marry at all, or to her life experiences as a single parent will be passed on to her children who will have non-conformist attitudes and behaviours in areas such as gender roles (Kurdek and Siesky, 1980a; Ambert, 1985; Kiecolt and Acock, 1988; Demo and Acock, 1991) and the acceptability of divorce (Greenberg and Nay, 1982). Third, the non-parental behaviour of the custodial parent provides the child with fewer appropriate guidelines for conducting adult life. For example, in the case of divorced parents, children are less involved in religious activity (Glenn and Supancic, 1984) and are taught ineffective ways of dealing with interpersonal conflict (Pope and Mueller, 1976). Bloom, Asher, and White (1978) suggest that persons who divorce or separate are often emotionally disturbed, either before marital disruption (and, therefore, its cause) or in the aftermath of the marital breakup. These three mechanisms vary in their impact on children depending on age at the time of marital disruption (Kurdek and Siesky, 1980b, 1980c; Kalter and Rembar, 1981), duration of one-person parenting, gender (Hetherington, Cox, and Cox, 1978; Wallerstein and Kelly, 1980; Guidubaldi and Perry, 1985), and gender-mix of the child and custodial parent (Santrock and Warshak, 1979) although same-sex role modelling may not matter as much as previously supposed (Amato and Booth, 1991).

The socio-economic perspective arose partly in response to the conservative ideological underpinnings of the social learning model and its failure to consider material factors. The socio-economic perspective holds that any negative effects of single parent family structure are due largely to the economic characteristics of female-headed families. Social economic status (SES) in childhood and adulthood affects adult adjustment (Acock and Kiecolt, 1989) and educational attainment (McLanahan, 1985). This perspective argues that SES is an independent variable that influences behaviour and attitudes, irrespective of economic factors associated with the formation of single parent families in the first place. McLanahan (1985) suggests three ways in which low SES could lead to low achievement among children in single parent families. First, similar to socialization theory, low supervision by the custodial parent related to the economic necessity of maternal employment is a factor. Second, children in single parent families, as a result of poverty, assume adult roles at young ages (e.g., working at a full-time job or looking after younger siblings) that interfere with school work and are associated with early school departure. This argument, in contrast with socialization theory, is that children in single parent families mature more quickly and display independence at younger ages (Weiss, 1979). Third, McLanahan suggests that the welfare state encourages dependency which, coupled with welfare stigma, erodes achievement orientation.

Methodological Issues

A crucial methodological issue concerns the conceptualization and measurement of family structure. Single parent family structure must be distinguished from its causes. Never-marriage is increasing with nearly 14% of Canadian single parent families created this way (Ram, 1990) but most single parent families are the result of an event that entails parent loss. Such an event is experientially different from its sequelae, family/household composition. Are the effects of family structure or the effects of parental loss being studied? Fuzziness in the independent variable creates confusion in the interpretation of findings (Parish and Kappes, 1980; Mueller and Cooper, 1986; Keith and Finlay, 1988). Further, with regard to separation and divorce, the effects of parental loss must be distinguished from the effects that result from the marital and family discord occurring prior to the marital dissolution (Fry and Addington, 1985).

A second issue concerns the potential diversity of intact families. Intact families are often assumed to be homogeneous when compared with other types of families (Parish and Kappes, 1980; Mueller and Cooper, 1986; Guttmann, 1988/89). They contain two biological or adoptive parents but intact families can vary along other dimensions of family structure such as the presence of other adults, number of children, and on dimensions of family interaction such as kin and social network embeddedness, degree of intra-familial conflict and unhappiness, and so forth (Booth and Edwards, 1989; Amato and Booth, 1991). Failure to consider the range of structural and interactive variation within intact families may result in an implicit framework that views intact families as ideal and other types of family structures as deviations that are necessarily deleterious for children. The links between family structure and child outcomes can only be established if the diversity and complexity of all families are incorporated both conceptually and empirically.

Third, many important aspects related to single parent family structure are typically not measured. These include length of time spent in various family types, the number of changes in family structure experienced during childhood, the extent and quality of contact with the non-custodial parent, availability of parent substitutes, and the general issues of family extension and family social support. Some of this information is available for children ages 11–16 in the United States (Furstenberg et al., 1983). In a related vein, the degree of economic change between the intact and non-intact state is rarely assessed.

The literature on dependent children frequently uses clinical samples (Demo and Acock, 1991) but this is not so much the case for research on adults. However, there are sampling problems that cross-cut with the type of information collected. On the one hand, some studies use small, non-representative samples and focus on the more subjective aspects of adult life (Parish and Kappes, 1980; Greenberg and Nay, 1982; Guttmann, 1988/89; Lauer and Lauer, 1991). On the other, some studies use large-scale national surveys that they are generally free of problems of non-representativeness but are limited in the types of information available for study and lack theoretically relevant variables (Glenn and Kramer, 1985; Keith and Finlay, 1988; Acock and Kiecolt, 1989; Thornton, 1991). In between are studies that use representative samples of limited categories of persons such as young adults (Mueller and Cooper, 1986; Amato, 1988b) or married persons only (Booth and Edwards, 1989).

The research design of most studies is cross-sectional, a major limitation when the subject matter is temporal by nature. Increasingly, longitudinal designs are being employed. In Britain, the National Child Development Study (Ferri, 1993) and in the U.S., data sets like the Panel Study of Income Dynamics, the National Longitudinal Survey of Youth, the National Longitudinal Survey of Young Men and the National Longitudinal Survey of Young Women (McLanahan, 1985; Michael and Tuma, 1985; Krein and Beller, 1988; Amato and Booth, 1991; Thornton, 1991) facilitate longitudinal analyses. Often these data sets are limited in information about family structure and in the types of dependent variables available for analysis. The Wallerstein and Kelly (1980) longitudinal data are of some use as the sample ages into adulthood, but are semi-clinical and lack a control group.

The statistical control of SES is not the pervasive problem that it is in studies of dependent children, although some studies (Parish and Kappes, 1980; Lauer and Lauer, 1991) fail to control for the SES background of family of origin. A more important issue is diversity in the measurement of SES, mostly the result of data availability. The educational level of the mother (and often the father) is usually controlled but occupational prestige of the father is often also used as part of the SES control (Glenn and Kramer, 1985; 1987; Amato and Booth, 1991) which creates inaccuracies depending on the degree of paternal involvement, financial or otherwise. Family income may or may be included. Other dimensions of SES, such as employment status of mother and welfare status of family, are rarely employed (McLanahan, 1985). Differences in the measurement of SES hamper comparability of findings and their interpretation.

Research Findings

Educational Attainment

A number of studies has shown that children from single parent families complete less formal schooling than children from intact families (Shaw, 1982; McLanahan, 1985; Mueller and Cooper, 1986; Wadsworth and Maclean, 1986; Keith and Finlay, 1988; Krein and Beller, 1988). The negative impact of single parent families varies with length of time spent in a single parent family (Hofferth, 1982; Shaw, 1982; Krein and Beller, 1988), number of children in the family (Wadsworth and Maclean, 1986), cause of the single parent structure with families resulting from death of one parent less affected (Wadsworth and Maclean, 1986), the ages at which a child lives in a non-intact family (Hofferth, 1982; Krein and Beller, 1988), and sex of the child with a greater impact on both males (Krein and Beller, 1988) and females (Keith and Finlay, 1988) reported. A recent meta-analysis shows that females are more educationally disadvantaged (Amato and Keith, 1991). As much as one-half of the difference between children from intact and non-intact families in likelihood of graduating from high school can be accounted for by family income (Astone and McLanahan, 1991). The remaining difference may be due to the school-related parenting behaviours and attitudes of single parents versus parents in intact homes. Astone and McLanahan (1991) report significant differences in parental supervision and monitoring of school progress and in parental educational aspirations but they found that these do not account for the lower educational level of children from single parent families.

Social Economic Status

Relatively little research documents the degree to which SES in adulthood is related to marital disruption and/or the single parent family experience in childhood. SES is more frequently used as a control variable (and viewed as a mediating variable) than as a dependent variable. Generally, results indicate that the adult children of single parent families have lower incomes than those of others (Mueller and Cooper, 1986; Wadsworth and Maclean, 1986), are more likely to have collected welfare in the past year, and are less likely to be homeowners (Mueller and Cooper, 1986). There is some suggestion that the income of men is negatively affected by family disruption due to divorce or separation only if their family of origin is blue-collar (Wadsworth and Maclean, 1986). On the other hand, the negative effect of a single parent family background on occupational prestige holds only for women (Mueller and Cooper, 1986). Both men and women fail to compensate in adulthood for the loss in SES experienced with parental divorce or separation (Wadsworth and Maclean, 1986).

Divorce Proneness

It is widely held that persons whose parents have divorced are more likely to experience divorce themselves. Although this general finding is reported (Pope and Mueller, 1977; Mueller and Cooper, 1986), evidence regarding intergenerational transmission of divorce is complicated. Studies indicate that the relationship holds for white women (Glenn and Kramer, 1987; Keith and Finlay, 1988; McLanahan and Bumpass, 1988) and for lower SES men (Keith and Finlay, 1988) but not for white men or blacks (Glenn and Kramer, 1988) and black women (McLanahan and Bumpass, 1988). Moore and Waite (1981) reported that divorce heritage exists only among those who marry at average ages, and not for persons who marry young. Others find that the transmission of divorce does not hold when age, education, SES, and place of birth are controlled (Heekerens, 1987). Researchers both favour (McLanahan and Bumpass, 1988) and reject (Glenn and Kramer, 1987) a role modelling and socialization theory explanation. Booth and Edwards (1989) found that persons from unhappy, intact homes have greater marital instability and dissatisfaction, as well as more negative family relationships than do adult children from divorced homes. Despite this, the offspring of unhappy, intact homes do not have a greater propensity to divorce, thus suggesting that toughing out an unhappy marriage is passed along from generation to generation.

Other Marriage-Related Behaviours

Some studies have found persons from divorced homes and single parent families are more likely to marry at younger ages (Mueller and Pope, 1977; Glenn and Kramer, 1987; Keith and Finlay, 1988; McLanahan and Bumpass, 1988). This has been attributed to low educational attainment (McLanahan, 1985; Keith and Finlay 1988), escape from an unpleasant home environment, emotional neediness that leads to early heterosexual relations (Wallerstein and Kelly, 1980; McLanahan, 1985), and/or parental inability to control dating behaviour (McLanahan and Bumpass, 1988). Other studies (Michael and Tuma, 1985; Mueller and Cooper, 1986) report no relationship between living in a single parent family and timing of marriage. Thornton (1991) found parental marital disruption to be associated with likelihood of cohabitation; perhaps it is not age at marriage that is affected, but rather the pathway to marriage, resulting from the transmission of more permissive attitudes toward sex outside marriage (socialization model). Both young age at marriage and cohabitation before marriage are associated with higher divorce probability (Balakrishnan et al., 1987; Thornton and Rodgers, 1987; Booth and Johnson, 1988), and could play a role in the greater propensity to divorce among children of parental divorce. Persons from disrupted homes, either due to death or divorce, are more likely to be involved in an intimate relationship such as legal or common-law marriage or steady dating, than persons from intact families, a finding that has been attributed to an intimacy deficit within non-intact homes (Lauer and Lauer, 1991). Quality of the relationship, however, does not vary by family background (Lauer and Lauer, 1991).

Attitudes to Marriage

Mixed findings are reported in studies of marriage attitudes among persons who have experienced parental divorce. Some have reported that the effects of parental divorce on adult attitudes towards marriage are weak; the children of divorced homes are not anti-marriage (or pro-divorce) (Amato, 1988b) and they are as desirous of marriage and as likely as persons from intact families to expect their marriages to last (Guttmann, 1988/89). On the other hand, there is evidence that persons who experienced the divorce of their parents have more favourable attitudes towards divorce (Greenberg and Nay, 1982) and cohabitation (Thornton and Camburn, 1987).

Adult Adjustment and Well-Being

Research on adult adjustment tends to focus on the long-term effects of the experience of parental marital dissolution, particularly divorce, rather than the effects of childhood family structure. Overall, results suggest a small, negative impact of marital dissolution on psychological well-being in adulthood, but the topic is fraught with controversy. Kulka and Weingarten (1979) used U.S. samples from 1957 and 1976 and found few differences between adults from divorced and intact families on measures of adult adjustment, after current life circumstances and social background variables were controlled; men, however, fared somewhat worse than women. Acock and Kiecolt (1989) report few significant differences, and no differential impact by gender, on five adjustment indicators, after SES controls are introduced to their analysis. Amato (1988a) reports no difference in self-esteem among adults who grew up in intact homes, those who experienced a parental divorce, and those who experienced a parental death. A significant difference in sense of power disappeared when education was introduced as a control.

Amato and Booth (1991) compared persons whose parents had divorced with persons brought up in intact families and found modest, but significant, differences in psychological, social, and marital well-being. But adults from intact, but unhappy, homes scored as low as adults from divorced homes. Also, the circumstances of divorce matter; persons who experienced multiple parental divorces and a loss of closeness to parents are at particular risk in terms of adult well-being. In contrast, adults who experienced a low stress parental divorce fare better than those who grew up in unhappy intact homes. This provides some empirical support for the belief that it is better for children to have their parents divorce than to live in an unhappy family situation. While the bulk of research shows small effects on adult adjustment, some studies report different conclusions. Nock (1982) reports positive effects of parental divorce on subsequent adult adjustment and suggests that coping with parental divorce equips one with the psychological skills and adaptability to deal with problems later in life. His findings are consistent with Veevers' (1991) notion of divorce as a developmental paradigm. On the other hand, Glenn and Kramer (1985) found significant negative effects on psychological well-being that are stronger for women than for men and that are due to parental divorce itself and not to post-divorce living arrangements.

Summary

Research indicates that single family parent homes and marital disruption have a modest, negative impact on adult children. Many aspects of adult life, however, have not been examined; these include parenting behaviour, caregiving to elder kin, involvement in community and voluntary associations, leisure activities, migration behaviour, religiosity, political involvement and attitudes, and health-related behaviours. No set of results is entirely consistent from the limited range of life dimensions that have been researched. Single parent families (and marital disruption due to divorce or separation) appear to be associated with lower educational attainment, lower income and SES in adulthood, higher likelihood of divorce especially for white women, younger age at marriage, and somewhat lower well-being. The findings do not hold for all categories of persons but the overall thrust cannot be ignored, particularly given the length of time between childhood background family situations and adult measurement. No theoretical perspective is able to account for the diversity and complexity of results. Theoretical refinement is required; a blending of socialization theory and the socio-economic perspective may be fruitful as results show some support for both models. Also, more attention to methodological issues is needed; the potpourri of methods used, which contribute to non-comparable findings, is an impediment to sorting out adult outcomes. No direct relationship between findings and methods is evident although how-we-know and what-we-know are not independent (Kanoy and Cunningham, 1984).

Examination of Canadian Data

Measurement of Family Background Status

The 1986 Canadian GSS–2 provides data on selected social characteristics and activities for a random sample of persons aged 15 and over, excluding residents of the Yukon and Northwest Territories and full-time residents of institutions (n = 16,390; response rate = 79%). Respondents were asked: "When you were 15 years old, did you live with your own father?" and "When you were 15 years old, did you live with your own mother?" Adoptive parents are included as own mother or own father. Respondents who did not live with both parents at age 15 were asked if the reason was due to death, to divorce or marital separation, or some other reason. These questions allowed for the classification of respondents into three types of family status at age 15: (1) persons living with both parents (intact families); (2) persons living with only one parent as a result of death; and (3) persons living with only one parent as a result of divorce or separation. Cases in which respondents do not fall into any of these categories such as living with neither parent or living with only one parent as a result of never-marriage, were excluded due to small numbers. Single parent families due to never-marriage are a rare occurrence for the age groups considered. Cases where the respondent and parents were temporarily living apart, such as child at boarding school or father in military service, were included in the intact category. The distribution of the sample into the three types is given in Table 19-1.

This measure of family status, although commonly used in the American General Social Surveys, contains important limitations, apart from the obvious one that a cross-sectional design is used although a longitudinal design is more appropriate. Wojkiewicz (1992) points out that it is a fairly accurate structural measure for persons in intact families (most persons who were in an intact family at age 15 had lived their entire lives in it) but is imprecise and fails to capture the diversity of the family life course for persons in non-intact families. For example, a person in category 3 may have experienced one parental divorce and one subsequent single parent family situation; another may have lived in a number of one- and two-parent situations, as parents separated and reconciled, or as the custodial parent

Table 19-1:

Family Status at Age 15, by Age and Sex

Age[a]	Intact Families	Broken by Death	Broken by Div./Sep.	Chi-Square
Males				
15-24	(1,365) 21.8%	(72) 14.1%	(160) 46.1%	
25-39	(2,153) 34.4%	(146) 28.6%	(107) 30.8%	
40-54	(1,358) 21.7%	(137) 26.9%	(56) 16.1%	
55-69	(1,014) 16.2%	(90) 17.6%	(24) 6.9%	
70+	(369) 5.9%	(65) 12.7%	-	
Total	(6,260) 100.0%	(510) 100.0%	(346) 100.0%	200.27***
Percent	88.0%	7.2%	4.9%	
Females				
15-24	(1,502) 20.2%	(70) 9.9%	(199) 43.4%	
25-39	(2,536) 34.1%	(156) 22.2%	(188) 41.0%	
40-54	(1,502) 20.2%	(171) 24.2%	(50) 10.9%	
55-69	(1,257) 16.9%	(193) 27.4%	(14) 3.1%	
70+	(640) 8.6%	(114) 16.2%	(7) 1.5%	
Total	(7,438) 100.0%	(703) 100.0%	(458) 100.0%	384.87***
Percent	86.5%	8.2%	5.3%	
Total (both sexes)	(13,698) 87.2%	(1,213) 7.7%	(804) 5.1%	557.57***

[a] Data not age-standardized.

Number of missing observations = 675.

*** p < .001♦

went through a number of legal or consensual marriages. The GSS–2 did not ask about the timing of family disruptions due to death or divorce or separation. Therefore, the duration of periods of single parent family living in relation to age of child cannot be assessed. The trichotomization does not correspond closely with living arrangements or family structure at age 15. Not all persons in groups 2 and 3 were living in single parent family arrangements. Respondents in these two groups were asked if, when they were 15, a male/female took the role of their father/mother. Information presented in Table 19-2 shows a replacement father cited by more than 20% of respondents in group 2 and approximately one-third of persons in group 3. Whether the replacement parents were step-parents, relatives, or friends, or if they resided with the respondent at age 15 is unknown. The degree of parental loss associated with divorce or separation, which could range from complete parent-child dissociation through varying amounts and

Table 19-2:
Replacement Mother/Father by Family Status
at Age 15, and Sex

	Broken by Death	Broken by Div./Sep.	Chi-Square
Replacement Mother [a]			
Males (n = 203)	56.7%	[b]	
Females (n = 308)	47.7%	[b]	
Chi-square (sex)	2.52 (ns)		
Replacement Father [a]			
Males (n = 629)	22.7%	32.3%	6.78**
Females (n = 851)	22.7%	33.1%	10.90***
Chi-square (sex)	0.00 (ns)	0.02 (ns)	
n =	409	241	65.32***

[a] The GSS-2 question asked "Was there a male/female who took the role of your father/mother?"
[b] Too small to report, by Statistics Canada guidelines.
** p < .01
*** p < .001 ♦

kinds of parent-child contact, is not known. Further, there is no information on variations on marital and familial conflict or happiness in intact families.

Why proceed given these limitations? The GSS–2 provides the only Canadian data that allow for any examination of adult outcomes of marital disruption and single parent families. There are no longitudinal data sets. The two Statistics Canada surveys that collected information on family history, the 1990 GSS–5 (Family and Friends) and the 1984 Canada History Survey (FHS), do not contain data on childhood family structure or parental marital history.

Outcome Variables

Three types of dependent variables are considered: behavioral variables, satisfaction variables, and religiosity. Behavioral variables include educational attainment, individual income, SES, and current marital status. The GSS–2 asked four questions related to educational attainment; these questions were combined to create a three-fold categorization as cell sizes do not allow for a finer education breakdown. Individual income was derived from the question "What was your income before taxes from wages, salaries and self-employment during the past twelve months?" The before-tax income of individuals was distributed into quartiles with differing breakpoints (provided in Table 19-4) for men and women. SES was measured by the Pineo scale (Pineo and Porter, 1967) and distributed into quartiles with differing ranges (given in Table 19-5) for men and women. Current marital status was collapsed into three categories to preserve cell size. Respondents evaluated their degree of satisfaction on a number of life domains. In addition, two broader questions were asked concerning satisfaction with one's self and with life in general. All responses were measured on a five-point scale ranging from very satisfied to very dissatisfied. Due to the distribution of responses, satisfaction was treated as a dichotomous variable — very satisfied vs. all other categories — and comparisons were made across the very satisfied category. Religiosity was measured by two questions in the GSS–2. Respondents were asked "What, if any, is your religion?" A choice of eight religious groups, plus a response category of no religion and the opportunity to write in another type of religion, was provided. Responses were categorized as no religion vs. all other categories and comparisons were made across the no religion response. Respondents who indicated a religion were also asked their frequency of religious attendance on a five-point scale ranging from at least once a week to never; this was collapsed into three categories.

Age Standardization

The age composition of the three groups varies. Persons who were not living with one of their parents due to divorce are likely to be younger than persons in the other two groups, given the relative recency of easy divorce in Canada. Robinson and McVey (1985) show the counterbalancing effects of increased divorce, on the one hand, and decreased widowhood, on the other, on marital dissolution trends in Canada over the period 1921–81. Table 19-1 reveals a significant difference across the three groups in age composition. Age standardization was performed to eliminate the confounding effect of age. Cases were weight-adjusted by age group within each family status category while controlling for sex. This ensures that the age-family status distribution is the same as that of the weighted population for each sex. Ideally, this analysis should, also, control for childhood SES. However, GSS–2 questions on education of mother and father contained high percentages (25–33%) of unusable responses, making the statistical control of childhood SES subject to unacceptable risk of error. The effect of not controlling for childhood SES is to inflate differences across family status categories to an unknown degree. However, analysis controlling for adult education (not presented here) revealed no discernible inflationary effect.

Findings from the Canadian Data

The majority of persons lived in an intact family at age 15 regardless of current age. Approximately 84–89% were in intact families among all age groups; Table 19-1 shows no variation by age. In the sample as a whole, 8% experienced a parental death by age 15 and 5% at least one parental

Table 19-3:

Educational Attainment by Family Status at Age 15, by Sex

Education	Intact Families	Broken by Death	Broken by Div./Sep.	Chi-Square
Males				
Less than high school	37.3%	45.5%	35.2%	
High school	16.5%	13.0%	21.1%	
Some post-secondary	46.2%	41.5%	43.7%	
n =	6,206	501	324	19.24**
Females				
Less than high school	37.2%	44.2%	36.7%	
High school	18.2%	15.0%	23.2%	
Some post-secondary	44.5%	40.8%	40.1%	
n =	7,361	702	456	22.03**
Chi-square (sex)	7.43*	.98 (ns)	1.08 (ns)	

Number of missing observations = 820.
* p < .05
** p < .01 ◆

divorce/separation. The likelihood of parental death by age 15 is higher for older persons and the likelihood of parental divorce/separation is higher for younger persons, which is in keeping with mortality and divorce trends. There is a slight tendency for females to be more likely to experience a parental divorce/separation than males. Nearly 60% of the persons under age 40 who saw a parental marital breakup due to divorce or separation by age 15 were female. This fits with U.S. research (Morgan, Lye, and Condran, 1988) indicating that fathers are more reluctant to leave a marriage if there are sons.

Information on replacement parents is shown Table 19-2. Mothers are more likely to be replaced than fathers, indicative of the better remarriage chances of previously married men with children compared with previously married women with children. Men are also likely to be more desirous of another marriage. Marriages broken by death are less likely to have replacement parents than marriages broken by divorce and separation, at least replacement fathers for whom there is complete data. This may indicate that the widowed have better support networks to assist in childrearing (Acock and Kiecolt, 1989) or that persons who are widowed have less desire to remarry compared with those who divorce. Last, the gender of the child has no impact on the likelihood of having a replacement parent for either category of disrupted marital family status.

Table 19-4:

Income Grouping of Individuals by Family Status
at Age 15, by Sex

Income Quartile [a]	Intact Families	Broken by Death	Broken by Div./Sep.	Chi-Square
Males				
First	23.9%	29.9%	25.7%	
Second	24.7%	21.5%	27.3%	
Third	24.1%	25.0%	23.3%	
Fourth	27.3%	23.6%	23.6%	
n =	5,565	469	288	12.92*
Females				
First	41.1%	41.5%	40.7%	
Second	7.1%	6.8%	-[b]	
Third	23.4%	25.2%	24.8%	
Fourth	28.4%	26.6%	26.7%	
n =	6,707	628	405	2.54 (ns)
Chi-square (sex)	891.48***	55.27***	51.30***	

[a] Break points for males are $2,000, $18,000, and $30,000; break points for females are zero income, $1,500, and $12,984. Income refers to income before taxes.

[b] Too small to report, by Statistics Canada guidelines. Number of missing observations (including "don't know") = 2,308.

* $p < .05$
*** $p < .001$ ♦

Table 19-3 indicates significant differences in educational attainment across the three family status groups for both men and women. Men from disrupted family backgrounds have lower levels of educational attainment than men from intact families; the broken by death group are particularly disadvantaged. The picture is mixed for women. Women from intact homes have the most education but women from broken by death homes are not as negatively affected as the broken by divorce group. The effect for women who had a parent die is only evident for low levels of educational attainment; they are not less likely to receive post-secondary education than women whose parents divorced or separated. The overall educational disadvantage of persons who had a parent die during their childhood is contrary to other work that shows that marital disruption due to divorce is more deleterious to educational attainment (Wadsworth and Maclean, 1986). This finding may be due to the lower likelihood of remarriage of the widowed parent, relative to the divorced parent, and accompanying limited financial resources for

Table 19-5:

SES (Pineo) by Family Status at Age 15, by Sex

SES Quartile [a]	Intact Families	Broken by Death	Broken by Div./Sep.	Chi-Square
Males				
First	28.0%	27.8%	24.1%	
Second	24.2%	25.1%	30.3%	
Third	22.9%	25.9%	16.8%	
Fourth	25.0%	21.2%	28.8%	
n =	5,174	404	274	15.32*
Females				
First	26.0%	19.8%	20.6%	
Second	19.1%	21.6%	22.7%	
Third	31.5%	28.1%	35.4%	
Fourth	23.4%	30.4%	21.2%	
n =	4,492	419	282	23.02**
Chi-square (sex)	100.59***	13.74***	25.32***	

[a] For males, the Pineo values for quartiles are: first quartile = values 2-6, second quartile = values 7-10, third quartile = values 11-13, fourth quartile = values 14+.
For females, the values are: first quartile = values 2-6, second quartile = values 7-11, third quartile = values 12-13, fourth quartile = values 14+. Values refer to current or last job. Number of missing observations = 5,325.
* p < .05, ** p < .01, *** p < .001♦

education. Significant gender differences in educational attainment exist only for persons from intact families with females more likely than males to graduate from high school but less likely to pursue post-secondary schooling. There is no significant gender difference for the other two groups. The broken by death group displays the same general pattern as the intact group; men are more likely than women to have some post-secondary education for those in the broken by divorce group. The latter finding fits U.S. research that indicates non-custodial fathers are more likely to finance the education of sons (Amato and Keith, 1991).

Table 19-4 shows that family status in childhood has a weak negative impact on adult income for men. There is a slight tendency for men from homes broken by death to have lower incomes than men from families broken by divorce or separation. No significant differences and no pattern exists for women. Thus, Canadian data do not show an impact of family status on income to the degree observed in the U.S. The data in Table 19-4 show that men's income is considerably higher than women's, even with

Table 19-6:

Current Marital Status by Family Status at Age 15, by Sex

Marital Status	Intact Families	Broken by Death	Broken by Div./Sep.	Chi-Square
Males				
Married/Com. Law	65.3%	59.4%	61.6%	
Sep./Divorced	3.2%	*	*	
Other	31.5%	33.0%	34.6%	
n =	8,253	672	430	29.17***
Females				
Married/Com. Law	62.5%	61.0%	55.8%	
Sep./Divorced	5.4%	7.0%	*	
Other	32.1%	32.1%	36.8%	
n =	8,379	793	515	11.22**
Chi-square (sex)	41.39***	.36(ns)	5.45(ns)	

* Too small to report, by Statistics Canada guidelines.
Number of missing observations = 687.
** p < .01, *** p < .001♦

different quartile break points for men and women. The gender differential in income occurs in all three groups; thus, family status background exerts no exacerbating effect.

SES, as measured by the Pineo scale and presented in Table 19-5, varies to a significant degree across the three family status groups for both men and women. The relationship between SES and family status as children is ambiguous and not strong. The relative ranking of the three groups is not readily apparent but men from broken by divorce families are not disadvantaged — they are least likely to be in the lowest SES quartile and most likely to be in the highest SES quartile. Results indicate a slight SES advantage for women from non-intact families. Gender differences in SES are significant for all three family status groups. The results favour women, which may be due to the differential SES quartile groupings by gender and/or to the large number of missing observations in the analysis.

Current marital status is presented in Table 19-6; both men and women from non-intact family backgrounds are less likely to be in either a married or common-law union. This is contrary to U.S. findings that persons from disrupted homes are more likely to be in relationships due to a possible intimacy deficit (Lauer and Lauer, 1991). The data suggest that persons from disrupted families are somewhat more likely to be divorced or separated, but cell sizes are too small to make statements with any certainty. The GSS–2 data do not contain information on marital history; thus, neither divorce

Table 19-7:

Satisfaction with Selected Life Domains by Family Status
at Age 15, by Sex

Percent Very Satisfied	Intact Families	Broken by Death	Broken by Div./Sep.	Chi-Square
Males				
Health *(n = 7,014)*	59.0%	56.0%	53.3%	5.61(ns)
Job *(n = 7,011)*	46.8%	49.8%	39.5%	8.65*
Family *(n = 7,004)*	69.6%	64.0%	59.3%	20.69***
Self *(n = 7,007)*	59.4%	57.1%	55.5%	2.70(ns)
Life *(n = 7,020)*	48.2%	45.7%	41.0%	7.02**
Females				
Health *(n = 8,463)*	54.8%	50.0%	50.1%	9.04*
Job *(n = 8,462)*	49.3%	47.6%	48.0%	1.01(ns)
Family *(n = 8,454)*	73.0%	66.0%	68.4%	18.86***
Self *(n = 8,427)*	55.7%	50.6%	46.3%	20.75***
Life *(n = 8,491)*	48.7%	42.8%	39.0%	23.61***
Chi-square (sex)				
Health	24.54***	4.02*	0.65(ns)	
Job	8.59**	0.47(ns)	5.17*	
Family	18.29***	0.42(ns)	6.33*	
Self	18.06***	4.70*	6.04*	
Life	0.42(ns)	0.94(ns)	0.23(ns)	

Number of missing observations ranges from 859 to 936.
* p < .05, ** p < .01, *** p < .001 ♦

proneness nor differences in age at marriage can be studied. The GSS practice of combining married and common-law categories does not allow for an examination of differences in likelihood of cohabiting.

A significant gender difference in current marital status exists only for those from intact families, with men more likely to be in a married or common-law union and less likely to be divorced or separated.

Table 19-7 shows that satisfaction with life domains of health, job, and family is highest among both men and women from intact families. Differences are particularly large for the family domain; persons from non-intact homes are less likely to report that they are very satisfied with family life. Among men, the broken by divorce group is the least satisfied; among women, it is those who lost a parent through death. Comparisons on global satisfaction with self and with life again favour persons from intact homes. Differences are particularly large for women and the pattern of results for both satisfaction measures is consistent; the highest amount of satisfaction occurs for women from intact homes and the lowest for women from families experiencing a parental divorce. These results are consistent with some U.S. research (Glenn and Kramer, 1985) reporting that parental divorce negatively affects adult well-being, particularly for women. In general, men are more satisfied than women; this is more the case for persons from intact homes than for those from the other two categories.

There is a strong relationship between family status and religious self-identification, particularly for men, as shown in Table 19-8. For both men and women, persons from intact homes are the least likely to state that they have no religion and persons from divorced homes are the most likely to do so. For men, the percentage with no religion nearly doubles, from 13% to 23%. Persons from families broken by death have intermediate levels, but are closer to the figures for persons from intact families than for those with a parental divorce, particularly among women. Gender differences in religious self-identification are highly significant for all three family status types; thus, gender differences in not having a religion are not mediated by family status background. Religious attendance varies significantly by family status for both women and men and corresponds to the information on religious self-identification. Those from intact families are the most frequent attenders and persons with a parental divorce are the least frequent attenders. Unlike religious self-identification, differences by family status are as large for women as they are for men. The low religiosity of persons from homes experiencing parental divorce could be due to a socialization effect. Glenn and Supancic (1984) and GSS–5 data show that persons who divorce are less religious than persons who do not divorce. Thus, the children of divorce were probably raised in homes with less religious involvement and commitment and carry this non-involvement into adulthood. That persons who had their families disrupted by death display relatively low religiosity, compared with persons from intact homes, suggests that the loss of a parent and/or the subsequent single parent family experience may exert an independent effect on religiosity. Gender differences in religious attendance vary by family status. The greater religious involvement of women compared to men is highly significant for those from intact families only. The relationship disappears for persons from families disrupted by death. Why family status mediates gender differences in church involvement is not known.

Conclusion

Childhood family situation has some negative effects in adulthood. Non-intactness of the family unit in childhood affects dimensions of adult life regardless of cause (death or divorce/separation), but the effects

Table 19-8:

Religiosity by Family Status at Age 15, by Sex

	Intact Families	Broken by Death	Broken by Div./Sep.	Chi-Square
(A) Percent stating no religion:				
Males (n = 6987)	12.5%	18.3%	23.4%	42.26***
Females (n = 8478)	7.2%	7.9%	9.8%	13.15*
Chi-square (sex)	107.44***	33.15***	26.86***	
(B) Religious Attendance:[a]				
Males				
At least weekly	28.9%	25.0%	17.6%	
Less often	53.2%	53.4%	54.7%	
Never	17.9%	21.5%	27.7%	
n =	5,375	409	241	65.32***
Females				
At least weekly	34.2%	29.4%	25.3%	
Less often	49.4%	50.0%	45.5%	
Never	16.4%	20.5%	29.2%	
n =	6,788	644	410	56.99***
Chi-square (sex)	38.04***	2.41(ns)	6.62*	

[a] Frequency of attending services/meetings other than on special occasions such as weddings, funerals, etc. Distribution excludes persons who stated they had no religion.
Number of missing observations (A) = 904.
Number of missing observations (B) = 584.
* $p < .05$, *** $p < .001$ ♦

surrounding divorce/separation appear greater. The major effects of non-intactness are lower levels of educational attainment, income for men, current married/common law status, satisfaction, and religiosity. There are similarities with the results of U.S. research but there are also enough differences to suggest that adult outcomes may be bound up with the wider social, economic, and political context of a nation. More knowledge is needed about the consequences for individuals of varying forms and developments in the welfare state.

Results for persons who are presently adults may not hold for today's young children when they are adults. Some of the negative effects, particularly for children from divorced families, may disappear given increased acceptance and decreased stigma of variant family forms and marital arrangements. The meta-analysis performed by Amato and Keith (1991) shows less impact of divorce on adult well-being in the more recent research, which they attribute to increased frequency and social acceptance of divorce. A lessening impact on individuals can be expected in the future to the degree that the effects of family non-intactness are related to societal devaluation or a perception of being different.

Better baseline Canadian data are necessary to separate the consequences of marital disruption from the consequences stemming from living in a single parent family as well as for testing theoretical propositions related to socialization theory and the socio-economic perspective. Canada truly lacks the data with which to address issues dealing with the adult outcomes of childhood single parent family structure. The data presented here are the only available Canadian data and do not provide the necessary information upon which to make informed policy choices. What is needed? A first step is a large data base that will allow a critical mass of researchers in government, educational, and non-profit sectors to examine the complex questions involved in this issue.

20

The Relationship of Mother's Marital Status at the Time of Her First Child's Birth to Socialization and Development

Elizabeth McNaughton

The 1970s saw a large increase in the number of single women giving birth. The number of births to unmarried women continued to grow in the 1980s although the rate of growth in single mother births declined. The increase in births to single mothers has been accompanied by a decline in the number of children being placed for adoption. These trends have given rise to concerns among health and social services professionals about the families headed by unmarried mothers, particularly young unmarried mothers, and the ability of existing services to meet their needs (Clark, Dechman, French and MacCallum, 1991, Chap. 1).

This paper focuses on the socialization and development of children of unmarried mothers by examining their contact with adults, participation in leisure activities, and emotional and intellectual development. The findings are based on a longitudinal study of a sample of unmarried mothers and married mothers who gave birth to their first child in 1978–79 in Nova Scotia. The most recent phase of this study was conducted in 1988; most of the mothers were no longer single parents, but there were differences in the experiences and development of children who were born to unmarried parents.

Study Design

This research project followed a longitudinal quasi-experimental design. An experimental group of 416 unmarried mothers and a quasi-control group of 403 married mothers were selected from among women who gave birth to their first child in a Nova Scotia hospital between July 1, 1978 and February 28, 1979. A comparative methodology was used to determine whether the needs of unmarried mothers were significantly different from their married counterparts. A longitudinal format was used to track life cycle developments. Four data collections occurred from 1978 to 1988: within 6 weeks after birth, at 9 months, at 18 months, and between 9 and 10 years. Young married mothers were under represented in the sample; thus, the fourth data collection was expanded to include an additional 70 young married mothers who were 19 years of age or younger at the time their first child was born. The response rate for the fourth data collection was 73%; 84% of the married mothers were located and agreed to participate compared to 62% of the unmarried mothers. Respondents and non-respondents were compared on demographic factors; no significant differences within either the married or unmarried groups were found.

Data collection included interviews with the mothers using structured questionnaires containing both open and closed questions to obtain information on the mother, the child and their interaction. Some identically worded questions were retained throughout the four research periods to ensure the collection of comparable information. Other questions were designed to obtain retrospective accounts of experiences. In addition, a sub-sample of 223 children were given psychological and educational assessments. These assessments were conducted by a psychometrist, under the direction of a psychologist, and took place in the school the child attended. All the analysis is based on the original marital status and age of the mother. The younger mothers were 19 years of age and under at the time of the birth of the child, while the older mothers were 20 years and older.

Family Structure

Any study of the single parent family experience is complicated by the fact that children in single parent families are likely to experience more than one family structure during the course of their childhood (Caple, 1988). Although 38% of women who participated in the most recent phase of the study were single when the research began in 1978, less than 8% were still single in 1988–89. Over the 10 year period, 81% of the unmarried mothers changed their marital status by marrying or entering a common-law union. In contrast, only 18% of the married group changed their marital status.

Of the unmarried mothers who married, two-thirds ended this relationship within seven years. Some of these mothers later remarried or entered a common-law union. Of the married women who experienced a change in marital status, approximately 30% (33% for the younger mothers and 29% for the older mothers) changed their marital status again within one year or less and most did so within the study period. The second change was usually marriage or the formation of a common-law union. As a result of changes in family structure during the ten years since their birth, 82% of all the children in this study were living in two-parent families at the time of the fourth interview.

Socialization Experiences

The relationship of family structure to socialization is unclear (McLanahan and Booth, 1989). Some studies suggest that in single parent families there is less parental involvement in schoolwork, less supervision, and less parental influence (McLanahan and Booth, 1989). However, parents are not the only persons involved in childcare. Eichler suggests that "it is at present the normal pattern rather than the exception that a child is taken care of by somebody other than the mother during significant periods of his or her working time" (1988). Childcare is frequently complex and may consist of multiple arrangements (Kamerman and Hayes, 1982). This section examines patterns of caregiving and the leisure-time activities of the children, including help received with homework, to determine if the experiences of the married and unmarried mothers differ.

Caregivers

The mothers in the study were asked to identify who had assisted them with child care responsibilities at each phase of the study. At the time of the first interview, 72% of mothers said that they were the sole caregiver compared to 57% at the second and third interviews and 17% at the final interview. Shortly after the child's birth, even a number of the married mothers saw themselves as sole caregivers. Not surprisingly, more of the unmarried mothers (25%) compared to the married mothers (13%) saw themselves as sole caregivers at the time of the last interview. Assistance with caregiving is provided by husbands, relatives, friends, babysitters and day care. Husbands constitute 70% of the group providing assistance, with other relatives providing 14%, friends babysitters and formal child care 13% and the child's father (when he and the child's mother are not married) 3%. A number of the mothers reported having more than one person to assist with child rearing.

Mothers are the primary although not necessarily the sole caregivers. All mothers spend a considerable amount of time with their children. On school days the mothers are most likely to spend between 4 and 6 hours a day with their children, averaging 5.25 hours. On Saturdays two-thirds of the mothers spend more than 8 hours with the children for an average of 10.2 hours compared to three-quarters of them who spend more than 8 hours with their children on Sundays for an average of 10.5 hours. There were no significant differences between the married and unmarried mothers. The study indicates that husbands usually give assistance daily. On weekdays, husbands average 3.5 hours with the children; on Saturdays, 8.6 hours and on Sundays, 9.7 hours. The average time spent with children by husbands of the married

Table 20-1:

Percentage of Mothers Receiving Help with Caring for Their Children from Relatives, Babysitters and Day Cares, by Child's Age, and Mother's Original Age and Marital Status

	19 Years and Under			20 Years and Over		
	Married	*Unmarried*	*(n)*	*Married*	*Unmarried*	*(n)*
Children Aged 0-2 Years						
Relatives	85.4	88.9	(194)	72.1	78.3	(205)
Babysitters	30.2	27.0	(63)	58.9	38.3*	(152)
Day Cares	0.0	6.3	(8)	5.0	5.0	(14)
Other	2.1	0.8	(3)	0.0	1.7	(1)
Children Age 2 Until Starting School						
Relatives	91.7	88.1	(199)	75.3	83.3	(215)
Babysitters	51.0	45.2	(106)	67.6	61.7	(185)
Day Cares	39.6	41.3	(90)	61.2	50.0	(164)
Other	0.0	0.0	(0)	0.0	0.0	(0)
Children Since Starting School						
Relatives	85.4	86.5	(191)	77.2	85.0	(220)
Babysitters	71.9	63.5	(149)	80.4	73.3	(220)
Day Cares	4.2	10.3	(17)	7.3	13.3	(24)
Other	1.0	3.2	(5)	1.4	0.0	(3)

Note: From *Mothers & Children: One Decade Later* (p.172) by S. Clark, M. Dechman, F. French and B. MacCallum, Nova Scotia Department of Community Services.

*Phi = .16, Significance of Chi-square < .01. ◆

and originally unmarried mothers varies little, averaging only 6 minutes difference on weekdays. The husbands of married mothers spend an extra 25 minutes on Saturdays and 40 minutes on Sundays with the children, but these differences were not statistically significant.

The pattern of assistance from helpers, other than husbands, varies depending upon the age of the child (see Table 20-1). Close to 80% of the mothers received help from relatives at all three stages. When the children were under two, 87% of unmarried mothers compared to 76% of married mothers received assistance from relatives (Phi = 0.11, significance of Chi-square < 0.01, n = 501). This difference decreases over time. Babysitters and day care were used more extensively at different stages. For the first two years, only 43% of mothers use babysitters compared to 58% when the children were between two and school age and 74% once the children started school. More married mothers than unmarried mothers use babysitters — 52% compared to 31% when the children were under two years of age. The older mothers used babysitters more than the younger mothers and the older married mothers used them significantly more frequently than the older unmarried mothers. The difference among the younger mothers was not significant. Babysitters are used more frequently by all mothers when the children are between age 2 and school age. The married women are significantly more likely to have used this form of child care and it is the older women who are considerably more likely to employ babysitters than the younger ones. Once the children have entered school, a majority of mothers receive help from babysitters but there is still a significant difference between married mothers and unmarried mothers; 82% of married mothers compared to 69% of unmarried mothers use babysitters for school age children.

The pattern for the use of day care is different than that for babysitters. Day care is most frequently used for children between the age of 2 and school age with 51% of the mothers using day care for this age group compared to 4% of mothers when the children were under 2 and 8% for children of school age. Married mothers (57%) were more likely to use day care than unmarried mothers (45%). Older married mothers (61%) were the most likely to use day care. The high percentage of mothers using day care may reflect the broad definition used in the study; nursery school programs, pre and post school programs, and summer programs were included as day care programs.

Data were also gathered on the number of child care arrangements that the mothers had made over the 10 years. These ranged from three mothers who had done everything themselves to one mother who had had 37 different arrangements. Two-thirds of the mothers (68%) report between one and seven different arrangements with the remaining third of the mothers reporting eight or more arrangements. Less than 5% of the mothers report

14 or more arrangements, while only 10% had two or fewer arrangements. There was no significant difference between the married and unmarried mothers with respect to the number of arrangements. Seven or fewer arrangements were used by 69% of the married mothers compared to 72% of the unmarried mothers. The unmarried mothers are somewhat more likely to have two or fewer arrangements (15%) compared to the married mothers (7%). Large numbers of child care arrangements, 14 or more, are also slightly more characteristic of unmarried mothers.

Leisure Activities

Leisure activities are a factor in the socialization of children. The mothers in this study were asked to identify their children's leisure-time activities and indicate the number of hours they spent on these activities in a week. Table 20-2 indicates that virtually all children play with their friends and watch television during the week. The other most frequent activities are reading, doing or being helped with homework, and playing alone (with at least 83% of the children in these activities). The least frequent activities are lessons and organized sports with fewer than 41% of the children participating in these activities. In two areas, lessons and groups, the participation rate of children of married mothers was significantly lower than for children of unmarried mothers. When age is taken into consideration, differences appear between the older married and unmarried mothers. The children of older married mothers are more apt to be helped with homework (Phi = .13, significance of Chi-square < .05) and to engage in lessons outside of school (Phi = .17, significance of Chi-square < .01) than the children of older unmarried mothers.

There is similarity among the children with respect to the amount of time spent on various activities (see Table 20-3). The children spend considerably more time playing with friends and watching television (35–40 hours a week) than in any other activity. An average of less than an hour a day was spent on any other activity. Reading, playing alone, and homework consume the next most amount of time. The least amount of time was spent on lessons, groups, organized sports and being read to. Differences between the married and unmarried group were small. The children of unmarried mothers spend over one hour more a week watching television and over two hours less playing with friends than did the children of married mothers. There was also some variation among those activities that consumed less time. The children of unmarried mothers receive more help with homework and spend more time with organized sports while the children of married mothers spend more time on lessons and with groups.

Research on the leisure activities of children is limited but information from a national survey of 9 to 12 year olds does provide a partial comparison. Two common activities, watching television and reading were compared.

Table 20-2:

*Participation Rates of Children in Leisure-Time Activities by
Mother's Original Age and Marital Status*

Activity	Married (n)	Unmarried (n)	Total
T.V.	99.4 (313)	100.0 (186)	99.6
Reading	95.5 (313)	93.5 (185)	94.8
Read to	56.9 (313)	59.7 (186)	57.9
Homework	95.2 (313)	90.3 (186)	93.4
Help with homework	89.1 (313)	85.4 (185)	87.8
Play with Friends	100.0 (313)	100.0 (186)	100.0
Play alone	83.1 (313)	83.2 (185)	83.1
Organized sport	41.0 (313)	40.3 (186)	40.8
Lessons	45.0 (313)	28.5[a] (186)	38.9
Groups	60.7 (313)	48.9[b] (186)	56.3

[a] Phi = 16, Significance of Chi-square < .001
[b] Phi = 12, Significance of Chi-square < .05 ◆

The children in the study are similar to Canadian children as a whole with respect to watching television. The number of hours spent reading, however, is less than the Canadian average for both 9 and 12 year olds. The findings that the children of unmarried mothers watch television more than those of married mothers is consistent with other research (Messaris and Hornik, 1983: 51).

Child Development

Psychological assessments were completed on 223 of the children. These were selected so that each of the four age and marital status categories were equally represented. The assessment included (a) the Wechsler Intelligence Scale for Children (WISC-R, Wechsler, 1974) to determine intelligence quotient, (b) the Peabody Picture Vocabulary Test (PPVT-R, Dunn and Dunn, 1981) to determine vocabulary, (c) the Beery Developmental Test of Visual-Motor Integration (Beery, 1982) to determine the level of eye-hand coordination, (d) the Basic Achievements Skills Individual Screener (BASIS, Psychological Corporation, 1983) to determine academic achievement in reading, math, spelling and writing, (e) the Piers-Harris Self Concept Scale (Piers, 1984) to determine self-image and (f) the Achenbach Child Behaviour Rating Scale (Achenbach and Edelbrock, 1983) to determine both teachers' and mothers' perceptions of behaviour in the areas of social withdrawal, aggression, and activity, and teachers' perceptions of attention. The study

Table 20-3:

Average Hours Per Week Spent by the Children in Leisure-Time Activities by the Mother's Original Age and Marital Status

	19 Years and Under				20 Years and Over			
Leisure Activity	Married	(n)	Unmarried	(n)	Married	(n)	Unmarried	(n)
Watching T.V.	17.49	(95)	17.23	(126)	15.45	(218)	17.21	(60)
Reading	5.86	(95)	5.70	(126)	5.21	(218)	5.33	(59)
Being read to	1.54	(95)	1.67	(126)	1.32	(218)	1.53	(60)
Homework	3.64	(95)	3.30	(126)	3.24	(218)	3.37	(60)
Being helped with homework	1.99	(95)	2.51	(126)	1.83	(218)	1.88	(59)
Play with friends	21.66	(95)	18.21[a]	(126)	20.15	(218)	18.72	(60)
Play alone	3.65	(95)	4.72	(126)	4.81	(218)	5.26	(59)
Organized sports	1.20	(95)	1.78	(126)	1.55	(217)	1.73	(60)
Lessons	0.42	(95)	0.55	(126)	1.16	(218)	0.48[b]	(60)
Groups	1.13	(95)	0.98	(126)	1.54	(218)	1.20	(60)

Note: From *Mothers & Children: One Decade Later* by S. Clark, M. Dechman, F. French and B. MacCallum, Nova Scotia Department of Community Services (p.217).

[1] t = 2.18, p < .05
[2] t = 4.13, p < .01 ◆

indicates that there are differences between the children of married and unmarried mothers with respect to intelligence, performance, and social adjustment. While age also contributed to the differences, maternal education was the most significant factor affecting children's performances on intellectual and emotional variables (Clark et al., 1991: 206).

Marital Status

The mean level of ability of the children of both married and unmarried mothers was within the average range, between 85 and 115. However, a wide range of IQ and verbal comprehension on the WISC-R scores was found within the total sample; some children performed well below average and others performed well above average. Approximately 14% of the sample scored below average on the verbal IQ and approximately 10% scored below average on the full scale IQ. The children of unmarried mothers performed significantly lower on the full scale IQ (t = 2.06, p < .05, n = 218), verbal comprehension (t = 2.43, p < .05, n = 218), receptive vocabulary (t = 2.58, p < .05, n = 222), reading (t = 1.34, p < .01, n = 216) and visual-motor integration (t = 2.90, p < .01, n = 195). Teachers rated the children of unmarried mothers as more socially withdrawn (U = 4066, p < .001, n = 213), inattentive (U = 378.5, p < .0001, n = 213), overactive (U = 4651, p < .05, n = 213), and aggressive (U = 4116, p < .001, n = 213). The only area where there was a significant difference between the ratings of the mothers was on the nervous-overactive scale. The unmarried mothers rated their children as more overactive than did the married mothers (U = 4936, p < .05, n = 222).

Age and Marital Status

Table 20-4 indicates some differences between the younger married and unmarried mothers and the older married and unmarried mothers. The children of younger unmarried mothers rated significantly lower than children of younger married mothers on receptive vocabulary and reading, teachers perceived them as more socially withdrawn (U = 1047, p < .05, n = 111) and inattentive (U = 1012, p < .05, n = 111), and mothers perceived than as more hyperactive (U = 1079.5, p < .05, n = 115). The children of the older unmarried mothers had lower performance on verbal comprehension and visual-motor integration than the children of the older married mothers. The children of the older unmarried mothers were also perceived by teachers to be more socially withdrawn (U = 984.5, p < .05, n = 102) and inattentive (U = 871.5, p < .05, n = 102) than the children of the older married mothers.

Education

Mothers education was divided as those with 11 years education or less and those with 12 years education or more. Table 20-5 shows that children

Table 20-4:

Performance of Children on Cognitive Measures by Mother's Original Marital Status and Age

	19 Years and Under		20 Years and Older	
	Married (n)	Unmarried (n)	Married (n)	Unmarried (n)
WISC - R				
Verbal IQ	100.1 (59)	97.8 (53)	104.7 (60)	100.6 (46)
Performance IQ	105.6 (59)	112.9 (53)	106.9 (61)	103.9 (46)
Full scale IQ	102.7 (59)	99.2 (53)	106.2 (60)	102.3 (46)
Verbal comprehension	40.9 (59)	38.8 (53)	44.4 (60)	40.7 (46)[a]
PPVT - T				
Receptive Vocabulary	100.5 (59)	95.7 (55)[b]	103.6 (61)	99.1 (47)
Basis				
Reading	103.2 (59)	94.9 (53)[c]	104.1 (59)	98.8 (45)
Math	98.3 (59)	94.4 (53)	98.3 (59)	95.9 (46)
Beery				
Visual motor	17.6 (53)	16.9 (45)	17.8 (52)	15.8 (41)[d]

Note: From *Mothers & Children: One Decade Later* by S. Clark, M. Dechman, F. French and B. MacCallum, Nova Scotia Department of Community Services (pp. 190-191).

[a] t = 2.07, p < .05
[b] t = 1.98, p < .05
[c] t = 2.93, p < .01
[d] t = 3.44, p < .001 ◆

Table 20-5:

Performance of Children on Cognitive Measures According to Mother's Current Educational Level

	11 Years or Less (n)	12 Years or More (n)
WISC - R		
Verbal IQ	95.8 (80)	104.2 (117) [a]
Performance IQ	101.9 (80)	106.9 (118)
Full scale IQ	97.6 (80)	106.1 (117) [b]
PPVT - R		
Receptive vocabulary	104.0 (80)	110.7 (121) [c]
BASIS		
Reading	95.2 (78)	103.6 (117) [d]
Math	92.9 (78)	99.3 (118) [e]
Beery		
Visual motor	16.3 (72)	17.7 (107) [f]

Note: From *Mothers & Children: One Decade Later* by S. Clark, M. Dechman, F. French and B. MacCallum, Nova Scotia Department of Community Services (pp. 197-199).
[a] $t = -4.64$, p. < .001
[b] $t = -4.24$, p. < .001
[c] $t = -3.93$, p. < .001
[d] $t = -3.33$, p. < .001
[e] $t = -2.86$, p. < .01
[f] $t = -3.22$, p. < .01 ♦

of mothers with 11 years or less of schooling obtained significantly lower scores on all factors relating to intelligence and ability except the performance IQ. These children were also rated as more socially withdrawn ($U = 3532.5$, $p < .05$, $n = 195$) and less attentive ($U–3358.5$, $p < .05$, $n = 195$) by teachers. In addition, children of mothers with lower education reported a statistically significantly lower self-image on behaviour, happiness, and total self-image.

Education, Marital Status and Age

The greatest number of differences appear between the children of married and unmarried mothers in the higher education group when education and marital status are examined concurrently. There were no significant differences in either group in the areas of intelligence and ability. However, the children of the better educated, unmarried mothers were rated more socially withdrawn ($U = 1220$, $p < .05$, $n = 120$), inattentive ($U = 1014$, $p < .01$, $n = 120$) and aggressive ($U = 1131$, $p < .05$, $n = 120$) by teachers and more hyper-active ($U = 1261$, $p < .05$, $n = 121$) by mothers. The children of the less educated, unmarried mothers were also rated more aggressive ($U = 478$, $p < .05$, $n = 75$) by teachers.

When age is also taken into consideration, no significant differences related to marital status were found for the children of young mothers with the lower education. However, the children of the better educated, young mothers had a poorer performance in reading ($t = 2.02$, $p < .05$, $n = 48$) and were rated more socially withdrawn ($U = 174.5$, $p < .05$, $n = 49$), inattentive ($U = 174.5$, $p < .05$, $n = 49$), and aggressive ($U = 177.5$, $p < .05$, $n = 49$) by teachers. The mothers rated them as more socially withdrawn ($U = 190.5$, $p < .05$, $n = 50$) and hyperactive ($U = 145.5$, $p < .01$, $n = 50$). The children of the older, better educated, unmarried mothers were rated more inattentive ($U = 340.5$, $p < .05$, $n = 70$) by teachers while the children of the older unmarried mothers with lower education had a lower self-image ($U = 19.0$, $p < .05$, $n = 27$).

Conclusions

Few differences in the socialization experiences and the development of the children of married and unmarried mothers emerged in this study. However, there was some variation in the experiences of the children suggesting that the marital status of the mother when her first child is born has some effect. The measures used to assess socialization were quantitative, and it was not possible to determine the quality of the relationships and experiences. Some differences may not have been apparent because of this. A more in-depth view of the development of the children was obtained through the psychological assessments. Overall, the ability, achievement, and behaviour of the children who participated in the study is largely positive. Average ability and achievement performance was observed and few differences emerged between the children on the basis of their mothers' marital status and age at the time their first child was born. However, the children of the younger, less educated, and unmarried mothers are at greater risk for lower performance in the areas of ability, achievement, behaviour, self-image, hand-eye coordination, and vocabulary than are the children of older, married, and more educated mothers (Clark et al., 1991: 207–209). As well, the child of the younger, unmarried, less educated mother is at a greater risk for difficulties than one would expect to find in the general population. Marital status of the mother at the time of birth does have implications for the child even though most of the mothers in the study were married 10 years after the birth of their first child. Families in which the mother has never been married continue to be formed and are becoming one of a number of family structures in our society. Understanding of the needs of these families is essential for society to develop the supports necessary and to ensure that all children have an opportunity to develop to their fullest potential.

21

Socialization Experiences of Children: Summary Policy Implications and Research Agenda

Joe Hudson and Lise Lavoie

Themes Regarding Effects on Children

What are the effects on children who experience life in lone parent families? This seemingly simple question is the central concern of the chapters by Elsa Ferri, Ellen Gee and Elizabeth McNaughton. These researchers use different approaches to address questions about the impact of lone parent family structures on children and summarize research finding from Canada, Britain, and the United States. Research approaches and results are described, including confounding factors that make any conclusions reached tentative and suggestive at best, and future research directions are outlined.

Research Summary

Ellen Gee reviews results from U.S. studies on the effects of childhood lone parent family structures on adults and presents information based on analysis of data from the 1986 Canadian General Social Survey. The U.S. studies show small negative effects on adult children who were raised in lone parent families. She emphasizes limitations in the research methods used and identifies differences in results according to a number of confounding factors. The 1986 Canadian General Social Survey was done at a single point in time; a random sample of Canadians were asked whether they lived with their own father and mother at age 15 and, if not, whether this was due to divorce, death, separation, or other reason. Respondents were classified into three categories: persons living with both parents at age 15; persons not living with both parents at age 15 due to the death of one parent; and persons not living with both parents at age 15 due to divorce or separation. Among the results of this cross-sectional study are that educational achievement varies across family groups according to sex and reason for family disruption, that family structure has no significant effect on adult income, and that adults from intact families generally report greater degrees of satisfaction with health, job, and family than persons from non-intact families.

Elsa Ferri complements Gee's research by presenting results from a British longitudinal study that followed all children born during one week in 1958. Ferri reports results from the five successive follow-ups done in 1965, 1969, 1974, 1981, 1991. Most of the results concerning the consequences of family disruption on children are mixed but Ferri emphasizes two conclusions. First, socio-economic differences between lone parent families and intact families account for more of the outcomes on children than family structure itself. It is not so much family structure that has effects on children as it is the economic difficulties experienced by lone parent families. Second, family disruption at an early age can have long term effects on children's development, other things being equal.

The chapter by Elizabeth McNaughton presents results of what is probably the only longitudinal study done in Canada aimed at understanding the life circumstances of unmarried mothers and their children. This study involved a population of married and unmarried mothers who gave birth to their first child in July 1978 through February 1979. Each mother was followed for 10 years with follow-up information collected when the child was 6 weeks, 9 months, 18 months, and between 9 and 10 years of age. The ongoing cohort of mothers was supplemented at the fourth wave of data collection with an additional sample of 70 young married mothers so as to provide sufficient numbers in this group to carry out detailed analysis of the independent effects of age and marital status. Comparisons are made between the groups of married and unmarried mothers, as well as between younger married and unmarried mothers (under age 20 at time of first birth) and older married and unmarried mothers (age 20 and over at time of first birth). Generally, the results show few significant differences in the development of children born to the group of married and unmarried mothers. Comparisons made controlling for education, marital status, and age, however, show that the children of younger, less educated, unmarried mothers are at greater risk for lower performance across a number of areas, including achievement, behaviour, and self image, than are children of older married and more educated mothers.

Research Methods Used

What is known from these chapters, and the degree of certitude of knowing about the effects of lone parent family structures on children, is a function of the way research questions are framed and the methods used to answer them. Knowledge is a function of research approaches. The issues reviewed here run through the three chapters, and the authors carefully qualify the reported results, but these qualifications need to be emphasized to understand that there are no simple answers to questions about the effects of family structure on children.

These papers describe two general ways of answering questions about the effects of family structure on children. One is the cross-sectional approach illustrated by the Canadian General Social Survey data used by Ellen Gee. The other is the longitudinal type of research design employed in the Nova Scotia study reported by Elizabeth McNaughton and the National Child Development Study described in Elsa Ferri's chapter. Ellen Gee notes that the non-experimental, cross-sectional design has been the most frequently employed research design in the study of lone parent families. To some extent this is because clinical data or official report data have been the most common sources for research on lone parent families. There are, however, a number of inherent weaknesses in this design and these are often exacerbated by the sampling and data collection techniques employed. Cross-sectional designs limit the investigator's ability to determine the time order of the variables studied. For example, in the Canadian General Social Survey, respondents were asked to identify who they lived with at fifteen years of age and the reason for this type of living arrangement. This ignores the fact that family structure changes over time. Evidence on this is given in McNaughton's chapter where she reports that, over the ten year period covered by the Nova Scotia study, 81% of the unmarried mothers changed their marital status and almost one-fifth of the married mothers experienced a change in their status through divorce, separation, or death. A further problem with cross-sectional studies is that any results from such an approach are limited by the reliability and validity of respondent recall. Long-term memory can be faulty, and there is always the likelihood of respondents telescoping events from the past into the present, or the reverse.

A longitudinal design, particularly a panel design, is the best way of resolving issues about temporal ordering and change of behaviour. The advantages of longitudinal surveys lie in their ability to provide detailed information about developmental histories. Longitudinal surveys can show the incidence of specific behaviours and achievements, such as officially recorded delinquencies, school completion, occupation, income, and help determine the extent to which one event precedes or follows another in developmental sequence. In this way such surveys can be useful in drawing conclusions about cause and effect. The limitation of longitudinal research is the expense and difficulties associated with following subjects over a long period of time. Large samples are required and issues of funding and management become complex.

Common Themes

The enormous diversity of lone parent families is a common theme running through these chapters. There is no such thing as the lone parent family in the form of a unitary, homogenous, and precisely defined family type used as an independent variable amenable to careful investigation. Instead, there are a wide variety of families, both lone parent and two parent.

Lone parenthood is reached in a variety of ways, ranging from death, divorce, and separation to deliberate choice; each of these may have different effects on children. Ferri's research, for example, shows that children living with widowed mothers or born to unmarried mothers differed little from children from intact homes. She also reports that, at age 11, children whose lone mothers were divorced or separated tended to do somewhat less well than children from intact families, and at age 23, male children whose parents had divorced were more likely to have left schools than children from intact homes and female children more likely to have had a first child. Ferri notes that the age of the child at the time of marital disruption is an important factor in determining the effects of the marital disruption on the children, whether through parental death or divorce.

Lone parent families also differ significantly in respect to the length of time spent in this type of family structure, as well as the number of changes experienced. Ferri, Gee, and McNaughton note that both elements are likely to have consequences for the children. The Nova Scotia study found that over a ten year period, 81% of the unmarried mothers changed their marital status and, of these, two-thirds did so within three years of the birth of the first child. A third of these mothers remained in this relationship after seven years. Eighteen percent of the married group changed their status through divorce, separation, or death and one-third of those changed marital status within one year. Over four-fifths of the children in the study were living in two-parent families at the end of the 10 year follow-up. Lone parent families differ on other key dimensions such as the gender of the lone parent, amount and type of contact the child has with the non-custodial parent, availability of parental substitutes such as extended family members, and amount and type of other forms of social support available to the custodial parent. All of these are likely to have significant effects on children.

Socio-economic status is the key dimension of lone parent families that has effects on children. Ferri notes that socio-economic factors accounted for more of the differences found between children in lone parent and intact families than did family structure. Similarly, the Nova Scotia study found that over two-thirds of the unmarried mothers received social assistance benefits sometime during the 10 year study period as compared to 13% of the married mothers. Two-parent families also vary in many respects such as the number of children, amount and type of family interaction, degree of family conflict, nature and amount of involvement with extended family members, and so on. All of these factors can have consequences for the life chances of children. This heterogeneity of one and two-parent families for research means that a host of variables need to be measured and controlled in studies aimed at assessing the effects of family structure on childhood outcomes. Failure to do so may result in confusion about the phenomenon studied and produce misleading results.

Policy Implications

This research suggests that children in single parent families experience negative effects when compared to their peers in dual parent families but that these effects are more likely to be explained by the poverty and socio-economic disadvantages of single parent families compared to dual parent families. These findings suggest two markedly different policy responses. One response is to argue that the resources of two parents are necessary to raise children outside of poverty and disadvantage; in dual parenting situations two adults are contributing to the support and care of children. This argument suggests public policies should be put in place to deter the development of single parent families and to increase the probability that children will receive care and support from two parents. An alternative approach is to recognize the deleterious effects of poverty on children and to pursue policies that assure a minimum level of financial support for children. These policy responses are likely to appeal to persons of different ideological persuasions and may be incompatible. Policies designed to deter the formation of single parent families may be inconsistent with policies designed to assure a minimum level of support for children in these families and they may serve as an incentive for this type of family formation.

A second important finding is that these families are not necessarily isolated and, to varying degrees, are imbedded in social networks involving extended families and friends which provide informal social support as well as formal social supports in the form of housing, child care, and so forth. The impact of public policies on existing and developing social support systems needs to be clearly assessed and evaluated both at the policy design stage as well as implementation of public policies and programs. Hopefully, public policies and programs will strengthen and enlarge social support systems made available to single parent families rather than replacing or detracting from these systems.

Research Needs

Recent research has addressed questions about the consequences for both parents and children of experiencing life in lone parent families. The view that children from lone parent families, particularly children of divorce or unmarried mothers, have lifelong damage done to them has become almost a truism. However, there is little hard evidence to indicate what proportion of children actually experience negative effects, and why others do not. Some recent attention has been given to the whole area of the effectiveness of various forms of intervention with families experiencing difficulties. Researchers and clinicians are interested in the effectiveness and impact of various intervention strategies but there is very little information relating to different approaches. What research is needed on lone parent families for use in developing adequate social policies and programs?

Research and Different Types of Single Parent Families

There are a number of different ways to become a single parent — divorce, death of a partner, children outside marriage. Each is likely to have different consequences for children. The life circumstances of young unmarried mothers are quite different from widows or from older unmarried mothers and these different forms of lone parent families may have much less in common than they would appear to have if we lumped them under the same type of family structure. Researchers can help provide useful policy guidance by focusing on specific forms of lone parents rather than treating lone parent families as a generic category.

Further, special populations of lone parent families have generally been neglected in research. Research needs to be directed to such groups as:

- older unmarried mothers;
- mothers who are incarcerated in correctional institutions;
- lone fathers;
- lone parent mothers who, as children, were raised in the custody of the state;
- the special difficulties of aboriginal lone parents who reside both on and off reserve.

We lack information about the development of children in such families, the special difficulties and challenges that confront them and their parents and the long-term effects of such experiences for both parents and children.

Longitudinal Studies

Each of the chapters in this section emphasizes the importance of employing longitudinal designs in Canada. The problems of fielding such designs are many but there are many advantages in being able to examine change over time and in studying the effects on children, as well as other effects, of changes and transitions in their families over time. These studies cannot be done with cross-sectional data. Panel and cohort studies are necessary if knowledge of lone parent families in Canada is to be advanced.

Borrowing from American and British efforts in conducting longitudinal survey research relating to family structure will generate comparable data to make cross-national comparisons. Some of the core elements of such a longitudinal data base will need to include:

- childhood family situation, including age, cause of lone parenthood, sex of custodial parent, consistency of custodial parent, number of parental marriages, quality of relationships with former spouse, duration of lone parenthood, family financial situation;
- income, employment, education of parents;
- family responsibilities for children;
- the amount and quality of contact with the non-custodial parent, as well as on the type of social support available and used by the family;
- parenting practices;
- family conflict/unhappiness;
- nature of unions such as marriage, cohabitation, common-law, and so forth;
- measures of adult well-being, attitudes, self-concept; and
- parental remarriage.

This kind of longitudinal data can be particularly important in determining the consequences for children of either marital disruption or living in single parent families.

Research about Services Provided to Single Parent Families

Research also needs to be directed to the services provided to lone parent families as well as all types of families. Specific types of research efforts would include:

- What are the effects, both intended and unintended, of different forms of public response to lone parent families? What are the discrepancies between available resources and needed services? Can lone parent families be better assisted by targeting services to them as compared to making services universally available to all families? Can services be targeted to lone parent families without the stigma often associated with the provision of such services?
- What is the nature of social agency involvement with children in lone parent families? What is the nature of the experiences of youth with state agencies at different times in their development?

Research needs to explore the perspectives of children and their parents by obtaining and carefully considering the viewpoints of children, parents and other members of their social networks. What are the views of lone parents and their children about the effects of social policies and programs?

Qualitative and Quantitative Methods

Full understanding of lone parent families will not come solely from longitudinal survey data. A multi-faceted approach is needed. It is essential that research on Canadian families include both qualitative and quantitative methods. This type of triangulation can bring into focus different aspects of family structure that may be hidden. In short, a variety of approaches needs to be taken to provide more comprehensive information about lone parent families in Canada. Smaller-scale studies using qualitative methods can supplement longitudinal research and provide in-depth understanding of the lone parent family experience. Small scale research projects can address the actual processes involved with different family environments acting to produce particular types of outcomes. For example, Ferri notes that we have very little information about the changes in household roles that are experienced in the transition to lone parenthood and back to two-parent families. From this perspective, families can be seen as moving through a series of changes, each of which may have measurable impacts preceding and following formal ruptures. An actual divorce may best be seen as a formal ceremony that is much less important than the events and processes leading up to it and those that follow from it. The relationship between the children and each of the parents, the relationship between the former spouses, and the adjustments which occur when one or both of the parents enter a new partnership, are all important matters that need to be addressed. These will be brought out by viewing families as sets of interacting elements in an on-going process. An important question concerns the implications of lone parenthood for the socialization of children, particularly in terms of balancing the instrumental needs of providing discipline and control and the affective needs of nurturance and care while handling inadequate finances and feeling alone.

What Promotes Successful Outcomes?

A related research area is to examine those factors that promote successful outcomes for lone parent families. What is it that enables some lone parents to have successful outcomes despite the difficulties associated with their parenting role? Addressing this type of question could help balance research that has focused on identifying factors associated with problematic outcomes in lone parent families. A related need is to gain a better understanding of the experiences of children, as perceived and reported by children, in single parent families. What is the role of siblings in lone parent families? Research needs to be sensitive to how siblings may provide care within lone parent families and the effects of siblings taking responsibility for parental roles.

Facilitating Use of Research Findings

Much more effort needs to be given to collaborative research that is comparable across jurisdictions. Comparative research that is inter-disciplinary would assist in widening perceptions about the phenomenon of lone parent families and highlight situations peculiar to countries. Particularly important here are questions about the consequences for lone parent families of social policy developments in different places so as to tease out the wider social and economic factors that impact upon families in different countries. A key question is always the pragmatic one of how to get funding for research while ensuring independence and relevance. How can government be stimulated to fund research that has the potential for producing critical findings, particularly in an era of limited funds?

A related issue concerns the dissemination of research findings, particularly in terms of facilitating the use of research findings by policy makers and practitioners. Too often, the presentation of research is incomprehensible to practitioners and the practical implications of the findings are either not presented in a simple and direct manner or get lost in the complications of the report. Research reports must be written as research and development documents, keeping the consumer in mind, not solely research colleagues. To facilitate this, universities must give greater credit to academics for producing information in popular media as well as in professional and academic journals. Involving practitioners and policy makers in the early stages of research planning efforts can also be useful in helping ensure that the research meets the needs of diverse audiences.

PART VI

CONCLUSIONS

22

Directions for Future Research

Joe Hudson and Burt Galaway

Several themes on the single parent family in Canada emerge from the research presented in this volume. These themes, as well as their social policy implications, are summarized in this chapter, along with a suggested agenda to guide future research on the single parent family in Canada.

Themes from the Research

The findings from the research are organized in relation to seven major themes: growth in the numbers of single parent families, characteristics of single parent families, changing reasons for single parent family formation, transitional nature of single parent families, poverty and single parent families, resource deficiencies of single parent families, and the consequences of single parent family experience for children.

Growth of Single Parent Families

The rate of single parent family formation has been accelerating in Canada since 1976, the number of single parent families now exceeds one million, is growing at three times that of husband-wife families, and now constitutes 14% of all families in Canada (McKie; Lero and Brockman; Spector and Klodawsky). Between 1951 and 1986 the number of male-headed single parent families increased by 103% and the number of women-headed families increased by 180% (McDaniel). These Canadian trends are paralleled in the United States and Britain. In 1990 approximately six million families in the United States were headed by single mothers representing nearly 25% of all families with children (McLanahan and Garfinkel). The number of lone parent families in Britain more than doubled in the past twenty years; in 1990, 19% of British families with dependent children were headed by lone parents (Ferri).

Characteristics of Single Parent Families

Single parent families are usually headed by women (McKie; Lero and Brockman; McDaniel) with only 18% headed by lone fathers (McKie). This pattern is also true in Britain where nine out of ten lone families are headed by a mother (Ferri). There are no indications that lone parents are conspicuously drawn from visible minorities (McKie) and there are relatively few lone parents with children under age 15 who have immigrated to Canada (McKie). In 1986, however, 23% of Aboriginal families living off reserves were headed by lone parents (McKie). Lone parents are decreasing in age in both Canada (Lero and Brockman; Dooley) and in France (Lefaucheur and Martin). Female lone parents are more likely to have their first marital or common-law union at a younger age than wives (McKie). Most lone parents have only one child under 13 whereas two-parent families are more likely to have two or more children under 13 (Lero and Brockman).

Changing Reasons for Single Parent Family Formation

Eichler points out that lone parent families can come into existence through the death of a married parent, separation or divorce of a married person, dissolution of a common-law relationship, birth to an unmarried woman, or through adoption of a child by a single parent. The reason for lone parent family formation in Canada has changed. Prior to 1966 most lone parent families came into existence because of death of one of the partners in a marriage; since then marital disruptions and childrearing by never married women have become the predominant reason for single parent family formation (Lero and Brockman; Marcil-Gratton; McKie; Spector and Klodawsky). Today approximately 66% of Canadian single parent families result from separation or divorce (Spector and Klodawsky). Of those resulting from childbearing by unmarried mothers, 68% of the unmarried mothers had not planned nor wanted to become pregnant (Clark). The changing nature of single parent family formation in Canada is also occurring in Great Britain (Ferri), France (Lefaucheur and Martin), and the United States (McLanahan and Garfinkel).

The proportion of Canadians who have ever lived in a common-law relationship is also rising rapidly (McKie), as is the proportion of children born to at least one parent who had ever lived in cohabitation (Marcil-Gratton). Marcil-Gratton found that this phenomena hardly existed in the early 1960s but that 43% of the children born in a 1987–1989 cohort had been born in a situation in which at least one parent had lived in cohabitation. These children are born out of wedlock, but in a family created by cohabitation (Marcil-Gratton). The proportion of children born into families with both their biological parents present has remained as high as previously but the framework of the parents' union has changed from marriage to cohabitation (Marcil-Gratton).

Single Parenthood as a Transitory Arrangement

Single parent families are often a transitory phenomena with the single parent frequently ending the status by entering into a new relationship either through cohabitation or marriage (Ferri; Marcil-Gratton; Eichler; McKie; McNaughton). A Nova Scotia study found that over a ten year period, 81% of the unmarried mothers changed their marital status (McNaughton). Single parenthood among fathers, which usually occurs later in life than single parenthood among mothers (McKie), is also more likely to be more transient because single parent fathers are more likely to remarry quickly (McKie) or return to relationships through cohabitation (Marcil-Gratton). Marcil-Gratton found that the average length of time a child spends with a single mother is 4.9 years, and with a single father 2.7 years, prior to the creation of a new union. Families created through cohabitation, however, tend to be unstable, resulting in children experiencing a succession of family forms from single parent to new unions formed through cohabitation, often back to single parenthood, followed by another union (Marcil-Gratton). This results in a complex set of networks for children (Marcil-Gratton) as well as the recognition that household and family membership is often not congruent (Eichler) so that an adult may be providing parenting responsibilities even though not living in the household.

Poverty and Single Parent Families

A markedly higher proportion of women-headed single parent families live in poverty in Britain (Ferri), the United States (McLanahan and Garfinkel), and in Canada (Dooley; McKie; Lero and Brockman; McDaniel; Spector and Klodawsky) than do other families; this is not, however, the situation in France because of the more generous income transfer programs and much higher probability that single parents will be in the labour force partly because of the universal availability of day care (Lefaucheur and Martin). In 1990 female-headed single parent families in Canada represented about 35% of all low income families (McKie) and over 50% of single parent families headed by women had incomes below the low income cutoff (Spector and Klodawsky); single parent families living in poverty tend to be families with a young child (Lero and Brockman; Dooley).

The annual income of single parent fathers, while less than that of two-parent families, is higher than that of the single parent mothers; in 1985 single parent families headed by fathers averaged $31,252 annual income compared to $19,177 for single mothers (McKie). The poverty status of women-headed single parent families relates to labour force participation, adequacies in child support, and inadequacies in public transfer of payments. Between 1973 and 1988 single parents over 35 experienced substantial earnings growth, those between 25–34 experienced stagnant earnings, and single parents under 25 experienced a large decline in earnings and a large increase in transfer payments (Dooley). During this same period the employment rate for all women with children grew from 40% to 73%, increased for all single mothers from 57% to 67%, but declined for single mothers under 25 from 63% to 48% (Dooley). Ninety-six percent of single mothers in 1990 who did not work for pay were below the low income cutoff (McKie). Single parent fathers are much more likely to participate in the labour force than single parent mothers (McKie; Lero and Brockman). The low labour force participation of single parent mothers relates to the presence of a young child at home, lack of suitable child care, low education, and lack of job opportunities (Lero and Brockman; Dooley; Clark). Employed single mothers earn less than single parent fathers and also earn less than married mothers (Spector and Klodawsky; Clark).

Failure to provide for adequate child support in divorce situations, compounded by the failure to vigorously enforce court orders, further contributes to the poverty of women-headed single parent families (Pask; McLanahan and Garfinkel). This is further aggravated by failure to equitably share other resources of the marriage such as the family home (Pask). If men were to uniformly pay one-third, instead of less than one-fifth, of their gross income as support, the percentage of women and children in poverty would be reduced from 58% to 26% and non-custodial fathers would, on average, have annual gross incomes after paying support, of $8,000 above the poverty line (Pask). The disparities of incomes and standards of living between the custodial and non-custodial household after divorce is further aggravated by the tax code which treats child support payments as a tax deduction for the non-custodial parent, but as taxable income for the custodial parent resulting in further disadvantaging the single parent (Zweibel).

The poverty of young single parent mothers has long term negative consequences for their retirement. The middle years of life are a time of asset accumulation, through home ownership, savings, and investment in retirement accounts. Few low income single parent families own homes (Pask; Spector and Klodawsky) and fewer have access to retirement accounts; thus these women will not have adequate means of support for their later years (Pask; Spector and Klodawsky; McDaniel). Inability to accumulate assets in the form of housing and retirement plans results in these women remaining very poor at later stages of their lives (Spector and Klodawsky).

Resource Deficiency

The only variable that consistently differentiates the single parent family from other types of families is that one adult carries sole responsibility for the day-to-day care of children (Eichler); this may lead to a condition of resource deficiency as the adult tries to balance and meet the demands of providing economic support, care for children, and other types of supports and services needed to maintain a family (Spector and Klodawsky). Single parent families allocate almost twice as much of their income to housing than two-parent families (Spector and Klodawsky), are more likely to have difficulty securing adequate housing (Clark), and are more likely than two-parent families to be tenants rather than home owners (McKie; Spector and Klodawsky; Ferri). Single parents are less likely to have a car and less likely to have adequate home furnishings than married parents (McKie; Spector and Klodawsky). Single parents have less housing choice than married parents and, thus, are less likely to have housing that is accessible to transportation, with adequate play areas for children, and with the security and privacy necessary for raising children (Spector and Klodawsky). Further, the absence of a second adult may reduce capacity to maintain shelter arrangements and provide support such as transportation (Spector and Klodawsky). Changes in residence often follow divorce and are one of the forms of social instability for single parent families (McLanahan and Garfinkel).

Single mothers with preschool children and single mothers with more limited educational backgrounds are less likely to be employed or enroled in educational institutions; a third of the single mothers who are not employed want a job (Lero and Brockman). The most common reason for not wanting or not being able to take a job is the mother wanting to stay and look after children (Lero). Availability of child care is of crucial significance for the employment and education of single parent mothers (Ferri; Lero and Brockman; Clark). Single mothers have more difficulty combining a job with child care responsibilities than married mothers; for married mothers, husbands and relatives often constitute the major source of help with children (Clark). Single mothers on social assistance seek and engage in a range of activities with the hope of permanently ending their need for social assistance (Gorlick and Pomfret). Social support, especially the provision of information, influences the likelihood that single parent families will engage in activities designed to exit from social assistance such as job training and education (Gorlick and Pomfret; Lero and Brockman).

The social and economic instability associated with single parenthood have direct implications for mental health; epidemiological surveys show higher rates of anxiety and depression among single mothers than for married women and married men (McLanahan and Garfinkel). Single employed mothers have a significantly higher score on general work-family tension than employed married mothers (Lero and Brockman). Single parents register more negatively than others in relation to their satisfaction with finances, housing, friends, self-esteem, job or main activity, and life as a whole (McKie). Single parents of both sexes spend more time alone than do their married counterparts (McKie); female single parents employed with at least one child under five report an average of only 1.3 hours per day of free time and, if not employed, 3.9 hours of free time daily (McKie). The individual responsibility model of the family underlies many public policies but may disadvantage women because it assumes both parents are equally responsible for themselves and for their children and does not recognize a social responsibility for the cost of raising children (Eichler).

Consequences for Children

There is growing evidence in the United States (McLanahan and Garfinkel), Britain (Ferri) and Canada (Gee; McNaughton) that negative consequences for children may be associated with single parenthood. American children of single parents are disadvantaged by being less likely to graduate from high school, more likely to have children as teenagers, to give birth out of wedlock, and to be involved in delinquency and crime (McLanahan and Garfinkel). British children from single parent families have lower school attainment and poorer behavioral adjustment than those in two-parent homes (Ferri), however the differences attributed to family situations are smaller in magnitude than those accounted for by economic factors. Studies of adult outcomes in Britain suggest that children in single parent families, especially those created by divorce, experience adverse adult outcomes in areas such as school leaving, lack of qualifications, and low employment status although these may be linked to economic disadvantages in early life rather than the direct influence of family structure or family conflict (Ferri). Children from single parent families complete less formal school than children from intact families (Gee). Children from divorced homes and single parent families are more likely to marry at younger ages and to have intimate relationships at younger ages (Gee). Satisfaction with life domains, health, job, and family is highest among both men and women from intact families (Gee). Both men and women from intact homes are less likely to state that they have no religion than persons from divorced homes (Gee). Children born of unmarried mothers are rated more overactive than children born to married mothers and are perceived by teachers to be socially withdrawn and more inattentive than children born of married mothers (McNaughton). Children of younger, less educated, unmarried mothers are at greater risk of lower performance in the areas of ability, achievement, behaviour, self-image, hand-eye coordination and vocabulary, than are the children of older, married, and more educated mothers (McNaughton). It is unclear, however, as to whether the differences noted can be attributed to family structure, family conflict preceding breakup, or to the general economic disadvantage of single parent families.

The number of children experiencing multiple family forms is still relatively small, but is a rapidly accelerating proportion of the total (Marcil-Gratton). American demographers estimate that half of all children born in the 1980s will live in a mother only family at some point in their life before reaching 18 (McLanahan and Garfinkel). Estimates in Britain are that 37% of marriages will end in divorce and that one child in five will experience parental divorce by the age of 16 (Ferri). In 1991 in Canada there were about 1.5 million children living in single parent families and all but 275,000 of these were with their mother (McKie). Children in single parent families are likely to experience more than one family structure and a complex set of relationships during the course of their childhood (McNaughton; Eichler; Marcil-Gratton).

Public Policy Considerations

Legislation and programs must be adjusted to more equitably meet the needs of single parent families. Much of current Canadian social policy is based on the two-parent family which can only result in the continued impoverishment of generations of children and their parents. There are over one million single parent families in Canada, 1.5 million children are part of these families, and many of these adults and children are poor. Their current needs must be met, not only for their own sakes, but also for the future of the country. The single parent family is not a stable family form. Families and their members regularly move in and out of this status. This raises the question of whether the single parent family is an appropriate or even useful unit for the design of public policy and programs. Perhaps the whole matter needs to be put into a broader context of family policy realizing that all families have support needs, some of which can be met by formal programs, and recognizing that these needs will change over the life cycle of the family.

Public policy in Canada must be built upon a balance in the distribution of private and public responsibilities and policy makers challenged to articulate the respective roles of the state, parents, and other kin in ensuring the well-being of families and their members. Heterogeneity of the population of single parent families, and of two-parent families as well, demands a greater degree of consideration of how different kinds of families are affected differently by public policies. Single parent families, like families in general, are differentiated one from another by virtue of relationship histories, ages of members, heritage, structural and membership characteristics of the immediate family and kin networks, socio-economic status, geographical location, availability of resources, patterns of family functioning, and distribution of household labour. Polices to respond to the economic support needs of single parent families need to address the adequacy of the support, dependability of the support, and empower the parent to exercise control over resources. Detailed consideration of the interrelatedness of social and economic policies and the part they play in shaping the life chances and opportunities of single parents and their children is necessary to better understand the dynamic nature of families. Appreciation of families in context calls for analyses of how the roles and experiences of men and women are moulded differently in both the public and private spheres of activity. The metaphor of need and dependency that has guided much of public policy with regard to single parent families is limited, potentially dehumanizing, and ultimately counter-productive. The metaphor of social investment is preferred and emphasizes the potential of single parents and their children.

The matter of resource deficiency was one of the central themes across the research. Resource deficiency does not refer to a deficiency within a person but rather to the recognition that one person is expected to carry responsibilities normally handled by two adults. Public policy can be directed towards remedying these deficiencies. The formal supports necessary to meet these needs should be integrated into a system of supports. The presence of adequate child care, housing, and transportation are essential to the economic support provided by employment. Providing job training and employment assistance will be of relatively limited effectiveness unless supports relating to housing, transportation, and child care are available. Because responsibility for these various support services cut across different jurisdictions, public policies may be inconsistent and contradictory. There is a clear need to examine both intent and effects to determine whether public policy is moving in a consistent, coherent direction.

There is also a need to agree upon and articulate common policy goals. Agreement may not exist on what these goals should be in relation to the single parent family or to families in general. Is the goal of policy to promote the healthy development of young children? Or should policies promote the economic independence of single mothers? Or should policies permit parents to spend more time with their young children or promote stability in the lives of young children? Public policies directed towards permitting parents to spend more time with children and to secure stability in the lives of children may not be consistent with the notion of promoting economic independence for single parents. Should any of these policies be targeted exclusively to single parents, or is it more appropriate that policy focus on the larger population of families?

This research suggests that children in single parent families experience negative effects when compared to their peers in dual parent families but that these effects may be explained by the poverty and economic disadvantages of single parent families compared to dual parent families. These findings suggest two markedly different policy responses. One response is to argue that the resources of two parents are necessary to raise children outside of poverty and disadvantage; in dual parenting situations two adults are contributing to the support and care of children. This argument suggests public policies to deter the development of single parent families and to increase the probability that children will receive care and support from two parents. An alternative approach is to recognize the deleterious effects of poverty on children and to pursue policies that assure a minimum level of financial support for children. Policies designed to deter the formation of single parent families may be inconsistent with policies designed to assure a minimum level of support for children in these families.

Single parent families are not necessarily isolated nor are they passive recipients of services. They are imbedded in social networks involving extended families and friends providing informal social support as well as formal social supports in the form of housing, child care, and so forth. The impact of public policies on existing and developing social support systems needs to be clearly assessed and evaluated both at the policy design stage as well as implementation of public policies and programs. Public policies and programs should strengthen and enlarge informal social support systems made available to single parent families rather than replacing or detracting from these systems.

Research Agenda

Longitudinal Research

Canadian families move through a variety of transitions which cross-sectional studies are not able to adequately analyze. A national longitudinal database is needed to identify the incidence over time of conditions and events, analyze how life events, behaviour and values are linked, and provide information on processes of household formation and dissolution. The design of a national longitudinal panel study should consider major surveys underway in other countries so as to ensure that the information produced can assist in making comparisons across different countries, as well as across different provincial and regional jurisdictions of Canada. In this way, questions can be addressed on the consequences of different policies and programs between and within different national jurisdictions.

(1) A longitudinal panel study on Canadian families should be designed to ensure comparability with relevant British and American longitudinal research, particularly the National Child Development Study in Britain and the U.S. National Longitudinal Survey of Youth.

(2) The specific focus of the proposed longitudinal panel studies should be on a cohort of children born during a specific time period, with regular follow-ups conducted.

(3) Key elements to be included in a Canadian national longitudinal panel study include:

- Health and physical development of children;
- Educational achievements of children;

- Lifestyles, attitudes, and behaviours of children;

- Occupational aspirations, training, and work histories of children;

- Marital changes, family formation and home ownership;

- Beliefs, attitudes, and values in respect to personal and family relationships, skills and work, social and political views;

- Current and previous employment/unemployment, education and training, literacy, family formation, housing, income and wealth, health, recreational and leisure activities, and community participation;

- Motor and social development, behavioral problems, nature and quality of the home environment, pregnancies and child birth, child care arrangements, parenting practices, and stress and conflict;

- Nature and amount of supports needed, available, and used.

(4) There is no single, discrete entity called a single parent family, but rather a series of family structures that change over time. Consequently, it is important that similar definitions be used for central concepts and common measures be employed so as to avoid confusion and contradiction within the field of study. The development of a national longitudinal panel study should provide the basis for researchers to begin employing common definitions and measures in respect to the single parent family.

Existing Data Sources

A considerable amount of data relevant to the single parent family currently exists in different government data sources including the Labour Force Survey, Census Surveys of Consumer Finance, General Social Surveys, and Family Expenditure Surveys. Much of this data can provide useful information about single parent families. Government officials and researchers share responsibility for making greater use of these data sources. As well, provincial data sources, particularly those dealing with social assistance should be made more available to researchers interested in the movement of single parents into and out of income maintenance schemes.

Multiple Research Methods

While national longitudinal survey data is sorely needed to provide information on the changing status of families in Canada, other approaches should be implemented to supplement panel studies. Only by using a variety of research methods can comprehensive information be generated about single parent families in this country. Attention needs to be given to the actual processes involved with different family environments that act to produce particular outcomes. Critical questions to be addressed include:

(1) Family violence and single parent families

- Role of family violence in the creation of single parent families;
- Life history of single parent families that come into existence subsequent to family violence compared to those which come into existence when divorce or separation was not linked to family violence.

(2) The perspectives of children and their parents as they move through a series of transitions

- Views about family experiences, particularly the range and impact of different sources of stress;
- Views about the effects of social policies and programs;
- Views about household roles as a result of family transitions;
- Views about events preceding and following from family transitions;
- Views about adjustments that occur when new partnerships are formed and old ones dissolved;
- Views about care provisions within single parent families, particularly in terms of the role of siblings and the types of social supports needed, available, and used.
- Views about how employed single parents make the psychological transition from home to work in the mornings and from work to home in the evenings.

(3) Greater attention in small-scale research studies needs to be given to special family populations, including:

- Mothers sentenced to correctional institutions;
- Mothers who, in childhood, were placed in the custody of government child welfare authorities;
- Aboriginal single parents residing both on and off reservations;
- Immigrant lone parent families;
- Unmarried older mothers;
- Single parent fathers.

Evaluation Research on Family Policies and Programs

Three general categories of evaluation research need to be undertaken:

(1) Process or implementation evaluations aimed at both providing information about the manner and extent to which programs and policies directed to single parent families are translated into operations, as well as to assist in using findings from outcome evaluations of family policies and programs.

(2) Outcome evaluations aimed at providing information about the results, effects, and impacts of family policies and programs. A necessary precondition for carrying out this type of evaluation is the development of well specified outcome criteria, clearly defined policies, and programs implemented consistent with the policies.

(3) Meta evaluations that will involve empirical re-analysis of multiple data sets about similar programs and policies. Common issues across comparable programs can be identified, the strength and integrity of findings produced can be generalized beyond a particular study done in a specific locale, and directions identified for future evaluation work.

Some of the specific areas to which evaluation research efforts need to be directed are:

(1) Child and spousal support:

- The nature of support orders, as well as factors associated with arriving at support levels;

- The frequency of joint and sole custodial arrangements, the court process and procedures leading up to the divorce, the content of divorce agreements, nature and extent to which families with various custody agreements return to court to either enforce or change their agreements;

- The effectiveness of different approaches for collecting awarded child support payments;

- The impact of public policies on the economic situations following from separation and divorce;

- The process of determining revision benefits and effects that follow from these;

- The effects of tax policies on single parents and their children;

- The effects of family law provisions on single parents and children, particularly matrimonial property legislation — the criteria applied and results of different valuation methods, division and distribution.

(2) Employment and labour market policies and programs. The economic insecurity of single parent families and the manner and extent to which government policies and labour markets impact on this condition need to be addressed, including questions about:

- Alternative policy impacts to enhance wage-earning capacities of single parents;

- The impact and effects of gender-based wage-inequities on the economic circumstances of single parent families;

- Disincentives and barriers to education, training, and employment opportunities following from governmental social assistance polices;

- Impacts of employee policies aimed at reducing the tension between work and family responsibilities of mothers.

(3) Impacts and effects of care provider, housing and support policies and programs. Three program and policy domains are particularly critical — child care, housing, and a variety of other formal and informal supports. Critical questions needing to be addressed include:

- The impacts and effects of alternative ways to finance and structure child care arrangements;

- The adequacy of low income housing for child rearing by single parents;

- The effect of formal and informal support systems, as well as the way in which public policies and programs can be used to generate more community-based approaches to supporting families in need.

(4) Impacts, effects, and processes involved in the educational and socialization roles of families. Questions needing to be addressed include:

- The impacts and effects of supplementary educational programs for children at risk and their parents;

- The efficacy of alternative sex education programs aimed at preventing unwanted births;

- The impacts of children on single parents, particularly the influence of child characteristics and behaviour.

(5) Impacts and effects of policies and programs, including those administered by criminal justice agencies, to respond to family violence:

- The impacts these programs and policies have on the vulnerability of women and children;

- The impacts on the economic conditions of women and children;

- The role these programs and policies play in either advertently or inadvertently contributing to the creation of single parent families;

- The impacts and effects of alternative public responses to family violence.

Research Directed Toward Successful Outcomes of Single Parent Families

Not all children suffer similarly from difficulties experienced by their parents and some may do better in the new family environment than would have been the case in the stressful environment of the initial family. Research needs to be directed at addressing questions about circumstances that permit families in transition to respond adequately to the needs of children. For example:

- What are the factors that tend to promote successful outcomes for children and parents in single parent families?

- How do successful single parents deal with the many difficulties associated with their parenting role?

- What are the nature of stressful experiences of single parents that produce competence as compared to those that give rise to dysfunction in children?

Research and Policy

Questions must be addressed in a way that is sensitive to political constraints to increase the probability of the use of research findings on single parent families. A collaborative approach is necessary with policy makers intimately involved in working with researchers to frame the questions to be answered, the methods to be used, and the timing of results. Key to this approach is the need for policy makers to clearly think through the specific actions to be taken, given the production of the research results. Both researchers and organizations funding research need to exercise greater efforts to facilitate the use of research findings by policy makers, practitioners, and citizens.

(1) Researchers need to present their methods and findings in a simple and direct manner that is comprehensible to policy makers, practitioners and citizens.

(2) One means of facilitating the wider dissemination of research findings would be for universities to disseminate information in popular media, in addition to communications through scholarly venues.

(3) Relevant practitioners and policy makers should be involved during the early planning stages of research efforts so as to help ensure that the findings produced have relevance to their information needs.

(4) The federal government should continue efforts at establishing National Research and Policy Workshops on significant issues as a major means of sharing information between researchers, policy makers, and program practitioners.

References

- A.C.T. (1984). *Recherches sur l'efficacité économique et sociale de l'Allocation de Parent Isolé.* Paris: Rapport de recherche pour la CNAF.

- A.C.T. (1987). *Les conditions de vie et les stratégies des familles monoparentales.* Paris: Rapport de recherche pour la CNAF.

- Abella, R.S. (1984). *Equality in Employment. A Royal Commission Report.* Ottawa: Ministry of Supply and Services.

- Abella, R. (1981). Economic adjustment on marriage breakdown: Support. *Family Law Review* 4: 1–10.

- Acock, A.C., and Kiecolt, K.J. (1989). Is it family structure or socioeconomic status? Family structure during adolescence and adult adjustment. *Social Forces* 68: 553–571.

- Adams, O.B., and Nagnur, D. (1989). Marriage, divorce and mortality: A life table analysis for Canada and the regions, 1980–1982. In J. Legare, T.R. Balakrishnan and R. Beaujot (eds.), *The Family in Crisis: A Population Crisis?* Ottawa: The Royal Society of Canada, 191–212.

- Advisory Council on the Status of Women (1992 May). Workshop on Child Support Guidelines, Ottawa.

- Ahrentzen, S., and Franck, K. (eds.) (1989). *New Households, New Housing.* New York: Von Nostrand Reinhold.

- Allen, D. (forthcoming). Welfare and the Family: The Canadian experience. *Journal of Labor Economics.*

- Amato, P.R., and Booth, A. (1991). Consequences of parental divorce and marital unhappiness for adult well-being. *Social Forces* 69: 895–914.

- Amato, P.R., and Keith, B. (1991). Parental divorce and adult well-being: A meta-analysis. *Journal of Marriage and the Family* 53: 43–58.

- Amato, P.R. (1988a). Long-term implications of parental divorce for adult self-concept. *Journal of Family Issues* 9: 201–213.

- Amato, P.R. (1988b). Parental divorce and attitudes toward marriage and family life. *Journal of Marriage and the Family* 50: 453–461.

- Ambert, A.M. (1985). The effect of divorce on women's attitudes towards feminism. *Sociological Focus* 18: 265–272.

- Anderson-Khlief S. (1981). Housing needs of single parent mothers. In S. Keller (ed.), *Building for Women.* Lexington: Lexington Books.

- Anthony, K., Weidemann, S., and Chin, Y. (1990). Housing perceptions of low-income single parents. *Environment and Behavior* 22 (2): 147–182.

- Astone, N.M., and McLanahan, S.S. (1991). Family structure, parental practices and high school completion. *American Sociological Review* 56: 309–320.

- Aubin, J., and Paquin, G. (ed.) (1986). *Discrimination, harcelement et harcelement sexuel—rapport de l'enquête: Femmes et logement.* Montréal: Comité Logement Rosemont en collaboration avec the Front d'Action Popularie en Réaménagement Urbain (FRAPRU).

- Austerberry, H., and Watson, S. (1985). A woman's place: A feminist approach to housing in Britain. In C. Ungerson (ed.), *Women and Social Policy: A Reader.* Basingstoke and London: Macmillan.

- Baar, E., and Moore, D. (1981). Ineffective enforcement: The growth of child support arrears. *Windsor Yearbook on Access to Justice*, 1, 94–120.

- Bakan, Joel (1991). Constitutional interpretation and social change: You can't always get what you want (Nor what you need). *Canadian Bar Review* 70: 307–328.

- Baker, J. (1991). Family Policy as an Anti-Poverty Measure. In M. Hardey, G. Crow (eds.), *Lone Parenthood: Coping with Constraints and Making Opportunities.* New York, London: Harvester Wheatsheaf, 110–125.

- Balakrishnan, T.R., and Beaujot, R. (1989). Introduction. In J. Legare, T.R. Balakrishnan and R.P. Beaujot (eds.), *The Family in Crisis: A Population Crisis?* Ottawa: The Royal Society of Canada, 6–13.

- Balakrishnan, T.R., Rao, V., Lapierre-Adamcyk, E., and Krotki, K. (1987). A hazard model analysis of the covariates of marriage dissolution in Canada. *Demography* 24: 395–406.

- Banting, K. (1982). *The Welfare State and Canadian Federation.* Kingston: McGill-Queen's University Press.

- Bassuk, E.L. (1991). Homeless families. *Scientific American* (December), 66–74.

- Bastard, B., Cardia-Vonèche, L. (1991). *Les femmes, le divorce et l'argent.* Genève: Labor and Fides.

- Bastard, B., Cardia-Vonèche, L. (1988a). *Les familles monoparentales face à leur situation économique.* Paris: Centre de Sociologie des Organisations. Rapport de recherche pour la CNAF.

- Bastard, B., Cardia-Vonèche, L. (1988b). Des familles monoparentales face à leurs difficultés économiques: des stratégies diverses. *Dialogue* (Paris) 101 ("Parents seuls. La famille après le divorce"): 45–64.

- Bastard, B., Cardia-Vonèche, L. (1987). La situation économique des familles à un seul parent. Réflexions sur l'appauvrissement. *Les Cahiers médico-sociaux* (Genève) 31 (2) ("Familles monoparentales"): 109–118.

- Bastard, B., Cardia-Vonèche, L. (1984). Le coût du divorce. Une analyse de la redistribution différentielle des ressources familiales. *Dialogue* (Paris) 86 ("Le temps du divorce"): 75–85.

- Battle, K. (1990). *Child Benefits Reform: A Report Prepared for the Standing Senate Committee on Social Affairs, Science and Technology.* Ottawa: Queen's Printer for Canada.

- Bernéche, F. (1990). *Problématique de l'habitation pour les ménages formant la nouvelle immigrations à Montréal: Eléments d'information et d'intervention.*

Montréal: Regroupement des organsimes du Montréal ethnique pour le logement (ROMEL) and Service de l'habitation et du développement urbain, Ville de Montréal.

- Blau, F., and Ferber, M. (1986). *The Economics of Women, Men and Work.* N.J.: Prentice-Hall.

- Bloom, B.L., Asher, S.J., and White, S.W. (1978). Marital disruption as a stressor: A review and analysis. *Psychological Bulletin* 85: 867–894.

- Booth, A., and Edwards, J.N. (1989). Transmission of marital and family quality over the generations: The effect of parental divorce and unhappiness. *Journal of Divorce* 13: 41–58.

- Booth, A., and Johnson, D. (1988). Premarital cohabitation and marital success. *Journal of Family Issues* 9: 255–272.

- Bourguignon, O., Rallu, J.-L., and Théry, I. (1985). *Du divorce et des enfants* (Travaux et documents No. 111). Paris: Institut National d'Etudes Démographiques.

- Bradshaw, J., and Millar, J. (1991). *Lone Parent Families in the UK* (Department of Social Security Research Report No. 6). London: Her Majesty's Stationery Office.

- Brandwein, R. (1977). After divorce: a focus on single parent families. *The Urban and Social Change Review* 10 (1).

- Brittan, A. (1973). *Meanings and Situations.* London: Routledge and Kegan Paul.

- Bumpass, L. (1984a). Children and marital disruption: A replication and update. *Demography* 21 (1): 71–82.

- Bumpass, L. (1984b). Some characteristics of children's second families. *American Journal of Sociology* 90 (3): 608–623.

- Bumpass, L. (1981). *Demographic Aspects of Children's Experience: Experience in Second Families* (CDE Working Paper No. 81–33). University of Wisconsin: Center for Demography and Ecology.

- Burguière, E., Seydoux, A. (1973). École maternelle et milieu familial. *Cahiers du CRESAS* (Paris) 10.

- Burke, M.A., and Spector, A. (1991). Falling through the cracks: Women aged 55–64 living alone. *Canadian Social Trends* 23: 14–17.

- Burke, M.A. (1986). Families: Diversity the new norm. *Canadian Social Trends* 1 (Summer): 6–10.

- Burtch, B., Pitcher-LaPrairie, C., and Wachtel, A. (1980). Issues in the determination and enforcement of child support arrears. *Canadian Journal of Family Law*, 3, 5–26.

- Canada Mortgage and Housing Corporation (1991a). *Evaluation of the Public Housing Program.* Ottawa: CMHC Program Evaluation Division.

- Canada Mortgage and Housing Corporation (1991b). *Evaluation of the Federal Co-Operative Housing Program.* Ottawa: CMHC Program Evaluation Division.

- Canada Mortgage and Housig Corporation (1991c). *Canadian Housing Markets.* Ottawa: CMHC Market Analysis Centre.

- Canada Mortgage and Housing Corporation (1991d). *Annual Report, 1990.* Ottawa: CMHC.

- Canada Department of Justice (1990). *Evaluation of the Divorce Act. Phase II: Monitoring and Evaluation.* Ottawa: Queens Printer for Canada.

- Canadian Institute for Research (1981). *Matrimonial Support Failures: Reasons Profiles and Perceptions of Individuals Involved*, 1 (Summary Report). Edmonton: University of Alberta Institute of Law Research and Reform.

- Caple, F.S. (1988). Restructuring family life. In E.A. Mulroy (ed.), *Women as Single Parents: Confronting Institutional Barriers in the Courts, the Workplace, and the Housing Market* (pp.73–98). Dover, MA: Auburn House.

- Cashmore, E. (1985). *Having to: The world of One Parent Families*. London: Counterpoint.

- Central Statistical Office (1989). *Family Expenditure Survey*.

- Centre d'Étude des Revenus et des Coûts (1989). *Le veuvage avant soixante ans: ses conséquences financières. II. La deuxième année du veuvage*. Paris: La Documentation Française. (Documents du CERC n°95).

- Centre d'Étude des Revenus et des Coûts (1987). *Familles nombreuses, mères isolées: situation économique et vulnérabilité*. Paris: La Documentation Française (Documents du CERC n°85.

- Centre d'Étude des Revenus et des Coûts (1986). *Le veuvage avant soixante ans: ses conséquences financières. I. Les premiers mois du veuvage*. Paris: La Documentation Française. (Documents du CERC n°81).

- Centre for Equality Rights in Accommodation (1992). *Interim Report to the Ontario Ministry of Housing*. Toronto.

- Chambers, D.L. (1979). *Making Fathers Pay: The Enforcement of Child Support*. Chicago: University of Chicago Press.

- Cherlin, A.J., Furstenberg, F.F., Chase-Lansdale, P.L., Kiernan, K., Robins, P.K., Morrison, D.R., and Teitler, J.O. (1991). Longitudinal studies of effects of divorce on children in Great Britain and the United States. *Science* 252: 1386–1389.

- Chester, R. (1977). The one parent family: Deviant or variant? In R. Chester and J. Peel, *Equalities and Inequalities in Family Life*. Academic Press.

- Ciuriak, D., and Sims, H. (1980). *Participation Rate and Labour Force Growth in Canada*. Ottawa: Department of Finance, Long Range and Structural Analysis Division.

- Clare, Kim, and Glossop, Robert (1993). Canadian public policy impacts: Summary, policy implications and research agenda. In J. Hudson and B. Galaway (eds.), *Single Parent Families: Perspectives on Research and Policy*. Toronto: Thompson Educational Publishing.

- Clark, S.M. (1993). Support needs of the Canadian single parent family. In J. Hudson and B. Galaway (eds.), *Single Parent Families: Perspectives on Research and Policy*. Toronto: Thompson Educational Publishing.

- Clark S., Dechman, M., French, F., and MacCallum, B. (1991). *Mothers and Children: One Decade Later*. Nova Scotia Department of Community Services.

- Cohen, S., and Wills, T. (1985). Stress, social support, and the buffering hypothesis. *Psychological Bulletin* 98: 310–357.

- Colletta, N.D. (1979). Support systems after divorce: Incidence and impact. *Journal of Marriage and the Family* 41: 837–845.

- Commaille, J. (1982). *Familles sans justice. Le droit et la justice face aux transformations de la famille*. Paris: Le Centurion. (Collection "Justice humaine").

- Conway, J.F. (1990). *The Canadian Family in Crisis*. Toronto: James Lorimer and Co.

- Cook, C. (1989). Components of neighborhood satisfaction. *Environment and Behavior* 20 (2): 115–149.

- Co-operative Housing Federation of Canada (1991). *Response to the Draft CMHC Evaluation of the Co-Operative Housing Program*. Ottawa: Co-operative Housing Foundation of Canada.

- Crellin, E., Pringle, M.L.K., and West, P. (1971). *Born Illegitimate*. Slough: National Foundation for Educational Research Publishing Company.

- Davie, R., Butler, N.R., and Goldstein, H. (1972). *From Birth to Seven*. London: Longman.

- Davies, C. (1985). Principles involved in the awarding of spousal support. *Reports of Family Law* 46 210–221.

- Decoin: J., Keil, M. (1983). L'A.P.I., une allocation qui dérange. *Bulletin*, CAF, 8, ("Les parents isolés"). Paris: Caisse Nationale des Allocations Familiales, 109–117.

- Demo, D.H., and Acock, A.C. (1991). The impact of divorce on children. In A. Booth (ed.), *Contemporary Families: Looking Forward, Looking Back* (pp.162–191). Minneapolis: National Council on Family Relations.

- Department of Finance (1985). *Account of the Cost of Selective Tax Measures*. Ottawa: Department of Supply and Services.

- Department of Health and Social Security (1985). *Low-Income Families*. London: Her Majesty's Stationery Office.

- Department of Health and Social Security (1974). Report of the Committee on one-parent families. London: Her Majesty's Stationery Office, 2 vols. (The Finer Report).

- Department of Justice (1992). Report of the Federal/Provincial/ Territorial Family Law Committee. *The Financial Implications of Child Support Guidelines: Research Report*. Ottawa: Ministry of Supply and Services.

- Department of Justice (1991). Report of the Federal/Provincial/ Territorial Family Law Committee. *Child Support: Public Discussion Paper*. Ottawa: Ministry of Supply and Services.

- Department of Justice, Bureau of Review (1990). *Evaluation of the Divorce Act - Phase II: Monitoring and Evaluation*. Ottawa: Queen's Printer for Canada.

- Department of Justice, Bureau of Review (1987). *The Evaluation of the Divorce Act, Phase I: Collection of Baseline Data*. Ottawa: Ministry of Supply and Services.

- Desrosiers, H., Le Bourdais, C., and Péron, Y. (1992). *La dynamique de la monoparentalité féminine au Canada*. Manuscript submitted for publication.

- Dooley, M.D. (1993). Recent changes in the economic welfare of lone mother families in Canada: The roles of market work, earnings and transfers. In J. Hudson and B. Galaway (eds.), *Single Parent Families: Perspectives on Research and Policy*. Toronto: Thompson Educational Publishing.

- Dooley, M. (1992a). *Gender, Age and Poverty in Canada*. Hamilton: Department of Economics, McMaster University.

- Dooley, M. D. (1992b). *The Converging Market Work Patterns of Married Mothers and Lone Mothers in Canada*. Unpublished manuscript, McMaster University, Department of Economics, Hamilton, Ontario.

- Dooley, M. (1991). The demography of child poverty in Canada, 1973–1986. *Canadian Studies in Population* 18: 53–74.

- Dooley, M.D. (1989). Changes in the market work of married women and lone mothers with children: 1973–1986. (Research Report No. 254, Program for Quantitative Studies in Economics and Population). Hamilton, Ontario: McMaster University.

- Dumas, J. (1990). *Rapport sur l'état de la population au Canada 1990* (Statistique Canada, Catalogue No. 91–209F). Ottawa: Ministère des Approvisionnements et Services Canada.

- Dumas, J. (1986). *Report on the Demographic Situation in Canada*. Ottawa: Statistics Canada.

- Duncan, G., and Hoffman, S. (1985). A reconsideration of the economic consequences of marital dissolution. *Demography* 22: 485–98.

- Economic Council of Canada (1992). *The New Face of Poverty: Income Security Needs of Canadian Families*. Ottawa: Minister of Supply and Services. Catalogue N. EC22–186/1992E.

- Edwards, M. (1986). Child support assessment, collection and enforcement: Issues and possible directions for reform. *Windsor Yearbook on Access to Justice* 6: 93–140.

- Eichler, Margrit (1993). Lone parent families: An instable category in search of stable policies. In J. Hudson and B. Galaway (eds.), *Single Parent Families: Perspectives on Research and Policy*. Toronto: Thompson Educational Publishing.

- Eichler, M. (1991). Family policy in Canada: From where to where? In J.E. Veevers (ed.), *Continuity and Change in Marriage and Family* (pp.417–429). Toronto: Holt, Rinehart and Winston.

- Eichler, M., and McCall, M.L. (1991, April). Father as a legal construct. Paper presented at the meeting of the Canadian Association of Law Teachers, Family Law Division, Montebello, Quebec.

- Eichler, M. (1990). The limits of family law reform or the privatization of female and child poverty. *Canadian Family Law Quarterly* 7 (1): 59–84.

- Eichler, M. (1988). *Families in Canada Today. Recent Changes and their Policy Consequences*. Toronto: Gage.

- Eichler, M. (1987). Family change and social policy. In K. Anderson, H. Armstrong, P. Armstrong, J. Drakich, M. Eichler, C. Guberman, A. Hayford, M. Luxton, J. Peters, E. Porter, C. Richardson, and G. Tesson (eds.), *Family Matters: Sociological and Contemporary Canadian Families* (pp.63–86). Toronto: Methuen.

- Elliott, B.J., and Richards, M.P.M. (1991). Children and divorce: educational performance and behaviour before and after parental separation. *International Journal of Law and the Family* 5: 258–276.

- Ellwood, D. (1988). *Poor Support*. New York: Basic Books.

- Emlen, A.C., and Koren, P.E. (1984). *Hard to Find and Difficult to Manage: The Effects of Child Care on the Workplace*. Portland, Oregon: Regional Research Institute for Human Services.

- Ermisch, J. (1990). Analysis of the dynamics of lone parenthood: socio-economic influences on entry and exit rates. In E. Duskin (ed.), *Lone Parent Families: The Economic Challenge.* Paris: Organization for Economic Cooperation and Development.

- Ermisch, J. (1986). The economics of the family: Applications to divorce and remarriage. Discussion Paper No. 40. London: Centre for Economic Policy Research.

- Essen, J. (1979). Living in one parent families: Attainment at school. *Child Care Health and Development* 5 (3): 189–200.

- Essen, J., and Lambert, L. (1977). Living in one parent families: Relationships and attitudes of 16-year-olds. *Child: Care Health and Development* 3, 301–318.

- Fallis, G. (1983). *Housing Decisions in a Life Cycle Framework.* Ottawa: Canada Mortgage and Housing Corporation, External Research Awards Program.

- Family Policy Studies Centre (no date). One Parent Families. Fact Sheet 3.

- Federal/Provincial/Territorial Family Law Committee (1992). *The Financial Implications of Child Support Guidelines: Research Report.* Ottawa: Queen's Printer for Canada.

- Federal/Provincial/Territorial Family Law Committee (1991). *Child Support: Public Discussion Paper.* Ottawa: Queen's Printer for Canada.

- Federal-Provincial Working Party on Income Maintenance. (1975). *Social Security Review Background Paper on Income Support and Supplementation.*

- Ferri, E. (1993). An overview of research and policy on the lone parent family in Britain. In J. Hudson and B. Galaway (eds.), *Single Parent Families: Perspectives on Research and Policy.* Toronto: Thompson Educational Publishing.

- Ferri, Elsa (1993). Socialization experiences of children in lone parent families: Evidence from the British National Child Development Study. In J. Hudson and B. Galaway (eds.), *Single Parent Families: Perspectives on Research and Policy.* Toronto: Thompson Educational Publishing.

- Ferri, E. (1984). *Stepchildren: A National Study.* Windsor: National Foundation for Educational Research-Nelson.

- Ferri, E. (1976). *Growing Up in a One Parent Family.* Windsor: National Foundation for Educational Research Publishing Co.

- Ferri, E., and Robinson, H. (1976). *Coping Alone.* Windsor: National Foundation for Educational Research Publishing Co.

- Festy, P. (1991). Biographies après divorce. In T. Hibert and L. Roussel (eds.), *La nuptialité: Evolution récente en France et dans les pays développés* (pp.193–209). Paris: Institut National d'Etudes Démographiques.

- Festy, P., Valetas, M.F. (1990). Contraintes sociales et conjugales sur la vie des femmes séparées. In France INSEE: *Données sociales 1990,* 301–305.

- Festy, P. (1988a). La place des pensions alimentaires. *Informations sociales* (Paris, CNAF) 4 ("Après la séparation"): 25–32.

- Festy, P. (1988b). Après la séparation: Diversité et stabilité des comportements. *Population* (Paris, INED) 3: 517–536.

- Festy, P., Valetas, M.F. (1987). Le divorce et après. *Population et sociétés* (Paris, INED) 215.

- Fine, S. (1992). Recession gnaws at family life. *Globe and Mail* 15 February: A1, A7.

- Fogelman, K., Power, C., and Fox, J. (1987). Family breakdown, social mobility and health inequalities (Working paper number 25). London: National Child Development Study User Support Group.

- Fogelman, K. (ed.) (1983). *Growing Up in Great Britain: Collected Papers from the National Child Development Study.* London: Macmillan.

- Fraser, N. (1989). Women, welfare and the politics of need interpretation. In P. Lassman (ed.), *Politics and Social Theory* (pp.104–122). New York: Routledge.

- Fraser, N. (1987). Women, welfare and the politics of needs integration. *Hypatia: A Journal of Feminist Philosophy* 2 (1): 103–121.

- Frazer, D. (1981). *Credit, A Mortgage for Life: A Review of Consumer Debt and Credit in Canada and the Impact of Increasing Shelter Costs.* Ottawa: Canadian Council on Social Development, Ottawa.

- Friendly, M., Rothman, L., and Oloman, M. (1991). *Child Care for Canadian Children and Families: A Discussion Paper.* Ottawa: Canada's Children.

- Frone, M.R., Russell, M., and Cooper, M.L. (1992). Antecedents and outcomes of work-family conflict: Testing a model of the work-family interface. *Journal of Applied Psychology* 77: 65–78.

- Fry, P.S., and Addington, J. (1985). Perceptions of parent and child adjustment in divorced families. *Clinical Psychology Review* 5: 141–157.

- Fuchs, V. and Rechlis, D. (1992). America's children: Economic perspectives and policy option. *Science* 3: 41–46.

- Fuchs, V. (1988). *Women's Quest for Economic Equality.* Cambridge: Harvard University Press.

- Furstenburg, F., Brooks-Gunn, J., and Morgan, S.P. (1987). *Adolescent Mothers in Later Life.* Cambridge: Cambridge University Press.

- Furstenberg, F.F., Jr., Nord, C.W., Peterson, J.L., and Zill, N. (1983). The life course of children of divorce: Marital disruption and parental contact. *American Sociological Review* 48: 656–668.

- Garfinkel, I. (1992). Assuring child support: An extension of social security. New York: Russell Sage Press.

- Garfinkel, I., and McLanahan, S. (1986). *Single Mothers and their Children: A New American Dilemma.* Washington, D.C.: Urban Institute Press.

- Garon, M. (1988). *Une expérience de testing de la discrimination racial et visibles dans le logement et pistes à Montréal* (Catalogue No. 122). Montreal: Commission des Droits de la Personne du Québec.

- de Gaulejac, V., Aubert, N. (1990). *Femmes au singulier ou la parentalité solitaire.* Paris: Klincksieck.

- Gautier, A. (1989). *Politique familiale et familles monoparentales en Guadeloupe.* Paris: Rapport de recherche pour la CNAF.

- Gee, Ellen M. (1993). Adult outcomes associated with childhood family structure: An appraisal of research and an examination of Canadian data. In J. Hudson and B. Galaway (eds.), *Single Parent Families: Perspectives on Research and Policy.* Toronto: Thompson Educational Publishing.

- Gee, E., and McDaniel. S. (1991). Pension politics and challenges: Retirement policy implications. *Canadian Public Policy* XVII (4): 456–472.

- Glenn, N.D., and Kramer, K.B. (1987). The marriages and divorces of the children of divorce. *Journal of Marriage and the Family* 49: 811–825.

- Glenn, N.D., and Kramer, K.B. (1985). The Psychological Well-Being of Adult Children of Divorce. *Journal of Marriage and the Family* 47: 905–912.

- Glenn, N.D., and Supancic, M. (1984). The demographic and social correlates of divorce and separation in the United States: An update and reconsideration. *Journal of Marriage and the Family* 46: 563–575.

- *Globe and Mail.* (1991). Attacking the core of child poverty. Editorial, 16 December 1991, A18.

- Goldberg, M. (1983). *The Housing Problem: A Real Crisis?* Vancouver: University of British Columbia Press.

- Gordon, L., and McLanahan, S. (1991). Single parenthood in 1900. *Journal of Family History* 16: 97–116.

- Gorlick, C., and Pomfret, D. (1993). Hope and circumstance: Single mothers exiting social assistance. In J. Hudson and B. Galaway (eds.), *Single Parent Families: Perspectives on Research and Policy.* Toronto: Thompson Educational Publishing.

- Gorlick, C., and Pomfret, D. (1991). Poverty and single mothers: Themes of voice and response. Paper presented at the National Social Policy Conference, Bishops University, Lennoxville, Province of Quebec.

- Gorlick, C., and Pomfret, D. (1988). Female single parents and their social support relationships. Paper presented at a joint session of the Canadian Association of Schools of Social Work and the Canadian Sociology and Anthropology Association, The University of Windsor, Windsor, Ontario.

- Grassby, M. (1991a). The dilemma of conflicting rights: Motions to reduce and cancel support. Unpublished paper. Montreal: Service de recherche de la Commission des services juridiques.

- Grassby, M. (1991b). Women in their forties: The extent of their rights to alimentary support. *Reports of Family Law* 30: 369–403.

- Graves, G. (1991). Single fathers: Demographic trends. Unpublished paper, Department of Sociology and Anthropology, Carleton University, Ottawa.

- Greenberg, E.F., and Nay, W.R. (1982). The intergenerational transmission of marital instability reconsidered. *Journal of Marriage and the Family* 44: 335–347.

- Greve, J., and Currie, E. (1990). *Homelessness in Britain.* York: Joseph Rowntree Memorial Trust.

- Grief, G. (1985). *Single Fathers.* Lexington, MA.: Lexington Book Press.

- Grindstaff, C. (1988). Adolescent marriage and childbearing: The long-term economic outcome, Canada in the 1980's. *Adolescence* XXIII (89): 45–58.

- Guidubaldi, J., and Perry, J.D. (1985). Divorce and mental health sequelae for children: A two- year follow-up of a nationwide sample. *Journal of the American Academy of Child Psychiatry* 24: 531–537.

- Gunderson, M., Muszynski, L., and Keck, J. (1990). *Women and Labour Market Poverty.* Ottawa: Canadian Advisory Council on the Status of Women.

- Gurstein, P., and Hood, N. (1975). *Housing Needs of One Parent Families.* Vancouver: Y.M.C.A.

- Guttentag, M., Salassin, S., and Belle, D. (1980). *The Mental Health of Women.* New York: Academic Press.

- Guttmann, J. (1988/89). Intimacy in young adult males' relationships as a function of divorced and non-divorced family of origin structure. *Journal of Divorce* 13: 253–261.

- Hanson, S. (1985). Single custodial fathers. In S. Hanson and F. Bozett (eds.), *Dimensions of Fatherhood.* Beverly Hills: Sage.

- Harrison, M., Snider, G., Milo, R., and Lucchesi, V. (1991). *Paying for the Children: Parent and Employer Experience of Stage One of Australia's Child Support Scheme.* Melbourne: Australian Institute for Family Studies.

- Harrison, M., Snider, G., and Milo, R. (1990). *Who Pays for the Children? A First Look at the Operation of Australia's New Child Support Scheme.* Melbourne: Australian Institute for Family Studies.

- Haskey, J. (1988). Trends in marriage and divorce and cohort analysis of the proportion of marriages ending in divorce. *Population Trends* 54: 21–28.

- Haskey, J. (1984). Social class and socio-economic differentials in divorce in England and Wales. *Population Studies* 38 (3): 419–438.

- Haskey, J. (1983). Children of divorcing couples. *Population Trends* 31: 20–26.

- Hasson, R.A. (1989). What's your favourite right? The Charter and income maintenance legislation. *Journal of Law and Social Policy* 5: 1–34.

- Hayden, D. (1984). *Redesigning the American Dream.* New York: W.W. Norton and Co.

- Hayden, D. (1981). What would a non-sexist city be like? In C. Simpson, E. Dixler, M. Nelson, and K. Yatrakis (eds.), *Women and the North American City* (pp.167–184). Chicago: University of Chicago Press.

- Heekerens, H.P. (1987). The rising risk of divorce — On intergenerational transmission of marital instability, *Zeitschrift fur Soziologie* 16: 190–203.

- Henderson, J., and Karn, V. (1987). *Race, Class and State Housing: Inequality and the Allocation of State Housing in Britain* (Studies in Urban and Regional Policy No. 4). Aldershot, England: Gower Publishing Co.

- Hernandez, D.J., and Myers, D.E. (1986, April). *Children and Their Extended Families Since the Great Depression.* Paper presented at the annual congress of the Population Association of America, San Francisco.

- Hetherington, E.M., Cox, M., and Cox, R. (1978). The aftermath of divorce. In H.J. Stevens, Jr. and M. Matthews (eds.), *Mother-Child, Father-Child Relations.* Washington, D.C.: National Association for the Education of Younger Children.

- Hofferth, S.L. (1982). Children's family experiences to age 18: A cohort life table analysis. Paper presented at the annual meeting of the Population Association of America, San Diego. Cited in Krein and Beller (1988).

- Hudson, Joe, and Lavoie, Lise (1993). Socialization experiences of children: Summary policy implications and research agenda. In J. Hudson and B. Galaway (eds.), *Single Parent Families: Perspectives on Research and Policy.* Toronto: Thompson Educational Publishing.

- Hunt, A., Fox, J., and Morgan, M. (1973). *Families and Their Needs*. London: Her Majesty's Stationery Office.

- Institut National de la Statistique et des Études Économiques (1991). *Les femmes. Contours et caractères*. Paris: INSEE.

- Institut National d'Études Démographiques (1986). *Quelques variables associées au montant et au paiement des pensions alimentaires*. Paris: INED, Rapport de recherche pour la CNAF.

- Jarvanainen, M. (1991). Suicide, sex, and social class in Finland. *Popnet (IIASA)* 20 (Fall): 6.

- Johnson, Laura C., and Galaway, Burt (1993). Social support needs: Summary, policy implications and research agenda. In J. Hudson and B. Galaway (eds.), *Single Parent Families: Perspectives on Research and Policy*. Toronto: Thompson Educational Publishing.

- Johnson, L.C., and Dineen, J. (1981). *The Kin Trade: The Daycare Crisis in Canada*. Toronto: McGraw-Hill Ryerson Limited.

- Jones, C., Marsden, L., and Tepperman, L. (1990). *Lives of Their Own: The Individuation of Women's Lives*. Toronto: Oxford University Press.

- Joshi, H. (1990). Obstacles and opportunities for lone parents as breadwinners. In E. Duskin (ed.), *Lone Parent Families: The Economic Challenge*. Paris: Organization for Economic Cooperation and Development.

- Kalter, N., and Rembar, J. (1981). The significance of a child's age at the time of parental divorce. *American Journal of Orthopsychiatry* 51: 85–100.

- Kamerman, S.B., and Hayes, C.D. (eds.) (1982). *Families That Work: Children in a Changing World*. Washington, D.C.: National Academy Press.

- Kanoy, K.W., and Cunningham, J.L. (1984). Consensus or confusion in research on children and divorce: Conceptual and methodological issues. *Journal of Divorce* 7: 45–71.

- Karn, V., and Henderson, J. (1983). Housing atypical households: understanding the practices of local government housing. In A.W. White (ed.), *Family Matters: Perspectives on the Family and Social Policy*. Oxford: Pergamon Press.

- Keith, V.M., and Finlay, B. (1988). The impact of parental divorce on children's educational attainment, marital timing, and likelihood of divorce. *Journal of Marriage and the Family* 50: 797–809.

- Kiecolt, K.J., and Acock, A.C. (1988). The long-term effects of family structure on gender role attitudes. *Journal of Marriage and the Family* 50: 709–717.

- Kiernan, K.E. (1992). The impact of family disruption in childhood on transitions made in young adult life. *Population Studies* 46 (2): 213–234.

- Kiernan K., and Wicks, M. (1990). *Family Change and Future Policy*. York: Joseph Rowntree Memorial Trust.

- King, A.J.C., Robertson, A.S., and Warren, W.W. (1985). *Summary Report: Canada Health Attitudes and Behaviours Survey, 9-, 12- and 15- Year Olds, 1984–85*. Ottawa: Minister of National Health and Welfare.

- Kitchen, B. (1986). The patriarchal bias of the income tax in Canada. *Atlantis* 11: 35–45.

- Klodawsky, F., and Spector, A. (1988). New families, new housing needs, new urban environments: The case of single-parent families. In C. Andrew and B. Moore Milroy (eds.), *Life Spaces Gender, Household, Employment.* Vancouver: University of British Columbia Press.

- Klodawsky, F., Spector, A., and Rose, D. (1985). *Single Parent Families and Canadian Housing Policies: How Mothers Lose.* Ottawa: Canada Mortgage and Housing Corporation, External Research Awards Program.

- Klodawsky, F., Spector, A., and Hendrix, C. (1983). *The Housing Needs of Single Parents in Canada.* Ottawa: Canada Mortgage and Housing Corporation, External Research Awards Program.

- Krein, S.H., and Beller, A.H. (1988). Educational attainment of children from single-parent families: Differences by exposure, gender, and race. *Demography* 25: 221–234.

- Krever, R. (1983). Support payments and the personal income tax. *Osgoode Hall Law Journal* 21: 636–700.

- Kulka, R.A., and Weingarten, H. (1979). The long-term effects of parental divorce in childhood on adult adjustment. *Journal of Social Issues* 35: 50–78.

- Kurdek, L.A., and Siesky, A.E., Jr. (1980a). Sex role self-concepts of single divorced parents and their children. *Journal of Divorce* 3: 249–261.

- Kurdek, L.A., and Siesky, A.E., Jr. (1980b). Children's perceptions of their parents' divorce. *Journal of Divorce* 3: 339–378.

- Kurdek, L.A., and Siesky, A.E., Jr. (1980c). Effects of divorce on children: The relationship between parent and child perspectives. *Journal of Divorce* 4: 85–99.

- L.A.S.A.R.E. Université de Nancy II: Rapport de recherche pour le Commissariat Général du Plan et la Mission Interministérielle Recherche Expérimentation.

- Lalonde, M. (1973). *Working Paper on Social Security in Canada.* Ottawa: National Health and Welfare.

- Lamb, L. (1987). Involuntary joint custody: What mothers will lose if fathers' rights groups win. *Horizons* Jan/Feb.: 20–23, 31.

- Languin, N., Von Allmen, M., Bastard, B., Cardia-Vonèche, L. (1990). Plus riche ou plus pauvre? Le divorce et l'évolution des ressources familiales à Genève. *Dialogue* (Paris) 109 ("Argent du couple et comptes familiaux"): 60–69.

- Lauer, R.H., and Lauer, J.C. (1991). The long-term consequences of problematic family backgrounds. *Family Relations* 40: 286–290.

- Le Gall, D., and Martin, C. (1991a). *Composer avec le logement: Recomposition familiale et usage de l'espace domestique.* CRTS. Université de Caen: Rapport pour le Plan Construction et Architecture. Ministère de l'Urbanisme et du Logement.

- Le Gall, D., and Martin, C. (1991b). L'instabilité conjugale et la recomposition familiale. In F. de Singly (ed.), *La famille: L'état des savoirs.* Paris: La Découverte, 58–66.

- Le Gall, D., and Martin, C. (1990). *Recomposition familiale, usages du droit et production normative.* CRTS, Université de Caen: Rapport de recherche pour la CNAF.

- Le Gall, D., and Martin, C. (1988a). *Le réseau de parenté après la désunion.* CRTS. Université de Caen: Rapport pour la CNAF.

- Le Gall, D., and Martin, C. (1988b). Le réseau parental après un divorce ou une séparation. *Dialogue* 101: 85–93.

- Le Gall, D., and Martin, C. (1987). *Les familles monoparentales. Evolution et traitement social.* Paris: Editions ESF.

- Le Gall, D., and Martin, C. (1986). *Familles monoparentales et action sociale.* CRTS. Université de Caen: Rapport de recherche pour la CNAF.

- Le Gall, D., and Martin, C. (1983). *Mouvance de la famille: réponse de l'action sociale.* CRTS. Université de Caen: Rapport de recherche pour la CNAF.

- Leavitt, J., and Saeggert, S. (1990). *From Abandonment to Hope: Community Households in Harlem.* New York: Columbia University Press.

- Leavitt, J. (1984). The shelter plus issue for single parents. *Women and Environments* 6 (2): 17–20.

- Lefaucheur, Nadine, and Martin, Claude (1993). Lone parent families in France: Situation and Research. In J. Hudson and B. Galaway (eds.), *Single Parent Families: Perspectives on Research and Policy.* Toronto: Thompson Educational Publishing.

- Lefaucheur, N. (1992a). French policy towards lone parent families. In The Joint Centre for Political Studies (ed.), *Poverty and Public Policy: Recent Experiences from the U.S., Canada and Western Europe.* Sage publications (In press).

- Lefaucheur, N. (1992b). Maternité, famille, État. In G. Duby, M. Perrot (eds.), *Histoire des femmes.* Tome V. F. Thébaud (ed.), Le XX° siècle. Paris: Plon, 411–430.

- Lefaucheur, N. (1991). Les familles dites monoparentales. In F. de Singly (ed.), *La famille: L'état des savoirs.* Paris: La Découverte, 67–74.

- Lefaucheur, N. (1989). *Dissociation familiale et délinquance juvénile: les avatars scientifiques d'une représentation sociale.* Paris: Rapport pour la CNAF.

- Lefaucheur, N. (1988a). Les conditions et niveaux de vie des enfants de parents séparés. In *L'enfant et ses parents séparés.* Paris: IDEF/CICERF, 135–168.

- Lefaucheur, N. (1988b). Rapport sur la situation des familles monoparentales en France. Paris: CNRS. Rapport à la Communauté Économique Européenne.

- Lefaucheur, N. (1988c). Les "familles monoparentales" en questions. *Dialogue* (Paris) 101 ("Parents seuls. La famille après le divorce"): 28–44.

- Lefaucheur, N. (1987a). *Les familles monoparentales: Une catégorie spécifique?* Paris: Rapport pour le Plan Construction. Ministère de l'Équipement et du Logement.

- Lefaucheur, N. (1987b). Quand leur situation était inférieure à celle de l'orphelin - ou le psychiatre, la marâtre et le délinquant juvénile. *Dialogue* (Paris) 97 ("Les beaux-enfants. Remariages et recompositions familiales"): 104–120.

- Lefaucheur, N. (1985). Familles monoparentales: Les mots pour les dire. In F. Bailleau, N. Lefaucheur, V. Peyre (eds.), *Lectures sociologiques du travail social.* Paris: Ed. Ouvrières/CRIV, 204–217.

- Légaré, J., and Desjardins, B. (1991). La monoparentalité: un concept moderne, une réalité ancienne. *Population* 46 (6): 677–1688.

- Léomant, C. (1974). Dissociation familiale et délinquance juvénile, remise en cause d'un stéréotype. *Annales de Vaucresson* (Vaucresson, France) 12: 19–141.

- Leonard, D., and Speakman, M.A. (1986). Women in the family: companions or caretakers. In V. Beechey and E. Whitelegg (eds.), *Women in Britain Today*. Milton Keynes: Open University.

- Léridon, H., Villeneuve-Gokalp, C. (1988a). *Enquête sur les situations familiales*. Paris: INED. Rapport de recherche pour la CNAF et l'INSEE.

- Léridon, H., Villeneuve-Gokalp, C. (1988b). Etre seul après la séparation. *Informations sociales* (Paris, CNAF) 4 ("Après la séparation"): 12–19.

- Léridon, H., Villeneuve-Gokalp, C. (1988c). Entre père et mère. *Population et sociétés* (Paris, INED) 220.

- Léridon, H., Villeneuve-Gokalp, C. (1988d). Les nouveaux couples. Nombre, catactéristiques et attitudes. *Population* (Paris, INED) 2: 331–374.

- Lero, Donna S., and Brockman, Lois M. (1993). Single parent families in Canada: A closer look. In J. Hudson and B. Galaway (eds.), *Single Parent Families: Perspectives on Research and Policy*. Toronto: Thompson Educational Publishing.

- Lero, D.S., Pence, A.R., Shields, M., Brockman, L.M., and Goelman, H. (1992). *Canadian National Child Care Study: Introductory Report*. Ottawa: Statistics Canada, Catalogue 89–526E.

- Lero, D.S., Goelman, H., Pence, A.R., Brockman, L.M., and Nuttall, S. (1992). *Parental Work Patterns and Child Care Needs*. Ottawa: Statistics Canada, Catalogue 89–529.

- Lero, D.S., Brockman, L.M., Pence, A.R., Goelman, H., and Johnson, K. (1992). *Workplace Benefits and Flexibility: A Parent's Perspective*. Unpublished manuscript. University of Guelph, Department of Family Studies.

- Lero, D.S., and Kyle, I. (1991). Work, families and child care in Ontario. In L.C. Johnson and D. Barnhorst (eds.), *Children, Families and Public Policy in the 90s* (pp.25–72). Toronto: Thompson Educational Publishing.

- Lero, D.S. (1985). *Parents' Needs, Preferences and Concerns About Child Care: Case Studies of 336 Canadian Families*. (Report prepared for the Task Force on Child Care, Series 5). Ottawa: Status of Women in Canada.

- Lippman, A. (1991). Prenatal genetic testing and screening: Constructing needs and reinforcing inequities. *American Journal of Law and Medicine* 17 (1 and 2): 15–50.

- MacDonnell, S. (1981). *Vulnerable Mothers, Vulnerable Children*. Halifax: Nova Scotia Department of Social Services.

- MacKay, H., and Austin, C. (1983). *Single Adolescent Mothers in Ontario*. Ottawa: Canadian Council on Social Development.

- Maclean, M., and Ekelaar, J. (1986). The financial consequences of divorce: the wrong debate. In M. Brenton and C. Ungerson (eds.), *The Yearbook of Social Policy*. London: Routledge and Kegan Paul.

- Maloney, M. (1989). Women and the Income Tax Act: Marriage, motherhood and divorce. *Canadian Journal on Women and the Law* 3: 182–210.

- Maloney, M. (1987). *Women and Income Tax Reform* (Background Paper). Ottawa: Canadian Advisory Council on the Status of Women.

- Marcil-Gratton, N. (1993). Growing up with a single parent, a transitional experience? Some demographic measures. In J. Hudson and B. Galaway (eds.), *Single Parent Families: Perspectives on Research and Policy*. Toronto: Thompson Educational Publishing.

- Marcil-Gratton, N., and Lapierre-Adamcyk, E. (1992). *Les modes de vie nouveaux des adultes et leur impact sur les enfants au Canada. Mise à jour 1990.* Rapport soumis au Ministère de la Santé et du Bien-être Social du Canada dans le cadre de l'Etude de l'évolution démographique et son incidence sur la politique économique et sociale, Département de démographie, Université de Montréal.

- Marcil-Gratton, N., and Lapierre-Adamcyk, E. (1988). *Les modes de vie nouveaux des adultes et leur impact sur les enfants au Canada.* Rapport soumis au Ministère de la Santé et du Bien-être Social du Canada dans le cadre de l'Etude de l'évolution démographique et son incidence sur la politique économique et sociale, Département de démographie, Université de Montréal.

- Marcus, I. (1983). The sexual politics of current child support. In Cassety (ed.), *The Parental Child-Support Obligation: Research, Practice and Social Policy* (pp.29–33). Lexington, Mass.: Lexington Books.

- Martin, J., and Roberts, C. (1984). *Women and Employment.* London: Her Majesty's Stationery Office.

- Martin, C. (1992). *Transitions familiales. Evolution du réseau social et familial après la désunion et modes de régulation sociale.* Université de Paris VIII: Thèse en vue du Doctorat de sociologie.

- McCall, M.L. (1991). Background paper: Options for reform of the law of spousal support under the Divorce Act, 1985. Calgary: Canadian Research Institute for Law and the Family.

- McCall, M.L., and Pask, E.D. (1990). Spousal and child support: Summary of recent research and suggestions for further inquiry. In K. Busby, L. Fainstein, and H. Penner (eds.), *Equality Issues in Family Law* (pp.118–128). Winnipeg: Legal Research Institute of the University of Manitoba.

- McCall, M.L., Hornick, J.P., and Wallace, J.E. (1988). *The Process and Economic Consequences of Marriage Breakdown.* Calgary: Canadian Research Institute for Law and the Family.

- McDaniel, Susan A. (1993). Single parenthood: Policy apartheid in Canada. In J. Hudson and B. Galaway (eds.), *Single Parent Families: Perspectives on Research and Policy.* Toronto: Thompson Educational Publishing.

- McDaniel, S.A. (1992a). Caring and sharing: Demographic aging, family and the state. In J. Hendricks and C. Rosenthal (eds.), *The Remainder of Their Days: Impact of Public Policy on Older Families.* New York: Garland.

- McDaniel, S.A. (1992b). Life rhythms and caring: Aging, family and the state (23rd Annual Sorokin Lecture), Monograph. Saskatoon: University of Saskatchewan.

- McDaniel, S.A. (1990). Towards family policy with women in mind. *Feminist Perspectives* #11: 1–24. Canadian Research Institute for the Advancement of Women, Monograph.

- McDonald, R. (1991). Canada's off-reserve Aboriginal population. *Canadian Social Trends* 23 (Winter): 2–7.

- McIninch, Fran, and Pentick, Maryanne (1993). Demographic trends: Summary, policy implications, and research agenda. In J. Hudson and B. Galaway (eds.), *Single Parent Families: Perspectives on Research and Policy.* Toronto: Thompson Educational Publishing.

- McKie, C. (1993). An overview of lone parenthood in Canada. In J. Hudson and B. Galaway (eds.), *Single Parent Families: Perspectives on Research and Policy.* Toronto: Thompson Educational Publishing.

- McKie, C., and Thompson, K. (1990). *Canadian Social Trends.* Toronto: Thompson Educational Publishing.

- McKie, C., Prentice, B., and Reed, P. (1983). *Divorce: la loi et la famille au Canada* (Statistique Canada, Catalogue No. 89–502F). Ottawa: Ministère des Approvisionnements et Services Canada.

- McKie, C., Prentice, B., and Reed, P. (1983). *Divorce: Law and the Family in Canada.* Ottawa: Ministry of Supply and Services.

- McLanahan, S., and Garfinkel, I. (1993). Single motherhood in the United States: Growth, problems, and policies. In J. Hudson and B. Galaway (eds.), *Single Parent Families: Perspectives on Research and Policy.* Toronto: Thompson Educational Publishing.

- McLanahan, S., and Booth, K. (1991). Mother-only families. In A. Booth (ed.), *Contemporary Families: Looking Forward, Looking Back* (pp.405–428). Minneapolis: National Council on Family Relations.

- McLanahan, S., and Booth, K. (1989). Mother-only families: Problems, prospects, and politics. *Journal of Marriage and the Family* 51: 557–580.

- McLanahan, S., and Bumpass, L. (1988). Intergenerational consequences of family disruption. *American Journal of Sociology* 94: 130–152.

- McLanahan, S. (1985). Family structure and the reproduction of poverty. *American Journal of Sociology* 90: 873–901.

- McLanahan, S. (1983). Family structure and stress: A longitudinal comparison of two-parent and female headed families. *Journal of Marriage and the Family* 45: 347–57.

- McNaughton, E. (1993). The relationship of mother's marital status at the time of her first child's birth to socialization and development. In J. Hudson and B. Galaway (eds.), *Single Parent Families: Perspectives on Research and Policy.* Toronto: Thompson Educational Publishing.

- McQuillan, K. (1988). *One-Adult and Two-Earner Households and Families: Trends, Determinants and Consequences: Part II Family Change and Family Income in Canada.* Ottawa: Report of the Review of Demography, Health and Welfare Canada.

- Mellett, C. (1983). *At the End of the Rope.* Halifax: Women's Emergency Housing Coalition.

- Messaris, P., and Hornick, R.C. (1983). Work status, television exposure, and educational outcomes. In C.D. Hayes and S.B. Kamerman (eds.), *Children of Working Parents: Experiences and Outcomes.* Washington DC: National Academy Press.

- Michael, R.Y., and Tuma, N.B. (1985). Entry into marriage and parenthood by young men and women: The influence of family background. *Demography* 22: 515–544.

- Michel, A. (1978). *Sociologie de la famille et du mariage.* Paris: Presses Universitaires de France (Le sociologue).

- Michelson, W. (1988). Divergent convergence: The daily routines of employed spouses as a public affairs agenda. In C. Andrew and B. Moore Milroy (eds.), *Life*

Spaces Gender, Household, Employment. Vancouver: University of British Columbia Press.

- Millar, J. (1989). *Poverty and the Lone Parent Family.* Avebury: Gower.

- Millar, J., and Glendinning, C. (1987). Invisible women, invisible poverty. In C. Glendinning and J. Millar. *Women and Poverty in Britain.* Brighton: Wheatsheaf.

- Moore, M. (1990). Women parenting alone. In C. McKie and K. Thompson (eds.), *Canadian Social Trends* (pp.121–127). Toronto: Thompson Educational Publishing.

- Moore, M., and McKie, C. (1990, June). The social rewards of family living: An analysis based on quality of life indicators. Paper presented at the Annual Meetings of the Canadian Sociology and Anthropology Association, Victoria, British Columbia.

- Moore, M. (1988). Female lone parenthood: The duration of episodes. *Canadian Social Trends* 10: 40–42.

- Moore, M. (1987). Women parenting alone. *Canadian Social Trends* 7 (Winter): 31–36.

- Moore, K.A., and Waite, L.J. (1981). Marital dissolution, early motherhood and early marriage. *Social Forces* 60: 20–40.

- Moran, B.I. (1989). Welcome to the funhouse: The incredible maze of modern divorce taxation. *Harvard Journal on Legislation* 26: 117–132.

- Morgan, S.P., Lye, D., and Condran, G. (1988). Sons, daughters, and the risk of marital disruption, *American Journal of Sociology* 94: 110–129.

- Moss, P. (1991). Day care for young children in the UK. In E. Melhuish and P. Moss (eds.), *Day Care for Young Children: International Perspectives.* London: Routledge.

- Mossman, M.J., and MacLean, M. (1986). Family law and social welfare: Towards a new equality. *Canadian Journal of Family Law* 5: 79–110.

- Mueller, C.W., and Cooper, P.W. (1986). Children of single parent families: How they fare as adults. *Family Relations* 35: 169–176.

- Mueller, C.W., and Pope, H. (1977). Marital instability: A study of its transmission between generations. *Journal of Marriage and the Family* 39: 83–93.

- Myles, J. (1991). Women, the welfare state and care-giving. *Canadian Journal on Aging* 10 (2): 82–85.

- Nakamura, A., and Nakamura, M. (1985). A survey of research on the work behavior of Canadian women. In W. C. Ridell (ed.), *Work and Pay: The Canadian Labour Market.* Toronto: University of Toronto Press.

- Nasdasdi, R. (1988). *Co-Operative Housing for Sole Parent Families,* M.A. Thesis, Department of Sociology, Acadia University.

- National Audit Office (1990). *Department of Social Security: Support for Lone Parent Families.* London: Her Majesty's Stationery Office.

- National Commission of Children (1991). *Beyond Rhetoric: A New American Agenda for Children and Families.* Washington: U.S. Government Printing Office.

- National Council of Welfare (1991). *Welfare incomes: 1990.* Ottawa: Minister of Supply and Services Canada. Catalogue H68–27/1991E.

- National Council of Welfare (1990). *Fighting Child Poverty.* Ottawa: Minister of Supply and Services Canada, Catalogue H68–29/1991E.

- National Council of Welfare (1990). *Women and Poverty Revisited.* Ottawa: Ministry of Supply and Services.

- National Council of Welfare (1987). *Welfare in Canada: The Tangled Safety Net.* Ottawa: Ministry of Supply and Services.

- Neyrand, G., Guillot, C. (1988). *La socialisation des enfants de parents isolés.* CIMERSS: Rapport de recherche pour la CNAF.

- Nock, S. (1982). Enduring effects of marital disruption and subsequent living arrangements. *Journal of Family Issues* 3: 25–40.

- Norvez, A. (1990). *De la naissance à l'école. Santé, modes de garde et préscolarité dans la France contemporaine* (Travaux et documents No. 126). Paris: Institut National d'Etudes Démographiques.

- Office of Population Censuses and Surveys (1990). *General Household Survey.* London: Her Majesty's Stationery Office.

- Ontario Standing Committee on the Administration of Justice (1982). *Report on the Ontario Housing Corporation and Local Housing Authorities.* Toronto.

- Osborn, A.F., Butler, N.R., and Morris, A.C. (1984). *The Social Life of Britain's Five-Year-Olds.* London: Routledge and Kegan Paul.

- Overall, C. (1991). *Ethics and Human Reproduction. A Feminist Analysis.* Boston: Unwin Hyman.

- Parish, T.S., and Kappes, B.M. (1980). Impact of father loss on the family. *Social Behavior and Personality* 8: 107–112.

- Parliament, J. (1989). Women employed outside the home. *Canadian Social Trends* 13 (Summer): 2–6.

- Pask, E. Diane (1993). Family law and policy in Canada: Economic implications for single custodial mothers and their children. In J. Hudson and B. Galaway (eds.), *Single Parent Families: Perspectives on Research and Policy.* Toronto: Thompson Educational Publishing.

- Pask, E.D., and Hass, C.A. (1990). *Division of Pensions.* Toronto: Carswell Legal Publications.

- Pask, E.D. (1989). The effect of family breakdown on retirement planning. In J. Eekelaar and D. Pearl (eds.), *An Aging World: Dilemmas and Challenges for Law and Social Policy* (pp.855–872). Oxford: Clarendon Press.

- Pask, E.D., and McCall, M.L. (eds.) (1989). *How Much and Why? The Economic Implications of Marriage Breakdown: Spousal and Child Support.* Calgary: Canadian Research Institute for Law and the Family.

- Pence, A.R., Erickson, D., Gauthier, A.H., Glossop, R., Lapierre-Adamcyk, E., and Marcil-Gratton, N. (1990). *Childhood as a Social Phenomenon. National Report, Canada* (Eurosocial Report Volume 36/6). Vienna: European Centre for Social Welfare Policy and Research.

- Pettit, M.L. (1987). *Housing the Single-Parent Family: A Resource and Action Handbook,* Trenton: State of New Jersey, Department of Community Affairs, Division of Housing and Development and Division on Women.

- Pineo, P., and Porter, J. (1967). Occupational prestige in Canada. *Canadian Review of Sociology and Anthropology* 4: 24–40.

- Piore, M.J. (1971). The dual labour market. In David Gordon (ed.), *Problems in Political Economy* (p.92). Lexington, Mass: D.C. Heath and Co.

- Pool, I., and Moore, M. (1986). *Lone Parenthood: Characteristics and Determinants — Results from the 1984 Family History Survey.* Ottawa: Statistics Canada.

- Pope, H., and Mueller, C.W. (1976). The intergenerational transmission of marital stability. Comparisons by sex and race. *Journal of Social Issues* 32: 49–66.

- Poussin, G., Sayn, I. (1990). *Un seul parent dans la famille. Approche psychologique et juridique de la famille monoparentale.* Paris: Paidos-Centurion.

- Pupo, N. (1988). Preserving patriarchy: Women, the family and the state. In N. Mandell and A. Duffy (eds.), *Reconstructing the Canadian Family: Feminist Perspectives.* Toronto: Butterworths.

- Ram, Bali. (1990). *New Trends in the Family: Demographic Facts and Features.* Ottawa: Statistics Canada Catalogue No. 91–535E.

- Ray, J.C., Carvoyeur, L.S., Jeandidier, B. (1989). *Prestations familiales, activité féminine et isolement. Un parallèle Lorraine/Luxembourg.* ADEPS. Université de Nancy II.

- Ray, J.C., Carvoyeur, L.S. (1986). *Transferts sociaux et modes de cohabitation. Le cas des femmes ayant des enfants à charge.*

- Ray, J.C. (1985). L'allocation de parent isolé désincite-t-elle au travail? In *Evaluation des politiques sociales.* Paris: La Documentation Française, (Commissariat Général du Plan), 75–112.

- Ray, J.C., Carvoyeur, L.S., Liman Tinguiri, M.K. (1983). *Allocation de Parent Isolé et désincitation au travail,* L.A.S.A.R.E. Université de Nancy II: Rapport de Recherche pour le Commissariat Général du Plan.

- Reitsma-Street, M. (1991). Girls learn to care; Girls policed to care. In C. Baines, P. Evans and S. Neysmith (eds.), *Women's Caring: Feminist Perspectives on Social Welfare* (pp.106–137). Toronto: McClelland and Stewart.

- Revenue Canada (1991). *Federal and Provincial General Tax Guide 1991.*

- Richards, M.P.M., and Dyson, M. (1982). Separation, divorce and the development of children: a review. Unpublished report prepared for the Department of Health and Social Security.

- Rickel, A.V., and Langner, T.S. (1985). Short-term and long-term effects of marital disruption on children. *American Journal of Community Psychology* 13: 599–611.

- Robertson, I. (1984). Single parent lifestyle and peripheral estate residence. *Town Planning Review* 55 (2): 197–213.

- Robinson, B.W., and McVey, W.W., Jr. (1985). The relative contribution of death and divorce to marital dissolution in Canada and the United States. *Canadian Journal of Sociology* 16: 93–109.

- Rogerson, C.J. (1991a). Judicial interpretation of the spousal and child support provisions of the Divorce Act (Part I). *Canadian Family Law Quarterly* 7: 155–269.

- Rogerson, C.J. (1991b). Judicial interpretation of the spousal and child support provisions of the Divorce Act (Part II). *Canadian Family Law Quarterly* 7: 271–314.

- Roll, J. (1988). *Family Fortunes: Parents' Incomes in the 1980's.* London: Family Policy Studies Centre.

- Ross, D.P., and Shillington, R. (1989). *The Canadian Fact Book on Poverty, 1989.* Ottawa: Canadian Council on Social Development.

- Rossi, P. (1982). *Why Families Move Revisited.* Berkeley, California: Sage Publications.

- Sanik, M.M., and Mauldin, T. (1986). Single versus two parent families: A comparison of mothers' time. *Family Relations* 35, 53–56.

- Santrock, J.W., and Warshak, R.A. (1979). Father custody and social development in boys and girls. *Journal of Social Issues* 35, 112–125.

- Sarason, I., Levine, H., Basham, R., and Sarason, B. (1983). Assessing social support: The social support questionnaire. *Journal of Personality and Social Psychology* 44: 127–139.

- Schmitz, C. (1989, 8 September). Support deduction benefit is wiped out by latest tax reform? *Lawyers Weekly*: 6.

- Schnayer, R., and Orr, R. (1988/89). A comparison of children living in single-mother and single-father families. *Journal of Divorce* 12: 2–3.

- Schorr, A., and Moen, P. (1979). The single parent and public policy. *Social Policy* 9 (5): 15–21.

- Seglow, J., Pringle, M.L.K., and Wedge, P. (1972). *Growing Up Adopted.* Slough: National Foundation for Educational Research.

- Shaw, L.B. (1982). High school completion for young women: Effects of low income and living with a single parent. *Journal of Family Issues* 3: 147–163.

- Simon, J. (1986). Women and the Canadian co-op experience: Integrating housing and economic development. *Women and Environments* 8 (1): 10–13.

- Simon, J., and Wekerle, G. (1985). *Creating a New Toronto Neighbourhood: The Planning Process and Resident's Experience.* Toronto: Canada Mortgage and Housing Corporation, Ontario Region.

- Simon, J. (1982). Housing by and for women: the Constance Hamilton Coop, women in/and planning. In *Proceedings of the Canadian Architectural Association.* Toronto: Canadian Architectural Association.

- Smardon, B. (1991). The federal state and the politics of retrenchment in Canada. *Journal of Canadian Studies* 26 (2): 122–141.

- Smith, M.R., and Laramore, J. (1986). Massachusetts' child support guidelines: A model for development. In *Essentials of Child Support Guidelines Development: Economic Issues and Policy Considerations* (Proceedings of the Women's Legal Defense Fund's National Conference on the Development of Child Support Guidelines). Washington: Women's Legal Defense Fund.

- Social Assistance Review Committee (1988). *Transitions: Report of the Ontario Social Assistance Review Committee.* Toronto: Queen's Printer for Ontario.

- Social Planning Council of Metropolitan Toronto (1979). *Metro's Suburbs in Transition, Part 1: Evolution and Overview.* Toronto: Social Planning Council of Metropolitan.

- Societé d'Habitation du Québec (1991). *Evaluation of the Provincial Non-Profit Housing Program.* Montreal: SHQ Evaluation Branch.

- Soper, M. (1980). Housing for single parents: A women's design. In G. Wekerle, R. Petersen and D. Morley (eds.), *New Space for Women.* Boulder, Colorado: Westview.

- Spain, D. (1990). Housing among female households. In D. Myers, *Housing Demography* (pp.86–107). Madison, Wisconsin: University of Wisconsin Press.

- Spector, Aron N., and Klodawsky, Fran (1993). The housing needs of single parent families in Canada: A dilemma for the 1990s. In J. Hudson and B. Galaway (eds.), *Single Parent Families: Perspectives on Research and Policy.* Toronto: Thompson Educational Publishing.

- Sprague, J.F. (1990). *More than Housing: Lifeboats for Women and Children.* Boston: Butterworth.

- Stacey, J. (1990). *Brave New Families: Stories of Democratic Upheaval in Late 20th Century America.* New York: Basic Books.

- Statistics Canada (1992). *Earnings of Men and Women 1990* (Cat. 13–217). Ottawa: Minister of Supply and Services.

- Statistics Canada (1992). *Labour Force Annual Averages, 1991* (Cat. 71–220, Household Survey Division). Ottawa: Minister of Industry, Science and Technology.

- Statistics Canada (1991). *Income Distributions by Size in Canada 1988* (Cat. 13–207, Household Services Division). Ottawa: Ministry of Supply and Services.

- Statistics Canada (1991). *Postcensal Estimates of Families, Canada, Provinces and Territories* (Cat. 91–204). Ottawa: Statistics Canada.

- Statistics Canada (1991a). *1990 Household Income, Facilities and Equipment Micro Data File* (Computer Readable Data Tape and Documentation). Ottawa: Statistics Canada, Consumer Income and Expenditure Division.

- Statistics Canada (1991b). *1989 Survey of Consumer Finance Micro Data File* (Computer Readable Data Tape and Documentation). Ottawa: Statistics Canada, Consumer Income and Expenditure Division.

- Statistics Canada (1990). *Current Demographic Analysis: New Trends in the Family* (Cat. 91–535E). Ottawa: Ministry of Supply and Services.

- Statistics Canada (1990). *The Health Report* (Cat. 82–003S, Canadian Centre for Health Information). Ottawa: Ministry of Supply and Services.

- Statistics Canada (1990). *Income Distribution in Canada* (Cat. 13–210). Ottawa: Ministry of Supply and Services.

- Statistics Canada (1990). *Women in Canada: A Statistical Report* (Cat. 89–503E). Ottawa: Minister of Supply and Services.

- Statistics Canada (1990a). *Public Use Sample Tape (1986) Household File* (Computer Readable Data Tape and Documentation, 1986 Census of Canada). Ottawa: Statistics Canada.

- Statistics Canada (1990b). *Public Use Sample Tape (1986), Individual File* (Computer Readable Data Tape and Documentation, 1986 Census of Canada). Ottawa: Statistics Canada.

- Statistics Canada (1989). *Focus on Canada: Family Income* (Cat. 98–128). Ottawa: Ministry of Supply and Services.

- Statistics Canada (1989). *Families,* part 2 (Cat. 93–107). Ottawa: Ministry of Supply and Services.

- Statistics Canada (1988). *1986 Survey of Family Expenditures Micro Data File* (Computer Readable Data Tape and Documentation). Ottawa: Statistics Canada, Consumer Income and Expenditures Division.

- Statistics Canada (1986). *Lone Parenthood: Characteristics and Determinants: Results from the 1984 Family History Survey* (Cat. 99–961). Ottawa: Ministry of Supply and Services.

- Statistics Canada (1985). *Family History Survey: Preliminary Findings* (Cat. 99–995). Ottawa: Ministry of Supply and Services.

- Statistics Canada (1984). *Canada's Lone-Parent Families.* Ottawa: Ministry of Supply and Services.

- Status of Women in Canada (1985). *An International Survey of Private and Public Law Maintenance of Single-Parent Families.* Ottawa: Ministry of Supply and Services.

- Steward D.G., and Steel, F.M. (1990). *The Economic Consequences of Divorce on Families Owning a Marital Home.* Winnipeg: University of Manitoba.

- Stout, Cam (1991). Common law: A growing alternative. *Canadian Social Trends* 23 (Winter): 18–20.

- Sweet, J.A., and Bumpass, L. (1987). *American Families and Households.* New-York: Russell Sage Foundation.

- Tachon, M. (1989). *Quand faire, c'est dire. Les politiques locales d'action sociale en direction des familles monoparentales.* Lyon: AREPS. Rapport pour la CNAF.

- Théry, I. (1991). Trouver le mot juste: Langage et parenté dans les recompositions familiales après divorce. In M. Segalen (ed.), *Jeux de familles* (pp.137–156). Paris: Presses du CNRS.

- Théry, I., Dhavernas, M.J. (1991). *Le beau-parent dans les familles recomposées. Rôle familial, statut social, statut juridique.* Paris: CRIV/CNRS. Rapport de recherche pour la CNAF.

- Théry, I. (1987). Remariage et familles composées: Des évidences aux incertitudes. *L'année sociologique* (Paris: Presses Universitaires de France) 37, 119–152.

- Thornton, A. (1991). Influence of the marital history of parents on the marital and cohabitational experiences of children. *American Journal of Sociology* 96: 868–894.

- Thornton, A., and Rodgers, W.L. (1987). The influence of individual and historical time on marital disruption. *Demography* 24: 1–22.

- Thornton, A., and Camburn, D. (1987). The influence of the family on premarital sexual attitudes and behavior. *Demography* 24: 323–340.

- Tort, M. (1988). Les situations monoparentales et la question psychanalytique. *Dialogue* (Paris) 101 ("Parents seuls: La famille après le divorce"): 7–27.

- Tort, M. (1987). *Effets de l'inséparation. La question psychanalytique dans les situations monoparentales.* Paris: Rapport pour la CNAF.

- Townsend, P. (1979). *Poverty in the UK.* Harmondsworth: Penguin.

- Trussell, T.J. (1976). Economic consequences of teenage childbearing. *Family Planning Perspectives* 8 (4).

- Tuzlak, A., and Hillcock, D.W. (1991). Single mothers and their children after divorce: A study of those "Who made it." In J.E. Veevers (ed.), *Continuity and Change in Marriage and Family* (pp.303–313). Toronto: Holt, Rinehart and Winston of Canada.

- U.S. Bureau of the Census (1991a). *Current Population Reports*, Series P–60, No. 174, Money income of households, families, and persons in the United States: 1990. Washington: U.S. Government Printing Office.

- U.S. Bureau of the Census (1991b). *Current Population Reports*, Series P–60, No 175, Households, families, and persons in the United States: 1990. Washington: U.S. Government Printing Office.

- United Nations Children's Fund (1991). *The State of the World's Children 1992*. New York: United Nations.

- Ursel, J. (1986). The state and the maintenance of patriarchy: A case study of family, labour and welfare legislation in Canada. In J. Dickinson and B. Russell (eds.), *Family, Economy and the State: The Social Reproduction Process Under Capitalism* (pp.150–191). New York: St. Martin's.

- Veevers, J.E. (1991). Traumas versus strens: A paradigm of positive versus negative divorce outcomes. *Journal of Divorce* 15: 99–126.

- Villeneuve-Gokalp, C. (1991). Du premier au deuxième couple: Les différences de comportement conjugal entre hommes et femmes. In T. Hibert, L. Roussel, *La nuptialité: Evolution récente en France et dans les pays développés*. Paris: INED. ("Congrès et colloques" n°7), 179–192.

- Villeneuve-Gokalp, C. (1989). Garder son emploi, garder ses enfants: une analyse par catégorie sociale. *Cahiers québécois de démographie* Québec 18 (1): 87–112.

- Wachtel, A., and Bustch, B.E. (1981). *Excuses: An Analysis of Court Interaction in Show Cause Enforcement in Maintenance Orders*. Vancouver: United Way of the Lower Mainland.

- Wadsworth, M.E.J., and Maclean, M. (1986). Parents' divorce and children's life chances. *Children and Youth Services Review* 8: 145–159.

- Walker, A. (1991). The relationship between the family and the state in the care of older people. *Canadian Journal on Aging* 10 (2): 94–112.

- Wallerstein, J.S. (1991). Children of divorce: The dilemma of a decade. In G.W. Bird and M.J. Sporakowski (eds.), *Taking Sides: Clashing Views on Controversial Issues in Family and Personal Relationships* (pp.268–275). Guildford, Conn.: Dushkin.

- Wallerstein, J.S. (1991). The long-term effects of divorce on children: A review. *Journal of the American Academy of Child and Adolescent Psychiatry* 30 (3): 349–360.

- Wallerstein, J.S., and Kelly, J.B. (1980). *Surviving the Breakup: How Parents and Children Cope with Divorce*. New York: Basic Books.

- Wargon, S. (1979). *Children in Canadian Families* (Statistics Canada, Catalogue No. 98–810). Ottawa: Minister of Supply and Services Canada.

- Wedge, P., and Essen, J. (1982). *Children in Adversity*. London: Pan Books.

- Weiss, R. (1984). The impact of marital dissolution on income and consumption in single- parent households. *Journal of Marriage and the Family* 46 (1): 115–127.

- Weiss, R.S. (1979). Growing up a little faster: The experience of growing up in a single-parent household. *Journal of Social Issues* 35: 97–111.

- Weitzman, L. (1985). *The Divorce Revolution: The Unexpected Social and Economic Consequences for Women and Children in America*. New York: The Free Press.

- Wekerle, G. (1988). *Women's Housing Projects in Eight Canadian Cities.* Ottawa: Canada Mortgage and Housing Corporation, External Grants Program.

- Wheeler, M. (1980). *Separation and After.* Toronto: Ministry of Community and Social Services.

- Williams, R.J. (1988). Quantification of child support. *Reports of Family Law* (Third Edition), 18, 234–273.

- Williams, R.G. (1987). *Development of Guidelines for Child Support Orders: Final Report.* Washington, D.C.: U.S. Government Printing Office.

- Wilson, M.H. (1991). Letter dated April 18, 1991 to Glenda P. Simms, President, Canadian Advisory Council on the Status of Women.

- Wireman, P. (1984). *Urban Neighbourhoods, Networks, and Families.* Lexington, Massachusetts: D.C. Heath and Co.

- Wojtkiewicz, R.A. (1992). Diversity in experiences of parental structure during childhood and adolescence. *Demography* 29: 59–68.

- Wolfson, M., and Evans, J. (1989). *Statistics Canada's Low Income Cut-Offs: Methodological Concerns and Possibilities.* Ottawa: Statistics Canada.

- Zweibel, E. (1993). Canadian income tax policy on child support payments: Old rationales applied to new realities. In J. Hudson and B. Galaway (eds.), *Single Parent Families: Perspectives on Research and Policy.* Toronto: Thompson Educational Publishing.

- Zweibel, E. (1992). Compensating custodial mothers for the extra economic costs of child rearing. Unpublished paper. Conference on Child Support Guidelines. May 22–24, 1992. Ottawa.

- Zweibel, E. (1986). Income tax consequences of support payments. In J.D. Payne (ed.), *Payne's Divorce and Family Law Digest* (pp.E71–94). Toronto: Richard DeBoo.

Index